Geographies for advanced study
edited by Emeritus Professor S. H. Beaver, M.A., F.R.G.S.

Geography of Marketing

Geographies for advanced study

Edited by Emeritus Professor Stanley H. Beaver, M.A., F.R.G.S.

Geography of Marketing

J. Beaujeu-Garnier
Professor of Geography, University of Paris 1

Annie Delobez
Lecturer in Geography, University of Paris 1

translated by S. H. Beaver

Longman
London and New York

Longman Group Limited London

*Associated companies, branches and representatives
throughout the world*

*Published in the United States of America
by Longman Inc., New York*
English translation and new material
© Longman Group Limited 1979

First published as *Géographie du Commerce* by Masson S. A., Paris in 1977.
© Masson, Paris, 1977.
English edition first published 1979

British Library Cataloguing in Publication Data

Beaujeu-Garnier, Jacqueline
 Geography of marketing. – (Geographies for advanced study).
 1. Geography, Commercial
 I. Title II. Delobez, Annie III. Series
 380   HF1025   78–40863

ISBN 0–582–48991–1

Printed in Great Britain by Richard Clay (The Chaucer Press) Ltd., Bungay, Suffolk

Contents

List of figures

List of plates

(unless otherwise noted, photographs are by the authors)

Editor's preface

It has been a great pleasure to collaborate once again with Mme. J. Beaujeu-Garnier, in a translation of the third work under her sole or joint authorship to appear in the Geographies for Advanced Study series. To an even greater extent than the *Geography of Population* and *Urban Geography*, the present volume breaks new ground. Naturally enough, it makes extensive use of French examples and French research, and the bibliography contains numerous university doctoral theses that, though inaccessible to the English reader save by visiting the universities concerned, are indicative of the growth of French thought and methodology in the field of urban and commercial studies. It seemed appropriate, therefore, with the authors' consent, to inject some more British material, and for this the Editor is grateful to his former colleague Dr. P. T. Kivell of the University of Keele. Dr. Kivell's contributions are acknowledged on the relevant pages.

S. H. Beaver
Eccleshall, Staffordshire
August 1978

Author's preface

The term 'commerce' covers the whole complex of processes that intervene between production and consumption. Its importance in the life of communities has been appreciated to a much greater extent by certain theoretical economists than by geographers. In the past the latter have only interested themselves in it occasionally and in an incomplete fashion. In texts on general geography or on individual countries, scarcely more than a single chapter has traditionally been devoted to marketing, and then only to external trade. The organisation of internal commerce has been passed over in silence or referred to only in passing when dealing with transport or towns. As for inter- and intra-regional exchanges, that are so helpful in the understanding of links, disequilibria, complementarities and polarisations, these have only recently attracted the attention of geographers. And French geographers have been particularly slow to follow the lead given by their colleagues in the USA and Britain. Even among these latter, only certain aspects have received much attention, evidenced in articles on particular and specific themes such as the spatial distribution of markets, the hierarchy of commercial facilities and the size of their clientele. In other words, the spatial theme, or rather that of spatial structure, has been largely dominant, and description has been more important than the search for explanations. Authors have analysed the laws of centrality in all their many forms, and have argued interminably on the truth or otherwise of Christaller's theory; relations have been sought between the size and complexity of commercial establishments and centres of population. In a word, the links between commerce and consumption have been re-examined, in their outward expression at least, but there has been little study of the relations between production and marketing, and no analysis of the diverse mechanisms of exchange.

In this book we have limited ourselves to certain aspects, defined in the ensuing pages, which still however constitute a vast field of study. Our object is twofold: to document the nature of commercial structures in different types of societies, and to offer some reflections on the theoretical researches that have been devoted to localisation and commercial functions. Hence the division of the book, after the introductory remarks on commercial functions, into two parts, organisation and localisation. We do not claim that it is a complete and definitive synthesis; but we hope that it opens up new fields for geographical thought and perhaps for practical action.

J. Beaujeu-Garnier
A. Delobez

Introduction

Commerce

Definition

The term *commerce* is so familiar, and in such constant use, that even the best dictionaries only give trite and sketchy definitions. However, in reflecting on all the matters that could be included within this theme, it is necessary to be more explicit, and the following definition is proposed: 'commerce is the transfer of possessions through the medium of exchange'. An examination of each of the key words in this sentence will help to underline the complexity of the problem.

The notion of *transfer,* or passing from one possessor to another, invites enquiry as to the legal (i.e. individual or body corporate) and economic (producer, consumer or intermediary) status of the parties involved, and as to the mode of transfer (direct from seller to buyer, or through the operation of one or more middlemen). The transfer is almost always accompanied not only by a change of owner but by a change of place.

The term *possession,* in general, covers anything that may be held as property. But the process of trading changes the nature of such property, transforming it from something that has only use-value to something that has exchange-value. It is such transferable possessions that form the basis of commercial activity. They include *goods,* which comprise real estate as well as movable commodities such as raw materials and manufactured articles – and a monetary value can be attached to both of these categories; also *human energy,* in the form of a paid labour force; and finally *information* – ideas, documentation and organisational services. The field of commerce can thus include, in a mercantile society, almost the whole range of human activity. Nothing lies outside it except that which is not transmissible or, one might add, capable of being coveted. This, of course, is a very wide conception of the domain of commerce; it is more usual to limit it to the *transmission of goods,* or their ownership, *for a consideration,* i.e. through the *medium of exchange.* Whether the consideration be in the form of barter or a monetary transaction, it is the evaluation and acceptance of its amount by both parties that constitutes the basis of trade.

In this book we must also limit ourselves: we shall deal mainly with matters concerning the transfer of goods. But in glancing at the operations necessary to produce these goods, to prepare them for sale and to distribute them, and also taking into consideration the structure of trade, we shall be led to include certain related matters such as the work-force, that is human energy, and the many forms of commercial services. It is indeed impossible to disentangle such complex matters.

The three 'ds' of commerce

The basis of all trade is a *difference,* an inequality either real or imagined. One possesses what another lacks, and this raises the possibility of an exchange that may take place with or without the use of money. One may barter one surplus for another, but one may also sell it, receive monetary payment and buy something else; one may also sell one's labour, one's creative power or knowledge and thus obtain monetary gains that permit the purchase of goods. The inequality between production and consumption that creates surpluses or deficiencies is the first difference; the inequality between products of different character (food against materials, temperate products against tropical, equipment against consumer goods) is the second. But there are also 'artificial' inequalities resulting from fashion or advertisement – e.g. different makes of car or refrigerator, and all the other exchanges of sophisticated products that the industrialised countries make between themselves. All these differences may be effective at any level between the individual and the state; they create a 'potential' for trade.

However, between this potential and its realisation must come *desire.* The producer must be willing to sell the whole or part of his output, and conversely, the consumer must wish to buy; without this willingness, the commercial process cannot begin. This desire may be stimulated directly or artificially by price manipulation, by increased purchasing power, by fairs and travelling trade shows, and by advertisements. The arousing of the desire for certain objects, certain types of leisure activity, or other modes of life, is a private occupation as well as a public function, and the professionals of the private sector in capitalist regimes, together with the technocrats in all types of government, seek and utilise every possible formula, in their own interests, to mould the aspirations of individuals and groups. The role of certain types of suggestion in the arousing or suppression of desire is perhaps more important than any direct measures of stimulation or coercion. Naturally, *difference* and *desire* can either reinforce or oppose each other. It all depends on how the difference is felt, whether as a need or a satisfaction.

Intervening as a moderator between both these motivating factors in trade is the matter of *distance.* The maximum intensity of commercial exchanges will take place if the *difference* is pronounced, the *desire* is strong and the *distance* short. But if the first two are weaker, distance may become very important. Of course it is not just a simple question of straight-line distance but of all the other factors that may affect movement: the physical nature of the land surface, the quality and cost of the transport media, and even ideological or social prejudices such as 'keeping up with the Jones's'.

These three 'ds' will be constantly taken into account and illustrated, more or less explicitly, in what follows. But we have been at pains to emphasise them at the outset because, together with plain description, they form the foundation of all the theoretical approaches to the geography of commerce.

The commercial 'system'

If there is one branch of geography in which systems analysis may be developed, it is certainly the geography of commerce. There could be no better illustration than one in which we may readily perceive all the terms, for the organisation and functioning of commercial relations fall within a well-defined framework, and the involvement of money means that for the most part they can be quantified. Furthermore, the position of commerce as the intermediary between producers and consumers places it in a chain the links of which are closely interdependent.

Let us briefly recall the fundamental characteristics of the system. It is a complex of distinct *components,* which are connected by a series of *relations;* each component may of itself form a sub-system. Relations between the separate components, and between the components and the environment, are an essential part of the system; and the evolution of the relationships may be the result of internal modifications of the components, changes in the relations linking them, or interactions that may be established between the system and the environment. The components of the commercial system combine spatial locations (centres of production, means of distribution, places of trade) and structures, in a chain of greater or less length, linked at each of these stages and inter-related (producer, collector, transformer, wholesaler, retailer); the whole being linked in linear fashion and retroactively by financial operations or sales and purchases in succession from producer to consumer, with a profit being made at each stage. To this chain of transactions is added the inter-relation of the processes at each stage: the scale–purchase action at the producing end has repercussions both on the production process and on the subsequent operations, and so on. On the other hand, the sum total of the commercial activities is remarkably inter-correlated with the whole geographical environment, and any modification of the latter has repercussions on the manifestations of commercial activity. The rest of this book will illustrate this, but we must emphasise it at the outset. In actual fact the complexity of the repercussions is such that all those – whether geographers or economists – who have attempted to establish the laws governing them have been obliged to begin by making a series of simplifying hypotheses, which means that their conclusions, while of interest as pure theory, have but a limited practical value.

The functions of commerce

In order to appreciate what we have called the functions of commerce, it is necessary first to distinguish two approaches, one concerning the nature of commerce and the other its manifestations. The first of these is the fundamental structure, integrated into the general system of economic mechanisms; the manifestations are only secondary phenomena, interesting certainly and not without their significance in the life of communities, but dependent on and varying with the structure. They represent, actually and figuratively, the 'shop-window' set before consumers, the last outcome of a complex integrated activity, playing an intermediate role that is not simple and uniform but has repercussions at various levels. It would be a mistake, however, to consider only these apparent and easily recognisable characteristics, for in truth the effects of commerce penetrate deeply into the lives of men and even transcend political systems.

An examination of the nature of commerce will enable us subsequently to appreciate more easily its multiple effects.

The nature of exchange

Exchange is not an original and inescapable part of human activity. All men are both producers and consumers; if man wishes to survive he is condemned to production (unless of course he lives parasitically on other producers). And no one will contest the absolute necessity for consumption. But a system of self-subsistence is readily conceivable, and it has regulated more or less completely the lives of many rural communities. Even large states have recently attempted to live in autarky, which is the same thing at international level.

As Marx in particular has shown, exchange accompanies the division of labour, whether at the level of the individual, the group or the nation. From this moment, the producer is no longer self-sufficient in all his needs, but he specialises, producing certain commodities that he cannot consume, either because they are surplus to his own requirements or because they are not intended for his own consumption. Thus a product, which in the self-subsistent stage had a simple use-value, now acquires, partly or wholly, an exchange-value: trade is born.

When and how did this phenomenon occur? The study of history, like that of the development of primitive societies at the present time, enables us to suggest certain conditions favourable to the change. Contact between two modes of life is the determining element: a community of cultivators and a community of nomads in early times, but also two groups exploiting their territory in different ways by reason of natural conditions (soil fertility, altitude, microclimate), or because of unequal agricultural capacities resulting from race, customs and culture. As the facts of economic life become more complex, opportunities for exchange multiply: the products of crafts and industries for agricultural commodities, of raw materials for industrial products, or of one industrial product for another, or ultimately, labour for the necessities of life.

The multiplicity of exchanges is thus limitless, and particularly so in all developed societies. However, though their importance is universally recognised, the mechanics of their operation is subtle. Their structure is a matter of economics, but their implications are largely geographical, because of the traffic flows they engender and of their spatial repercussions, in both directions. Placed between production and consumption, commerce is at the same time initiated by the former, which provides the basis of its activity, and stimulated by the latter, which provides its outlet. The more the first develops, so it is necessary to increase the second, and as consumption grows, so the means of increasing production must be sought. Thus, according to Marx, 'consumption is itself a factor in productive activity'. The development of consumption by every possible means – as in our modern 'consumer society' – entails a corresponding stimulation of production. According to the celebrated formula of Quesnay, 'every sale is also a purchase', and there is no end to the process.

This production–consumption process may be complicated by the intervention of multiple patterns of distribution: the distribution of incomes, the grouping of the population, and the organisation of traffic routes, all of which have an influence on the methods of exchange, and thus on the relations between producer and consumer. Does this mean that the variations of the two ends of the process are always perfectly adjusted, while trade plays but a passive role as a conveyor-belt? Such an assertion would omit the intervention of contingencies of an economic, political or other nature.

In the capitalist system, the profit motive is dominant, and because of this, two extreme cases may develop: in the first, the lure of profit and the great appetite for increased sales may result in over-production; output is artifically stimulated while demand is excited to the maximum possible extent, but should the mechanism become disordered, the market is glutted, and prices and profits fall. Conversely, output may be reduced in order to create a scarcity and so raise the price; the profit per unit may thus be increased, but the overall gain may be limited. In other words, the price level exercises a considerable if not autonomous influence, operating on the two ends of the process so as to maximise profits. The interests of production and marketing are thus to some extent opposed, the opposition being more marked as the two functions are better organised, e.g. relation between producers and central purchasing agencies as against those between producers and small shopkeepers. However, save in the United States, the mass of consumers do not present a united front, and the possibility of opposition between marketing and the consumer is much weaker.

In the socialist system, ideally, production must be adjusted to the needs of the consumers. Exchange is the link between them, but it cannot have much influence, for it is only concerned with the transmission of goods, without involving any profit motive outside the strict minimum necessary for its functioning. That at least is the theory. But what is it like in practice? Another factor is interposed between producers and consumers, namely the State. The State has the responsibility of maintaining general economic equilibrium; it thus decides on priorities of production and this therefore determines the possibilities of consumption both in nature and quantity. In this case also, therefore, the free play of relations between production and consumption, in so far as these represent two integrated aspects of the same economic reality, is not assured.

But the situation is not the same in the two cases. In the capitalist system, it is commerce itself that ends by acquiring its own power. This situation is one of continual contest that leads to the formation of groups of producer-traders, cooperatives, direct distribution of certain products in times of crisis, and within the commercial profession, all possible manifestations of competition. Indeed, if these are destined to capture more efficiently the desired clientele, they also offer the possibility of seeing 'a kingdom divided against itself'.

So while commerce as an intermediary activity occupies an important place in economic life, we can readily perceive that as a speculative activity it exercises many other influences in societies founded on the capitalist system. But it must be pointed out also that traditions and international contacts are strong, and that most if not all socialist countries have been obliged, at various levels and in different ways, to adopt the same methods and to experience the same effects as have been noted in the West. We shall return to this point later.

The mechanisms of trading

Commerce is too often looked at only in its final stage, namely retail distribution. This is but a partial and insufficient view, for the whole process must be considered, from production to consumption. We may distinguish four aspects of the series of operations that characterise every commercial transaction: the making available of the saleable goods, the types of trading relationships and how they function, the mechanics of the exchange process, and the financial implications.

The *preparation of goods for sale* is the indispensable first stage in the whole commercial process. The characteristics of the production exercise a preponderant influence: the nature, quantity, dispersal or concentration of the goods generate flows, systems and processes of distribution that differ in extent and structure. This is the starting point of the 'circuit' of commercial relations.

The circuit may be direct from peasant producers to neighbouring urban markets, for example. If the distance between the two is greater, or the saleable produce more bulky, it is necessary to consider other arrangements, such as local collection, and employing the services of one or more intermediaries, in order to market the produce. The collection of produce may often necessitate some means of temporary storage (silos or warehouses), a local transport system and often some preliminary processing. This links industry and commerce and provides a spring-board for the latter, but one which involves the expense of an indispensable pre-sale organisation, such as packing or canning factories for some agricultural products, refineries for oil, and preliminary treatment of ores. This initial phase has the advantage of increasing commercial returns, for the production of basic low-value goods is subsidised by these operations that precede interregional or even international trade. In more advanced cases, industrial mass-production, after long and complex manufacturing processes, reaches the distribution stage. Often certain of these operations are performed within the same undertaking, either in premises in the same locality or in scattered factories that are integrated within the sphere of production. Commerce only enters when there are financial transactions accompanying the transfer from one stage to another.

The outcome is retail trade, which is thus, in the majority of cases, at least in developed countries, simply a secondary phenomenon.

The second operation in the commercial process, the *organisation of trade circuits,* results from conditions that differ from product to product. A typological hierarchy may be recognised. The simplest type is a direct relation between the producer-seller and the consumer-client; the transactions are usually of small dimensions, there is no tying-up of capital, and transport is limited both in distance and in quantity; personal ties are strong and individualised, the stability problematical. The second type assumes the existence of at least one intermediate stage concerned with the collection of produce. It offers a variety of forms, from the wholesaler who centralises the output of dispersed producers and distributes in the local region, to the double mechanism whereby a wholesaler first of all builds up stock to supply an intermediary who then through a sole agent achieves a widespread distribution. The succession of commercial operations, with the associated transport, results in the accumulation of profit margins on one and the same product that gives it a value of its own and enables it to pass from a diffuse production area, often badly organised, to a commercialised zone that is frequently better organised and more competitive. The simple laws of supply and demand are altered by the possibilities of storage, the cost of transport, the availability of capital – and also the action of speculators. The third type of trade circuit is much more

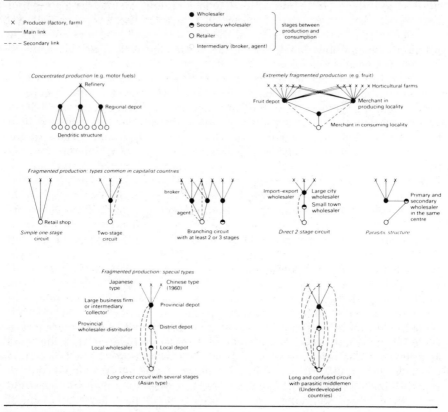

Fig. 1   Flow-diagrams of commercial circuits.

complex because it associates commerce with manufacturing. The operations described in the second type persist, but they are linked to others. Distribution at the retail stage is only effected after a manufacturing process; the workshop and the factory are concentration points for purchases and dispersion points for sales, and the commercial function that belongs to them is both secondary in relation to their *raison d'être* and essential in relation to their possibilities of existence. Commerce in this case is an accessory function that has really only been studied by economists under the heading of costs and their role in the localisation of firms and the formation of market areas. But in a study of commerce in its own right, it is necessary to remember the fact that these costs have a decisive influence on retail distribution. It is the framework of production that plays the determining role in the setting of the price level that is the essential element in sales to customers. Some undertakings, the possessors of 'trade marks', seek to impose selling prices on the retailers; they may also agree among themselves to avoid competition by giving different names to the same product. Some firms set up their own distribution organisation (e.g. for petrol or cars). However, distribution also plays a part, for producers may be subjected to competitive sales within a single specialised wholesale establishment (e.g. for television sets, domestic electrical appliances); others appear among the many producers of the lines of goods offered in multi-range shops, from the bazaar to the large department store. Finally the State itself may intervene to see that retail prices do not exceed or fall below certain limits, so that firms anxious to scoop the market do not use cut-price methods. The organisation of trade circuits is also reflected in the material aspect of commercialisation, e.g. large showrooms, chains of cold stores. These flows depend on a recurring series of gluts and shortfalls in production. There is almost always an alternation from one to the other.

After the initial purchase, collection and storage presuppose the existence of a convergent road system with lorries and vans playing an important role; but if it is a question of larger and more constant output, as in the case of ores or phosphates, specialised rail or water transport may be used. The first assembly point is a 'warehouse' – that may take the form of a silo, a stock-pile, a wine-cellar, a cold store; the commodities may here be re-sorted for direct sale, for forwarding, or for transformation, often after conditioning and re-valuing in accordance with the duration of storage. These depots or 'entrepôts' may take many forms. They are often situated at break-of-bulk points; they may be specialised or general warehouses; their functional organisation is varied, but always designed to encourage their use. They are an essential link in the wholesaling chain, and are to be found at different levels of the trading circuit. They are always accompanied by offices, where decisions are taken and orders given, regarding the transactions; the offices may be on the premises, in an uncomfortable corner, or in a separate place. The great commercial offices, seats of the wholesale merchants and of business enterprises at all levels, constitute a very characteristic domain. They may be in the heart of a town's central business district, in a great metropolitan centre serving a large region or a whole nation, or even in a foreign country, but wherever they are, they control all the ramifications of commercial exchanges like a spider at the centre of its web. The invisible links are also as strong and as active as the flow of merchandise from one depot to another, or from one depot to its subsidiaries. The activity of the intangible relations is greater and more efficient in the more developed countries; one might almost say that there is a substitution here, and that relations of this kind multiply as the actual transport of goods gets less. There is no need to see the goods before purchase, and an order from Chicago, London or Sydney can cause the fictitious movement of a cargo, buy or sell for future delivery, ruin a whole region or bring unexpected prosperity. All this is part of commerce, represented by financial exchanges, balance-sheets, and a multitude of implications that end finally in retail sales to individual consumers.

All this movement of goods is compensated by *movements of capital*; this is the real medium of exchange, except in the case of barter or in the 'clearing agreements' that are arranged by certain groups of states. The merchant receives from his clients certain sums of money that are deducted from the total resources of the organisation concerned. The merchant's turnover comprises two parts: the first is equal to the sum total of his own expenses, the rest is his 'profit'. The former represents the 'price' (not of production but at resale) of the goods, the latter comprises payment for his services, plus profit. The two aspects are commonly termed 'gross margin' and 'net margin'. This is the source of 'commercial capital' that, like any other form of capital, can grow, but has the additional advantage of great flexibility. The merchant can re-invest his profit in the business to amplify and improve it, and thus the commercial 'equipment' benefits directly. But he may also invest it in other directions, such as his own welfare, a second home, or the purchase of land, and in this case his profits go to swell the sum total of economic activity. Either way, unless it makes a loss, the business of commerce is a means of acquiring wealth, and so has its attractions. The circulation of money induces a whole chain of consequences: renewal of supplies, that activates the wholesale trade and so the producers; the financing of on-going operations that involve payments, interest, dividends, loans, bill drawing facilities and the whole range of banking activities without which commerce could hardly survive; a snowball effect indeed. The banking system may come to the aid of an enterprise that is expanding, multiplying its activities or acquiring shares in other companies. But it can also help in fostering the ambitions of large companies to occupy monopolistic positions that may enable them to act as pressure-groups at national or international level – such as the great oil companies, or the United Fruit Company.

The conclusion can be summed up in one sentence, written more than a century ago: 'The result to which we are led is not that production, distribution, exchange and consumption are all equal, but that they are parts of a whole, diversities in the heart of a unity' (Karl Marx, 1857).

Auxiliary functions of commerce

At the outset of this examination of the auxiliary functions of commerce, we might suggest two words that conjure up an image: commerce is a shop-window, and a cogwheel. As shop-window, it has a direct impact on the masses, and as cogwheel, it interlocks into the process of spatial organisation; and these two aspects make commerce a powerful agent in social transformation. In sum, the auxiliary functions are: animation and distraction, spatial organisation, information and transformation, and economic development.

Animation and distraction

This is the visible and outward face of commerce. The student of urban sociology is well aware of the animation created by the attraction of commercial activity. Shops are visited not only to make purchases but for other reasons as well. A commercial quarter exerts a considerable influence on its neighbourhood. The street provides a free side-show: the multiplicity of shops, their windows full of varied and tempting displays designed to catch the eye and arouse desire, and the shoulder-to-shoulder jostling of customers and strollers, create an atmosphere that entices the idler as well as the genuine purchaser. It is certain that shopping streets are much more frequented than others, and that commercial centres are veritable poles of attraction. It is the same for all forms of commerce, whether traditional or sophisticated. The market place was from the earliest times the only point of contact between rural and urban dwellers, as it still is in many parts of the Third World. But now we can witness the crowded pavements and the swarms of people in the shopping quarters of every large city in the world.

Animation and distraction go side by side. Young folk make the new shopping centres their rendezvous on Saturday afternoons in the United States as in France and Germany, and many families conclude their weekly shopping expedition with a visit to the cinema or the restaurant. The popularity of the traffic-free streets in old city centres, where festivities of one sort or another are frequent, is another aspect of the same phenomenon. While this movement of pedestrians characterises the retail shopping areas, it must not be forgotten that a similar animation is created by other forms of commerce: the lorries that come and go in the warehouse districts, and the intense traffic of all kinds that characterises the most active ports.

Spatial organisation

The attractive power of commerce is utilised to the full in all planning schemes; the 'business centre' is the key to the development of a focal point in urban life, particularly in new towns. The endeavour to counter rural depopulation also involves the creation, or the safeguarding, of relatively well-equipped shopping centres in the small market towns. Associated with the shopping centre are administrative, cultural and commercial functions that add to the feeling of centricity. What in former times arose spontaneously is now carefully calculated and planned, a very evident proof of the acknowledged importance of the trading function in spatial structure.

This particular example bears witness to the extraordinary dominating influence of commerce. So much so that studies of the frequency of shopping visits have been used both to establish the sphere of influence of a town and to determine the relationships that exist within a regional urban system. Because of its level of importance whether planned or unplanned, commerce occupies a pre-eminent position in the structuring of both real and perceived space: urban spheres of influence, the hierarchy of regional and national centres, the balance of trade flows between one district and another, the constitution of customs unions, organisation of produce or commodity markets that cross frontiers and transform political regimes. Even the socialist countries, after having attempted to organise themselves according to their own principles, have been led more and more to establish extensive commercial relations with the capitalist world while making concessions, in their own territories, to the production and distribution of consumer goods. And from one side of the globe to the other, more and more customs unions are coming into being.

Information and transformation

Information may be considered from two points of view: first the 'shop-window' aspect that is obvious to everyone, and secondly, less evident but no less fundamental, the aspect that relates to dealings, trade currents, agreements, everything concerned with the 'behind-the-scenes' operations of commerce that make or break trade flows, encourage speculation, and create prosperity or crisis.

The first aspect takes on different forms according to the level of technological development of the country concerned. It may involve the actual display of goods, or window-dressing, or alternatively advertising, bill-posting, radio and television. There are many variations, and consumers are bit by bit literally submerged by constant pressure. This bludgeoning by publicity gradually creates a new mentality, a psychological conditioning of the mind. By shop-window displays, demonstrations and explanations by the sellers or their agents, new products are made known, new fashions introduced; reputations are made or destroyed, crazes are created. Advertisements by word of mouth, in print, or by coloured posters, have the same effect. Individuals subjected to these techniques cannot remain indifferent; they cannot even retain their former personality, and one may speak of the *transformation* of the individual's mentality (it has even been called *derangement*). All kinds of extremes are possible, including the development of the 'throw-away' mentality and subservience to conditioned reactions; these are sicknesses of our consumer civilisation, that contemporary writers have not failed to condemn.

Thus, information spread directly or indirectly regarding commercial activities can lead either to progress or to subservience. These tendencies are not confined to the most developed industrial countries, but are even more strongly present in the developing countries. Even the socialist countries, where conditions are very different, cannot ignore their impact. Though we may condemn the excesses about which it is difficult to make an impartial judgement, we must recognise that we have here an auxiliary commercial function of considerable significance. The same thing is true of information that relates to technical and economic matters, and ensures the starting, continuation or cessation of commercial operations. Without such information, how could the producer be alerted to sales possibilities, the wishes of his clientele, or the price to fix? In the same way distributors or consumers benefit from the information and arrange for its improvement and wider dissemination. Thus information, whether we like it or not, engenders a progressive transformation of society; the reaction may be of acceptance (e.g. growth of consumption, diffusion of technical progress, modification of production, the appearance of new styles of living) or of dispute and rejection. It is therefore not only a psychological, technical and economic transformation of the average consumer that results from commercial advertising, but also a constant adaptation of the sectors of production and trade that rely for their outlets on retail sales. All this has its spatial effect, regional, national and international, in urban centres as well as among scattered populations.

Commerce and economic development
We must not conclude this introduction without enquiring about the role of commerce in *development*. Some extreme views have been expressed on this subject, in earlier centuries as well as in modern times. We may recall the celebrated phrase of the historian Pirenne: 'towns are the daughters of commerce'; and contrast it with the severe judgement of Benjamin Franklin: 'war is nothing but brigandage, and commerce just fraud and deception'.[1]

To give a more balanced view, we must once again avoid global judgements. The fields of action of commerce are so widespread, and at such different levels, the mechanics of its operation vary so much with politico-economic ideologies, and its functioning according to the degree of a country's development is so varied, that it seems impossible to give a simple interpretation.

From theoretical research, it is evident that commerce is a fundamental link in the chain of production–consumption relations and that in accordance with the perfection or disorder of its organisation, it can bring consequences that are either beneficial or catastrophic. Even in countries with a planned economy, the adaptation is far from perfect, and the bottlenecks that have been experienced bear witness to the lack of coordination between supply and demand for certain products that has on numerous occasions hindered economic expansion. To an even greater extent, as we have seen, the instabilities that result in western countries from over-production or speculation can be dangerous. But conversely, that is when the production–trade–consumption chain is working harmoniously, or better still if commerce, through individual initiative and the many auxiliary functions that we have recognised in free capitalist economies, acts as a stimulant to both production and consumption, its role in development, though somewhat unsteady, is definite.

The sum total of the major and auxiliary functions of commerce suggests the idea of a force moving in a kind of continuous spiral: the system rests on a complex of direct and reversible relations that is almost without any flaw. We cannot examine all aspects of this; we will simply cite the following appreciation, written by Scott (1972, p. 316) with regard to rural markets: (They) 'link exchange systems in such a way as to stimulate economic dependence on inter- and intraregional exchange. This, in turn, shifts the socio-economic basis of the community towards continuously expanding production and growth.'

How many families in the developing countries can make ends meet without engaging in petty trading? What would become of producers of all kinds and degrees of importance if they could not dispose of their wares? The repercussions of the rise in oil prices have burst open apparently impregnable situations, by provoking a veritable influx of industrial products into the suddenly expanded markets of the Middle East. And likewise Algeria finances its industry through the sale of its oil. A recent study, however, has shown the way in which, in the Ivory Coast, an expansion of agricultural production has engendered a new interior trade and the possibility of an export of agricultural products (Sawadogo, 1975).

Commerce thus has both directly and indirectly a powerful influence on economic structure and spatial organisation. As an intermediary operation, some would say parasitic, it is an element in the characteristic system of economic relations, strongly influencing the two ends of the chain of which it forms the middle link. In western countries one might accord it the status of driving-wheel, and this is without doubt a rather regrettable hypertrophy. But in any case no one can deny that it has contributed to the power and status of many towns, has swollen the coffers and has favoured good relations, even at the international level; but it may also ruin and destroy, as much for technical as for financial reasons or political changes. It is one of the great forces in all forms of civilisation.

Notes

1. The actual quotation is: 'Finally, there seem to be but three Ways for a Nation to acquire Wealth. The first is by *War* as the Romans did in plundering their conquered Neighbours. This is *Robbery*. The second by *Commerce* which is generally *Cheating*. The third by *Agriculture* the only *honest Way*.' ('Positions to be examined', 4 April 1769, in *The Papers of Benjamin Franklin*, ed. W. B. Wilcox, vol. 16, p. 109. Yale Univ. Press, 1972.) (Editor's note.)

Commercial organisation

Introduction: The diversity of commercial organisation

Despite the universality of some of its aspects, commerce plays a variable part in the activity of different countries, and expresses itself in diverse ways in the cultural landscape.

Even though in some backward regions the bulk of the population is still without shops and knows no form of exchange other than barter, or at most direct transactions between producer and consumer, there is no longer a single country in the world where one cannot discover examples of some stages in the commercial process, from various sorts of intermediaries to dealers, commission agents, forwarding agents, and usually wholesalers and retailers. There is no doubt that political or economic colonialism favoured the growth of the two-stage system of trading that was general at the end of the nineteenth century in the great European powers. But it is also true that the same model has been adopted by the socialist countries as a technical necessity, after some unconvincing attempts to short-circuit the process. This gives the world's commercial structures a measure of family relationship, noticeable whether one is considering certain commercial practices or the disposition of selling-places, small shops and markets in particular.

Outside these common features, however, the diversity of commercial organisations is very striking. The commercial traveller will not report in the same way on his relations with the business world in the Middle East, the United States and the Soviet Union, for example. Concerning the ordinary shops, he will write in the first case of poverty, of bric-à-brac, of the doubtful cleanliness of the premises, and the eagerness and loquacity of the proprietors; in the second, of the wealth, the functional modernity of the equipment, and the fewness and cool efficiency of the assistants; in the last, of the sober, stark and rather sad character of the shops, and the indifference and slowness of the employees. Likewise, no professional import–export agent would dream of seeking serious business relationships in a foreign country without having carefully studied its commercial organisation.

No one, looking at statistics of the structure of economic activity, would be tempted to put into the same class Nepal, Hungary and Australia (which have respectively 1.6 per cent, 5 per cent and 17 per cent of their active population employed in commerce), or Malawi, West Germany and Japan (with 8, 12 and 18 per cent of their gross national product derived from distribution). But who, having visited India, would not be surprised to learn that commerce contributes the same proportion of the gross domestic product (GDP) as in the United Kingdom, or that commerce occupies the same percentage of the active population, 11 per cent, in both Syria and Sweden, without coming to the conclusion that similar statistics do not correspond to similar realities?

For the geographer, an understanding of this diversity of commercial systems is fundamental. He cannot explain correctly the physical and functional variety of the 'equipment' (shop premises, stores, warehouses, supermarkets, etc.) if he has not grasped the main features of the structural organisation of distribution. The very low density of shops in the rural areas of the USA and the USSR, and the very high density in the central areas of western European cities and those of the Third World, have neither identical causes, nor similar significance. Both reflect divergent conceptions of the organisation of commercial activity that bear witness to different social structures and levels of economic development.

Commerce appears without doubt to be the element that expresses most faithfully the type of society in which it is implanted. It reflects at the same time the level of economic and technical development, psychological behaviour, social structure and political control. Furthermore, its evolution, which proceeds by complex mutations in space and in time, gives a picture not only of the actual state of affairs but also the dimensions of the changes that have taken place. Lastly, as an activity controlled not only by the laws of economics but expressing also the result of the constant interrelation between individuals or human societies whose interests are both opposed and at the same time coincident, it may be classed among the great social facts of a civilisation.

It would thus appear ambitious, even utopian, to offer in such a small volume an attempt at a synthesis of so vast and many-sided a subject. It is, however, possible to sketch in broad outline the heterogeneous commercial structures that co-exist in the modern world, for there are some characteristic types of organisation.

First it is necessary to enumerate the principal factors in this heterogeneity.

Major factors in the diversity of commercial organisations

In each country commerce constitutes a sub-system within the general structure of society, in time and space. Many factors help to control its role in spatial organisation.

The relations between commercial activity and the different elements of the societies concerned, whether socio-political, economic or cultural, are numerous, and so complex that any outline sketch is bound to be coarse and over-simplified. In the chapters that follow we shall endeavour to remedy this deficiency by a study of the major types of commercial organisation.

The main determining factor that indirectly controls the organisation of commercial activity is the *social system,* and whether or not it is founded on hierarchies of individuals, groups and social structures. It does not matter whether the criterion of strength is the labour force, intellectual capacity or the accumulation of material wealth: the power of the small shopkeepers, and through them the place of commerce in our trading communities, is proof of this.

From this derive the consequences related to economic structures. To demonstrate their range, we may distinguish three major themes: exploitation of part of the consuming population for the profit of groups of privileged entrepreneurs; sacrifice of the mass of consumers for the aggrandisement of the

State; equitable distribution among all the citizens of the goods produced, and the benefits that follow from this.

The degree and the means of *intervention by public authorities* in the socio-economic system and the planning of land-use, are no less important. Liberalism, planning, state control, are the keywords that represent fundamental ideas in the organisation of commerce: private or state control of the means of distribution, freedom or otherwise of enterprise and competition.

As a major component of the economic system, commerce also depends very much on the *functioning of the economy* and its level of development. It is important to know which of the three factors, production, consumption and trade (including the financing thereof), is dominant in the control of economic growth. In the developed countries, the industrial revolution gave this energising role to industry, but in the last few decades the business world of the great economic powers has staged a come-back and regained some of its lost influence. At the same time, consumers, by organising themselves, are developing a strength that they have never known hitherto.

As for *economic development,* it is well enough known that this is accompanied by a growth of production (and so of distributable goods); by an increase in the money supply (and so the amount spendable), either through the multiplication of jobs, or by the raising of wages and salaries for the same work; by the rising level of qualifications (and usually by all three of these); and in general by a greater control over the use of land and an intensification of inter-regional exchanges. An increase in consumption, a reorganisation of the shopping system and the modification of tastes and demands that result from this, are other allied factors. But changes in the shopping system are not linked in linear fashion with changes in the economy. A period of economic expansion may at first be accompanied, in a liberal economy, by a disorganised and excessive expansion of shopping facilities, to be followed a few years later by re-adjustment, with the disappearance of the least profit-making establishments and often the appearance of new types of shop – a re-drawing, indeed, of the map of commercial activity.

In a general way, it may be said that the greater the distance of producing centres, and the greater the number of producers that are attracted to one centre of consumption, the greater also will be the necessity for the multiplication of commercial intermediaries. Also, as self-sufficiency diminishes, so production becomes more diversified, both in respect of the nature and variety of goods and of the scattering or concentration of supplies; more efficient, too, become the techniques of long-distance communication, and more dense the transport and advertising networks; more liberal the political economy, with free trade and unrestricted competition; and more complex becomes the commercial system, with an intensification of trade, an expansion of shopping facilities, wider spheres of influence, and a lengthening and multiplication of the commercial arteries.

With such economic development, the need for a system of wholesaling becomes evident, indeed it is indispensable to the efficient functioning of a modern industrial economy, providing for the distribution, in accordance with consumer needs, of diverse mass-produced commodities. Under the heading of 'wholesale' are at least three types of specific service: the assembly of a great variety and considerable quantity of goods coming from many sources of production scattered over wide distances; the breaking up and preparation for sale of large consignments, thus relieving the producers from the necessity of sending out vast numbers of small packages; finally, and most important, with the great increase in the size of urban centres of consumption and of the industries that supply them, the control of distribution through the provision of warehousing facilities from which retailers can draw their supplies. If the stocking of saleable goods were to take place only at the production centres, public demand, which often fluctuates very rapidly, would suffer many interruptions of supply, for the resources of the retailers are very limited. Since the consumer cannot visit every factory, every agricultural cooperative – and certainly not every farm! – the provision of wholesale depots distributed at regular intervals over a large market area is revealed as an important auxiliary service within the economy. Of course, the wholesaling business is often encumbered with parasitic firms that through repetitive intervention lengthen the chain of transactions and thereby increase costs, but their existence may sometimes help to iron out blockages in the economic system such as inadequate output, lack of storage capacity, or poor transport. One could equally well question the use, or the parasitic character, of other intermediaries who spring up in a developing economic system, such as brokers and commission agents. Their presence is explained by the inadequate circulation of economic 'intelligence', a situation maintained without protest in countries with a free-competition economy, where the main object is not to ensure the best possible distribution of consumer goods but to procure more rapidly than one's competitor the information that will enable the maximum profit to be realised. The result of all this is a more attenuated relationship between producer and consumer.

Another aspect of economic development is the use of economic profit-earning capacity as the main if not the only criterion in the organisation of commerce as in other types of activity. This is a fact that merits much closer attention, and we shall study its implications in our detailed treatment of French commerce.

Economic development and *technical development* proceed side by side. If we understand by technical development the whole range of human progress, the effects on commerce are virtually limitless. We can group them under three headings: those developments that are reflected in the processes of distribution, those that influence the frequency of shopping expeditions, and those that affect the demands of the customers.

Industrialisation, that has led to the great expansion of towns and cities, accompanied by the development of urban transport, resulted first in a rapid growth in the traditional forms of trading, and then in the eruption of new methods, such as the department stores of the nineteenth century, and the one-price shops in the early part of the twentieth. But let us make no mistake: these new techniques have also been favoured by the transformation in production methods, for we have passed during the same period from crafts to industry and from the almost unique article to the standardised, mass-produced goods of today.

The same thing is true of the evolution of banking methods and the processes of the formation of cooperative societies or capitalist enterprises that permit access to almost limitless credit, to very large investments and to new forms of partnership and management. More recently, the use of computer techniques in the most developed countries has accelerated the concentration and integration of trading activities into larger units.

We must not forget also that technical progress has permitted the construction of vast storage depots and refrigerated warehouses, and this has revolutionised wholesaling in terms of the collection, storage and speculative redistribution of agricultural and industrial products.

It is not only the technical innovations in other sectors of activity that have caused changes in the organisation of distribution, but also the evolution of the commercial methods themselves, such as the introduction of self-service, the development of 'marketing' (that is, the whole process of encouraging sales), new forms of specialisation or of de-specialisation in the range of goods offered in the shops. Traditionally, specialisation was in terms of the nature of the goods offered, with commodity subdivisions corresponding to those of the manufacturers; but more recently specialisation has been in catering for particular types of clientele such as mothers-to-be, children, teenagers, and so on, or particular uses to which a variety of goods may be put, such as household equipment, garden requisites, and a variety of leisure occupations. In this way, under the combined influence of technical progress and the absolute necessity for profitability, the notion of an optimal size for shops is gradually veering in favour of larger units, and this has had an important effect on the distribution-map of shopping facilities. We must emphasise that the attitude adopted by economic advisers and commercial managers with regard to specialisation and de-specialisation, and to the multiplication of very large units, has much more serious consequences than might appear at first sight. It would be easy to demonstrate that a high degree of specialisation in individual shops, and also, though to a different degree, the cult of sheer size, accentuate the phenomenon of centrality, and thus aggravate the inequalities of service, rendering large areas, in particular the rural countryside, unattractive. The choice made is in some respects the choice of society as well as of the business promoters.

Numerous authors have discussed the consequences for commercial activity of technical progress in the control of environmental space, particularly through transport developments. The opening of new railway lines, networks of bus routes, the growth of individual car ownership, the development of motorways, and of short-distance as well as long-distance air services, all play a fundamental part in commercial activities. And we may add that the possibility of parking is becoming as important as the possibility of rapid movement. The progress of telecommunications is not less vital. First the telephone and now 'telex' enable orders to be transmitted over vast distances, through national and international markets, without the purchaser taking a single step. Thus the power and the radius of influence of a commercial centre can be measured just as much by the flow of orders or the size of the financial transactions as by the physical presence of customers or the concentration of goods for sale.

Consumer demands have encouraged this use of technical progress: modern man – at least in the Western World – is only satisfied by being able to move about with ease, to pay the best price without haggling, and to have the maximum possible choice of a wide range of good-quality products. So he gets into his car, takes advantage of free parking, assembles all his purchases that do not require special services, and pays by cheque or credit card; when he returns home, a refrigerator and a deep-freezer enable him to store his food purchases for a short or a long time, while the standardisation of his domestic appliances permits their repair and renewal by articles bought at the same place.

Thus distribution is deeply indebted to a whole range of technical developments, but conversely the transformation of commerce favours the diffusion and sophistication of technology. The standardisation of products, and the speeding up of their distribution by trading, lead to a monotony that forces countries in the forefront of technical progress, if they are not to perish from sheer boredom, to replace diversity in space by diversity in time, with the development of gadgetry and constant changes of fashion.

Commercial structures also bear the imprint of the *variety of cultural heritage*. Psychological behaviour depends as much on cultural antecedents as on biological controls. This is evidenced by, among other things, the attitude of social groups or even whole races towards the notion of profit (and religious culture plays an important part in this), and towards commercial occupations (and with regard to the latter, it must be emphasised that the role of women in the commercial activities of different countries is not related simply to the level of economic development and the labour market). The influence of cultural heritage is evidenced, too, in the relations between sellers and buyers, in which the practice of bargaining is a good example; and also in the ethics of traders, and in consumer behaviour (including the habits of saving as well as of spending).

Social structure also influences consumption, and thus commerce, in many ways. Behaviour varies as between social classes and modes of life. It is not only a question of financial means but of basic attitudes, and this is partly cultural. Economics, culture and psychology are all involved. It is surely in the developing countries that the impact of social evolution on the organisation of commerce has been most striking in recent years.

It is important not to forget that a commercial structure exists both in time and in space. It is exceptional for a country to be able to wipe out the past and reorganise its commercial system from scratch; only the socialist countries have attempted such an experiment in recent years, as we shall see. As a general rule, present systems always include some features inherited from the past, and often these weigh so heavily that one is faced with what is almost a double structure of commercial activity.

A commercial system is not just an abstract conception; it is evident in space by the location of all the commercial establishments that form the network. But this space is not a neutral factor. It has dimensions that may exercise some constraint on the development of the system. The area of a country and the distances involved in inter-regional or international trade, require the existence of a number of wholesale depots as well as retail outlets. Thus the distances that separate the retailers from their suppliers compel the latter, for technical and logistic reasons, to organise intermediate links in the chain, such as regional depots for the manufacturers, and branch warehouses, or, in the case of the larger merchants, to make use of lesser wholesalers. Space is thus by no means a negligible factor in the structure of commerce, for beyond a certain threshold, economic concentration, to the extent to which it is accompanied by the growth of giant-sized production units and wholesale depots, has as an inevitable consequence the appearance of supplementary relay-stations in the trading system. The disposition of pipelines and storage depots belonging to oil companies is the best example, but there are numerous other examples among wholesalers dealing in goods that are in constant demand whose business is sufficiently large to warrant the establishment of local warehouses. The effect of this phenomenon on the planning of land-use is not negligible: a degree of evenness in the distribution of centres of production may reduce the length of trade flows, but on the other hand, it may result in the multiplication of commercial intermediaries in order to facilitate the maintenance or reinforcement of the economic concentration of production in a few points only within a country or region; it remains to be seen which is the least costly in financial and human terms.

Space, however, has also geographical aspects: natural conditions, the configuration of built-up areas, the communications network, the distribution of producers and consumers, and in particular the density of population. These are also constraints that influence the organisation of buying and selling and the location of shops. Land values, which vary widely, often influence commercial structure by controlling the location of establishments, particularly in a free economy: the great growth of peri-urban hypermarkets, with their consequential effects, is a recent proof of this.

Finally, it could be said that the extent to which a country opens its doors to external trade, and the geographical situation of its trading partners, together with the nature of the relations that it maintains with them (equal partners, or a dominant or subordinate role), are also not without influence on the organisation of commercial structure (for example, the presence or absence of a wholesale export–import sector, that we shall study in the underdeveloped countries), and on the location of commercial centres at frontier posts and especially at ports.

The above paragraphs give some idea of the complexity of the factors influencing commercial activity. They enable us to affirm that while there is a fundamental relationship between the importance and localisation of commercial establishments and the size and distribution of the populations they serve, any model of the spatial distribution of shopping facilities that does not take into account the multitude of other variables is of little interest or value.

It may be true that in certain countries the population no longer has a sufficiently dominant role in the spatial distribution of commerce, which is entirely dependent on economic laws; but the solution to this problem is a matter of community choice.

As we have seen, the main factors in the organisation of commerce are as much political as technical. This is why our typology of the world's commercial organisations is based essentially on socio-economic systems, and then on the level of economic development. We shall thus analyse the commercial structures of the capitalist world, then those of the socialist countries, distinguishing the underdeveloped countries (at least in the first group, into which they mostly fall) and the industrialised nations.

Chapter 1

Commercial organisation in capitalist industrial countries

The commercial system of the United States

This operates under two banners: a hierarchical management system of oligarchic type, and free competition, characterised by a market economy and unfettered private enterprise that does not, however, exclude the possibility of state interference to regulate competition. The commercial organisation is powerful and dynamic. The average turnover in 1967 (the last available census of distribution) of all the wholesale and retail businesses was $312,000, a figure more than three times the French equivalent, and this was obtained with only 46 employees per 1,000 inhabitants (cf. France, 56 per 1,000). The whole system is the best actual example of a free capitalist economic organisation, in the service of a rich consumer society, but still dependent to some extent on foreign trade, that helps to swell the importance of commerce in the general economic life.

A powerful commercial system, always expanding

The importance of the activities of commercial enterprises is impressive. In 1973, retail sales amounted to $338 billion,[1] and wholesale to $365 billion. Already, in 1966–7, for a population four times that of France, retail trades in the USA had sales receipts 6.8 times that of their French counterparts, and wholesalers 5.6 times. The size of these figures results from the number of consumers, their high and constantly rising standard of living, and an economic organisation founded in the complementarity of producing areas that are becoming ever more specialised. It is true that this application to space of the division of labour principle, if carried too far in the direction of mono-production, may be dangerous in times of recession, but in normal times it has great advantages.

Organisation of wholesale trade
The abundance and variety of merchandise, and an economic policy founded on freedom of trade, render the operations of the wholesale sector particularly necessary. The extreme variety of products is due to advanced technology as well as to the diversity of centres of production, in a country that covers 9 million square kilometres. The complete abandonment of any notion of local or regional autarky, together with the giant growth of many of the producing units, results in an exceptional intensification of internal trade.

However, wholesaling does not always appear to the producers the most efficient channel for distribution. In 1967, only 45 per cent of the wholesale trade was done by merchants, while 40 per cent was effected by the commercial services of industrial or petroleum companies, 13 per cent by commercial agents or brokers, and 2 per cent by agricultural cooperatives. Nevertheless, an important part of the enormous external trade passes through the hands of import–export firms, and importer-distributors, who then supply other wholesalers or large retail companies, or through the hands of wholesale importers and exporters. External trade, indispensable to the national economy, is considerable, and it makes possible the high average standard of living; it represented 13 per cent of the world's total imports in 1972, and 12 per cent of the world's exports.

The 1960s were often difficult for the wholesalers, because they had to rethink their role in order to adapt to the changing structures of both production and retailing. For some industrial firms, the wholesaling business was too traditionalist to enable them to quicken their penetration of consumer markets, and insufficiently provided with large warehouses to permit distribution to take place in a rational and cheap manner without bottlenecks. The factories, becoming ever larger, wished to disperse their output rapidly so as not to be encumbered with large stocks, while at the same time continuing their rhythm of production with better and more efficient equipment. Many of them have thus, with the increase in economic concentration, endeavoured to create their own distribution system, or have sought contacts with trade customers or with large retail organisations (the evolution of which we shall study later) to deliver directly, with profit to both sides, from the factories.

However, in 1967 the wholesaling business in the United States was still very solidly based; the average turnover was $967,400. Twenty per cent of the businesses, representing 78 per cent of the total wholesale turnover, exceeded this level,[2] whilst 2.9 per cent, responsible for selling 25 million items of merchandise a year, divided 40 per cent of the wholesale market between them. At the summit of this pyramid, 760 firms had a turnover of more than $20 million, capturing between them 20 per cent of the total trade sales.

It is true that the competition of industrial warehousing has not hindered the growth of the wholesaling business during the past decade, but the expansion of the latter, which from 1945 onwards had been more rapid than that of industrial production, has been slowed down, especially during the period 1965–8. Thus, taking 1963 as 100, the comparative indices of wholesaling and industrial production in subsequent years were as follows:

	1965	1967	1969	1972
Wholesaling	119	121	150	189
Industrial production	117	131	145	151

Since 1969, forecasts of the virtual disappearance of the wholesaler have been proved false. The experience of several firms has shown that the alternative system of distribution was generally more expensive than using the services of the wholesaler. Moreover, despite their difficulties, the merchant-wholesalers have maintained their market share and have even improved their position. In 1948 they effected 42.4 per cent of primary sales; in 1963, 43.9 per cent; and in the 1970s more than 45 per cent. But the difficult times have produced an increasing aggressiveness in some merchants, and a more rapid concentration of businesses – which has pleased the manufacturers. There has also been a decline in the part played by merchant-wholesalers in sales of non-durable products, from 58.1 per cent of the wholesale trade in 1960 to 54 per cent in 1973. The food trade has been most affected by reason of the development of large chains that are more highly integrated. On the contrary, wholesale trade in durable goods, especially vehicles, for which the demand has enormously expanded, has increased. Within this field, the most noticeable development is the growth of trade in the products of technology – materials, spare parts, machines and special equipment for industry. In the past, trade in such goods has been almost entirely by direct negotiation, but the diversification in international sources of supply renders an intermediary more useful.

Recently, too, the energy crisis has been particularly beneficial to merchants dealing in vehicles; because of the high cost of transport, retail branches have been more willing to use their services rather than the depots of their parent firms, which may often be more distant.

Retail trade
Retail trade (that in the United States supplies almost the whole population) owes its dimensions not only to the mass of consumers – 210 millions of them – but also to their high standard of living; one of the highest in the world and still rising. In 1973, the gross domestic product (GDP) was $6,167 per inhabitant, a figure that allowed a personal income of $4,950 (of which $260 were saved). The average family income was $12,050, but a privileged 40 per cent of families had over $15,000. There is thus nothing astonishing in the figure of one car to 2.1 persons, or one telephone to 1.6 persons. However, only 48 per cent of personal spending was on material goods (food, clothing, domestic equipment); housing, transport and other items such as leisure and health playing an important part. This is why, between 1963 and 1972, the expansion of retail trade remained slightly less than that of the GDP. It was none the less remarkable, however, for in real terms it maintained a growth rate of 5 per cent per annum as against a population increase of only 1.1 per cent. The rising standard of living was reflected, as far as retail trade is concerned, by the increasing proportion of durable goods: 19.6 per cent in 1958 and 22 per cent in 1973.

Retail trade attains the profitability that is its ideal, thanks to an increasing economic and geographical concentration of its business units. In 1967, half the businesses, representing 94 per cent of national sales, had an annual turnover of more than $50,000; 10 per cent of them, each with a turnover of more than $300,000, took two-thirds of the trade.[3] It is not only the size of the multiple chain-stores that has caused this economic concentration. In the field of specialised retailing, for example, 6 per cent of the 42,000 shops selling female clothing do 47 per cent of the business; 10 per cent of the 33,000 furniture stores have 44 per cent of the trade; 5.5 per cent of the 40,000 wine and spirit stores take 33 per cent; 3 per cent of the 23,000 jewellers take 29 per cent; and even 8 per cent of the drug stores take 27 per cent of the trade. Certain sectors, however, retain a looser structure: there are 218,000 groceries and 94,000 bookshops.

Between 1963 and 1967, although employment in retailing rose from 5 to

5.4 per shop, the turnover, thanks also to a slight increase in productivity, rose by 9 per cent (in constant dollars). We can better evaluate the role of the large establishments by noting that 30 per cent of the retail businesses had more than 3 employees and were responsible for 80 per cent of the takings, while 5.4 per cent, employing each at least 20 persons, were responsible for half the purchases of the entire American population. These large enterprises continue to strengthen their hold on the market; even in 1963 they represented only 4.5 per cent of the number of businesses but had 43 per cent of the sales.

The growth in the capacity of large stores was accompanied by a thinning-out of small shops.[4] Also, the relation between shops and population has changed from 1 shop per 148 inhabitants in 1948 to 1 per 175 in 1967 – a figure that compared with France's 1 per 88. Between 1956 and 1974 the number of food shops has declined from more than 300,000 to a little over 200,000. The disappearance of the small shop, which has been going on for 20 years, has been accompanied by a progressive growth of large stores. Already we may infer from the statistics that the proportion of shops belonging to firms having more than 10 branches has passed from 9 per cent in 1948 to 12.5 per cent in 1967, and their percentage of the total sales from 30 to 40. Since that time, until 1973, their volume of business, at current prices, has increased more rapidly than the total retail trade – to the extent of 81 per cent as against 60 per cent. Further, it is the most powerful of the chain-store companies that have increased their hold on the market more rapidly: undertakings with more than 100 branches had 12.3 per cent of the total sales in 1948, 18.6 per cent in 1967, and probably almost 25 per cent in 1973.

None of the major European businesses can compare with the 10 principal United States distributors, whose ranks include the great mail-order and department store firm of Sears Roebuck (turnover $13 billion in 1975), and the three major chains of supermarkets, Safeway Stores (with 2,373 branches), Great Atlantic and Pacific Tea, commonly known as A & P (with 3,680 branches), and J. C. Penney, a group of department stores that, copying the methods of Sears Roebuck, has attained this eminence in a few years. Each of these organisations sells more than three times as much as the West German firm of Karstad Kepa, the principal European retail business (see Table 1 on p. 24).

Although operating within a free system, in fact the actions and decisions of this oligarchy weigh heavily on the functioning of the whole commercial organisation. However, by reason of the severity of the competitive system, these companies are sometimes giants with feet of clay. At the end of 1975 the large and popular chain-stores firm of W. T. Grant went to the wall in the most spectacular bankruptcy in the history of United States retailing. Like S. S. Kresge in 1960, Grant's could not withstand the competition of the discount-stores. While the Kresge management (which controlled 1,257 shops with a turnover of $5.5 billion in 1975, a year in which it built 950,000m² of new shopping space, more than either Sears Roebuck or J. C. Penney) decided to enter the discount market, Grant's had opted for a policy based on quality. As a result, with 1,180 shops and 60,000 employees, their turnover was a mere $1.7 billion.

The process of population drift towards the towns and cities (73 per cent of the population was urban in 1970) facilitates the creation of sales organisations of ever increasing size, and the restructuring of the distribution system. This movement towards the economic concentration of retailing is but one example among many of the capitalist process of profit accumulation in the hands of the most economically efficient enterprises, and is in part a consequence of the earlier concentration that gave many branches of American industry the most powerful production units in the world, anxious to sell their wares rapidly and in large quantities. Now the techniques of salesmanship are evolving in the same way, as we shall see.

A competitive system, dynamic and efficient, with a great capacity for innovation in the interests of economic expansion

American commercial enterprises are factors in the national economic expansion; they are not content merely to cater for their clients' needs, but to an increasing extent are engaged in conditioning consumers in order to facilitate the expansion of production. To this end, and to increase the rapidity of their turnover, they concentrate on improving their efficiency.

American commerce during the past half century has been characterised by the mystique of 'marketing'; all the constraints hindering the expansion of sales have acted as stimulants to the imagination of the marketing services that, as in industry, became attached to the business houses. The almost complete freedom of pricing policy has allowed this imagination to run riot in the promotion of commercial activity.

Transformation of wholesaling

Stimulated by the danger of finding themselves supplanted, in relation to their traditional clientele, by the commercial services of the big industrial firms, the wholesalers first attempted to improve their own management by modernising their warehousing and packaging. This involved, during the early 1970s, a 10 per cent reduction in their manpower, but it was followed by increased profitability. Recently, the more dynamic among them have had a fresh objective, a broadening of their economic role. Market research has shown them how to counter the pressure imposed upon them by the establishment of more direct relations between production and retailing, by enlarging the scope of their services, giving technical advice to professional clients and small merchants, assisting retailers in the management of their stocks, the programming of new sales lines so as to avoid immobilising their shelves with superfluous stock, or planning promotional campaigns and seasonal sales.

All these services, however, are not available to small, isolated wholesale businesses, and the result has been the development of large firms or groups. In fact, the American wholesalers have promoted strong contractual relationships between themselves and the retailers through the expedient of voluntary chains.[5] The first of these were formed during the First World War, and by the early 1960s they were fairly numerous, especially in the food and hardware trades; since then, however, they have spread rapidly to most other sections of commercial activity. In general, the collaboration between wholesalers and retailers is also improved by the reduction in the number of retail outlets, for this enables the wholesaler to devote more time to the technical advice that he gives to the retailer.

Though 'cash and carry' has existed for a long time in the United States, the multiplication of this form of trading is of less significance than in those countries where very small shopkeepers are more firmly entrenched.

Evolution of retailing

Retailing, in the United States, is the active intermediary between supply (producers) and demand (consumers), but its bias is more towards supply than towards demand. It provides an even more striking illustration than wholesaling of commercial dynamism. A rapid glance at its evolution will show the inventive force that since the last century has animated the business of retailing in the search for greater efficiency.

The United States has become the great laboratory in which new forms of economic marketing have been evolved. During the last 30 years especially, innovations have succeeded each other with great rapidity, generally without destroying what was there before; they have developed side-by-side, but all have had the objective of transforming the human being into a robot purchaser. The creativity of the Americans in this field is not an accident; it results from a culture moulded by the profit motive, which applies to all the personnel of commercial enterprises and is accompanied by the ruthless elimination of inefficient elements; a policy of encouraging individual initiative in the removal of blockages in the system, together with a good internal information service.

The main characteristics in the evolution of business practices in the United States are their diversification, with a growing standardisation in part of the system – that concerned essentially with normal consumer goods – contrasting with an often narrow specialism of other establishments, and commercial concentration. We have already noted, from the available statistics, the growing importance of department stores, drugstores and mail-order firms: 15.5 per cent of all retail sales in 1958 and 21.7 per cent in 1973. Unfortunately the American commercial census omits 'self-service' stores; it is certain that their number is increasing daily.

In fact, since the end of last century, all the main innovations in the commercial system, whether in ways of conducting business, in relations between undertakings, in sales methods or in types of business equipment, have led to decreasing specialisation of shops.

The evolution took place in three stages, from 1860.

The two phases in the development of the main shopping types, 1860–1950 The great urban explosion at the end of the nineteenth century (19 per cent of the population were town-dwellers in 1860 and 40 per cent in 1900) provided the first incentive, followed by the difficulties created by the economic crisis of 1930, and finally the extraordinary economic expansion that America experienced thanks to her engagement in the Second World War. The year 1930, in fact, is the hinge between the first phase and the second, which ended with the termination of that war in 1945.

First phase of innovation: branch-shops, single-price shops, voluntary purchasing-chains Although, in the rural areas, the non-specialised 'general store' or 'trading post' was traditional, it was not until after 1860 that it appeared in the towns in the form of branch-shops. In this system of 'chain-stores' the dispersion of the sales points, geared to local requirements was balanced by the centralisation of management and warehouses. This arrangement contributed to low prices, thanks to the advantages obtained by producers in the form of large orders, and to the reduction in distribution costs facilitated by the integration of the wholesaling stage, that sometimes even extended back into manufacturing.

Shortly after this, two other novel forms of commerce increased the number of non-specialised shops. In 1874, in imitation of the Paris *Bon Marché,* the first American department store opened. Then, in 1879, F. W. Woolworth, having developed the idea of a one-price cheap shop, in which the customer could also handle the goods on display, launched his first 'five and ten cents' store; very soon he was at the head of a vast chain of such stores, with a central management and many branches.

For the independent shops, the competition of the chain stores became more serious with the advent in 1924 of the 'combi' (combination stores, shops of 150 to 200m²), selling, in addition to basic foodstuffs, pharmaceuticals, tobacco and newspapers. The 'combis' combined the functions of two other types of independent shops introduced after 1920, the 'foodstore' and the 'drugstore'.

The success of the integrated chains was based, in part, on two aspects of their business – lack of specialisation, and cheapness. The retailers most affected, chiefly at first the food shops and then more specialised shops, chose to counter-attack on the second front, combining in order to buy more cheaply. The first such group, created in 1925, was the Independent Grocers' Association, a purchasing cooperative of retailers. While in the beginning these organisations dealt with wholesalers, they soon short-circuited them.

The wholesalers replied with an enormous development of retail outlets that assured them not only of a clientele of retailers, but gave them the power to organise and coordinate the two types of business.

In a more negative reaction, the traditional business community secured the passing of the anti-trust laws that obliged the chain-stores to refrain from reducing their profit margins below 21 per cent. This figure was still lower than the 25 per cent normally realised by the independent retailers, but the chain-stores lost the advantage of a price differential sufficiently large to be very attractive and thus to enable them to continue their spectacular progress.

One could say that the great economic crisis of the early 1930s brought to an end this extraordinary first phase in the transformation of commercial activities, which at this date were characterised by the three principles that had been 'invented' during the period: standardisation, integration and economic concentration. The story had been unfolded in classical fashion – important innovations at the end of the nineteenth century, free expansion of new methods in the first quarter of the twentieth century, and finally reaction (from about 1925); the reaction came first from the most dynamic of the pre-existing organisations, and was then helped, through political pressure, by government intervention.

The golden age of supermarkets   In 1930, the appearance of the first supermarket heralds a new phase, that of self-service and the expansion of shop floor-space. The innovations of the preceding phase were further developed, with less hindrance from the weight of tradition and more emphasis on economic efficiency (in the interest of both the business and, in principle, of the consumer), to the detriment of certain services to clients. Besides, to the extent that they patronised the new sales methods, purchasers at the same time accepted the gradual sacrifice of the traditional shopping services such as information (replaced for better or worse by trade marks or brand names), personal advice and indeed the service provided by the proximity of the shop to the customer.

The manager of a chain of branch shops, Michael Cullen, had the idea of combining various successful methods borrowed from several kinds of trading. From the general stores he adopted the limited array of ordinary foodstuffs; from the large department store, the notion of having everything on view; from the 'one-price' stores that of a large sales area, not so imposing nor so constrained by localisation and investment problems as the big shops, only 500–600m², but still more than 10 times the size of the traditional shop; he added the 'self-service' principle that had first been tried in California in 1912, the system of limited exits first developed at Memphis in 1916, and an idea of his own, the 'semi-discount' (300 articles at cost price and the next 200 at 5 per cent discount).

He did not succeed in convincing his employers, so in 1920, with much publicity, he opened his own 'supermarket' on Long Island, New York. It was a commercial triumph, for his methods were well suited to the reduced purchasing power that accompanied the Great Depression. By 1932 he had 8 supermarkets. And by 1936, in which year the Supermarket Institute was created, there were 1,200 of them in the United States.

The techniques of establishment, organisation and management of supermarkets and the range of goods offered have evolved since then, particularly with creation of adjacent parking lots as the motor car became an essential part of the American way of life, and the introduction of lines other than foodstuffs, thus giving rise to the in-store specialist shops for particular goods franchised by the supermarket; but the basic principles have not changed.

Already, before the war, the supermarket companies had secured sufficient financial standing and commercial ascendancy to be a serious hindrance to the pre-existing chain stores. In 1937, A & P, chief of the latter, decided to close nearly 1,000 of its smaller shops in eastern USA, replacing them by 200 supermarkets.

As for the independent traders, the most enterprising opened 'superettes', with self-service on a smaller scale, thus requiring less capital and having a turnover at this period only one-sixth that of the supermarkets. But once again, their principal action was political: they succeeded in getting many municipal councils to impose heavy taxes on the supermarkets – though this did not really hinder the expansion thereof, any more than the restrictions on the setting up of new ones were to do, after 1945.

In 1953 the 'superettes' were responsible for 35 per cent of national food sales, and the supermarkets for 48 per cent. By 1959 the latter, now numbering 22,253, took 70 per cent of the trade.

In the United States, although one may regard as a supermarket any self-service store with a floor space of over 400 m², the main criterion in the delimitation of different types of self-service stores is financial. The thresholds have altered with inflation, which makes a study of the growth difficult; but in 1975, the small self-service shops had a turnover of under $150,000, the supermarkets over $500,000, with the 'superettes' somewhere in between.

A review of the situation in the commercial world of the United States in 1973 reveals the importance of these first two periods in the history of modern trading.

From the 5,800 department stores issued 32.3 billion dollars' worth of merchandise, or 10.4 per cent of the total retail sales; 700 of them, situated in the 21 largest cities, accounted for half this figure. Their gross profit margin averaged 40 per cent, whereas that of the supermarkets was only 18 per cent. These large shops were developing self-service within their premises, and half their receipts now came from departments functioning in this way; but conversely they transformed other departments into specialty shops, thus assuring customers of individual attention.

The check-out desks of the 41,000 supermarkets collected $113 billion, entirely from foodstuffs; this figure represented 78.8 per cent of the total for this type of trade (the remainder being 11.3 per cent by the superettes and 9.9 per cent by small traditional shops) compared with 75.4 in 1970. But this gain was due only to the largest supermarkets, the 'superstores' (a term applied to those having a weekly turnover of more than $100,000). For there was an over-supply of supermarkets, sometimes as many as four or five in one business district; for this reason, and because of the economic recession, their net profit (i.e. after tax and interest payments) fell to 2 per cent in 1956, and further to 1.5 per cent in 1972 and 0.8 per cent in 1973. They were closing at the rate of 1,500 a year, with the prospect of 1,800 closures a year in the future owing to the development of the superstores. This has created serious problems, since most of these establishments are in premises with at least 15-year leases; and of the supermarkets in existence in 1971, 30 per cent were less than five years old. It is probable that many of them will be sub-let to specialist traders in such things as hardware, cycles, flowers – which are becoming great consumers of space.

The chain-stores, that is, in the official terminology, companies with more than 10 branches, representing 20 per cent of the total number of sales points for foodstuffs (53 per cent of the supermarkets, 30 per cent of the superettes and 5 per cent of the small shops), received half the sales income from this sector. They were slowly increasing their share every year, at the expense of the 'independent' concerns, mostly small enterprises. Furthermore, they were becoming important, outside the food sector, in the clothing and motor accessories trades.

Recent changes in the structure of retail trade   As it became more and more difficult to keep on selling more to a population with the highest standard of living in the world, it seems that the American marketing specialists, from 1950 onwards and especially during the past decade, have directed all their ingenuity towards this goal. Their dynamic approach, continually stimulated by the spirit of competition and by research, has been sharpened recently by new obstacles due to the economic crisis and the development of 'consumerism'.

Consumers to whom it is becoming difficult to sell 'any old thing'   'Consumerism' in the United States has nothing revolutionary about it; it is simply concerned with combating monopolies, of both production and distribution, in the interests of free enterprise. In a short time it has become an irreversible movement, ever since the first great international combine, General Motors, was obliged to bow before Ralph Nader. Forced by this young lawyer in 1965 to withdraw from sale a potentially dangerous make of car, the firm failed in its endeavour to discredit him, and with him consumerism. Since then, Nader has succeeded in promoting seven important laws concerning the protection of the environment and the health of consumers. Though he was dealing with producers rather than traders, his action was not without significance for the latter, for it gave fresh life to the consumer movement.

In the United States, the first comparative test of merchandise had been made in 1928 by the Consumers' Research Association, which split in 1936 into two private groups. Since Nader became associated with one of them, the Consumers' Union, this body has tested 2,000 products a year and published a review read by two million families. But in this liberal democracy, it was only quite recently that consumers began rather timidly to become partners in the whole commercial process, instead of merely submitting to it, and some years elapsed before they were sufficiently organised and informed to be able to become an effective force. This was especially so since recent presidents have appeared to be opponents rather than arbiters, and have refused to create a federal agency for the protection of consumers.

Henceforth, as well as the producers, the more realistic of the traders have abandoned their policy of disregard for the consumer; the new methods adopted are no longer only directed towards maximisation of profit from the flow of commodities, but increasingly also towards maintaining a profit while catering for the needs of their clientele. One minor aspect of this, but significant in that it increased operational expenses, was the introduction in 1975, by the chains of supermarkets, of 'hostesses' whose function is to inform and advise customers.

Post–1950 commercial innovations   In order to increase sales, the new line adopted by the traders has been to adapt themselves more closely to the life-style and purchasing habits of consumers – and perhaps also to transform them! For a growing number of shoppers the main object is to purchase the maximum amount of goods and services in the shortest possible time. The traders, for their part, seek to develop impulse-buying in order to maximise the potential of their premises and displays.

How can the functional attractiveness of the shop be improved, save by diversification of the counters and services? The motto of the distributors is a kind of commercial version of the classical rule of drama: 'unity of time, place and action': arrange the place so that the act of purchasing may be as frequent as possible in the time that the customer has at his disposal.

The diversification of the kinds of goods and services that can be obtained, depending on the size of the shop, may be effected either by abandoning specialisation or by setting up a coordinated series of specialised shops. The de-specialisation of shops has gained much ground in recent years; already, by 1967, for example, only 22 per cent of the male ready-to-wear sales were in shops devoted exclusively to this type of merchandise, and comparable figures were 28 per cent for shoes, 35 per cent for women's clothing, 41 per cent for furniture, and 42 per cent for electrical goods including radio and television. This phase of increasing diversification is also accompanied by the growth of self-service stores, by the establishment of giant 'shopping centres' or 'discounters' and more recently of 'home centres', 'warehouse stores' and 'superstores', together with the development of various forms of unspecialised sales, of different kinds but all derived from nineteeth-century or pre-war types such as door-to-door sales, mail-order sales, 'catalog show-rooms', and automatic vending machines.

To counterbalance this growth of the unspecialised store, there has been an increase in specialty shops. This has clearly involved a widening in the nature of specialist trading, that in itself reflects the growing variety of goods manufactured to supply a consumption-oriented society.

All these developments have been accompanied by an intensification of advertising, about 50 per cent of it in the daily papers and 30 per cent on television. In 1974 the food trades devoted $80 million to this end – but this sum still only represented 0.07 per cent of their annual turnover. Experience has shown that any reduction in advertising produces a serious fall in sales in many types of shop.

Evolution of self-service stores   This may be summarised in four points:

1. *Increased attention to de-specialisation.*   This is effectively demonstrated in the internal look of supermarkets by the growth of the non-food sectors; the term 'combination store' is applied to such shops of over 400 m² floor space occupied by a single tenant. In much the same way the supermarkets have linked themselves with shopping centres, in order to get facilities that they could not themselves provide for their clients.

2. *Growing attention to the services provided.*   This is another form of de-specialisation, extending the purely commercial area into the whole realm of tertiary services used by the public. It includes the traditional commercial services such as advice, credit (though now with the use of credit cards), home delivery of goods purchased, and so on, but also, in the more important stores, allied services such as banking counters and the hiring of equipment, or, in the major business centres, association with a growing number of service shops (e.g. travel agents). In the smaller supermarkets (under 1,500 m² floor space), in recent years, some 20 to 25 per cent of the takings have been derived from these services, and the proportion rises to 35–40 per cent in the larger ones (over 1,800 m²).

Some self-service stores are now offering other types of service as well. Thus the 'convenience stores' are small 'emergency' shops, offering a relatively limited range of brands and varieties, but open very early in the morning and late at night. Their turnover is of the order of $200,000. They provide the first example in the United States of a return to the 'corner shop' principle – though they are far removed from the traditional corner shop, since they have parking lots and high price mark-ups. From only 500 in 1957, they rose in number to 20,300 in 1973, and they sold 3.8 per cent of all the foodstuffs. Since 1972 they are, with the superstores, the only type of shop to have increased the volume of their sales.

There is a general tendency also for a lengthening of the opening hours of shops; more of them are remaining open day and night, including Sundays.

3. *Increase in shopping floor-space.*   This results in large measure from the previous tendencies. Very large figures have only been reached in the last few years: in 1973 the supermarket average was 1,744 m², but from 1970 a number have been built with selling areas of 2,200 – 2,500 m². However, this is the beginning of the age of superstores, that we study below.

4. *Improvement of the quality and atmosphere of shops.*   This is general, and is aimed at putting the client in a state of euphoria, ready for impulse buying. In many subtle ways individual shops endeavour to create a strong and distinctive personality of their own – a kind of 'trade mark', in fact.

Rapid multiplication of giant stores   Beginning shortly before the Second World War to serve the characteristic loosely knit suburbs of detached houses, increasingly distant from the central business districts of the towns, the 'shopping centres' mark the commencement in the United States of modern urban commerce. One of the pioneers was Victor Gruen. His architect planners were inspired more by the creations of the remote past – the Greek *stoa* (public hall), the Roman arcade, the oriental bazaar – than by the markets of mediaeval Europe.

One of the fundamental aspects of the study of these shopping centres is their localisation, for they are major elements in the whole commercial network. We shall study this in Part II of this book. Here we are concerned with them simply as elements in a commercial system.

The 75 centres of the first generation (pre-1950) were mainly small open markets, covering 4 to 10 hectares, and with 15 to 30 individual shops including one small department store, and parking space for 500 to 1,000 cars. Only a few had regional significance; the most successful was the Cross County Yorkers, near New York; here, on 15 hectares, were more than 50 shops and two large department stores, served by 3,000 to 10,000 parking spaces.

The second generation were mainly regional centres, built between 1950 and 1960. There are more than 2,000 of these, distinguished from their predecessors by greatly increased dimensions (about 100 shops facing on to an open or covered mall), and the presence of two large department stores, of which one was often constructed later in order to increase the attraction of the centre. One of their main defects was the spread of the parking lots, that sometimes necessitated a 10- or 15-minute walk to the centre. In this group may be included Old Orchard, in Chicago, Tri County, near Cincinnati, Evergreen (Chicago) and Roosevelt Field (New York).

After 1960, though further shopping centres of this type were opened, as well as smaller ones serving particular quarters of cities, the trend was for the building of immense covered markets, architecturally planned, extending over 20 hectares. Constructed usually on two floors, with one or more levels of underground parking, these centres, forming part of long-term city planning, make themselves more attractive by incorporating the shops of competing chain-store businesses. One of the first such centres was Randhurst (Chicago), opened in 1962; it has 110,000 m² of floor space, of which one-half is occupied by three large department stores and the rest by 90 smaller shops; there are 7,400 parking spaces, and its plan envisaged that 10 per cent of the sales would be from food shops, 40 per cent from the large department stores, and the rest from non-food shops.

In 1973 the United States had more than 14,000 shopping centres of all sizes, but mainly medium and small; some 500 of them provided air-conditioned accommodation. Between them they accounted for 43 per cent of the national retail sales. The biggest one of all is in the suburbs of Chicago: it has 220,000 m² of floor space, 211 shops, including 4 large department stores, and 20 restaurants; it demonstrates clearly that such regional centres are becoming new poles of economic and social life.

It is envisaged that by 1980 there may be 22,000 shopping centres, having one-half of all the retail trade. At the present time, about half the new retail outlets are in shopping centres, which are becoming a grave menace to the traditional central business districts of cities; an example is furnished by the gift-shops – those in central districts now only take 44 per cent of the total receipts.

Another aspect of the tendency for gigantism is the opening of department stores with very extensive floor-space. With many departments spread over a sales area of over 3,000 m², they have one thing in common – the giving of discount.[6] But this, at first applying to all goods on sale, is becoming less and less systematic, as once again the emphasis is veering towards quality, the tone of the shop, and service to the customer. Most of these large-area shops belong to chains. They are of two types.

The first are general stores, and these again are of two kinds: 'cargos' and superstores. The cargos, originating less than twenty years ago, comprise a series of small one-owner shops; these are really covered markets with rudimentary facilities, standing isolated on one or two hectares of land, often in the open countryside. They give discounts of about 20 per cent on all goods, which leaves them with a profit margin lower than 12 per cent on foodstuffs (as low as 5 per cent on preserves), compensated by that on other commodities. The superstores were until a few years ago just large supermarkets. Now, however, as in the hypermarkets of Europe, they are giant department stores in which the non-food sectors are of great importance. The 'Grand Bazar' of the Jewel organisation, opened in 1973 in a Chicago suburb, is the prototype of this new generation of superstores; still the unique American example, it is, in its area of 9000 m², in its decor, the range and assortment of its merchandise, the importance of fresh and frozen foods, and the layout of its various departments, an adaptation of the French type of hypermarket. As such, it is the first example since the end of the nineteenth century of an American import of a commercial technique. The superstores, as a group, now provide 7 per cent of the sales points for groceries, and receive 16 per cent of the takings; despite discount rates that are less than those given by the cargos, but are still large, their gross profit margin is 23 per cent (30 per cent on non-food goods, 16 per cent on groceries and 20 per cent on meat). It is reckoned that by 1985 the superstores may control 50 per cent of the national food trade, with less than 10,000 premises. This will result in the closure of almost half the existing supermarkets (by 1975, A & P had already closed 1,300 of the 4,500 that it controlled a few years earlier). It is probable that the hypermarkets, by their very nature, will never yield the returns that made the fortune of the supermarkets, so long advantaged by the absence of real competition; the superstores are in competition with the cargos and the commercial centres. The consumer is the beneficiary of this real struggle for his custom.

The other large-area stores are more specialised, and all reflect the evolution of a way of life that is geared to the development of the individual house-property,[7] to increased leisure and higher incomes. As well as 'garden centres', more than 3,000 'home-centres' have appeared since 1960, devoted to furnishing, equipment and 'do-it-yourself' repairs; of all the branches of retail trading, it is this that gives the greatest profit margin. Other new shops are the 'warehouse stores', specialists in furniture, adding the attraction of discount to the vast array of stock; customers have to pass through the warehouse in order to reach the showroom, and may have the goods delivered. Then there are sales centres for sports, camping and toys (veritable mini-Disneylands); and hobby centres that combine these branches; in the 1960s there were some small ones (500 with 1,400 m² floor-space), but the majority of those opened in the last few years (at the rate of one a day!) are larger than 3,000 m².

The progress of certain revived sales techniques   Since the greatest efficiency is achieved by not requiring the client to go to the shop, the sales processes designed to touch the customer wherever he may be, at home or away, but in places where he does not intend to make purchases, are exploited more and more vigorously by this American system, that is anxious to expand.

The *mail-order sale* business, launched by the big stores more than half a century ago, has staged a considerable revival. It is currently used by the publishing trade, in hotel furnishing, by hospitals, many consumer-goods industries, and by servicing companies. There are 5,900 firms specialising in mail-order sales, and their turnover now represents 10 per cent of the national retail business, as against only 4 per cent in 1970. Contrary to the general trend, the mail-order business is growing more rapidly than the average for retailing. The five major concerns are the large store proprietors Sears Roebuck, 20 per cent of whose income comes from mail-order, Montgomery Ward, J. C. Penney, Spiegel and Ardens.

To increase the size and profitability of their prospecting for custom, the firms use various commercial card-indexes; they purchase these, using for example the index of credit-card holders from certain petrol companies; but recently they have developed a new technique that is partly derived from the mail-order business and partly from the discount stores. This is the 'discount catalog showroom', the latest in the long list of American sales devices. It consists of the setting up of a shop in which are displayed samples of all the items in a particular catalogue. The customer can purchase on the spot; the existence of stock in reserve reduces the inconvenience of breakages and loss of price-tags, which are the plague of self-service stores; but he can also order by correspondence in the full knowledge of what he is getting, thus avoiding the major hazard of purchasing from a catalogue. The prices are subject to discount, but have the additional advantage of stability, since they correspond to the printed catalogue. There were 1,200 catalogue showrooms in the United States in 1973, effecting 0.5 per cent of the total retail sales; but their number had risen to 3,000 in 1974. The principal firm, Consumer's Distributing, has 52 showrooms in the US and 115 in Canada. The present classification of catalogue showrooms by type of commodities shows that 20–30 per cent deal in jewellery, 12–14 per cent in household electrical goods, 6–11 per cent in silver table-ware, 7 per cent in photography and binoculars, and the remainder in gifts, games and leather goods; about half the turnover is effected during the last three months of the year, the present-buying season. The running costs of this type of establishment are lower than all other types, and the profits higher, so that the 1973–4 average of pre-tax dividends was 10 per cent.

Home sales by canvassers is a universal practice, but it is the business of certain important companies such as Avon, Revlon and Fuller Brush, as well as numerous smaller ones, numbering in all some 77,000 in 1967, with an annual turnover of $2.5 billion.

Finally, more than 10,000 firms are engaged in the *automatic vending* business, in public places and in places of work, or even at the entrance to certain shops to facilitate out-of-hours shopping. This system began at the end of last century in the United States, and in 1972 it accounted for $7 billion of sales, one-third being cigarettes and one-third drinks; this sum represents (at constant value) more than double that of 10 years earlier, and it led to pre-tax dividends of 4 to 6.5 per cent.

All these variations in the internal trading system of the United States tend to reinforce its role in the national economy. It is difficult to express this quantitatively, but one may appreciate the growth in employment, particularly of salaried personnel. Between 1950 and 1972, the Federal Bureau of

Economic Analysis recorded a 50 per cent increase in employment in commerce, more rapid in wholesaling and less so in retailing (if, as before, we exclude restaurants and the automobile trade). Furthermore, the ratio of salaried employment to wage-earning has risen from 4 to 1 in 1948, to 5.7 to 1 in 1967. All this corresponds to a much greater expansion in business, for it must not be forgotten that there has been a great increase in productivity due to the use of business machinery and the rationalising of management. Unfortunately, there has also been an acceleration in the rhythm expected of the labour force during its hours of work. According to the Harvard Business School, the average turnover per square metre of floor-space in specialty shops and department stores will grow by 20 per cent, assuming a constant dollar, between now and the late 1980s, without any alteration in the part played in general running expenses by salaries (presently 19 per cent).

Just as the structure of the commercial system influences the organisation of shopping types, in particular by imposing limits of viability according to the type of population grouping in which they are set up, so the evolution of the commercial system is accompanied, as we shall see in Part II, by a remodelling of the spatial distributions of the shopping network.

Table 1. The major Western commercial firms

Ten largest retail enterprises in USA in 1973			
Name of firm	Turnover (billion French francs)	Net profit (% of turnover)	No. of employees
1. Sears Roebuck	57.9	5.5	401,000
2. Safeway Stores	31.9	1.3	117,221
3. A & P	31.7	0.2	113,800
4. J. C. Penney	29.3	3.0	200,000
5. S. S. Kresge	22.1	2.9	125,000
6. Kroger	19.8	0.7	50,400
7. Marcor	19.2	2.4	142,184
8. F. W. Woolworth	17.5	2.5	213,414
9. Fed. Dept. Stores	13.9	3.8	86,500
10. Rapid American	11.0	1.3	90,000

Twelve largest retail enterprises in western Europe, 1972		
Name of firm	Country	Turnover (billion French francs)
1. Karstad Kepa	W. Germany	9.0
2. Kaufhof-Kaufhalle	W. Germany	8.1
3. Printemps-Prisunic	France	8.0
4. Hertil Bilka	W. Germany	8.0
5. Quelle	W. Germany	6.8
6. Marks and Spencer	UK	6.4
7. Migros	Switzerland	5.8
8. Galeries Lafayette -Monoprix	France	5.5
9. C & A Brennink Meyer	W. Germany	5.4
10. Great Universal Stores	UK	5.2
11. Nouv. Gal. Réunis-Uniprix	France	4.8
12. G. B.-Inno-B.M.*	Belgium	4.8

* The amalgamation of these three did not take place until 1973.

Source: Distribution d'aujourd'hui (Belgium), volumes for 1974 and 1975.

The commercial system of other developed capitalist countries

The countries to which we now turn are all adherents to the capitalist system, and have long been politically independent; they are certainly not underdeveloped, for their GNP exceeded $1,000 per inhabitant in 1974, and they all have the example of the United States as their aim, in commerce as in other spheres. Their civilisations, following revolutions in industry and in transport, have developed a mercantile economy. Among the examples cited we shall find that the principal differences of commercial organisation stem from the peculiarities of the traditional system of exchange; from the extent to which, for various reasons, an integrated commercial system and American-type sales techniques have been developed; and finally, the degree of control exercised over commercial enterprises, albeit within these liberal economies, by public authorities.

In western European countries

Consumer behaviour and sales techniques have a degree of similarity in western Europe that is a reflection of a common culture. But although the commercial systems have the same origins and the same goals as in the United States, the system of commodity distribution shows notable differences from that which we have described above. These differences in the degree of economic or spatial concentration of the trading facilities, and in the modernisation of sales techniques, in other words the sum total of the productivity of the personnel and the distribution of shops, also vary from country to country. They result from disparities in the level of economic development, but also, to a greater extent than one might imagine, from national psycho-sociological, and therefore political characteristics.

The role of commerce in the national economy does not always attain the same importance, and it has developed in different ways. One need only examine Table 2, looking particularly at the United Kingdom and Belgium, to realise that beyond a certain level of consumption, there is no systematic correlation between the size of the GNP and commercial activity, nor of the value of the former as a guide to the national employment figure.

Table 2. Role of commerce in national economy

Country	GNP per inhabitant in dollars, 1971	% of secondary sector in GDP		% of commerce in GDP		% commercial employment/total employment	
		1961	1971	1961	1971	1961	1971
W. Germany	3,571	54.6	53.5	13.2	12.2	12.6	13.1
Denmark	3,507	39.0	36.5	14.7	13.0	14.6	13.0
France	3,175	47.3	46.4	11.7	10.5	10.1	11.4
Belgium	3,007	40.6	41.5	12.2	13.2	13.5	15.1
Netherlands	2,818	44.1	42.4	12.1	11.7	13.8	16.0
UK	2,454	41.9	37.5	10.5	8.9	13.6	12.8
Italy	1,887	41.0	41.5	11.8	12.0	9.8	11.1

Sources: Gross National Product: *United Nations Statistical Yearbook.*
Gross Domestic Product: *National Accounts of OECD countries.*

In all countries the contribution of agriculture to the national product is declining; it is everywhere inferior to commerce (except in Italy in 1961); whilst the part played by private and public services is increasing. With regard to commerce, the position is not the same in all the countries. Certainly the variations in the relative importance of industry and commerce are in step, an increase in the production of goods implying the establishment of adequate sales outlets. We may also note that the role of industry, like that of commerce, is not increasing except in Belgium and Italy; elsewhere it is losing ground to other services. It is no longer the standard of living but the degree of modernisation of the economy, that differentiates these capitalist countries. This modernisation is characterised at the moment by an expansion of services more rapid than that of goods, and by improvements in quality rather than quantity. Commerce is clearly not a spearhead in the modernisation of national economies. There is also a disharmony between total national output and commercial employment: productivity increases much more slowly in distribution than in other branches of the economy. However, once a certain threshold in the modernisation of commercial 'equipment' has been passed, commercial activities become less demanding in manpower. So far, only the United Kingdom and the Scandinavian countries have reached this point. Jefferys and Knee (1962) estimated that employment in the distributive trades in the whole of western Europe represented 8.9 per cent of the total employment in 1930, 10.3 per cent in 1950, and 11 per cent in 1955. At the moment the figure is probably 12 per cent, but this may well fall in the future.

Though the standard of living of the population does not automatically influence the modernisation of commercial activities, there are several points at which its influence is dominant: thus the lower the standard, the higher is the proportion of foodstuffs in the total volume of sales, and the higher the male employment role in commerce.

We can distinguish several types of commercial structure in the countries of western Europe, depending on the degree to which they have followed the lead of the United States in the modernising process.

In a first group we may include the Mediterranean countries, which have the

Table 3. Commercial concentration

Country	Proportion of integrated businesses in total retail sales (% 1971)	Employees per establishment		Number of inhabitants per	
		Retail 1971	Wholesale 1970	Retail shop 1971	Self-service stores 1971
Italy	8.8	2	5	57	36,550
Belgium	17.3	2.5	4.1	65	3,181
France	28.7	3.4	8.7	98	2,340
Netherlands	29.1	3.7	8.5	88	1,400
W. Germany	32.6	5	10.8	125	712
UK	50.3	5	18.8	65	3,181
Switzerland	35.8	?	?	156	1,100
Denmark	23.2	4	8.4	95	941
Sweden	38.4	4	?	110	946

lowest per capita incomes in western Europe: Italy, Greece, Spain, Portugal. To this list Belgium must be added, though its standard of living is higher. In all these countries, the processes of distribution, though in course of transformation, retain a much more traditional pattern than elsewhere, a pattern more like the age-old model that made the fortunes of Europe's merchants. Small family businesses, independent and old-fashioned, are still dominant.

Table 4. Integration and voluntary association (Percentage of national market served by different types of commercial organisation, 1971).

Country	Large-scale businesses			Mail-order sales	Associations of independent retailers
	Chain-stores	Department stores	Consumer cooperatives		
Italy	3.0	3.9	1.7	0.2	5
Belgium	9.9	8.2	2.4	0.8	8
France	15.2	9.5	2.9	1.1	19
Netherlands	20.3	6.3	1.6	0.9	30
W. Germany	14.6	10.3	3.0	4.7	35
UK	29.1	10.3	7.1	3.8	14
Switzerland	6.6	11.8	16.7	0.7	?
Denmark	6.0	5.6	11.4	0.2	17
Sweden	6.6	13.0	17.0	1.8	26

In the Mediterranean countries, the general level of economic development is reflected in the degree of involvement in modern capitalist commerce. On the contrary, in Belgium psycho-sociological and political factors have contributed to the survival of outmoded forms, a survival that surprisingly conceals a genuine dynamism.

A second group includes Switzerland and the Nordic countries, which are all moderately well-off, though the level of affluence in Sweden is double that of Finland and Iceland. These countries have some relatively novel commercial organisations, and some consumer power is beginning to temper the excesses of commercial enterprise.

The last group includes the 'consumer societies'. Freedom of enterprise has fostered creativity, but the business magnates have been content to reproduce, some two decades later and with some minor differences due to various factors, the models provided by the United States. The Netherlands, France and Western Germany are following the United Kingdom, where the transformation of the commercial system is most advanced.

The 'traditionalist' group
In the Mediterranean countries, expenditure on foodstuffs continues to represent more than half the total amount spent in shops, and food shops remain slightly more numerous than non-food shops. The most common form is the grocery, which is often in fact a miniature general store. Trading occupies more men than women. The shopkeeper, known personally to all his customers, renders numerous and various services. In 1974 there were no less than three such stores to every thousand people, and in Portugal almost six. All

the large Mediterranean towns have had their department stores and *magasins populaires* (variety stores) for a long time. In Italy, the seven large stores of La Rinascente and the 300 variety stores controlled by the Standa and UPIM groups have a high reputation. The investment policies of large organisations such as Fiat and Montedison have helped the growth of these trading firms. The feeble investment capacity of the small traders, the inadequate standardisation of saleable products, the dislike of the Latin peoples for any form of shopping that does away with human contacts, and the low income level of many households have hindered the development of the self-service principle. It is in Spain that self-service is best developed, with one *autoservicio* to 4,500 people in 1972 – but fewer than 100 supermarkets; the government encourages the spread of small units, particularly in the tourist areas. Elsewhere there is at the most one self-service store to 35,000 inhabitants. There are about 100 supermarkets in Portugal, and a few in Greece, that are frequented by the wealthier section of the population that is accustomed to foreign travel. Italy is better provided with large shops, and has 700 supermarkets. Hypermarkets have made their appearance thanks to Brazilian investments in Portugal, and French in Spain and Italy (two Carrefour establishments in 1972); but in the latter country the threat of such foreign competition has stimulated the local organisations, and in 1975 Rinascente opened its second hypermarket near Brescia.

Signs of economic concentration within the sphere of selling are more apparent in the non-food sector than in foodstuffs, and this applies both to retailing and to wholesaling, which still has a superabundance of units. Integrated commerce nowhere reachers 10 per cent of the total sales, and even this is largely due to the activities of such international groups as SPAR and V.G. Chain-stores are more important than cooperatives. The resistance of the small traditional shops to the rise of large capitalist undertakings is stronger than elsewhere in Europe in these countries, where concealed unemployment still induces many workers to emigrate. It finds an echo in political circles. In Italy, the fear of aggravating the already numerous social tensions led the government to pass a law in June 1971 requiring local authorities to make plans every four years for the development of the system of distribution. This law has certainly brought about a stagnation of commercial structures, for in the absence of a plan it is forbidden to grant new licences – and few communes have made any plans. There is stagnation too in the field of economic capitalism, for preference is always given in the case of new developments to consumer cooperatives or groups of small retailers.

The modernisation of the selling business is certainly more advanced in Belgium than on the shores of the Mediterranean. But on the other hand the integration is no greater, either in retailing or in wholesaling. A multitude of small shops, very well maintained, conserves the vitality of every town centre. The 'cultural landscape' of commerce has an air of permanence, and a high density of sales points, with a high intensity of service to the population, are still characteristic of Belgian commerce. Although food shops no longer number more than half the total, there are 2.8 general food stores to every 1,000 inhabitants. This is all the more surprising since the nature of consumption differs but little from that of neighbouring countries such as The Netherlands, West Germany or even France, where the commercial structures have advanced considerably since the last war.

Jeanneney (1954) showed that even in 1947 the feeble integration of commercial equipment (3.4 establishments per 100 inhabitants), and the low productivity of distribution workers, put Belgium in a class well below the United States and Sweden (1 shop to 100 people), and also below the other western European countries with a comparable standard of living (under 2 shops to 100 people). The difficulty of getting food supplies during the war and post-war periods, as is well known, had favoured the multiplication of small middlemen living on the 'black market' (Michel and Vander-Eycken, 1974). But the same was true in France, where however, the plethora of small shopkeepers did not reach the same proportions as in Belgium. The difference stems from a law passed in Belgium in the 1930s – by a democratically elected parliament, be it noted, and thus representing a certain national mentality – protecting the traditional commercial system. Thus because liberalising influences have not run their normal course, Belgium possesses this peculiar commercial structure, somewhat archaic in appearance, from which it is now trying to extricate itself. In the early 1930s the economic depression led, in many parts of the world, to measures of interference with the complete freedom of the economic system, in particular as regards external trade, but in no other country did the break with liberalism have more serious consequences for internal trade than in Belgium. Not without reason was the word 'padlock' applied to the decision to prevent the opening of new shops employing more than 5 persons, or the expansion of existing ones, in towns of over 100,000 population, or even 3 persons in other communes. Despite some relief between 1944 and 1959, this draconian measure remained in force until 1961. It is not surprising that in 1955 the structure of Belgium's internal trade appeared more old-fashioned than that of the Mediterranean countries, though with a generally higher productivity, resulting from a higher standard of living, in other sectors of the economy, and a body of tradespeople more competent than those of the Mediterranean area.

Table 5

Country	Number of people per retail shop	Number of employees per shop	Total sales per shop ($)
Belgium	34	1.6	11,497
Spain	105	2.4	13,611
Italy	59	1.8	10,320
Portugal	89	2.2	8,969
Greece	84	1.7	6,970
France	57	2.3	20,253

Source: Jefferys and Knee (1962, p. 37).

During the same period France, at the tail-end of the group of other developed countries of western Europe, was already in process of freeing itself from the effects of the black market.

The fact that it became possible after 1961 to open large retail shops in Belgium rendered acutely necessary the adoption of parallel measures to prevent a catastrophic slaughter of small shops. Various edicts concerned with taxation and credit favoured small independent shop-keepers. A more unusual 'establishment law' was passed in 1958 (and completed in 1970–1), designed to improve the health of the business profession by imposing on those who wish to set up shop on their own account, levels of investment and experience of management. Unfortunately these measures have remained something of a dead letter.

Between 1962 and 1971, the directors of the more dynamic commercial enterprises endeavoured to catch up on the delays, which had been caused by governmental restrictions, to the organisation of distribution in the American style. And as often happens when an economically backward country suddenly finds the means of remedying its deficiency, it is the very latest techniques that have been tried out, with the help of the banks and of large industrial firms who, conscious of the poor shape of the distribution process in Belgium, have been quick to take advantage of any loophole in the regulations. With one supermarket to every 20,000 people, and one hypermarket to 175,000, Belgium has, since 1972, risen to the top of the western European league, alongside West Germany. The sales area of the large shops (supermarkets, hypermarkets and department stores) has trebled between 1960 and 1972, reaching a figure of 1,435,000 m², and their proportion of the national retail turnover has risen from 7 to 16 per cent (compared with 25 per cent in the USA), with a rise from 5 to 25 per cent in the food sector. Despite all this, however, shops with a turnover greater than $100,000 scarcely represented 5 per cent of the national total, as against more than half in the United States. In the matter of the concentration of retail distribution, Belgium is about 25 years behind the USA (Michel and Vander-Eycken, 1974). Between 1961 and 1972 the takings of the big shops have expanded more rapidly (5.7 per cent increase) than in the Mediterranean countries, and actually more rapidly than in the United Kingdom, The Netherlands or Luxembourg, but the rate has been lower than in France and West Germany (increase 9 per cent), or in the Scandinavian countries (increase 7 per cent). The small independent shops that in 1973 still effected 80 per cent of the national retail sales remained, with those of The Netherlands, the most hostile in Europe towards the idea of cooperation, especially in the non-food sector, thus proving that the psycho-sociological factors that have contributed to the repeated extension of the 'padlock' regulations are still very much in evidence.

Nevertheless, one can find examples in Belgium of all the new types of sales units that have come out of the United States since the last war: auto-centres, garden centres, home centres, hobby centres, drugstores. A dozen shopping centres of moderate size (between 10,000 and 30,000 m², as at Woluwe, Anderlecht and Courtrai) have been created, thanks to the participation of large distribution firms: G.B.-Inno-B.M. (which is twelfth in size in Europe, see Table 1). Delhaize le Lion, and Sarma,[8] each having a turnover of 10 billion Belgian francs, and Louis Delhaize. Only one large retailing firm, Colruyt, specialising in discount and in cash-and-carry, has not participated in this development. Thus it seems that to a greater extent than in other European countries, the leaders of Belgian commerce have been fascinated by everything American.

This wave of new creations, especially hypermarkets, has clearly excited a movement of protest among the independent shopkeepers, and as in France, in 1962 and again in 1972, new laws were passed regulating the establishment of new commercial enterprises, and a committee was set up, 'to make a comprehensive study of the distribution of shopping facilities, with short-term and medium-term plans' (Michel and Vander-Eycken, 1974). Even though the smallness of the national territory facilitates such a study, this concern with spatial organisation is interesting, because it is relatively uncommon in capitalist countries.

The lack of concentration in Belgian retailing is partly responsible for a similar situation in wholesaling, the structure of which also reflects the abnormal circumstances resulting from the 'padlock' law. With many small businesses satisfying a multitude of retailers, the average individual wholesaler employs no more people than his counterpart in Italy, and many fewer than in other Common Market countries. However, 60 per cent of those employed in wholesaling are in firms with more than 10 employees (West Germany and The Netherlands have 70 per cent, the others much less). The importance of wholesaling in the total commercial activity shows clearly that Belgium remains a nation of shopkeepers, with 14.7 employees in commerce to every 1,000 inhabitants, a figure more than double that of the Mediterranean countries, greater than France (13.1) and the United Kingdom (13.9), and surpassed only by West Germany (19.4) and The Netherlands (20). The opening in 1975 at Heysel of the Brussels International Trade Mart, the largest building devoted to import and export trade in Europe, and open all the year, unlike other trade fairs, is a sign of Belgian desire to create a new image as a trading country.

Commercial systems characterised by a socialising liberalism
1. One might hesitate to include *Switzerland* in this group, but the important growth of consumer cooperatives and the concern of the public authorities for the consumer place it in a transitional category, more closely akin to the Scandinavian countries than to the industrialised Common Market countries.

In Switzerland, integrated commerce already holds a fair share of the market. Even in 1960 it effected 27 per cent of the total sales, a figure that placed it third in the world after the USA and the UK. Its share has increased slowly and fairly regularly in all forms of distribution, though not without some difficulties for the chain stores, which are tending to specialise in the face of competition.

One of the main characteristics of Swiss commerce is the part played by consumer cooperatives, more particularly by two large groups, Migros (with a turnover of 5.4 billion Swiss francs in 1974) and U.S.C. (turnover 4.7 billion). The latter, a union of small rural cooperatives, employs 32,000 people, has over 1,800 sales outlets and serves nearly a million households. As for the better-known Migros, it has 500 shops (including 142 supermarkets that have half the total turnover, 13 hypermarkets, 80 specialised shops and 100 mobile shops). The descendant of a limited company founded in 1925 by Duttweiler, that from 1930 marked its perishable products with a terminal sales date, it became a cooperative in 1942, and is now a federation of twelve cooperatives, serving 700,000 members. In order to work on small profit margins, Migros has established a number of factories for the treatment of produce. It also runs its own bank, an insurance company and a tourist agency called Hotelplan. For a long time it has had a policy of worker-participation. Being wedded to the ideal of consumer health, Migros refuses to sell alcoholic liquor, tobacco, or polluting forms of petrol, and will not use plastic bottles; 1 per cent of its turnover is devoted to the development of cultural activities, and it has founded two research institutes, one for socio-economic enquiries and the other for the scientific investigation of nutritional problems.

Certain other larger and prosperous store-owing companies are also investing in self-service stores: Jelmoli (with a 1974 turnover of more than 800 million Swiss francs), with Credit Suisse as the principal shareholder, has shown much initiative in actually opening branches abroad, for example, one in the Part Dieu at Lyon, France.

Switzerland is the country with the highest density of retail shops: one shop and seven employees to every 170 inhabitants. The density of food shops is also high – one to 480 persons in 1973. But the re-fashioning of the network of retail food outlets is also more rapid than elsewhere in Europe, for in 1970 there was one to 400 persons. This evolution has been accompanied by the growth of self-service, that in 1970 could be found in only 35 per cent of the shops (compare 73 per cent in West Germany and 53 per cent in The Netherlands). Half the self-service shops were at that time independent, though it is true that most of them were affiliated to purchasing groups or to voluntary chains,[9] either regional (USEGO, ALRO) or international (V.G.). On the other hand, the 400 or so supermarkets, of moderate dimensions, were almost all owned by big commercial firms.

The first shopping centre, Glatt, opened in 1968 at Zurich, had by 1975 become the largest in the country, with 50,000 m^2 of floor space. Since two more, actually situated opposite each other, have subsequently been opened in the same city, this market is to some extent saturated.

Swiss consumers are very quality-conscious, and the authorities encourage this tendency; in the canton of Vaud, for example, the education of children as future consumers starts in the schools at the age of ten.

2. The *Nordic countries,* despite differences in consumption levels and in local commercial structures, can be said to constitute another type. We take Sweden as an example, since it has been and remains a model for the neighbouring countries, because its remarkable economic development that has given its citizens the highest standard of living in the world (the GNP in 1973 was $6,185, as against $6,167 in the United States) has not brought about the elimination of the socialist principles that have influenced the organisation of its internal trade for more than a century.

We must make it clear at the outset that in comparison with Sweden, the Danish and Norwegian systems of internal distribution have a weaker development of the cooperative movement, together with a dynamic independent sector that is sustained by active professional associations and powerful purchasing groups. Moreover, Norway has hardly yet begun to develop very large stores and shopping centres (the only one of any significance in 1971 was at Moss, some 50 km from Oslo). As for the Danes, while they have taken to shopping centres of 10,000 to 20,000 m^2, they are opposed to the development of hypermarkets. In Finland and in Iceland, internal trade is dominated, to a greater extent than in Sweden, by cooperatives that are responsible for 40 per cent of the total sales; some shopping centres are being planned, and large discount shops have found favour among Finnish customers. Consumer protection seems less well organised by the public authorities in these four other Nordic countries than in Sweden, and perhaps that is why one finds consumer associations as in other industrial countries.

In Sweden, not only has the cooperative movement dominated the world of shopping since 1850, but, unlike the situation in the United Kingdom, it retains an appreciable momentum. Its proportion of total sales rose from 14.5 per cent in 1960 to more than 17 per cent in the mid-1970s, and in foodstuffs its proportion was 25 per cent. The major organisation is K.F., a politically and religiously neutral body created in 1899, that now includes almost all the consumer cooperatives in the country, numbering 222 in 1971. It is remarkable that such a fragmented structure can wield effective economic power. With a clientele of 1.6 million members in 1970 (expanded from 1 million in 1950), K.F. was among the first European retail undertakings to adopt self-service and to adjust its organisation to changes in methods of distribution and the evolution of the purchasing habits of its customers; it had 8,000 sales outlets in 1950, but only 2,500 in 1975, of which nearly 200 were the popular *Domus* shops, together with the *Konsum* supermarkets and several large discount-stores. Its present policy is to build very large shops, and at the same time small ones with a limited range of goods, like the American 'convenience stores'. The group employs 60,000 salaried personnel. Like those of Migros in Switzerland, its activities are many and various, for it is concerned not merely with satisfying the present needs of its customers, but also with assuring them of a certain quality of life. The strength of the cooperative movement has not prevented the growth and prosperity of the variety stores, which had 4.5 per cent of the total turnover in 1962 and 10.6 per cent in 1973, nor of the large department stores whose share rose from 2.1 to 4.3 per cent in the same period. Only chain-stores have made little progress; there is but one major business, that of Metro which controls some 80 supermarkets.

The second chacteristic of Swedish distribution is the purchasing association formed by groups of independent shop-keepers. The principal organisation is the retailers' cooperative, I.C.S. that supplies more than 5,000 shops and has a turnover equal to three-quarters that of K.F. Voluntary chains have less influence. There are also important groupings of wholesalers, such as A.S.K. and S.A.K.O., which serve most of the remaining independent shops. Small and completely isolated shopkeepers are becoming increasingly rare.

This sense of unity among the independent shop-owners explains the rapid adaptation of the whole commercial system to modern techniques. Only one-quarter of the general food shops have not yet adopted self-service. In retailing as a whole there is now one self-service shop to every 900 inhabitants. And they are not merely small ones. Sweden has four times as many supermarkets as Switzerland, though its population is only one-fifth larger and the density eight times less. Generations of urban dwellers from many countries have walked round the shopping centres of Sweden, that were established very early. The largest centres are at Skärholmen, 12 km from Stockholm, with 60,000 m² of floor space, and Västra Frölunda, 7 km from Göteborg. The majority of them, however, cover only 10,000–20,000 m². Moreover, in 1974 it was officially decided not to build any more of over 20,000 m². With a sense of proportion as well as of democracy, the Scandinavians are anxious to avoid spatial disequilibrium of shopping facilities.

The last specific trait of the Swedish commercial system is the existence of an effective 'consumerism', the influence of which is increasing because of official support. There are no large national consumers' associations as in the USA or the UK, but the protection of consumers is assured by three forces: the central bureau L.O. that deals with claims; the cooperative movement whose function is to dispute and take action; and above all the government, led from 1932 to

1975 by the Social Democratic party, that has build up an efficient institutional and juridical framework to give consumers real power in matters of production and trading. We might perhaps add the mass media as a fourth force, creating a large audience for matters concerned with the defence of consumers and of the environment.

In 1973 the government included within the 'National Consumer Office' a whole apparatus that it had built up slowly from 1940, the date of the first 'information bureau' for giving advice to householders. The principal items in this were an Institute of Labelling founded in 1951, the office of consumers' *Ombudsman*, dating from 1954, and the Consumers' Institute founded in 1957 to disseminate information. The objects of the Office are threefold: to develop new means of action so that the population will no longer feel an unequal partner in the producer–consumer relationship, to give assistance to the poorest consumers, and to create a regional organisation to assist consumers to resolve their problems locally. The State has devoted five times more money to this project than has France (Doyère, 1975). Although agreement between the different parties is the method advocated by the administration, authoritarian measures, such as that relating to the size limit for shopping centres, are not excluded. It must be added that in this country, long accustomed to genuine democracy, the decisions of the government are respected.

Despite all these measures, the population has not really the power to take up arms on equal terms against the forces of production and trade. The contestants thus do not lack spokesmen who denounce the publicity given to a policy of protection that according to them is derisory. Bjorn Gillberg, the Swedish counterpart of the American Nader, regards as a piece of humbug the 'consumers' congress' organised by K.F. in 1971, where, however, the whole cooperative movement was put in the dock, accused of having lost sight of its democratic objectives, of having allied itself with private capitalism, and of being more concerned with profit than with the well-being of the consumer, and with publicity rather than objective information. It is true that since this congress K.F. has not changed its basic policy; but what the protesters were demanding savoured less of 'social democracy' than of a socialist policy concerned not only with man but with the whole environment. This sort of thing does not figure among the objectives of liberal socialist commercial systems, for the economy of the undertaking remains the keystone of all social organisations; only the excesses are barred.

The liberal system of the great European powers
The commercial systems of these countries resemble each other because in regard to the main influential factors, the situations are similar: comparable levels of economic development, free capitalist enterprise, and a heritage of mercantile tradition. Another common feature is that at the end of the last century, when their economic policies still ruled the whole world, they gave birth to integrated commerce and allowed it to develop in conditions of free competition. Today, big-business trading holds one-quarter of the market, and chain-stores over 10 per cent. The generally high standard of living allows the non-food sector to rise well above that of foodstuffs, in the number of shops as well as in turnover.

The example of France will enable us the better to understand the evolution of commerce, and its problems, in those industrial countries where, in economic terms, the innovatory forces, to an even greater extent than in the United States, have clashed with those of conservatism, but where the occasional intervention of the state has never systematically favoured the latter as in Belgium.

These diverse national organisations each have their own characteristics, however, that we may briefly outline.

The Netherlands remains a mercantile country with a dynamic wholesale trade, in which retail distribution is seeking a middle course between the two major goals of maximum profit and the best possible service to customers. Since 1960, integrated concerns have doubled their share thanks to the growth in towns of chain-stores and large department stores. The chain-store sector, indeed, is particularly strong in the foodstuffs line, with 35 per cent of the total retail takings in 1972. At the same time the number of independent food shops has diminished by half, from 81,000 to 42,000. Company-owned shops are also increasing, especially in the rural areas.

The Dutch have freely adopted the most modern sales techniques: there are now 27 Albrecht 'baby sharks', and six Litha 'catalogue showrooms', the first of which opened in 1975. Development has been progressive and orderly, avoiding gigantism and anarchy. Thus in the self-service sector, that now represents 85 per cent of food sales, there is one shop to 8,000 inhabitants, for the sales floor-spaces are mostly of small or medium size; in 1970, 93 per cent of the self-service shops were smaller than 400 m^2, and 85 per cent of them were independently owned; in 1971, there were only 18 hypermarkets compared with 55 in Belgium. Much effort is also being expended on the renovation of traditional shops, on converting town-centres into pedestrian zones, only opening shopping centres when such a course appears necessary, and then only small ones. The two main associations of consumers, formed in the 1950s, are very powerful and are encouraged by the government, which regularly consults them and offers them membership of committees concerned with consumption.

In the *German Federal Republic,* the integration of commerce on capitalist lines is more advanced, and it has increased particularly in the last decade or so: a growth of 9 per cent between 1962 and 1971. This is all the more remarkable since the chain-stores and large department stores had a difficult time after 1945, though they are now prosperous; on the contrary, the variety stores have progressed but little. The density of self-service shops, whether large or small ones, has no equivalent elsewhere in the world, and 90 per cent of food sales are effected therein. Independent shopkeepers are grouping themselves to a greater extent, either in association with the two great purchasing cooperatives established early this century, or with the dozen or so voluntary chains opened since 1950, six of which have nation-wide influence. West Germany, together with the United Kingdom, remains at the head of the mail-order business, which employs 62,000 persons in four large firms. The largest of these had a turnover of DM 2 billions in 1973, the seventh largest in Europe. Shopping centres have developed at an increasing rate during the last 20 years, both in number and size; the largest, Ruhr Park at Bochum, opened in 1964 with 21,000 m^2 and now has 70,000 m^2; in 1974 there were fifteen others larger than 15,000 m^2. Recently, however, because of several bankruptcies, it has been decided to slow down the rate of progress and to build smaller centres of

20,000–40,000 m², to put them not only in suburban fringes but in city centres, and to concentrate more on quality and the traditional service.

Up to the present, the effective collaboration between consumer associations, of which the largest has 7 million members, and the national or local governments that largely support them, has been concerned only with problems of the quality and price of goods; trading firms are still completely free to set up shop wherever they like.

It is in the *United Kingdom* that the copying of the United States model has advanced furthest, even to the point of going beyond the model except in the field of technical innovation. Indeed, since the 1950s integrated commerce has achieved 40 per cent of the retail turnover, a figure reached nowhere else outside the United States. This situation need cause no surprise. For though Great Britain has faced many difficulties since the Second World War, and occupies only tenth place in Europe in GNP per inhabitant, it was for a long time, before the loss of its empire, a rich country, the economic leader of industrial Europe, and this explains the progressive nature of its commercial system.

The distributive trades in the United Kingdom*

By whatever criteria one adopts, the distributive trades present a very substantial sector of economic activity in the UK. In 1976 they accounted for 9.5 per cent of the GDP and provided employment for 2.7 million people. Throughout the economic vicissitudes of the past decade, including many profound changes within the distributive trades themselves, these figures have remained remarkably constant.

Traditionally, distribution has been divided into wholesaling and retailing. Today the division is less clear cut, and some observers would even suggest that wholesaling is declining as a separate function. For the sake of clarity however, they will here be treated individually.

Wholesaling

The role of the wholesaler in the overall pattern of distribution has attracted relatively little attention from geographers (but see Vance, 1970; Thorpe and Kirby, 1972). Normally concerned with stockholding, forward purchasing and the distribution of commodities to independent retailers, the wholesaler operates in the competitive no-man's-land between manufacturer and retailer, but recently he has come under pressure from both directions and as a result has undergone numerous changes.

Because of this fluid and rapidly changing situation, it is not easy to make valid generalisations about the structure of wholesaling. Certainly it is true to say that it is less important in the UK than in most other European countries, but this is largely a reflection of differences in the retail structure, especially the size and importance of large-scale retailers. The ratio of wholesale to retail employees is lower in Britain than in any of our EEC neighbours and while many of them were increasing their employment in wholesaling during the 1960s, Britain's numbers declined. The relatively minor importance of wholesalers, at least for one region of the UK, was outlined in the 1971

---

* This section has been contributed by Dr. P. T. Kivell.

National Economic Development Office report.[10] Over a wide range of selected products, 71 per cent were delivered direct from the manufacturer to the retailer while the wholesalers' average share was only 26 per cent; ranging from 16 per cent for clothing to 31 per cent for grocery and 37 per cent for 'other household items'. The same report showed that, contrary to widely held opinion, the position is fairly stable and the wholesalers' share of the market had not slipped significantly. The proportion of food sales, for example, had declined only modestly, from 37 per cent in 1938 to 31 per cent in 1969. Wholesalers rely upon independent retailers for a high proportion of their trade and a major problem currently facing them is the continuing decline in the independent retailers' share of the market.

Among the most important trends prompted by changing trading conditions, we can identify a decline in the number of wholesalers coupled with an increase in average size, the growth of voluntary wholesale chains, especially for food, the growing participation of wholesalers in retailing, and the increasing organisational efficiency of wholesaling operations. One particularly notable development, stemming from the decision of wholesalers to impose a minimum order size, or dispense entirely with travelling representatives, free deliveries and other selling costs, has been the growth of the cash-and-carry warehouse. Operating mainly within the food sector, cash-and-carry warehouses experienced an explosive growth in the late 1960s. Estimates of the total number vary, but the consensus view suggests about 625–650 by the early 1970s, with relatively few additions more recently.

In many ways the reorganisation of wholesaling reflects the changes within retailing, with increases in unit size, the development of chains and associations, and the substitution of the customer's own effort in place of paid labour being particularly important trends. Many of these processes can be illustrated by reference to the example of the merger announced in 1978 between two of the largest food wholesalers, Linfood and Wheatsheaf. In addition to specific financial advantages, this merger will result in the new company having a very broad range of interests in the distribution chain. It will account for 12 per cent of the delivered wholesale market, 16.5 per cent of the cash-and-carry sector and nearly 2 per cent of the retail food market through SPAR and V.G. associations together with their involvement in the Gateway chain of stores and Carrefour hypermarkets.

Retailing
The evolution of retailing in Britain has been well documented (Smith, 1947; Jefferys, 1954; McClelland, 1964; Stacey and Wilson, 1965; Scott, 1970; Davìes, 1976) and the intention here is merely to summarise the organisational structure and identify some broad, contemporary trends. Within the European context, British retailing has established a reputation as one of the largest and most efficient systems, having played a pioneer role in many aspects, notably the growth of the cooperative movement, the development of department stores, the strength of large multiple organisations and the spread of supermarkets. Average shop sizes and numbers of employees per shop are both among the largest in Europe.

Conventionally, retailing is subdivided according to the way in which it is organised, and three main groups are recognised. Table 6 details the breakdown of the total retail trade between these groups and it clearly shows one of the most consistent long-term trends in British retailing, that is, the decline of the independents' share of total sales and the increase of the multiples.

Table 6. Structure of retail trade in Great Britain.

	% of total retail turnover			
	1900	1961	1966	1971
Cooperatives	6.0–7.0	10.8	9.1	7.1
Multiples	3.0–4.5	29.2	34.5	39.0
Independents	86.5–90.0	60.0	56.4	53.9

Source: Jefferys, 1954.
1971 Census of Distribution, Part 1, Table 3.

Independents   Independent retailers, normally defined as operators with less than 10 outlets, are numerically the commonest form of retail organisation in Britain. Out of a total of 473,000 shops in Britain in 1971, approximately 83 per cent were operated by independent retailers, but as Table 6 shows their share of the total retail trade was only 54 per cent. This represents a fairly steady decline of their share of the total turnover throughout the course of this century. Jefferys (1954) has suggested that the independents accounted for 86–90 per cent of the total in 1900, and that they began to feel the most severe effects of competition from the multiples and cooperatives from the 1930s onwards. Although defined as operators with less than 10 outlets, the majority (84 per cent) are in fact single-shop traders and their average size is small. Almost 90 per cent of all shops in Great Britain possessed less than 92.8 m² of selling space in 1971 and it is in this size range that the independents are concentrated. Berry (1977) has shown that the smallest one-third of shops accounted for only 5 per cent of total sales. The trading position of the small shop has become more difficult in recent years due to a number of changes in virtually all aspects of their business environment and attention has been drawn to these problems in studies by Kirby (1974) and Berry (1977).

Independent retailers are represented in all sectors of retailing but their importance varies. Currently they are most important in the newsagents/confectioners/tobacconist and the 'other non-food' sectors, where they account for 84.2 and 70.8 per cent of turnover respectively. In these areas small size, specialisation and personal attention are benefits which the individual shopkeeper can still capitalise upon. At the other end of the scale, the independent retailer has seen his share of the mass food market in the grocery and provision sector shrink to 37.5 per cent (in 1975) under the onslaught of the multiples and cooperatives who are able to offer economies of scale and lower prices on standard items.

One response of the independents has involved the growth of voluntary groups since the mid-1950s. The 1971 Census of Distribution recognises two distinct kinds of voluntary groups:

1. Wholesaler-sponsored groups which are associations between wholesalers and retailers throughout the chain of distribution. Thus there is a close cooperation within the group upon purchasing, display materials, stock control, brand presentation, financing and standardised accounting. The best known groups of this kind are Mace, SPAR and Vivo.

2. Retail buyers' groups in which independent retailers agree to joint purchases of some supplies to obtain the benefits of bulk buying. Such groups are usually restricted to a single town or sub-region.

Such associations have evolved particularly in the food sector and Mersey (1973) suggests that in 1970 one-third of independent grocers were group members and they accounted for over one-half of the grocery turnover in the independent sector.

There is not a great deal of regional variation in the representation of independent shops but they achieve their greatest share of trade in the older industrial cities and dispersed rural settlements of the North West, Yorkshire–Humberside, and Wales; and not surprisingly the average shop size is also smallest in these three regions.

Multiples Multiples are defined by the Census of Distribution as firms, other than cooperatives, having 10 or more establishments. Their origins in Britain can be traced back to the beginning of this century with the emergence of such firms as Liptons, Home and Colonial, and Marks and Spencer. The competitive efficiency of multiple stores with their ability to operate scale economies, specialised facilities, and to purchase, or even create, prime sites has given them a strong trading position and in 1971 they accounted for two-fifths of the total retail turnover (Table 6). More recent figures produced by Berry (1977) suggest that by 1975 they had virtually caught up with the independents, with a market share of some 45 per cent. The importance of large-scale multiple retailers is often cited as one of the strengths of the British retail system.

In some cases multiple organisations have grown from a single base which simply increased its number of outlets, but the processes of amalgamation and takeover have been important, often resulting in complex holding groups. Thus, for example, the United Drapery Stores group embraces such well known 'high street' names as Alexandre, John Collier, Richard Shops, Wm. Timpson, Swears and Wells and Wm. Whiteley.

Although strongly represented in most sections of retailing, it is within the intensely competitive food sector that the multiples have made their greatest recent gains. Multiples, with a 22 per cent share of the grocery and provision market in 1961, had almost doubled their share to a figure of 39 per cent by 1971, notwithstanding a decline in their number of outlets. The number of outlets is of course a very crude guide to relative trading positions. Thus, for example, an Institute of Grocery Distribution survey shows that of 7,100 multiples in March 1974, 450 had closed by March 1975. The closures, however, averaged 140 m² and 175 new stores which opened in the same period averaged 930 m², a net gain in floor-space of 100,000 m². The other sectors in which the multiples are particularly strong include general stores (both department and variety) and clothing and footwear. Indeed, as Scott (1970) has pointed out, it was the footwear trade which was the first in Britain to adopt multiple trading on a substantial scale.

With their aggressive policies in food retailing, plus expansion into other fields, particularly hardware, furniture, photographic goods, books and stationery and electrical goods, the multiples have had a far more dynamic trading record in recent years than any other major kind of organisation. In contrast to the cooperatives and independents whose shares of total trade declined between 1961 and 1971 the multiples moved ahead strongly

(Table 6). In addition, they were the only major sector not to experience a reduction in their number of outlets; the loss of outlets in the food sector being exactly counterbalanced by a gain in the number of non-food shops. To some extent the greater involvement of the multiples in non-food retailing, including the expansion of traditional grocery retailers into durable goods (e.g. Tesco's home and wear departments) is a deliberate attempt to capitalise upon changing expenditure patterns, whereby food has been taking a progressively smaller proportion of total consumer expenditure.

One of the most intensely competitive areas of multiple trading is the food sector, and this has been the driving force behind the development of self-service stores and supermarkets now operated by multiples, independents and cooperatives alike. The early involvement of the multiples with convenience goods, especially food, is not surprising since this is where their advantages of bulk buying, standardised presentation, rapid turnover and competitive prices could be used to greatest advantage.

Since the war, multiple food retailers have undertaken heavy capital investment programmes to increase efficiency. Most companies which participated in the most anarchical expansionary period of the 1950s and 1960s have, in the 1970s, been trying to rationalise their locational pattern and increase the average size of their outlets. Tesco, for example closed 182 of its smaller stores between 1971 and 1975, and the average size of their new supermarkets opened during the year rose from 1,094 m² in 1971 to 2,975 m² in 1975. In 1976 only 194 of Tesco's 744 outlets were under 186 m², and 54 were over 1,858 m² – but their shares of the group's turnover were 4 per cent and 31 per cent respectively.

In addition to the changes within retailing itself, there are several trends within the pattern of consumer behaviour which have favoured the multiples. Thus the tendency for more women to have full-time paid employment, the trend towards convenience foodstuffs, increasing motor-car and deep-freeze ownership, bulk buying and increasing cost-consciousness have all steered more trade towards the multiples, largely at the expense of independent food retailers.

As far as the spatial pattern of multiple retailing is concerned, one or two tentative conclusions may be drawn. Mills (1974) points out the strength of the multiples in the South East region, an impression which is strengthened by the 1971 Census of Distribution which gives a figure of 46.8 per cent for the multiples' share of total trade in the South East compared with a range of 32.5–40.1 in the other standard regions. Hall, Knapp and Winston (1961) point out that there is also a rural–urban difference, with multiples being more strongly represented in towns than in the countryside, and Metcalf (1968) confirms the importance of population density, income levels and economic growth in converging large-scale retailing.

Cooperatives   From their basis in the North West of England, where they emerged largely to serve the mid-nineteenth century urban working class, the cooperatives have spread geographically throughout the country. Notwithstanding minor regional variations, the cooperatives remain a fairly small element of the retail system compared with independents and multiples, and in 1971 they accounted for only 7 per cent of total turnover (Table 6). They are heavily committed to the food sector, and this in 1971 accounted for four-fifths of their turnover. Even so, they were able to claim only 13 per cent of the total grocery turnover.

In the past the cooperatives have had a notable record of innovation; for example, the Co-operative Wholesale Society which was an early development of vertical integration, the federations of cooperative laundries, bakeries and dairies during the inter-war years, and the pioneer role in the self-service revolution of the early post-war years. However, during the past two decades the movement has seen its market share falling sharply: in the ten-year period 1961–71 alone it lost 30 per cent of its overall market share and closed 40 per cent of its outlets. The reasons for this decline are many, but among the most important are its dependence upon food, conflicts between members' interests and multiple-operation techniques, the autonomous outlook of small societies, and the lack of new investment caused by the distribution of profits as consumer dividends rather than for re-investment.

Through the 1960s and early 1970s the movement was revitalised. A reduction in the number of societies from a peak of 1,400 at the turn of the century, to 1,001 in 1952 and 224 in 1976, coupled with a more aggressive marketing policy, including the substitution of trading stamps for consumer dividends, and a vastly increased investment programme is beginning to bring results, and in 1975 the cooperatives had the largest increase in turnover in both food and durable goods (Berry, 1977). A 1975 plan envisages only 26 regional societies for the whole of England and Wales.

Department stores   Department stores are not a separate form of retail organisation as they are run by all three major groups, independents, multiples and cooperatives, but they do represent a distinctive form of trading.

Table 7. Department stores 1971

	Number	Turnover (£ million)
Cooperatives	233	159
Multiples	242	360
Independent	343	429
Total	818	950

Source: 1971 Census of Distribution.

After a surge of development in the inter-war years, their post-war experience has been somewhat mixed. They are mainly tied to central business district locations, often in outdated premises, and they have been particularly vulnerable to the rising costs of their traditionally high standard of service. In the face of strong competition from the multiples which sell many of the same kinds of goods, the department stores have managed to retain a fairly stable 4–6 per cent of the total market. Many department stores are part of a larger holding group in which the method and degree of integration varies, but currently four groups, Debenhams, House of Fraser, John Lewis Partnership and Sears Holdings, control approximately one-half of the total of department stores.

Special trading   The 1971 census records a further group of highly specialised retail types. Briefly these comprise mail order, vending machines, credit traders calling on customers, and mobile shops. Between them these types have a turnover of some £800 million, or 0.5 per cent of the total, with mail-order companies being by far the most significant.

The legislative environment

Although it provides enormous scope for individual initiative and enterpreneurial skills, retailing in Britain takes places within an ever-tighter legislative framework.

Ever since the Addison Act of 1919 banned corner shops from new public housing estates, town planners have exercised increasing control over the location of shops. The growth of town planning after the Second World War, together with the urgent need to rebuild many damaged shopping centres, increased this involvement, and in retrospect the planners' attitude towards retailing can be seen largely as a preservation of the existing pattern. The most recent piece of substantial legislation, the Town and Country Planning Act of 1968, together with the structure plans which stem from it, confirm the planner's task. Implicitly he is expected to be concerned with retail provision in order to ensure reasonable access to facilities for all members of the community, to protect the environment and balance social costs and benefits. Explicitly this normally involves identifying an existing hierarchy and then, by means of population forecasts, per capita expenditure patterns and an analysis of trading areas, producing an estimate of future requirements in terms of retail floor-space and preferred locations. Although providing a valuable strategic framework for future retail patterns, the structure-plan process, especially in its present transitional phase, is often criticised for being too slow and cumbersome to respond to the rapidly changing demands of both retailers and consumers. For the most part, retail planning in this sense is carried out at county or sub-regional level, but occasionally advisory policies, such as the renowned *Development Control Policy Note No. 13* (1972) on 'Out of Town Shops and Shopping Centres', emanate from central-government sources.

Retail prices are another aspect of the business which have seen increasing government intervention of one kind and another. Notable among the moves in this field was the Resale Prices Act of 1964 which formally ended Retail Price Maintenence (RPM), a system which was in any case beginning to collapse naturally. Today, only books and pharmaceutical products are still subject to RPM. Additional controls on profits and prices of selected items, mainly food, have also been a feature of the inflationary period of the mid-1970s through the operation of temporary subsidies and the workings of the Prices and Incomes Board.

Selective Employment Tax (SET) and Value Added Tax (VAT) were two further measures which had profound repercussions for retailing. Introduced in 1966, SET was in effect an employment tax levied on non-manufacturing industries with the intention of improving labour efficiency. The precise effects are difficult to estimate, even the official report (Reddaway, 1970) found it difficult to separate the effects of SET from the abolition of RPM, but many commentators suggest that it hastened the trend towards self-service. Together with purchase tax, SET was replaced by VAT in 1973, largely in order to bring Britain into line with other EEC members. It is perhaps too soon to estimate the full effects of VAT, but the added accountancy burden which it brings has often been cited as a factor in the high closure rate of small shops.

Britain has a long history of legislation in the field of consumer protection, from the Weights and Measures Acts of the closing quarter of the nineteenth century to the flurry of legislation which in the 1970s produced such important advances as the appointment of a Minister for Trade and Consumer Protection (1972) and the Fair Trading Act of 1973. In addition to government measures, various other bodies, such as the Association for Consumer Research with its journal *Which?*, have emerged to champion the consumer's cause, and there is no doubt that the shopper of today is better informed and more carefully protected than at any time in the past.

Contemporary trends

As far as the organisation of retailing in Britain is concerned, the past quarter century represents a very dynamic period. It has seen the intensification of some previously established trends, but also the development of some new ones.

From a peak of 583,000 shops in 1950, the number had declined to 439,000 in 1975 (Berry, 1977), a 25 per cent decline in the same numbers of years. A process of deliberate rationalisation, especially within the multiple and cooperative sectors, together with a cessation of trading by many independents, largely account for this decline, but as Kirby (1974) has pointed out the magnitude of the decline has not been uniform throughout the country or the various retail organisations and trades. Undoubtedly some of the most severe contraction has taken place among independent retailers unable to take advantage of scale economies, unable to respond to changing consumer demands and shopping behaviour, and unable generally to compete with the more successful multiples. Perhaps surprisingly against this background of shops closures, total retail employment has remained remarkably stable, largely as a result of more complex shift working, the spread of six-day opening and the increased staff demands of specialised and department stores.

Associated with the decline in the number of outlets is an increase in the average size of the remainder. Details on floor-space are not given by any of the Censuses before 1971 so detailed comparisons are difficult. Clearly though, most operators, particularly within food retailing, were revising their optimum store sizes upwards and the present-day superstores and hypermarkets must be seen as a natural extension of this policy. Davies (1976) shows that whereas 15.9 per cent of new supermarkets in 1969 exceeded 929 m^2, by 1972 the figure had risen to 26.5 per cent.

The ascendancy of self-service forms of retailing is closely related to these trends. Compared with the USA self-service was a late development in Britain. The pioneer in this field was the cooperative movement in the early 1940s, but 10 years later the experiment was still being viewed equivocally by many retailers. The development of self-service methods of selling and of supermarkets blossomed together, largely in the food trade, and by the late 1950s both were firmly established. The most significant period of increase came between 1958 and 1967, during which period the numbers of self-service stores and supermarkets increased from 4,500 to 22,500 and 175 to 2,800 respectively[11] with the most rapid proportionate increases concentrated between 1959 and 1963. By 1973 Davies (1976) estimated that there were 5,000 supermarkets.

Much of this discussion on the organisation of retailing has pointed to the growing importance of multiple trades and the decline in the share of total turnover taken by independents. Indeed, given the trends summarised immediately above, this process appears almost inevitable. The overall picture is clear from Table 6, but more recent figures produced by the Economist Intelligence Unit in 1976 suggest that the gap between the multiples and independents has narrowed further, with 1975 shares being 45 per cent and 48 per cent respectively and a stabilisation of the cooperatives' share at 7 per cent.

A final caveat should perhaps be entered, concerning some of the traditional divisions used in retailing. With more traditionally non-food retailers like Marks and Spencer and Woolworths selling food lines, and food retailers like Tesco branching out into consumer durables, and with the emergence of hypermarkets selling virtually everything, a pattern of scrambled merchandising has become widespread. It therefore becomes increasingly difficult to classify and generalise. Marks and Spencer, for example, is no longer simply a multiple, nor is it the 'bazaar' it once was; rather it is a cross between a department store and a specialist multiple, but the position is still somewhat fluid.[12]

The commercial organisation of France

The domestic trade of France, as in other capitalist industrial countries, has been in a state of perpetual change for over a century; but it is only within the last two decades that it has become a really dynamic sector of economic activity. While it is customary to remark that it is still well behind the United States, it is less frequently noted that in fact the changes have been far more fundamental than those across the Atlantic. For it is infinitely more difficult to substitute one structure for another than to start afresh in a young country that is still growing up. There is always the inertia of the existing establishments; it is rare for them to evolve if their immediate environment changes but little. As in the case of other European countries, French commercial structures have changed mainly as a result of external factors concerned with the transformation of society and the economy. And the changes have been mainly imitations of American technology.

Causes of the transformation of commercial structures
But for the rural exodus that reduced the population of the countryside from 27 millions in 1870 to 15 millions a hundred years later, resulting in the closure of many traditional shops, and without the urban growth that entailed the setting-up in towns and their suburbs of shopping facilities indispensable for the provisioning of 13 million extra customers between 1870 and 1946, with a further 13 millions in the much shorter period 1946–70, the transformation of the commercial structures would have made but little progress. The evolution of the numbers and spatial distribution of the population, by altering the map of commercial equipment, has helped in the economic restructuring of those facilities. As proof, the small, traditional and often economically marginal shop is no longer to be found except in the regions suffering from depopulation, in some rural areas, and in the older quarters of towns.

Since the beginning of the century, the development of motor transport, and during the last few decades the use of the private car for shopping expeditions, have also facilitated the structural changes. With one car to 3.4 persons in 1976, it is possible to regard the vast majority of households as no longer dependent on their nearest shop. Motorisation, giving mobility to the clientele and favouring the growth of commercial centres that offer a variety of shops, either within or on the periphery of towns, has contributed to a reduction in the level of services provided by local shops in the countryside, and has thus accelerated their rate of closure.

Other factors, as in the United States, have contributed even more directly than by the upsetting of the existing regime of shopping to the economic modification of the whole system. Some of these factors have necessitated the opening of new types of shop: first, for example, the technological developments that have placed new products on the market; then the great increase in the proportion of the population leading an urban way of life, that demands what may be called 'leisure goods'; and thirdly the modification in the socio-professional composition of the French population. The last of these does not merely involve a diminution in the agricultural population – and only 3 millions still get a living off the land – it is characterised by a rapid increase in the number of 'white-collar' occupations, and more than 8 millions are now so employed, a figure that has risen by 20 per cent between 1962 and 1968. The tertiary sector alone (as officially defined) held 25 per cent of the employed population in 1900 and twice that percentage now with an active population of roughly the same size. But the shopping expenditure of the different socio-professional classes is very varied. According to an enquiry by INSEE (Institut National de la Statistique et des Etudes Economiques) among households in 1970 (Kagan and Bergé, 1972), while the average expenditure on food was the same for the white-collar worker and the agricultural peasant, expenditure of the former on clothing was 1.8 times higher; on hygiene and health 2.7 times; and on culture and leisure 2 times higher. Further, the general rise in the standard of living (since 1900 personal incomes have trebled in France, and between 1970 and 1975 purchasing power increased by an average of 4.7 per cent per annum) has been accompanied by an enormous growth in the demand for the less commonplace goods, and so in a multiplication and a diversification of shops to sell them. The modification of the national pattern of consumption is significant. According to the latest reports, the changes between 1959 and 1975 were as follows: a decrease in expenditure on food, from 37.3 to 25.5 per cent, and on clothing from 11.5 to 9.1 per cent; and a rise in all other groups, especially 'hygiene and health', that increased from 8.3 to 15 per cent. Going back a little further, before the Second World War expenditure on food still accounted for one-half of the average family's income.

The development of consumer habits is also not without its consequences for the appearance of new kinds of trading: take for example the case of young people. The numbers of 'under-twenties', though proportionally slightly less than at the beginning of the century, are now much greater – 16 millions as against 13.3 millions in 1900. But what is more important is that most of these youngsters, formerly supplied by their parents, have now themselves become customers for particular types of goods,[13] to such an extent that some shop-keepers have come to specialise in their requirements, or have actually opened new types of shop.

That the evolution of shop-types should be facilitated by the diversification and expansion of what has become a phenomenon of mass-consumption is not the only explanation. There are other factors involved, such as the new orientation of industry towards mass-production, the growing influence of the financial world in the business of trading, the changed behaviour of a clientele that is adopting a new life-style, and the effect of the mass media. The first two of these have favoured the concentration of commercial enterprise and the shortening of distribution circuits; the third results in the increasing size of shops, and the last, like all the others, is conducive to the modernisation of sales techniques.

The development of the processing of agricultural products, the concentration of industrial undertakings, technical progress and the constant increase in the size of factories, and the strengthening of foreign competition (in particular from Common Market countries) by the lowering of tariff barriers, have led to the mass-production of a whole series of new commodities, both foodstuffs and non-food, in standardised and pre-packed form. In order to reduce the selling costs of these products, more and more large factories are endeavouring to deliver in as large quantities as possible, giving their clients more favourable terms for large and regular orders for a single commodity. This results in unequal competition between large and small distributors. It is the small shopkeepers that bear the brunt of this difference in the cost of obtaining their supplies, for the wholesalers, like the producers, and for the same reasons, scale their prices according to the volume of the orders. Given that price is for most customers the main reason for the choice of shop, this practice has resulted in the elimination of many small retailers, and has contributed to the concentration of distribution, to the development of integrated businesses, and to the growth of voluntary associations.

The attitude of the large banks, formerly swayed by social considerations in making financial decisions relating to a locality or region, but now only disposed to sustain dynamic and profitable businesses, has amplified this movement towards concentration. Their influence has been even more pronounced, since they have taken part in the creation of new enterprises (hypermarket companies in particular) or large and equally novel forms of development such as regional shopping centres whose promoters they have financed.

The very great increase in the numbers of people now influenced by an urban life-style has also helped in the proliferation of very large unspecialised stores. After the Second World War, the change in the form of urbanism from small houses to blocks of flats modified the commercial environment of the suburbs, making it profitable to create medium- and even large-sized neighbourhood shops. Furthermore, living in these new suburbs and working in the town entailed fixed hours, time-consuming journeys, fatigue and less opportunity for shopping expeditions during normal opening hours. And, since most family shopping is done by the housewife, it is pertinent to note that in the urban agglomerations, and particularly the largest of these, female employment is greater than elsewhere. Thus in 1968, 35 per cent of the female population in the Paris region were in employment, compared with 25 per cent in the rest of the country. Any effort by the shops to economise the housewife's time spent in making her purchases is thus welcome. The grouping of shops in shopping centres, the display of a vast array of sales lines under one roof, and self-service, have all made their contribution; and profitability has been assured by a growth in the average size of the undertakings and the shops.

The expansion of self-service has been rendered easier, as much by the spectacular development of mass-advertising that has accompanied the standardisation of consumption, as by the adoption of trade-marks or brand-names that absolve the merchants from their former advisory function concerning many types of goods. Advertising, more a fact of life for the town dweller than for the countryman, cost 5 billion francs in 1970. More than half the receipts of the shops selling 'daily' requirements, and about one-third of those of 'periodic' shops, came from branded articles. On the other hand, advertising that encourages purchasing may also create false needs. Thus, together with the rise in incomes and the decline in thrift, it has contributed, though in a way that is difficult to quantify, to the increase in consumption. So, too, has the growth of credit sales of durable and semi-durable goods.

The increase in profits resulting from these diverse developments has facilitated the transformation of the types of shop. In parallel, the necessity for shops to increase their profitability in order to get a better position in the economic circuit, technical progress in distribution and the improvement of management have worked in the same direction. However, too many retailers are content to refurbish their shops at frequent intervals rather than modernise their commercial practices.

All these factors have combined, in various and often complex ways, to prepare the marketing structures for important changes. These changes have come about the more easily because other changes have taken place at the same time: the frontiers of the whole Western bloc are now open to the penetration of capital, techniques, competitive products and economic intelligence; international relations have quickened; and businessmen have been prepared to take the financial risk of innovations.

In France, there has been a general modification in the conservative attitude of the financial backers of commercial enterprise; it was indeed as late as the end of the 1950s before the traditional model gave way to the introduction of new trading methods. Doubtless this is but one aspect of the change in mentality that, especially since 1945, made people more interested in novelty than in the preservation of the past. The movement accelerated within the last ten years or so with the arrival on the economic scene of a generation of young and dynamic personalities, brought up in the post-war cult of the infallibility of anything emanating from the United States. Among such remarkable individuals, though with different backgrounds and ideas, are E. Leclerc, M. Fournier (Carrefour) and A. Essel (FNAC), whose names will go down to posterity as marking this period of profound change in French commerce.

Though human initiative exercised the determining role, little would have been possible without capital. Loans have greatly increased, to a figure of 3,500 million francs in 1975. The banks have certainly played a large part in this, but an even larger share has been taken by the specialist credit organisations, notably the *Crédit national*. Up to 1968, taking one year with another, it had financed between 60 and 75 per cent of the developments, while the ordinary finance houses had provided only a quarter. After that date, the respective proportions were nearer 50 and 35–40. It is apparent that the bankers waited for the new types of shop to prove themselves before investing more generously.

Recent changes in marketing equipment[14]
These are of two kinds, and are mainly repetitions of those experienced in the United States. On the one hand, they involve sales techniques and types of

shop; these are changes that effect the consumer directly. On the other hand, they are part of the increasing emphasis on economic concentration; this is the main factor in the transformation of the commercial system, and even of the national economy, in which distribution businesses have an increasingly controlling influence. Of this the public at large has scarcely yet become aware.

Evolution of sales techniques and shop types   Decline of the traditional shop   We are witnessing a spectacular increase in selling methods that reduce the contact between buyer and seller, both in wholesaling and retailing. In wholesaling, however, self-service remains of limited importance: the 340 'cash-and-carry' depots sell mainly goods in constant demand; in 1971 they only had 1.5 per cent of the national wholesaling turnover.

The loss of human contact with the purchaser is much more noticeable in retailing. While in 1972, 92.5 per cent of retail sales were still effected in ordinary shops, the six other main forms of trading, the market stall (3.9 per cent), mail-order (1.5 per cent), travelling salesmen (1.2 per cent), canvassing (0.7 per cent), orders placed in shops (0.2 per cent), and vending machines (less than 0.1 per cent) (Quin, 1973), were slowly gaining ground; their overall share went up by 0.5 per cent between 1970 and 1972, but at unequal rates. Market stalls in towns, and travelling salesmen in rural areas, have just about maintained their position. On the contrary, the mail-order business is constantly growing – from 0.55 per cent of the total turnover in 1960 to 2 per cent in 1975 (and 4.13 per cent for non-food goods). La Redoute, the principal French mail-order firm and the third largest in Europe, had a turnover of 1.77 billion francs in 1975, which put it among the first 10 distribution companies in France.

It is really within the shops themselves that the dehumanisation of trading is most marked. On the other hand, the development of self-service (17.5 per cent of the retail turnover in 1972), that allows a reduction in the general expenses of distribution points, has undoubtedly facilitated shop-based selling in the face of competition from other forms of trading. Launched in France in 1948 by the Goulet-Turpin chain stores, there were 1690 self-service shops by 1960, 10,000 by 1965, and 26,000 in 1975, or one shop to every 2,000 inhabitants. Self-service yielded 2.5 per cent of the retail turnover in 1960 (4.5 per cent in food lines) and 17.5 per cent in 1972; it is especially widespread in the sale of foodstuffs, in which it represents 36 per cent of the turnover.

Another sales technique imported from the United States is 'discount' – selling with a reduced profit margin. This began a successful expansion in 1960, after being authorised by a government regulation that suppressed the imposition of prices by producers. It is often associated with self-service, but not strongly, since some department stores use it, though employing sales persons, in lines such as domestic electrical goods, leisure articles and furniture. From 0.35 per cent of total sales in 1962 it rose to 1 per cent in 1970, but must be much greater now since most of the large stores have adopted it.

Creation of large unspecialised shopping units   From the Middle Ages when the shop began to replace the pedlar, to about 1955, France was the privileged domain of the small, specialised shopkeeper. Except in the case of department stores (with more than 2500 m² selling area and 175 employees), variety stores (over 300 m²) and some important non-food shops (such as Galeries Barbès for furniture), selling areas seldom covered more than 100 m².

But in 1972, 18 per cent of retail sales (22 per cent in food and 15 per cent in other goods), and in 1975, about one-quarter, were effected in unspecialised shops of over 400 m².

Variety stores first appeared in France in 1927; they numbered 135 in 1945, and 600 in 1966; but by this time some of them had already gone over to self-service, wholly or partially, and this furthered their multiplication.

Indeed, what is most striking about the medium- and large-sized self-service stores is not their size, but the rapidity of their diffusion. Originating in the United States, 'superettes' (120 to 400 m²) and supermarkets (over 400 m²), though large consumers of space, multiplied in small towns as well as in cities. Even more remarkable, in towns of over 100,000 population, has been the growth of the hypermarket (with over 2,500 m² of floor-space); this is an essentially French development, differing from the other two types not only by its great size but by the proportion of its selling area (up to one-third) devoted to non-food goods. In 1975 there were 5,000 superettes, occupying 1 million m², or 17 per cent of the national self-service total, and employing 34,000 persons. In 1977, the 3,358 supermarkets (with 95,000 employees, 6 per cent of the French retailing total) and the 370 hypermarkets (with 5 per cent of the wage-earners) took respectively 10 and 9 per cent of the total retailing receipts (19 and 12 per cent in the case of foodstuffs). If we recollect that in 1960 only 0.9 per cent, and in 1961, 6.1 per cent of expenditure in retail shops took place in supermarkets and hypermarkets, we can realise the extent and rapidity of the growth – for in 1965 there were only 584 supermarkets and but one hypermarket.

The rate of construction of large self-service stores accelerated sharply after 1971: in the record year of 1972, no less than 277 new supermarkets and 67 new hypermarkets were opened. The Royer Law of 1973 (see p. 54) and some saturation of the market rendered the continuation of such a rate impossible; 51 hypermarkets were opened in 1973, 14 in 1975, and 30 in 1977; the law not only made such developments subject to planning control, but by bringing back the 30-day limit on payment for perishable goods, resulted in a net diminution in the cash-flow of the companies concerned, and hindered their expansion. Supermarkets and hypermarkets, especially important in food sales, are not the only large-area shops to have grown up in the last dozen years. More than 1,500 shops selling home furnishings and domestic electrical equipment (equivalent to the American 'home-centres'), 550 hardware and 'do-it-yourself' shops ('hobby centres') and 300 'garden centres' have been opened. All offer discounts to a greater or lesser extent.

This boom in giant self-service stores has stimulated creative activity among the traditional department-store organisations: three department stores a year were being opened between 1965 and 1968, and six or seven a year between 1969 and 1975; more than two-thirds of these were in large provincial cities. However, the department-store companies, of which the chief are Nouvelles-Galeries, Printemps and Galeries Lafayette, still only represent 3.6 per cent of the national retail sales. As for variety stores, their rate of expansion remained high until 1965 but has since slackened.

For many reasons, the large traditional and modern stores constructed since 1955, unlike their predecessors, have been built on the periphery of towns. For one thing, the suburbs have, since 1945, become the centres of demographic growth. And further, the very size of the new stores has denied them a place in city centres, for two reasons: the streets of the central areas, already crowded, could not have sustained the traffic flow that such establishments normally create, and besides, the scarcity of sites in city centres, and their very high cost, in any case obliged the promoters of large stores to seek peripheral locations. The tendency for department-stores companies to re-invest in central areas is explained partly by the relatively poor results obtained from such establishments in the suburbs, and partly by the policies of many local authorities, who seek to avert the decline of their central areas (but, in marked contrast to the United States, the conservation of historic centres will prevent the complete gutting of such areas and the construction of new central business districts that include modern shopping precincts).

Until the end of the 1960s, the main characteristic of hypermarket sites was their isolation, both from traditional shopping areas and from other shops. But the majority of the new giants constructed since 1971 have been regarded as the beating hearts of commercial centres. Before 1971, scarcely one-quarter of the hypermarkets were situated in commercial centres, but 65 per cent of those built between 1971 and 1974 were so located (Coquery, 1976).

The desire of the suburban-dweller to make shopping an expedition, to have the possibility of choosing between one shop and another, and to have other distractions available as well as shops, in other words, to find in the shopping complex a miniature central business district, has led to the success of 'shopping centres'. The first of these were simply neighbourhood centres, of less than 1,500 m², with up to 20 small shops grouped around a self-service store, and serving the blocks of flats constructed after 1950. Then certain promoters, inspired by the American example, were quick to see the profits that might be reaped from shopping centres serving a much larger area or even a whole region. Public authorities, anxious to foster peripheral commercial development, encouraged them. In 1974, there were 239 shopping centres of over 1,000 m², of which 140, mostly opened since 1970, had over 10,000 m². They totalled 3.5 million m² of selling area, about 12 per cent of the national total. Of 10 centres of over 50,000 m² that had regional significance, 8 were in the Paris area.

The cult of gigantism and regrouping has not only affected retail trade. It is evident also in wholesaling, particularly in the construction of regional and even international wholesaling centres. The initiative, in the first case, came from the public authorities. A decree of 1953 led to the opening of some 20 wholesale markets dealing in perishables. Some of these were '*marchés d'intérêt national*' (MIN), the most famous of which is Paris-Rungis. These constructions enabled the regrouping of merchants on sites well provided with appropriate infrastructure and services, and so helped to balance the crumbling regime of wholesaling in production centres (such as Avignon, Châteauroux) and centres of consumption (such as Paris, Lyons, Bordeaux). It was hoped also to reduce the costs of marketing and simplify the mechanism of intermediary transactions.

Following on the example of these great wholesale establishments for food products, but this time on the wholesalers' own initiative, a series of wholesale centres was created during the 1960s. On sites of 3–20 ha, groups of non-food merchants have congregated, mostly moving from urban sites that were too small to permit further development. These centres, numbering 22 in 1972, are mostly in provincial centres (Lyons-Caluire, Nantes-Carquefou, Orleans-St Jean de la Ruelle, Bordeaux, Toulouse) rather than in the Paris region (Rosny,

Rungis). More recently still, centres of international trading have been proposed, on the lines of the American 'world trade centers'.

All these types of large commercial equipment have proved their profitability (except for some financed by local authorities!), and this explains their rapid proliferation. But their creation has required a capacity for investment that is rarely possible for small shopkeepers. Their realisation has been possible to the extent that a strong concentration of commercial enterprises was previously effected, usually with the object of creating large establishments.

Growth of economic concentration The success of the large stores has been followed by an acceleration of economic concentration. This is manifested in several ways: a shortening of the distribution circuits through the growth of large integrated concerns, a concentration of purchasing through the medium of central warehouses, and a reduction in the number of enterprises and sales points. Some reduction in prices to the consumer has resulted, since there is still some competition. But there are fears that if concentration continues, some integrated companies will achieve a quasi-monopolistic position, which may be unfortunate for the consumer. Coquery (1976) has been at pains to show, in a study of the development policies of certain commercial groups, that such organisations are tending to carve up the French market between them.

The rise of integrated commerce All forms of integrated commerce, with the exception of the cooperatives, have taken part in the general progress, sometimes with great rapidity: their share of the total retail trade was 11.1 per cent in 1950, 15 per cent in 1960, 27 per cent in 1970 and 28.5 per cent in 1972 (Quin, 1973). However, most department-store companies have been in a sorry plight since 1973; and the economic recession has not helped. Such difficulties are not confined to France: they are worldwide.

If we compare sales in 1950 with those in 1976, chain stores increased from 4.5 to 8.5 per cent, department and variety stores rose from 3.5 to 5.5 per cent, and consumer cooperatives from 1.7 to 2.5 per cent; the cooperatives now fall below the undertakings that sell through agents (4 per cent) but are still ahead of mail-order firms, though probably not for long. The principal chain-store company, Casino-Epargne (with a turnover of 4.7 billion francs in 1974) had 2,000 branches, 55 supermarkets and 8 hypermarkets in 1975. In total, the chain stores now control about 100 hypermarkets and 700 supermarkets. For their part, the cooperatives have already launched 21 'Rond Point' hypermarkets and 300 supermarkets. This has naturally resulted in a concentration of businesses: the number of chain-store companies has fallen from 125 in 1946 to 81 in 1974, and of cooperative societies from 608 in 1958 to 204 in 1975, despite their democratic principles that are opposed to gigantism.

Thus, little by little, there is a growing concentration of retailing in the hands of large companies, with important financial groupings that result in the formation of commercial colossi.

In 1972, the top 12 integrated businesses, each with a turnover of more than one billion francs, achieved 6.5 per cent of the national retail sales; the next 33 on the list, each with receipts of over half a billion francs, achieved the same percentage. In all, the 100 largest firms in the distribution trade had about one-fifth of the turnover.

What is more, the capital of many of these businesses is controlled by a few among them. We are thus witnessing, in France, as in the United States and other industrialised countries, the creation of powerful financial groups in the distribution sector. 'Their aim is to extend and reinforce their commercial activity, by taking control of companies that will increase their financial resources, their sales strength and their field of activity' (Quin, 1971). The five principal groups in 1973, according to the magazine *Coopération* (October 1974) were Carrefour (turnover Fr 4.8 billion), Casino-Epargne (4.16 billion), Printemps-Prisunic (3.85 billion) Galeries Lafayette-Monoprix (3.38 billion), Nouvelles Galeries (3.36 billion). Mergers, absorptions, acquisition of majority interests, and the creation of subsidiaries, that lead to the formation of such groups, have proceeded at an increasing pace during the last decade or so.

Even more than the financial groups, the commercial groups have ambitions towards oligopoly. Originating usually from the necessity of grouping in order to buy most economically from important producers, the central purchasing agencies, the keystones of these commercial empires, are no longer concerned only with the supply function but offer numerous other services and tend more or less overtly to guide the commercial policy of their members, in order to reinforce the competitive power of the group. Thus seven large commercial groups in 1973 already controlled 15 per cent of French retailing. They were Paridoc (trade marks Mammouth, Suma, Record, Gem, Bagg; turnover 12 billion francs); Printemps-Prisunic (turnover 9.3 billion); Sgce-Coop (8.4 billion); Difra-Francap-Camas (trademarks Radar, Record, Gro, V2000; turnover 8 billion). Mergers and closures continue to reinforce this economic concentration.

The endurance of other forms of trading   Despite its rapid progress, integrated commerce (including the largest independent shops) still controls only 30 per cent of the distributive trade, for the traditional independent traders are offering more and more resistance. The competition of the big companies obliged the independents to react in various ways, of which the most effective was association – which is another form of concentration. This is certainly as true of wholesalers, through whom more than half the retailed food and one-third of the non-food goods pass, as of retailers.

Certain independent wholesalers have formed groups or voluntary chains, enabling them to secure advantageous terms from industrial suppliers and to obtain more outlets. However, the majority of wholesalers remain quite independent, and three-quarters of them are very small, with under five employees.

The independent retailers, comprising (in 1972) 92 per cent of the retail shops (82 per cent being fixed shops and 10 per cent market stalls), had 75 per cent of the non-food sales and 67 per cent of food sales. The non-fixed shops had 4 per cent of the total retail trade. Independents retained 90 per cent of the turnover in the case of bakeries, more than 80 per cent in cake-shops and butchers, but under 75 per cent in the case of goods purchased less frequently by the working classes, only 55 per cent for dry groceries and 40 per cent for manufactured drinks. In the non-food trades, in which production is less standardised and customers have need of guidance, the independents always have more than two-thirds of the turnover, except in the case of footwear and furniture, in which the integrated businesses take 60 and 40 per cent respectively.

In 1972, 10.3 per cent of food purchases in France were still made in the markets, the activity of which, after a period of decline in the 1960s, had become stabilised; and 2.7 per cent direct from the farms. The independent stall-holders even had a 17 per cent share of the fruit, vegetable and fish sales, 12 per cent of poultry and flowers, and 5 per cent of haberdashery, meat, clothing and footwear.

Most of the independent shops are small, in terms of selling area, turnover and employment. This is why, since the 1950s, reorganisation has been through association. Some independents have set up purchasing groups, which can hardly have pleased the short-circuited wholesalers, but others have formed voluntary chains – much more to the wholesalers' liking. Centralised purchasing arrangements of these two types have helped the members to improve their sales techniques, to modernise their shops (especially by introducing self-service), and have facilitated financial aid. Among the purchasing groups, in the food business, are the retailers' cooperative UNICO, with 6,500 members, and UNA, with 2,700. Of the voluntary chains, three have between 5,000 and 7,000 sales points: SEGEDES is affiliated to the European organisation that includes V.G., SPAR and Sopegros.

More than one-fifth of the independent retailers, with a turnover that is 15 per cent of the French distribution total, now take part in associations of one kind or another. The 400,000 small shops that remain completely independent no longer represent three-quarters of French retailing, and have only 55 per cent of the total sales as against 88 per cent in 1950 and 66 per cent in 1970.

Lastly, during the last dozen years the small shops have endeavoured to counter big business, not by economic concentration but by spatial concentration, that is by opening *centres collectifs d'indépendants*. In 1974, there were 62 such shopping centres, of which 21 had more than 5,000 m² of floor-space. The three largest are Mistral 7 in Vaucluse, with 66 shops and 30,000 m²; Barnéoud in Var, with 117 shops and 22,500 m²; and Barnéoud in Bouches-du-Rhône, with 153 shops and 14,000 m². If these MCI (*magasins collectifs d'indépendants*) have not always given good results (and Centor at Pau, and Drug-Tours at Tours, have failed), human problems (individualism and lack of enthusiasm among the participants), errors of location, and poor management, have been to blame.

General evolution of French marketing
The deflation of trading: a movement completed in 1975 The intense movement towards the vertical integration of commerce (the linking of wholesaling and retailing in many companies) has been accompanied by a movement towards horizontal integration (reduction in number of establishments and growth in their average size).

Table 8

	Number of undertakings		Number of establishments		
	1962	1966	1962	1966	1975
Wholesale	89,763	74,000	124,404	85,900	c. 81,000
Retail	543,906	507,700	677,445	556,200	c. 500,000

Source: 1962 and 1966, INSEE; 1975, estimated.

An analysis made by Coquery (1976) shows that the real mobility of the small shopkeeper is far greater than the figures indicate. Between 1963 and 1973, there were 620,700 new shops opened as against 615,000 closures, which is equivalent to a complete renewal, every five years, of the personnel of shopkeeping.

We can trace, since 1945, an evolutionary progress in French marketing activity. After the war, the sudden rise in consumption encouraged many persons with no professional qualifications, with a dislike for manual labour or the status of badly-paid employee, and with some small investable capital, to set up as shopkeepers. Deflation began in 1959–60 (with more than 4,000 closures a year), but was partly allayed by the influx of repatriates from North Africa. It was renewed in 1968–71, creating a grave social problem, partly by reason of the elimination of marginal businesses that followed the general introduction of VAT, but especially because of the growth of large stores that had made serious inroads into the 'daily purchases' market, especially foodstuffs. Since 1972, shop closures have been at a steadier rate, but the extreme mobility mentioned above indicates structural weakness.

The concentration of trading has been accompanied by a considerable rise in the numbers employed, from 1.7 millions in 1954 to 1.98 millions in 1962 and 2.25 millions in 1975, of whom 60 per cent were in retailing, which has as many women as men employed (under one-third are women in wholesaling). The total number in commercial employment now represents 17 per cent of French wage-earners.

At the present time distribution, thanks to the large companies and commercial groups and to the rationalisation of managements, is a force that producers must reckon with: hypermarkets alone handle one-quarter of the industrial output of articles in everyday use.

First attempts at limiting the power of the distributors   Rise of consumer-ism   For a long time, the 'Coops' were the only commercial organisations concerned with *not* exploiting their clientele, and they owe their growth in part to this principle. During the 1950s, some private associations undertook to promote consumer power. Many of them flourished in the French nation of individualists. Government help for them was meagre – a mere 900,000 francs in all. But in 1967 the INC (National Consumers' Institute) was created, to keep consumers informed. It distributed 280,000 copies of the handbook *50 millions de consommateurs* ('50 million consumers'), that yielded one-third of its budget, a further 11.7 million francs being contributed by the State.

Intervention of the State in commercial organisation.   French liberalism has not entirely excluded certain state intervention. Some state control has been exercised for a long time, thanks to regulations relating to sales taxes, the prevention of fraud, the control of competition, supervision of pharmacies, and so on, and to state monopolies such as tobacco, matches and explosives. More recently there has been control of urban commercial development. An Order of 1961 entailed, for the first time, that an urban plan must not neglect the commercial element. An Order of 1969 set up consultative committees in each *département* to give advice on all projects for shopping developments of more than 10,000 m².

Finally, the Royer Law on commerce and the working classes was passed in 1973. In Articles 28 to 36, this law controls the creation of new shopping facilities in a very restrictive fashion that favours the small shopkeeper. One of its major provisions was to enlarge the functions of the departmental committees on urban commercial development. These committees would henceforth decide on all projects for shop construction or extension involving more than 1,000 m² of selling space (a limit raised to 1,500 m² in communes of more than 40,000 people).

The development of national and international consumerism at last pursuaded the French government to make possible a more effective protection of the consumer: in 1976 the post of Secretary of State for the Consumer was created.

All these measures will certainly not prevent the large industrial and commercial companies from orienting consumption as they please, for their own profit rather than for the benefit of the consumer. It is indeed difficult for the government of a free capitalist country to intervene to prevent the creation of large commercial groups, for the groups will arrange their affairs, as in Japan, to get round the law. Likewise, it is not part of government policy to counter the excessive and growing disequilibrium of a spatial distribution of commerce that favours the urban agglomerations. This is, however, a contradiction of the avowed wish to revivify the rural areas. But an economy based on competition has its own laws, to which French society has decided to submit.

The complex organisation of commerce in Japan

Confused by the Japanese system of distribution, western exporters are inclined to regard it as archaic. It is true that the traditional channels, very diverse and often excessively long because of their hierarchic nature, are still preponderant. They are largely responsible for the fragility of the commercial structure, that has long been characterised, in the main, by the domination of the *shoshas,* large business houses, that have no equivalent in other capitalist countries, over the multitude of very small shops. In the changes that have taken place during the last 60 years or so – changes that could be summed up as 'americanisation' – these shoshas, together with the department stores, remain as strong points in the new commercial organisation.

The traditional structures
Trading occupies an important place in the national activity. In a state of continual expansion, it occupies 17 per cent of the working population (compared with 18 per cent in the United States) and accounted for 18 per cent of the GDP in 1973 (only 14 per cent in 1960). Although the recent development of foreign trade and the rising standard of living are partly responsible for placing Japan at the head of all the developed countries, a major factor is the lack of adaptation of the commercial structures to a modern capitalist economy.

The distribution circuits are for the most part oddly tortuous, and the intermediary transactions are numerous and costly, for wholesaling usually takes the form of an apparently unavoidable hierarchy of stages. In the United States sales at the wholesale level are 1.1 times those of the retailers, and in France 1.2 times, but in Japan the figure is 3.7. Most manufactured goods pass through at least two stages of wholesaling. The primary wholesalers have 53 per cent of the total wholesaling turnover. They act on a national scale as sales agents for both Japanese and foreign producers. Thirty per cent of their sales are destined for industry, 2 per cent for export, 25 per cent for retailers and 43 per cent for second-tier wholesalers. These latter control the regional markets: trading in Japan is very compartmentalised because of the persistence of local peculiarities. They are responsible for one-quarter of the national wholesaling turnover. Some 40 per cent of their sales are directed towards retailers, but 36 per cent go to yet other wholesalers.

Indeed, usually the trading circuit involves not two but a minimum of three intermediate stages, for the secondary wholesalers may have 'local wholesalers' as clients, and these latter do 22 per cent of the total wholesaling business. Much of the agricultural produce passes through several hands before reaching the retailer: brokers, wholesalers in the producing zones, wholesalers in the centres of consumption, and so on. There may even be a variety of circuits, all more or less long, for a single product. In general, when there are many producers, and the quality of the products is very variable, the commercial circuit followed is a long one.

This multiplicity of intermediary transactions was necessary in the past, when transport was difficult and social structures remained feudal. It is quite unjustifiable in a modern economy. However, such intermediaries still play an important part in the overall trading turnover in Japan: 33 per cent as against 15 per cent in the United States. It must be emphasised, too, that not only are the structures hierarchically organised, both in function and spatially, but 'the whole process of distribution . . . from manufacturer to retailer, is beset with feudal traditions dating from last century or earlier, including a whole complex of personal relationships' (Murata, 1973).

How can such a situation be explained? Certainly by the inadequate concentration of industrial undertakings, but also by the multitude of very small shops. The primary wholesalers will not deal directly with the shopkeepers, who order such small quantities because they have no storage space and often ask for credit. And they will not risk the absence of cash payment because they cannot possibly know the financial trustworthiness of so many small clients. They find it more advantageous to use the services provided by the secondary wholesalers who are better equipped to make deliveries in the narrow and tortuous streets of Japanese towns. Many of the retail shops are family businesses, 64 per cent of them have only one or two assistants and only 3.9 per cent employ more than 10 persons. In 1973 the average sales area was only 41 m² and almost one-third of the shops had under 20 m². The sales per square metre amounted to 320,000 yen a year. Such a trading structure suited the people's living style, that despite a rapid westernisation remained steeped in tradition. The very small size of most houses and apartments (averaging no more than 35 m²) and the preference of housewives for fresh food products leads to daily shopping expeditions for the most part. The customers make their purchases in shops close to their homes or to bus stops, for less than one-third of the households have motor cars. Thus the density of sales points, particularly for daily purchases, must be very high: in 1972, 48 per cent of the shops sold only food, and they realised only 30 per cent of the total retail turnover.

It is now clear why most of the wholesaling businesses are also small: 72 per cent of them employ under 10 persons and 21 per cent less than 3. Further, in

1972, there was 1 wholesaler to every 412 inhabitants, a most unusual ratio, that compares with 1 to 674 in the United States, a country in which the GDP per capita is almost twice that of Japan.

It is not true, however, that trading activity in Japan has traditionally remained only in the hands of the small shopkeepers. Other time-honoured types such as department stores and *shoshas* have respectively 10 per cent of all the retail transactions and one-third of the total trade.

The first department store was opened in 1904 by Mitsukoshi. Most of the others are post-1930 establishments. Their development provoked legislation in 1937 to protect the small shopkeepers. This law was repealed after the Second World War, but was replaced in 1956 by a very conservative measure, strictly regulating new foundations, expansions, mergers and opening hours, for all businesses having a sales area of over 3,000 m² and more than 50 assistants, in the six largest cities, and over 1,500 m² in other towns. In 1971 there were 261 department stores, employing 180,000 persons: 70 per cent of their business was done in the largest cities. The 11 principal firms, having 56 stores with an average sales area of over 23,000 m², were responsible for over half the total turnover of department stores. Nevertheless, the largest of them was only one-fifth the size of the US giant, Sears Roebuck (see Table 9). But the true situation does not accord with the official census figures, for many firms get round the law by opening, within the same building, shops for different specialties, each run by a separate company but all included in the same financial group. The sales figures for the department stores are increasing slowly but regularly, for their reputation is good, mainly by reason of the quality of their merchandise but also because of the other activities that they stimulate. One of them (Shibuya, in Tokyo) actually has a zoo on its roof; but they all offer attractions for a large number of casual visitors, more numerous at week-ends and especially on Sundays, when motor traffic is often forbidden in their vicinity. Ginza-Tokyo, Shinjuku-Tokyo and Shibuya-Tokyo have counted up to 200,000 visitors on a Sunday. The department stores sometimes get their supplies direct from the producers but for the most part they hand over the business of stocking and keeping the counters full to primary wholesalers on perhaps to the *shoshas*.

The domination of the commercial circuits by the *shoshas*, unchallenged until after the last war, has no parallel elsewhere in the world. They are super-wholesalers, being at the same time agents for import–export business, for interior distribution (between 44 and 64 per cent of the turnover of the 10 largest *shoshas* is derived from this), and having branches abroad. Traditionally, the functions of production and distribution were quite separate in Japan, and until the 1950s manufacturers entrusted almost all their business to specialist firms, both for the obtaining of raw materials and for the marketing of the goods. Thus the *shoshas* were often, though not necessarily, linked to industrial groups. The most powerful of them were federated within the great commercial empires known as *zaibatsus*. This was the case with the two largest – Mitsubishi and Mitsui, as well as Sumitomo (see Table 10). The boom in Japanese industry has enabled *shoshas* of this type to reinforce their role in the country's economic life, while those that were quite independent of producers have lost their influence: for example, Marubeni (which however has since 1965 been more or less attached to the Fuji Bank) or C.Itoh, the oldest of the great merchant companies. Depending on how they are defined – for it is not easy to distinguish the *shoshas* from the large wholesale businesses – the statistics reveal that there are between 4,000 and 9,000 *shoshas,* of which the largest have many-sided commercial activities (they will deal in anything that is saleable) and the smaller ones are more specialised; these latter, however, are only responsible for 10 per cent of the external trade. But a mere 39 of these organisations control 80 per cent of Japanese imports and 70 per cent of the exports; and indeed one-half of the external trade and 20 per cent of the domestic wholesale business is in the hands of only 11 of them. The largest employ over 10,000 people, and have between 70 and 100 foreign branches; and as a result of this system of international economic intelligence, and thanks to their financial power and organisational ability, they are becoming more and more active in initiating developments – in the provision of housing, for example, in data processing, space research and exploration of the oceans – in which they then take part. Ten of the fourteen principal economic enterprises in Japan, in terms of turnover, are *shoshas,* the others being industrial firms. But the chief of the latter, Nippon Steel, has only a quarter of the income of the Mitsubishi *shosha.*

The *shoshas,* which first appeared in the *Meiji* era, that is in the second half of the nineteenth century, perhaps owe their origin to the excessively craft-oriented character of production – or so runs the classic theory. But Setogawa (1975) regards them as 'colonial companies in reverse', originating in the necessity to have specialists to conduct business between two totally different worlds, a necessity that made itself felt when Japan began to trade with the West. However this may be, they do not appear today as the relics of another era, for they have evolved with the transformation of the Japanese economy and remain in control of Japanese trade.

Yet despite the undoubted dynamism of the *shoshas* and department stores, about half the shops in the traditional Japanese commercial system are family businesses, and economically marginal. What is more, most of them that employ assistants do not do so as part of a thought-out policy; they just do not know how to run their businesses efficiently. In fact, the shopkeepers have got into the habit of over-employment, during the time when unemployment was rife in Japan and the unemployed would be content with the very low wages paid in the commercial sector. Besides, in the absence of any professional organisation, not keeping separate accounts of wages and turnover, lacking business information, and generally inefficient, these small shopkeepers have 'a negative attitude towards innovation' (Tajima, 1971), and cannot devise methods of standardising their operations or investing in modern equipment. In 1967, moreover, some 44 per cent of the retailers had other activities as well, and 20 per cent derived more than half their income from such sources.

The Japanese rulers well understand that the transformation of the commercial structure is an urgent necessity; they consider that too large a part of the home market remains in the hardened arteries of petty shopkeeping and that this acts as a brake especially on the nation's industrial expansion.

Evolution of commercial organisation since 1960
The first feature, as in the industrialised countries of Europe, has been a concentration and a modernisation of retail shops, albeit very slowly, and a shortening of the supply lines.

Growing at about the same rate as the GNP, retail sales multiplied almost seven times between 1954 and 1973, under the combined influence of a slowing-down in the rate of population growth and a rapid rise in purchasing power. This growth in demand has been accompanied by a rather unusual development of the shopping facilities. As in other old mercantile countries that are now developing industrially, though to a smaller degree, there has been a modification in the structure by the concentration of undertakings. But unlike these other countries, the number of shops in Japan has continued to grow, which is not surprising in view of the boom in demand, a boom that has no parallel elsewhere in the world. Between 1954 and 1972 the number of wholesalers increased by 15 per cent, and that of retail shops by 16 per cent. In terms of employment, the corresponding figures were 57 and 48 per cent. It was the non-food shops (apart from clothing) that benefited most from this expansion. The first sign of deflation in retailing did not come until 1972, and then only in respect of fish, fruit and vegetables. The proportion of the undertakings employing less than 5 persons fell from 95 to under 85 per cent, and they only took 30 per cent of the trade instead of 55 per cent. But the average number of employees per shop only rose from 2.6 to 3.4 in 20 years. In the three years 1970–2, the size of the average shop increased from 37.2 to 41.4 m², and the average employment from 3.35 to 3.45. In wholesaling, there was a much stronger movement towards concentration, and the number of businesses employing less than 5 persons fell to 40 per cent of the total, while the average number of employees rose from 8.4 in 1954 to 11.5 in 1972.

In the field of retailing, the department stores and supermarkets are expanding rapidly. Although legislation has not exactly encouraged the department stores, their numbers increased by 67 per cent between 1960 and 1970, their employment roll by 69 per cent and their sales areas by 93 per cent. The rise and the success of the supermarkets, the dimensions of which enable them to escape the provisions of the law of 1956, has revitalised the big stores, causing them to increase the density and modernity of their network of branches. But this has only enabled them to increase very slightly their proportion of the national retail sales, from 9 per cent in the 1950s to 12 per cent in 1974. The competition of the supermarkets is severe. The first was opened in Tokyo in 1953; by 1962 they had already scooped 3.7 per cent of the retail market, and this figure rose to 11.3 per cent in 1973, and by now they are on level terms with the department stores. These supermarkets belong in general to large chain-store groups; they are relatively small, and have self-service; they have been opened mainly in peripheral suburbs of the great cities, and function as neighbourhood shops; but unlike their European and American counterparts, they sell non-food goods as well as foodstuffs. Some hypermarkets have been opened in city centres, but this is not a common development, for in general, Japan has little room available for such space-consuming users.

Although it has been rapid, the growth of supermarkets has been less spectacular than was at one time expected; the fragmentation of production that often forces the companies to get their supplies through wholesalers, prevents the adoption of a pricing policy as attractive as that practised by western supermarkets. They can, however, sell cheaper than the small shops since they do not have to go through the tertiary wholesalers, and rarely even the secondaries. Besides, little by little they have come to agreements with producers who furnish goods that can be sold under a brand name.

The competition of the supermarkets has also, as elsewhere, provoked discontent among the small shopkeepers. This led the government in 1974 to pass a new law requiring new supermarkets, as well as department stores, to get prior planning permission that is only granted after consultation with the local shopkeepers. Other measures have dealt with the promotion of small businesses, through aid given to voluntary chains and the creation of shopping centres for independent retailers, and the control of new developments by foreign firms. Although the Japanese market was until recently completely denied to them, foreign business houses can now hold up to 49 per cent of the shares in companies that have no more than 11 stores. Sears Roebuck (USA), Quelle (West Germany) and two British firms have already taken advantage of this breach in the barrier that formerly protected national commerce.

The shortening of the trade circuits may be regarded as the main transformation that has affected the Japanese commercial system during the last ten years or so. Many of the most active industrial firms have vied with the wholesalers for the control of trade flows by selling direct to the department stores or to central purchasing agencies that are increasing in number year by year. The latter serve the chain stores that have developed subsequently to the department stores and supermarkets, dealing in specialised goods such as electrical apparatus (where they now have 25 per cent of the sales), clothing, furniture, footwear, optical instruments and cameras. There are also central agencies for consumer cooperatives (which, however, only represent 1 per cent of the retail turnover), and for the voluntary chains that after a halting start have gained in efficiency. Commercial activities are certainly becoming more concentrated – though to nowhere near the same extent as in the western industrial countries – and the large companies and groups now control 20 per cent of the retail sales; this shortening of the circuits is a grave danger for the wholesalers. In general, the growth of integrated commercial undertakings may be regarded as a step in the right direction. It prevents the producers from taking hold of a large part of the distribution system, a danger that is far from being imaginary because of the fragility of the commercial structures. The department stores and the multiples that sometimes take over the factories or create their own distribution systems and develop their own brands, represent a power that can partially balance that of industry. For indeed some manufacturers, discouraged by the fragmentation of the commercial undertakings in certain sectors, have taken direct control of marketing by creating their own distribution systems, or more often by tying retailers to their own products (rather like breweries and public houses in Britain). Fortunately, perhaps, not many have sufficient financial resources to undertake such a scheme. They try instead, to a greater extent than in western countries because Japanese commercial structures are more decrepit, to control the merchants by staging publicity campaigns to advertise their products, and giving preferential treatment, in the form of substantial refunds, to certain wholesalers who are selected for their dynamic qualities. Such refunds often constitute the sole benefit reaped by the wholesale firms, since the industrialists tend more and more to fix retail prices by contract, a monopolistic practice that has obliged the public authorities to intervene to limit the number of such contracts.

This attitude on the part of the producers hastens the disappearance of the marginal merchants, and of those who cannot, since they have not the storage space, assume fully their function as stockholders – and this is indeed the case with the majority of Japanese wholesalers who are still located in town centres. So it looks as if, within the next decade, there will be a sharp decline in the number of secondary and tertiary wholesalers, so that the distribution channels will differ less and less from one product to another, and in general a weakening of the role of the wholesalers who since the *Meiji* era have dominated the trade flows within the country. Already, wholesale revenues have grown more slowly than retail, for in 1966 the ratio of the first to the second was 4.8, falling to 3.7 in 1972; and the movement is accelerating.

This tendency towards vertical integration is also seen, in the opposite direction, in the taking over by the *shoshas* of certain industries such as sugar, furniture, clothing. The *shoshas* are also investing, preferably by leasing, in the supermarket network, and are themselves developing shopping centres. Bearing in mind what we have said about the decline of wholesaling, it is remarkable that the *shoshas* maintain their hold not only on the trade circuits but also on the whole economic life of the country. Despite their antiquity, they appear to western industrialists, usually Europeans, who use their import–export services, to be the organisation of the future: 3 per cent of their turnover comes from transactions effected between Japanese producers and foreign buyers, and this part of their activity is expanding rapidly. Installed as they are in the world's markets, and with a reasonable understanding of the local trade flows and techniques in many countries, they always seem to be able to find a purchaser for whatever merchandise they have to sell. This is a valuable faculty, the efficiency of which can be measured by the degree of penetration achieved during the last ten years by Japanese goods in Europe and the United States. Particularly valuable, at a time when the industrial countries stand or fall by the expansion of their export capacity. The import–export firms, like those of the industrial west, have agents in foreign countries, but they are rarely located on the spot.

Another factor is beginning to play a fundamental role in the changing commercial organisation of Japan, and that is economic growth. It is in Japan that the GNP has risen fastest between 1967 and 1973. Taking 1967 as 100, the index in 1973 was 315, compared with 279 in West Germany, and under 200 in most of the other capitalist industrial countries. Wages rose by 30 per cent between 1973 and 1974. This rise in incomes is being expressed in an americanisation of the life-style. The Japanese are becoming a consumer society. Thus, little by little, the regional disparities in the markets are giving way to a standardisation of national consumption, that favours integration and the remodelling of the shopping system. Local shopping centres are pushing ahead with comprehensive construction schemes, particularly at crossroads sites. But space is lacking in Japan, 80 per cent of which is mountainous, for the kind of developments that are taking place in western countries. So there are only a few of these schemes, and the most noteworthy, now considered as models of urban commercial development, are those constructed underneath the great rail and road nuclei recently completed in Tokyo. On the other hand, all the other forms of trading and sales techniques imported from the United States seem destined for an even more promising future by virtue of the numbers of Japanese retail executives who have studied for upwards of ten years or received a portion of their training in America.

Some commercial experts regard these changes as dangerous, because in their judgement they have been inspired more by concern for the quality of life than for management, and it is precisely in the sphere of management that Japan lags so far behind the United States. It is true that after having meekly accepted the claims of advertisers (and advertising expenses trebled between 1963 and 1972, when they amounted to 900 billion yen) the Japanese consumer has become more critical as his standard of life has risen. There are now six important consumer associations. The oldest, Shufuren, the Housewives' Association, began in 1948; the largest now has 13 million members. They are having more and more impact on the population, and are becoming more efficient in their questioning of the quality and price of goods, even to the extent of organising purchasing boycotts. In 1957 the government passed a law concerning the 'inspection of exports', and this helped at the same time to improve the quality of products on sale in the home market. Since then, under pressure from the consumer lobby, it has taken several further steps in the same direction. And in 1972 it set up a safety council to draw together all the various measures into a comprehensive piece of overall legislation.

All these recent changes have brought the Japanese commercial system much closer to those of the other capitalist industrial countries. However, integrated commerce plays a smaller part, and industry and the wholesalers are still largely in control of the distribution circuits; but consumerism is more

Table 9. The eight leading retailers in Japan, 1972

Name	Turnover (billion yen)
1. Daiei (supermarkets)	744
2. Mitsukoshi (department stores)	744
3. Daimaru (department stores)	599
4. Takashimaya (department stores)	571
5. Seibu (supermarkets)	429
6. Matsurakaya (department stores)	423
7. Seibu (department stores)	412
8. Jasuko (supermarkets)	406

Source: Les Canaux d'importation au Japon, p. 24 Belgian Office of external trade.

Table 10. The six major trading companies in Japan, 1975

Name	Turnover (billion yen)	(billion dollars)	Employees
1. Mitsubishi	9,070	30.0	10,650
2. Mitsui	8,253	27.3	11,500
3. Marubeni	5,565	18.4	8,450
4. C. Itoh	5,416	17.9	7,950
5. Sumitomo Shoji	5,381	17.8	6,250
6. Nissho-Iwai	3,933	13.0	7,300
Total of 10 major companies	46,260	153.0	68,300

'Top Ten' sales in first six months of 1975 (per cent)
Domestic   69.9   (Home produced 48.5; imported 21.4)
Foreign   30.1   (Exports 20.3; Offshore 9.8)

Source: The Economist, 17 April 1976, p. 68.

aggressive. Yet the Japanese organisation will maintain, probably for a long time, a certain uniqueness that rests essentially on two facts. First, in a country that depends more than any other on its external trade, the *shoshas* have an influence on the economy and on government equivalent to that of the banks in Europe and the United States. Secondly, it is probable that spatial constraints rather than traditional purchasing habits will force the Japanese to maintain moderate-sized shops, and so to reflect American practice rather less than they would have wished.

Notes

1. For comparative purposes this figure includes only that which is regarded as retail business by the US census, i.e. it excludes the automobile trade ($93 billion), service stations ($34 billion), and cafe-restaurants ($38 billion).
2. In France only 8 per cent exceeded this figure.
3. In France, at this time, only 0.27 per cent of the companies engaged (and what would it be for individual shops!), had a turnover greater than 1 million francs (=$200,000), and 0.71 per cent had more than 19 employees.
4. Especially if businesses connected with automobiles and restaurants are excluded, as has been done.
5. These are chains of owner-managed shops that draw stocks from central warehouses – cf. SPAR in England.
6. Discount is a remission of 15 to 20 per cent on the published price, on almost all articles; this formula appeared in the late 1940s in small and medium shops specialising in electrical goods, radio and photography. Now about 15 per cent of the turnover of all retail trade in the United States is effected on this basis, and it is forecast that by 1980 the percentage will be 25.
7. As L. Wegnez remarks 'The average American stays only five years in any one house, but he adds numerous accessories to it, that increase its saleable value.' And 'The Americans now devote 10 per cent of their gross national product to the pursuit of leisure.'
8. Sarma was taken over by the English company Penney, as was Anspach by Sears Roebuck in 1971, and the Grand Bazar by the Swiss firm of Jelmoli.
9. A 'voluntary chain' comprises two or more wholesalers each with its associated independent retailers. See Scott (1970), p. 44.
10. *Channels and costs of distribution of the N.E. region.* Distributive Trades E.D.C., NEDO, 1971.
11. 'Ten Years of Retailing', *Retail Business,* **121,** March 1968.
12. It is also international: apart from its total selling area of 575,000 m² in the UK, it has 8,650 m² in Europe and 155,000 m² in Canada. In 1977 it opened a new store of 2,500 m² in Rosny II, Paris (Marks and Spencer, *Annual Report,* 1978).
13. An INSEE enquiry in 1971 showed that customers under 25 years of age purchased more than their elders in the following sectors: 'culture and leisure', transport, housing and clothing; but much less on food and 'hygiene'.
14. A very full account of the organisation of distribution in France is given in Dayan (1975).

Chapter 2

Commercial organisation in poor countries with a free economy

The medley of organisational forms that one finds in the trading systems of those Third World countries moving within the orbit of the capitalist industrialised powers cannot conceal the fundamental characteristic of their commercial system, which is an apparently dual structure. Every observer must be struck by the overwhelming importance of the local markets, of itinerant traders and of the tiny bazaars in the lives of the great majority of the population, in the towns as well as in the countryside, while only a very small minority of wealthy people, natives or foreigners, ever cross the thresholds of the urban stores that are better stocked, more modern and present in increasing numbers as the economic growth of the country proceeds.

We begin by evaluating the role of commerce in these non-industrialised countries. Then we shall demonstrate that the co-existence of two types of structure is not a disadvantage for they are in fact linked in a single system. We must not regard the poor petty trading only as the heritage of a traditional organisation that is in course of disappearing, but must understand that in these countries it forms, in company with modern commerce, a parallel system that is actually a contributory factor in underdevelopment. Finally we shall note the principal factors, historico-economic, psycho-sociological and political, that help to give a certain variety of form to the commercial structures of the underdeveloped countries.

Examples taken from several parts of the Third World will illustrate this rapid survey. If one excepts the data, of very unequal value, afforded by population censuses, statistics relating to the commercial activity in poor countries are rare, and on the whole so unsystematic that they are very difficult to use. Until the last decade or so, census officials working in these countries, not perceiving the economic importance of native petty trading, and influenced by their western background, only took into consideration the business of import–export and modern types of retailing. The unstable world of the petty trader does not fit easily into the matrices of the statisticians. Furthermore, economists, convinced of the universal and inescapable character of the type of evolution experienced by the developed capitalist countries, have often considered the traditional forms of commercial structure as economically condemned and therefore negligible, from the moment when competition from modern trading styles begins. Yet, as we shall see, not only does traditional trading remain very healthy, it also plays a large part in the economic organisation of the underdeveloped countries. Fortunately, the studies of marketing made by a commission of the International Geographical Union

(1974–6) and some recent publications are leading to a rapid increase in the availability of information.

The importance of commercial activity in poor countries

According to official statistics, the contribution of commerce to the GDP differs little, overall, from that in the industrialised countries, namely between 8 and 18 per cent. However, in some states its value exceeds that of other services and of industry, giving figures of over 28 per cent, rising even to 33 per cent in Mexico. To express reservations about the validity of these data, given the virtual certainty of incomplete recording, is but to imply that commerce always has a greater importance in the national economy than the statistics indicate. But of course similar underestimation occurs in other sectors of the economy as well.

If we compare these figures with those extracted from population censuses, which always show more than 10 per cent of the active population employed in commerce, it would seem that this branch of national activity is relatively one of the major sectors in the underdeveloped countries. In fact its proportion of the GDP is nearly always double its proportion of the total employment. This is not the case in the industrial countries, with a few exceptions such as the United States (where commerce employs 7 per cent of the population and is responsible for 17 per cent of the GDP), for in general the discrepancy between the two figures is very much less, only 2 or 3 per cent. But this kind of comparison can be very hazardous, for again the figures may not be very reliable. We cannot ignore the fact that lacunae in the demographic statistics are worse than in national accounting. Omissions and false declarations are not the only cause; it is virtually impossible to record irregular employment and secondary jobs. And in the underdeveloped countries, the occupation of salesman is frequently just a source of supplementary income, seasonally or even regularly, and is a stop-gap for many unemployed persons. However, in view of the generally low level of returns from agriculture and the services (in which domestic service holds pride of place), it seems not unreasonable to consider commerce as one of the most productive sectors of the economy in poor countries, and as such one of the generators of growth. We shall see, moreover, that this result is to be attributed mainly to commerce of the more modern type.

It is possible that commerce is only in fourth place, after agriculture, domestic service, and handicrafts and industry, as an employer in almost all poor countries, but its importance in the national activity derives more from its ability to absorb labour than from the number of jobs it offers. On the one hand, the overall task performed by trading activities is capable of an exceptional degree of fragmentation. On the other hand, one may become a trader with no training, no diploma, no shop, no employer and even without any personal capital. One may also quit at will, even if one is in debt. It is usually not like this in other sectors of activity (some domestic service excepted); to get a job it is necessary in the first place, perhaps, to visit an employment agency, or to have an available site, or a craft skill, or an assured employer, or more than one of these. All the studies that have been made in the towns of the underdeveloped countries show the important part played by new and inexperienced traders (Santos, 1975, p. 196). This 'last resort' aspect of trading is universal. But as one of the major consequences of underdevelopment is the inability to ensure full employment and to guarantee even a minimal standard of living for the majority of the population, it acts as a determining factor in the very organisation of commerce. This is particularly true in the towns, where individuals, cut off from the supplies that an agricultural mode of life provides, and totally dependent upon a money economy, must eke out a living either by using their physical strength as labourers or by using their wits.

We must not, however, lose sight of the fact that trading offers less employment, in proportion to the total population, than in the developed capitalist countries. Even if there is some doubt about the accuracy of the figures given in the *Statistical Yearbook* of UNO, where the recorded number of people occupied in commerce varies from 5 to 20 per thousand of the population in the poor countries, it is certain that an adjustment for underestimation would not bring the proportion up to the 35 to 70 per thousand characteristic of the industrialised countries. There is nothing surprising about this. The principal reasons are the low level of consumption in quantity and quality, of both individuals and undertakings, and the degree of self-subsistence. By low quality we do not mean the intrinsic quality of the products but rather their technological value and their lack of variety, reduced as they are to bare necessities only. As for subsistence, this is rapidly declining with the exodus of the rural population, but it remains in general more than 20 per cent, and sometimes up to 50 per cent of the GDP.

The peculiarity of the underdeveloped countries is not so much that there are so many people concerned with some form of trading, as that the sum total of products finally reaching the consumer remains so small. It is true that there are no accurate data on this point. But whether we base our measurement on the tonnages of goods, the number of articles, or more especially the total value of the merchandise, it is evident that the average productivity of commerce bears no comparison to that of the developed countries.

The same conclusion is reached if we consider not the quantity of merchandise but the clientele that is effectively served. In the absence of documentation on this point we can only make some general observations. As in the developed countries, trading in the Third World is essentially an urban phenomenon. An important difference, however, is that in the richer countries the clientele of the towns is regional, with the rural population coming into the urban centres for shopping, whereas in the poor countries it is purely local, that is almost exclusively urban, while the mass of the national population that is rural and produces well over half its own food, is very little concerned with urban commerce. It is thus clear that in these countries in which the majority of the inhabitants have not the means, either financial or in terms of transport to the urban markets, to play much part in a monetary commercial economy, a figure relating commercial employment to total population cannot take account of such a situation. If, on the other hand, we calculate the same figure in relation to urban centres such as Ibadan, Accra, Saigon or Mexico City, we get 63 to 75 employed in commerce per thousand population, in the same bracket as national and international centres like Paris, New York and Tokyo. Measured against the norms of the capitalist economy, the overemployment in the commercial sector in Third World cities is very evident. But when the observer from the western world is confronted and astonished by the multitude of stalls and traders in the urban streets of the underdeveloped world, he tends to forget the invisible mass of employees in the commercial offices of the developed countries.

Two different commercial structures, linked in a single system that generates economic growth but also perpetuates underdevelopment

The modern commercial undertakings that exist in almost all the underdeveloped countries hardly contribute at all to this inflation of employment in trading, for they are all very concerned about productivity. Moreover, in all their functional characteristics they are utterly different from all the other varieties of trading, both sedentary and itinerant. We have in fact two distinct structures. For reasons already discussed, economists have not been concerned with evaluating their respective roles. It seems that in general we can estimate that about 10 to 20 per cent of the employees in commerce are in the modern undertakings. But with only this small percentage of the labour force, they generate at least 60 per cent of the value of all commerce, if we are to believe the report on the development plan for Mali published in Paris in 1975; in this report, 46 per cent of the value added by commerce in 1962 was ascribed to foreign firms, 14 per cent to national public companies and only 40 per cent to the 'traditional' traders.

It is not inappropriate, in describing the duality of the commercial structures of the underdeveloped countries, to use antonymous expressions like 'traditional and modern', or 'poor petty trading and capitalist big business'. Nevertheless, this does not really take account of the specific nature of the situation, for the same terms are used with reference to the richer countries. But the cleavage is here more profound than in the industrialised world. In the latter it results essentially from the historical factors that affect the form of the distributive trades, whereas in the Third World it is concerned not only with the 'apparatus' but also, more consistently, with the clientele, thus dividing trade flows into two distinct circuits. The rupture is not, however, complete, for at the supply end there are overlaps and exchanges between the two structures. Thus we are not faced with two juxtaposed commercial systems that are independent and co-exist by accident. The two systems are dynamically inseparable.

Why do two circuits co-exist?

The answer to this question is that in the poor countries society is divided essentially into two camps, with no common measure between their standards of living. The enormous hiatus between the incomes of a small minority, with standards equivalent to those of the wealthy classes of the industrial countries, often with western contacts that given them expensive material and cultural tastes; and on the other hand the vast majority, whose financial resources are minimal, is sufficient to explain the existence of two markets that have but little in common. It is often the case that between 5 and 10 per cent of the active population will divide more than half the total income between them, while more than 60 per cent can hardly gain a living wage from less than a quarter of the total income. In Senegal in 1973, a small farmer (and 75 per cent of the population lives off the land) could only make 43,700 francs a year (including his own produce) while the average wage was 575,000 francs; but in the towns the majority of the wage-earners could earn less than 100,000 francs while the administrative classes, and especially the Europeans, were earning more than 2 million francs. Except for certain articles such as fruit and vegetables, and the products of native crafts, the wealthier people were just not interested in the poor-quality goods, often produced and sold under unhygienic conditions, consumed by the mass of the population. These latter simply have not the financial means to purchase high-quality goods, and furthermore, have to be content with only the bare necessities. The middle classes, as yet poorly represented, do not form a sufficiently large or wealthy clientele to command their own special market; so they visit both types, purchasing the least seedy-looking products in the traditional markets and the least expensive articles in the modern shops.

Though occasionally the native traders may have dealings with customers from widely differing income groups, the disparities in the means engender such great differences in the quality and quantity of consumption and in purchasing habits that a single commercial system could not possibly satisfy the two main types of consumer. Thus the structural model of trading exported by the capitalist industrial powers has not been able to attain full development in the poor countries, for its functional demands are incompatible with the servicing of a vast mass of poor people. On the contrary, the traditional local trading has always been directed towards this type of clientele. With every justification, Santos (1975) writes of an 'upper circuit' and a 'lower circuit' of commercial activity.

However, not being able to serve the mass of the population directly, modern businesses have tried to derive the utmost indirect profit by supplying the small traders, and thus to control the whole market. For all their appearance of distinctiveness, the two commercial structures are in reality just complementary sub-systems within the whole commercial realm.

How do the two forms of commercial organisation differ?

They differ in the first place through the motivation of the entrepreneurs. Obviously both the petty trader and the wholesale merchant hope to make money. But the fact is that retail sales to an impoverished clientele hardly yield sufficient profit to provide capital for investment in modern methods. And all those who embark on trading activities in the 'lower circuit' are well aware of this. We could summarise the situation by distinguishing 'subsistence trading' from 'business trading'. The main preoccupation of the petty traders who play a part in the commercial activity of the 'bazaar' is to assure the survival of their families by acquiring, from day to day, the cash that is indispensable in an economy that revolves more and more around the use of money. Quite otherwise is the objective of the enterprises included in what Geertz (1963) calls the 'firm centred economy' (as opposed to the 'bazaar economy'); this is to take the most of the invested capital by conducting business in a profitable manner and so lead to further expansion. The covering of expenses, including salaries, is but a preliminary in this case.

This difference in motivation is to be found not only in the commercial sector; it dominates all the secondary and tertiary activities that contribute to either one or the other of the two main sections of the economy in underdeveloped countries. Higgins (1956), Geertz (1963) and more recently Santos (1975), have given similar descriptions, if not identical interpretations; Santos has a penetrating analysis of the urban economic system of the Third World, in which he gives many examples of the functioning of commerce.

Higgins has summarised the main technological characteristics of the two forms of organisation, pointing out that the business firm is capital intensive while the bazaar is labour intensive. It is easy to distinguish a type of commerce that is run by an undertaking whose existence would be impossible without large capital resources, from one that depends mainly on its labour supply. The former has need of a large space (75 to 200 m² in most cases, but much more for department stores and some wholesalers), conveniently laid out. It must have stocks that assure a regular supply of all the goods that it displays – and this implies a volume that will avoid interruptions of supply, and excludes an ultra-rapid turnover. If these stocks are dependent on imports, very large amounts may be necessary: for example, at Abidjan, the stocks of the variety stores are double those of their equivalents in France. It also necessitates modern labour-saving equipment, and qualified assistants, in order to get the maximum profit. Subsistence trading can be accommodated in tiny shops (commonly between 5 and 30 m²), often hastily erected – when indeed it does not dispense with premises entirely (and as a general rule itinerant salesmen outnumber sedentary ones). They dispose of minute quantities of goods, sometimes miscellaneous, rarely regular and frequently replaced. They depend mainly on family labour and employ only unqualified assistants. Thus on the one hand we have the import–export businesses, the wholesalers and the modern retail shops (often small and specialising in good-quality imported products, or luxuries, or branches of varying sizes belonging to large firms), with other economic enterprises, industrial and financial, as neighbours. On the other hand, a multitude of small shopkeepers, stall-holders, pedlars, mingled with craftsmen and those who provide traditional services. It is, in sum, the classic division between large and small trading, with on the one side employees that are subjects of a tiered organisation, though assured of regular wages that, however low they may be, at least remove the fear of insecurity; and on the other side a large majority of independent traders whose resources are inadequate and uncertain. But we must reiterate that the great difference is that in the rich countries both large and small traders, with very few exceptions, serve the entire clientele. In the Third World this is not so.

If the chasm between the two types of trading is perfectly obvious when comparing the first African hypermarket (MBOLO at Libreville, with a building of 11,000 m², of which 4,000 m² sales area and 1,300 m² of cold store, and 200 employees of whom 10 are technicians from France), with the petty trader from Gabon who buys 1,000 francs'-worth of goods on credit, and sells them all from his home during the next two months for between 1,200 and 1,300 francs, it is a little less so when one is concerned with wholesaling and some forms of retailing. But it can still be seen if one dissects the mechanism of each circuit.

The implications of the major characteristics, as outlined above, are numerous, and the two structures are contrasted in terms of the mechanism of their operation, their behaviour and their relations.

The *organisation* of 'business trading' as opposed to 'subsistence trading' is in some ways cumbersome and constraining. If the need to get a sufficient return from the capital invested is not sufficient to enforce strict management, the supervision exercised by the banks to which it is necessary to turn for at least part of the financial support would certainly demand it, as an essential condition of further assistance. Further, the larger the business, the greater its bureaucratisation. In the search for economic productivity, the proprietors endeavour to reduce the number of employees to the absolute minimum, even though wages and social charges are less weighty items in the budget than in the industrial countries – at least as far as locally recruited staff are concerned. For the cost of management staff is high: large commercial firms in the underdeveloped countries have many foreign contacts and must employ competent people who will not be fleeced by the agents of big companies from the great powers. To secure managers with some knowledge of modern economics it is thus necessary to recruit from abroad, or among natives who have had a foreign education. If we add that this type of trading stands little chance of escaping the tax-man, because its location is fixed, and that it uses the most modern means of communication, it is not difficult to imagine that its general expenses are substantial, and this leaves little room for flexibility and improvisation. In the business game, financial success is what matters; the losers are eliminated, and this leads to an increasing concentration of the market in the hands of the more successful players.

The functioning of 'bazaar trading' is quite different. This is the realm of individual initiative and resourcefulness. Here the stakes are not the same. The loss of a day's trading simply means less to eat tomorrow, but does not prevent continuing with the occupation, provided that the salesman's capacity for hard work is retained. And as it happens it would not be noticed in these countries that have chronic unemployment and a constant rural exodus that fills the towns with job-hunters. Arising from the local condition of poverty that drives the people to adapt themselves to scarcity, bazaar trading is almost as important as a provider of a little employment for those who lack it, as in the distribution of goods. And by assisting in the circulation of money within local communities, it contributes to purchasing power, that is to its own growth. The bazaar is thus a major centre of employment. The domain of the petty trader, in which everyone, in a mainly free economy, has the opportunity of trying his luck, contains a large proportion of the self-employed, especially among the stall-holders and pedlars. But it is also the home of the family business, and the small permanent shops enable the maximum number in any family to eke out a bare living. Perhaps instead of 'labour intensive' we should call it 'labour *extensive*'! It does not come under the surveillance of the banks, which would not regard a capacity for hard work as sufficient guarantee for a loan. However, the operation of credit does have a crushing effect, even though it is concerned with loans arranged by word of mouth, on a personal basis, generally by suppliers to clients, implying a certain persuasive ability in the borrower and a degree of trust by the lender. Nevertheless, the latter is not a philanthropist, even though he risks only small advances, usually in kind rather than in cash, on a short-term basis and with a high rate of interest. Many itinerant traders spend much of their time trying to encourage a wholesaler, a dealer and a retailer to entrust them with a small quantity of saleable merchandise. Santos (1975, pp. 214–29) has made a study of the mechanics of financing petty trading. In such a system, writing and accounting have no place. Many traders can neither read nor write, and if they can at least count they have no idea of management or forecasting. Everything is carried in the head of the trader. This permits a very light and flexible infrastructure; and mobility is also a dominant characteristic of this 'bazaar trading'.

Mobility expresses itself in many ways: physical mobility of selling-places, as with itinerant traders, mobility in type of trade, with the nature of the goods sold varying from time to time, and mobility in terms of time, with many traders occupied irregularly during the day, the week, or seasonally in accordance with their momentary needs for ready cash. Even among the sedentary traders, the first two of these types of mobility are frequent, for the smallness of the investment and the lack of formal business structure make for easy changes of site or of specialisation. Mobility is also a way of avoiding taxes. In any case, the public authorities derive but little revenue from the traders. Thus in Morocco in 1965 (Beghin, 1974) there were 77,000 licensed traders and about 92,000 who were exempt.

The web of relations woven by each of the two main types of commerce differs profoundly, and the localisation of undertakings reflects this. 'Business trading' only utilises the products of the country in which it is located if the producers are capable of supplying goods of consistent quality at regular intervals and in sufficient quantity. This is in effect to say that since we are dealing with underdeveloped countries, the bulk of their supplies, particularly of manufactured goods but also of essential foodstuffs, arrive from abroad. All the local exports are also handled by a few business firms. With few exceptions, the whole of commerce depends on its links with the outside world. Doubly so, since much of its profit is invested abroad. Many firms in the 'upper circuit', often the most important ones, are part of integrated concerns that have their headquarters in a foreign country. Further, many wholesale businesses act as antennae for international organisations. All this pushes the local markets into an abnormally subordinate position that is all the more noticeable when, as sometimes happens, certain large firms, not content with merely associating with the banks, actually take them over. However far-flung, in spatial terms, may be the sources that supply the big business houses, their trade circuits are much shorter than those of traditional commerce, and every effort is made to shorten them still further, partly of course to make more profit, but also to reduce prices to the consumer.

The strength of the commercial links with overseas industrial countries and the marked dependence on a wealthy clientele explain the concentration of these large enterprises in the ports and major urban centres – which are often one and the same. Thus the Cape Verde peninsula, where 17 per cent of the population of Senegal resides, has three-quarters of the national commercial potential. As in all countries with a liberal economy, the network of modern business establishments reflects the urban hierarchy, and this is true even of the former colonial territories in Africa where large companies had opened trading posts in small country towns. And because all the households served are motorised and have domestic servants, most of the modern shops are located side by side in the heart of the cities, from which their influence extends over a wide radius. Centrality is more marked than in the rich countries.

'Subsistence trading' has no external linkages. Everything that it sells has been purchased from local producers or from merchants in the 'upper circuit';

or perhaps occasionally from ships in a kind of smuggling operation. But the goods only reach the final salesman after having passed through the hands of several intermediaries, wholesalers or retailers in the towns, carriers in the countryside. The trade circuits are long and rarely stable. In this connection we must emphasise that articles in rural shops are very dear. As most consumer goods (even those sold in the 'lower circuit', indirectly) are imported, districts in the interior of all the underdeveloped countries are at a distinct disadvantage, for they are ill provided with transport. In 1962, according to Hetzel (1972), 54 per cent of all the goods imported into Togo were sold in Lomé, that has only 6 per cent of the country's population, and 32 per cent outside the capital city, the rest being re-exported. Prices in the interior are raised even higher because the carriers, themselves often traders, take advantage of the situation. Frequently shopkeepers exercise a monopoly over vast areas where, because of the importance of subsistence and the very small returns obtained by agricultural producers who are exploited by wholesale firms that are often subsidiaries of the import–export companies that organise the collection of the produce, the extent of the market does not permit the creation and survival of other shops. In the Congo, in 1971 (Busaka, 1975), products were sold in the interior at three times their price in Kinshasa. Finally we may note that the merchants are frequently creditors of most of their clients, to whom they grant loans at high rates of interest on the security of future harvests.

It remains true, however, that in detail the location of sales points in the 'lower circuit' depends on the distribution of the population rather than of the suppliers. For the clientele has but little mobility. Its purchases are mostly bare necessities, mainly foodstuffs. The ordinary shop, except in the case of those in the permanent markets, does only a very local trade. As in any case each trader has scarcely the resources to supply more than a dozen or so families, the traditional trading system covers all the areas occupied by the ordinary people, and corresponds to the density of population, weighted by the general level of expenditure, which as we have seen is particularly low in the rural areas. Although the many pedlars play an important role in these rural areas, because of the absence of permanent shops, itinerant traders are specially numerous in the towns. In Singapore, 30 per cent of the pedlars are in the city centre. Indeed, places of traffic concentration – markets, stations, shopping streets and handicraft centres, and the central business districts – are the main haunts of the pedlars. And they often choose their stand to suit the wares they have managed to pick up.

The choice of commercial strategy differs radically in the two 'circuits'. Modern shops have policies akin to those of similar enterprises in western countries. Whether their wares are specialised or not, they are always better stocked than the traditional shops. The display is more orderly and attractive, inside the shop as well as in the window. A regular feature is the sale of standardised, pre-packed foodstuffs, mostly of average quality, originating in the industrial countries. Prices are fixed and goods are sold for cash. Working on a profit margin lower than usual in the 'lower circuit', these shops are assured of a large volume of sales, thanks to a relatively wealthy clientele that in many countries is captive because of the small number of such shops yet available. Economic growth and the expansion of urban areas are in general accompanied by more and more advertising as the shops endeavour to encourage consumption. Policies of expansion and modernisation, especially if put forward by the great integrated commercial firms, are readily agreed to by the public authorities, which may also allow aid in the form of tax relief or even subventions, and in some countries active participation. Thus in 1975 the hypermarket MBOLO was opened in Gabon, financed to the extent of 26 per cent by local public and private sources and for the rest of its 1,500 million francs by big French concerns.

To characterise the behaviour of the petty traders, whether sedentary or itinerant, it is only necessary to take each of the above points and proclaim the exact opposite. Offering, in a state of some chaos, a much reduced choice of oddly assorted commodities, of poor quality, the salesmen dispense rubbishy goods in minute quantities, often fragmenting standard packages. Stocking-up according to their available means at any moment, they are more concerned with finding something saleable than with quality or the maintenance of particular lines. In contrast with the 'upper circuit', neither the amount of work nor the time expended seem to enter into the selling price. Every sale is subject to a varying degree of subtle bargaining that often leaves the traders with a substantial profit margin. But they will also sell at cost price, or even at a loss, if they need ready cash; so that in the end, since they rarely have many goods to sell, and have high interest charges to pay, their annual profit is never great. Under these circumstances, word-of-mouth advertising is all that is possible. Nevertheless, if recourse to the mass media is out of the question for the small traders, they do benefit from the fall-out from the advertising campaigns for branded goods that incite even those who have not the means to purchase. When the public authorities begin to interest themselves in the small traders, it is a bad sign; particularly for the pedlars, for whom public authority equals police.

It may be said that the modern system of trading creates new structures rather than adapting itself to what already exists (Santos, 1975), while the traditional system just submits. But we must add that within each system, the dispositions are not uniform, and that two levels are discernible. The 'upper circuit' includes all the foreign-owned companies, often multinational, who handle the bulk of the imported merchandise. These effectively dominate the economic life of all those countries that depend largely on outside influences. Sometimes such undertakings have been nationalised by the governments of former colonies that have attained political independence. But there is in addition a further discrimination within the modern commercial sector, for the public authorities, while endeavouring to promote a liberal economy, give assistance only to state enterprises. The other less important businesses, usually wholesale but also retail, run more or less on the principles of rationality and efficiency laid down by western economists, mostly belong to foreign merchants, sometimes European but as often as not from the Third World – Syrians and Lebanese in West Africa, Chinese and Indians in East Africa and South East Asia – or to privileged nationals. Such enterprises adapt themselves to what they find rather than creating a new situation, and they can rely on only the moral support of the government.

Similarly, in the 'lower circuit' we can distinguish on the one hand the small traders, native or foreign, who work full-time and with no other occupation, and on the other those who are part-timers, including the numerous pedlars, mostly native or from neighbouring territories. In Cameroun, in 1970, the latter were classified as having an annual turnover of less than 100,000 francs. But some of the 16,000 shops came into this category as well as the majority of the 30,000 stall-holders.

The Third World countries thus owe both the top and bottom levels of their commercial equipment to the former or often continuing economic dependence imposed upon them by big business from the rich countries. This is direct in the first case, indirect in the second it we admit the clear showing by numerous authors that underdevelopment, if not actual poverty, stems in part from this economic dependence. In many underdeveloped countries throughout Africa and South East Asia, this dependence on the outside world is very evident, for it gives to both circuits one common feature, namely, that the majority of the most active businesses, and many others too, are run by foreigners. All the latter come from countries that have a long commercial tradition; but in the 'upper circuit' they come from the industrial nations whereas in the 'lower circuit' they come from relatively poor countries.

Is this a situation that will disappear as economic production increases in the countries concerned?

The answer to this question is a firm 'no', when the policy followed by the public authorities is balanced by a growth in the GNP that only benefits the rich. We may analyse the process.

The sales techniques developed in the capitalist world since the last century were spread in the Third World by western firms, formerly living on the slave trade, that are the remote descendants of the great European commercial companies of the sixteenth and seventeenth centuries. They have gained enormous profits through organising the exploitation of natural riches, obtainable at a low price in the underdeveloped areas of the world, for sale at a handsome profit in the industrial countries, offering the 'natives' in exchange manufactured goods, useful for the most part, it is true, but on terms wholly favourable to themselves and the manufacturers. This form of pillage was scarcely more difficult to control in the rare case of independent countries than in the colonies, since the exchange between unequal partners was always, until quite recent times, to the detriment of the weaker party. Not content with the profits derived from the import–export business, the commercial firms have established retail outlets, with single shops at first, and since the Second World War, department stores, multiples, and now supermarkets. While in Africa and Asia modern shops have often been created by and for Europeans, in Latin America the initiative and capital have come from the United States. In Venezuela, for example, Rockefeller has financed a chain of supermarkets (CADA) and Sears Roebuck has a large store. In 1962, the large warehousing firms in Lomé, Togo (Hetzel, 1974) sold one-third of their imports directly to their subsidiaries, most of them in the capital itself. In West Africa, variety stores, department stores and supermarkets, rapidly expanding as elsewhere in the Third World, are mostly in the hands of the French West Africa Company (CFAO), and the West African Commercial Company (SCOA). The Monoprix shops belong to CFAO because this company, with a turnover of 3,000 million francs in 1975, is a subsidiary of Galeries-Lafayette. SCOA, which is established in both French- and English-speaking countries, in Nigeria especially, also controls Printania since this is a subsidiary of Printemps-

Prisunic; it also has 170 branches of the Avion chain, established since 1956 in the Ivory Coast, and 75 SONADIS shops in Senegal; although in 1970 retail sales represented only 24 per cent of its turnover, 2,400 million francs, a figure double that of the Printemps chain in France, with 26 per cent derived from wholesaling and 21 per cent from road transport in Africa; between 1970 and 1975 its receipts doubled, and profits likewise, for the growth of the African market was especially favourable to the old firms. CFAO is also, since 1963, the supplier of a group of retail-purchasers, SAVE, that it has helped to modernise (Bonnefonds, 1968). It is from these great companies that the newly independent African governments have requested technical assistance and financial aid for the promotion of indigenous sales organisations. The response has always been positive, since this is the best, perhaps the only way in which the European companies can preserve their power over a distribution system that is in course of africanisation.

The development of bulk-trading through the use of chain-stores is much appreciated by families that have a regular income. But it also benefits the whole population indirectly, for it contributes to the formation and stabilisation of price levels: the proximity of a large modern store forces the traditional traders to review their prices.

Nevertheless, the development of modern trading methods is not usually accompanied by a dimunution in traditional petty trading. This is not so much because the latter reflects the tastes of the traditional customers, as because the numbers of the poor do not decline in most of the developing countries. Indeed, the temptations to which all Third World consumers are subject, from the introduction of well-made foreign goods, is a permanent obstacle to popular economising even when this is otherwise possible. In these underdeveloped lands the construction of factories that would help to lessen the dependence on foreign suppliers is only possible by recourse to foreign money-lenders – and in avoiding Charybdis they founder on Scylla. Besides, the investors who create the new factories naturally use the technologies of the West, that minimise the use of manpower. They also reserve the management posts for their own nationals. Nevertheless, as more and more are established in the Third World, just to benefit from labour which is very cheap compared with that in the industrial countries, they take on qualified workers. For these it means certain entry into the middle classes, but they are relatively few. Industrialisation is too mechanised to offer much in the way of employment for the masses, whose lot will thus not be improved. Quite the contrary, according to some economists, for whom 'climbing the social scale is selective and discriminatory, and merely creates a more acute pressure on the wages of the lower classes' (Santos, 1975, p. 175ff). If we add that fertility is particularly high among the poor, and that the influx of people from the rural areas into the towns only aggravates the disparity of living conditions, improving them for a minority who have regular jobs and lowering them for the unemployed, we can appreciate that the mass of the poverty-stricken who can only buy in the 'lower circuit' is not diminishing.

The commercial system of the 'lower circuit' is thus not simply residual, it is actually tending to expand, and remains very healthy. Though its methods may be largely traditional, that does not prevent it from adapting itself to changes in consumption, from improving its ways and means and using modern transport, for example, or even from making more radical changes when the competition of 'European' shops appears. In this case, the traders begin by revising their pricing policy, and then their business methods. Then they lean towards a degree of specialisation, and take more care over the display and the quality of their goods and the maintenance and lighting of their shops. This additional effort and expense enables them to retain their middle-class customers, but does not allow an increased turnover. In some countries such as the Ivory Coast, they even join forces in order to counter the competition of the modern shops. Besides, far from diminishing, the sales points in the traditional system actually multiply as the urban agglomerations expand. They are set up in the new towns built outside the gates of the old ones, and they prosper in the shanty-towns. Everywhere they assist the newly arrived immigrants to become part of the community. In the towns, where the constant display of the products of modern technology provokes desires, the poor will willingly sacrifice housing, and if need be food, in favour of other types of consumption that have been introduced with much publicity; and the conclusion has been reached that the increase in shanty-towns around Third World cities is linked with urban poverty and imported consumer habits (Santos, 1975, after M. Frankman, *Rapid Urbanization in Latin America: a Key to Development,* McGill University, 1970).

In concluding this analysis of the two commercial systems into which the internal trade of the poor countries is divided, it must be emphasised that they bear witness to the realism and the remarkable capacity for adaptation of the capitalist system. The 'lower circuit' in particular has a great social significance, for in enabling the poor to survive it acts as a safety-valve for an iniquitous system of exploitation. And it is not prejudicial to the economic efficiency of modern big business since it is the latter's customer.

So long as these countries choose to depend entirely on imported technology, to leave their market at the mercy of fluctuating prices, open to the speculators of the industrial nations, and the regulation of their trade flows in the hands of foreign businessmen who always favour the capitalist industrialised world, they will find it difficult, indeed impossible, to escape from the grip of underdevelopment, unless, like the OPEC countries, they discover some means of pressurising the industrial powers – or unless, in a utopian world, the latter renounce their commercial colonialism.

All the poor countries that have advanced some way along the road of economic development have witnessed the automatic decline of 'subsistence trading' with the rise of modern businesses. This has happened since 1955 in Singapore (Yue Man Yeung, 1973). Along with the growth of economic activity, private consumption has trebled, and the amount spent by businessmen and tourists has greatly increased. The number of trading businesses had also trebled, but this growth has been accompanied by variations in quality and in spatial distribution. Up to 1960, there were twice as many new businesses in the city centre as outside it, and most of them were of a modern type. Since 1960 developments have been almost equal in the two sectors, with the periphery only slightly less important than the centre; and on the city fringes, too, modern establishments have appeared, including large department stores. Everywhere the relative importance of food purchases has fallen, from 52 to 47 per cent in the island as a whole and from 46 to 40 per cent in the city centre. It is true that a grand programme of urban reconstruction, still in progress, has meant a reduction in the city-centre population, which now represents only 15 per cent of the island's 2.1 millions instead of 20 per cent a decade earlier. These population movements have entailed a slight diminution in the numbers of traditional shops and pedlars.

Conclusion: the causes of diversity in the trading systems of underdeveloped countries

The first peculiarity that enables us to distinguish the trading activities of one country from those of another derives from the diversity of the type of civilisation that has influenced the present social structure. For example, the place of women in trading differs widely from one country to another. In the Muslim countries it is virtually nil, whereas among certain non-Muslim tribes of black Africa it is very great, especially in the markets; half-way between these two extremes come many Asian countries where Muslim influence is slight. The apparatus of traditional trading also varies widely. The trading centre of the East is the unspecialised covered market, a characteristic feature of all Muslim countries; called a *suq* in the Arab lands, a *pasar* in Indonesia, where it is housed either in a permanent building or in a collection of wooden huts, it is but a rather distant copy of the original Persian *bazaar*. In the Philippines, where only the small island of Mindoro is Muslim, most of the retailers run '*sari sari* stores', in small huts strung out along the streets; as in other parts of the world, the ribbon arrangement of shops is more important than their concentration.

The nationality of the westerners who set modern commerce in motion is scarcely ever a differentiating factor. But occasionally one can detect it in the exterior or interior appearance of the shops or in the range of goods offered, when the colonial regime has impressed certain consumer habits upon the indigenous population.

On the other hand, the unequal aptitude for trading among the people of the Third World is striking. For example, the Latin American Indians, certain African groups, the Malays in Asia; none make good traders. The last of these, forming the bulk of the population in Sarawak and North Borneo, play almost no part in trading except in the villages, where the multiplicity of dialects makes things difficult for outsiders. Have some people a special gift for trading activities? Or perhaps some social or religious background that predisposes them towards it? The example of Mahomet perhaps attracts many Muslims towards commerce, but that is not to say that all Arab states are mercantile: thus in the Arabian Gulf, only the emirates of Bahrein and Dubai have had long experience in the world of trading. However, certain nations seem to be seed-beds of traders, who spread their activities throughout the Third World where they compete very successfully with the natives. Muslim and Chinese traders have had the most remarkable success in infiltrating into the commercial activity of many countries. They seem to have divided the world between them, so as to give a distinct flavour to trading in two great zones. The Middle East, North and West Africa are the field of the Muslims, particularly Syrians and Lebanese, who have even crossed the Atlantic to take over certain trading activities in Latin America, for example textile importing in Venezuela. East Africa and South East Asia are the domain of the Chinese, and to a lesser extent of the Indians; except for Uganda, that has recently expelled all foreign traders. In Senegal, 58 per cent of the wholesale businesses in the Cape Verde peninsula belong to 'Lebanese', who also control 10 per cent of the 300 retail shops, with a further 40 per cent in the hands of 'Moors', Muslims from other African countries. In Malaysia, where Chinese form one-third of the entire population, their commercial success has been spectacular, to the extent that they are popularly believed to control the economy; in fact the Chinese traders are mostly agents, pedlars or stall-holders in the markets (Dupuis, 1972). In Sarawak especially, Europeans are only concerned with the import of manufactures, while the Indians have cornered the retail trade in textiles and the Chinese have taken over both levels of retail shops and the export of local products.

The *level of economic activity* is also a differentiating factor of some significance. Within large zones of similar civilisation, the countries with a higher GNP, particularly if this has been the case for some time, have more quality shops in relation to the mass of consumers, and more supermarkets than in the other countries. For example, Venezuela, Brazil, South Africa, Gabon and Malaysia have richer economies than their neighbours. This is not to say that traditional trading is any less flourishing, for in these countries economic growth mainly benefits the wealthy; thus Venezuela, with a GNP five times greater than that of a country like the Philippines, has the same proportion – one-third – of the population with a per capita income of under 500 dollars, that condemns them to subsistence trading for the satisfaction of their needs. All the Third World countries in which western colonial settlement is of some importance appear to be better equipped with luxury or semi-luxury shops than the rest.

Another example bears witness to the effects of the sudden and dramatic rise in the GNP: the recent influx of petrodollars has led the rulers of the tiny Arab state of Qatar, with only 180,000 inhabitants and customs that are in many ways still mediaeval, not merely to import from the western world the most elementary products and the most sophisticated industrial goods, but also to open, in April 1978, the first hypermarket in the Middle East in which to sell these goods. Built in the desert, on the outskirts of Doha, it has a sales area of 7,855 m², and offers an assortment of 10,000 items, mainly imported by air from the United States in weekly consignments for perishable goods and monthly for other merchandise, which include such things as Maserati cars, luxury garments from Nina Ricci, and costly perfumes.

The *degree of interference by public authorities* is the last major diversifying factor in the free countries of the Third World. It is only a question of measures directed specifically at commerce, and not of general political decisions. The latter may, however, sometimes have important effects, as for example the law of 1944 that gave all Guatemalans equal legal status, and abolished forced labour and the indenturing of the aboriginals – a move that enabled many of these people to engage in commercial activities, with the consequential creation of many new fixed trading points in the mountain villages (Demyk, 1975). Direct government intervention is usually directed towards regaining control of national trade, and of modernising it. Actions of the first kind are seen especially in the former African colonies; here the africanisation of commerce is the main object. Decisions are sometimes categorical and definitive, as in Nigeria where since 1968 the import business is confined to natives, as it has been for much longer in Guinea: this creates many supply problems for these countries. Regulations are generally more flexible in most other countries, and also less effective. Thus in Senegal, since 1969, and especially since 1971, the profession of trader is subject to a licence that is designed, with some state aid, to facilitate the entry of selected Senegalese into the business world, and particularly into importing. But by reason of bilateral agreements it is difficult to refuse such licences to foreigners, or to impose quotas, without the danger of being cut off from certain western markets. While it may be difficult to retreat from the existing position, the general growth of foreign trade may make it possible to introduce a few Senegalese into the European business circle. Measures have also been taken to counter the technical incompetence of the native traders. Here the westerners are more willing to yield ground. The government, that has already assisted the 21 retail cooperative societies that were established in 1965, is in process of creating a chain of 500 shops, reserved for holders of the certificate of secondary education. It also encourages the setting up of central purchasing agencies, that will have access to foreign markets. In this respect Senegal is following the example of the Ivory Coast, which since the early 1960s has allowed the promotion of two retail purchasing groups. But the Ivory Coast economic distribution company is unfortunately only a subsidiary of SCOA; the 'Société commerciale et industrielle africaine de la Côte d'Ivoire' has much more independence.

Similar policies have been adopted to aid both the reorganisation of trade flows and the modernisation of the equipment.

Sometimes it is not by measures to direct the economy that the authorities seek to influence the organisation of commerce, but by the planning of land-use. This is the case in Singapore where the policy was introduced in 1959 with the accession to power of the Popular Action party.

Such, then, are the main factors that give character to the trading activities of certain countries. On the whole their impact is but slight, even when government action is involved; though such action remains the principal means of securing the development of the commercial system of these Third World countries that still have a liberal economy.

Chapter 3

Commercial organisation in socialist countries

The Soviet distribution system

The three principles underlying the whole economic structure of the USSR are reflected in the distribution sector by the central planning of trading, the hierarchy of commodity flows and the collectivisation of nine-tenths of the commercial equipment. It makes little sense to compare statistics for the USA with those for the Soviet Union, except perhaps to underline the disproportion between the roles of commercial activity in a mercantile economy and in one based on marxism. In 1972, the turnover of commercial enterprises in the USSR, serving a population of 240 millions, was only one-half and the numbers employed probably less than one-half[1] of those of the United States in 1967, that served barely 200 millions. The fact is that the Soviet rulers, faithful to the distinction established by Marx between 'complementary' aspects of distribution (processing, warehousing, transport) that are considered natural because they are a necessary extension of the process of production and add to the value of the goods, and 'pure' aspects, that are to be shunned because they are based simply in speculation, and so materially and socially unproductive, maintained until 1969 a system in which trading was nothing but an unavoidable and passive link in the distribution of the commodities produced. From a distrust of this sector of the economy that is so much a part of the capitalist system, to the extent of being, with banking, one of its two main attributes, they endeavoured to control it with a tight rein. As a result, bearing in mind the low developmental state of the Russia of 1917 and the priority accorded to capital equipment, it is not surprising that the supply of consumer goods has scarcely reached a level that would be regarded in the West as bare necessity.

In recent years, however, the Soviet commercial system has evolved, under the dual influence of a rise in consumption and the re-introduction of the profit motive as a stimulus to the economy. The Soviet system begins to look like a somewhat backward half-brother of that of the capitalist industrial countries. Nevertheless, in 1976 the system remained effectively the same as it had been ten years earlier, before the introduction of more flexible trading methods. We shall therefore, in the first place, and before analysing the nature and effects of the 1967 reforms, describe the commercial structure as it was prior to the reform.

The bureaucratic and centralised organisation of a passive process

Soviet trading is not in the hands of a single organisation, but of separate organisations for foreign trade, the internal distribution of equipment goods, and of consumer goods in rural and in urban environments. However, except for a very small proportion of the transactions, the controlling hands are identical.

External trade

This was declared a state monopoly in 1918, and has remained so ever since. In order to maintain the balance of trade, to avoid disruption of the domestic market, and to respond more readily to national equipment requirements, imports and exports, which amount to 3.7 per cent of the world's total, are effected under licence. Such licences are granted by appropriate departments of a federal ministry, in accordance with an annual plan approved by the government. The trade agreements with foreign suppliers and customers are made by commercial delegations acting as agents for 29 different State corporations or for the Central Union of Consumer Societies.

Under this system, wholesaling is a purely administrative function.

Domestic trade

A series of modifications introduced between 1956 and 1965 did something to simplify the Soviet system of commercial organisation, but it remained complex. Within the whole gamut of territorial divisions (the Union, republics, then various regional and local areas) there are two types of authority. The first, having a coordinating function, is the State Planning Board (GOSPLAN), which determines national needs and the distribution of resources; the second, subordinate in role, is concerned with sectors of the economy; it functions through ministries, each responsible for a section of the overall plan, such as the organisation of trade flows, the economic and financial control of undertakings and of prices, and lastly employment. Commercial activity comes under the tutelage of several ministries: the distribution of consumer goods is primarily the responsibility of the department of trade, but others involved are health and information; capital goods, since 1965, come under the State Commission for Material and Technical Supplies (GOSSNAB).

Distribution of capital goods   Until 1965 the system that had been established in broad outline in 1932 at the time of the first five-year plan (and thus during a period of extreme poverty that necessitated rigorous control of trading), had as its motive force the instructions of GOSPLAN, that assigned to each of the 30 ministries their customers, their suppliers and their objectives; under these instructions, each ministry organised some part of the exchanges. To minimise the inconvenience of such a fragmentation of the means of production, GOSSNAB was created, a kind of 'Ministry of intersector exchanges' independent both of GOSPLAN and of the other sectorial ministries. Its task was to coordinate transactions relating to more than 25,000 types of intermediate goods[2], centralising all the requests for the supplying of undertakings submitted by other ministries and responding thereto with either a refusal or a purchasing permit. This gigantic administrative task employed 700,000 people, with a central directorate organised into 'inter-industrial' sectors such as ball-bearings, agricultural materials, heavy engineering products, chemicals – 21 of them in all, with another 15 territorial directorates. A buying permit having been granted, the transactions are arranged directly between individual enterprises. The wholesaling stage is, as before, merely a piece of administration.

Distribution of consumer goods.   The domestic trade in wheat and other foodstuffs was nationalised in 1918, but this was countermanded by the NEP (Novaya Ekonomicheskaya Politika) in 1921. In 1923, however, concerned at the expansion of private trading, the government began to support the cooperatives, after some misgivings caused by the number of mencheviks in their ranks. Cooperatives were already numerous; they first appeared as far back as 1865 and by 1917 there were 35,000 of them, with 11 million members. In 1922, when private trading accounted for three-quarters of all the retail sales, the cooperatives represented only 11 per cent, but this figure rose to 30.7 per cent in 1924 and to a maximum of 74 per cent in 1931. By 1935 their share had been reduced to only 19 per cent of the national retail turnover, but this was due, not to the competition of traditional private enterprise, which had disappeared since 1931, but to that of the state shops, the turnover of which rose from 14 per cent of the national total in 1922 to 66 per cent in 1935, and of the *kolkhoz* markets. The latter, the only form of free commerce permitted, expanded between 1931 and 1934, when they achieved 18 per cent of the total retail sales, but subsequently they declined.

The decree of 1935, which gave cooperatives a monopoly of all trade in the rural areas and small towns, and transferred to the State all the shops in the larger cities, is the basis of the present system of internal trade. In the main, although the *kolkhoz* markets are still permitted, the system now depends on centralisation and state planning.

Despite certain reforms, it has been rare, until quite recently, to find articles which could move freely and directly from producers to retailers, without strict controls on their distribution. The authorities of GOSPLAN planned, at national level, the distribution of several hundred types of consumer goods, constituting almost two-thirds of all the articles of trade, and at republic level, that of most other commodities. It is within this already constraining framework that the organisation of the 'apparatus' of distribution has been organised – on a centralist model that enables the State to exercise a firm control over the whole commercial system. It is true that the direct hold of the Ministry of Trade on the organisation is statutory only in respect of state trading, but by its pyramidal structure, by the vigilance of members of the Communist party, and by the organisation of its supply-lines, the cooperative sector, as we shall see, does not escape state control.

Rural trading   This is in the hands of the central union of cooperatives which works in both the wholesale and retail fields.

Cooperative retailing   The proportion of the national retail trade done in the rural areas is declining as different regions become more urbanised and industrialised: from 25.4 per cent in 1940 to 21.8 per cent in 1974. Almost 9,000 village cooperatives, the SELPOS, each serving an average of five *sovkhozy* or *kolkhozy*[3], are concerned with supplying the entire needs, food and non-food, of more that 100 million rural dwellers. It is not necessary to belong to the cooperative in order to purchase there, but since products in short supply go first to the members, most of the peasants pay their contributions. In 1974 cooperative membership included 62 million households. Unlike the cooperatives in western countries, the Soviet societies refund only a tiny part of their profits to the customers, the rest going into further investment, the training of staff and the payment of incentive bonuses to the personnel. But in any case the profits are very limited because of price-control imposed by the State.

During the last fifteen years or so there has been a rapid concentration of SELPOS, by amalgamations. From 25,000 in 1947, their number fell to 15,000 in 1959, and in 1965 there were no more than 10,000. This movement is in part due to the diminution in the numbers of *kolkhozy*, which have also been subjected to consolidation.

Centralisation and a hierarchical form characterise the Soviet cooperative system. At the head is the central union of cooperatives (*Centrosoyuz*), the edicts of which must be faithfully carried out by the lower tiers, the pyramid of which is based on administrative divisions – unions in republics, in *oblasts* (provinces), *krai* (counties), and *rayon* (districts). At the base of the pyramid are the SELPOS. The weight of this organisation is justified by the extent of the territory, and its apparently authoritative centralisation is compensated by an intense and critical participation by the majority of the cooperators who elect the members of the various management committees. Although state trading and cooperative trading greatly resemble each other, the latter could certainly be described as a form of democratic centralism, while the former is entirely state controlled. However, while it never gives direct instructions, the Communist party plays a very great part in the cooperative movement; its watchdogs seek to prevent, and at times to remedy, discontent among the rural masses whose very existence depends largely on the good or bad functioning of the cooperative, which is the sole source of their supplies.

The cooperatives are autonomous in their organisation, but not as regards their sources of supply. On the one hand, the distribution of consumer goods as between state shops and the cooperatives is decided by the Council of Ministers, on the advice of GOSPLAN, which is informed of the wishes of both organisations. On the other hand, the cooperative union has no wholesale organisation of its own, for it is compelled to depend on the wholesale distribution functions exercised by state trading – functions that often include the supplying of rural shops in response to the requests made by the cooperatives.

In view of the cost of transport, which is necessarily higher in the case of rural trading than in the towns, prices in the cooperatives are appreciably higher than those in state shops.

To serve the dispersed rural population, scattered in 700,000 settlements over an area of 22 million km², the SELPOS had opened, by 1974, more than 300,000 rural shops (there were only 230,000 in 1962), employing 2,600,000 wage-earners of whom almost half were salesmen, the remainder office-workers, or employed in transport, the making-up of the saleable goods, or in the construction and maintenance of the shop buildings.

Most of the shops are small buildings of one or two storeys, usually without display windows – for there is no need for devices to attract the already captive customers! In the interior, the goods are carefully laid out, and there is a vast assortment, for it must cover all possible requirements in both food and non-food commodities; but the range of choice is very limited.

The nature of the shops is a response to the hierarchical framework imposed by the *Centrosoyuz*: mobile shops for hamlets of less than 200 people, a small unspecialised shop serving the current needs of each village – there were nearly 200,000 of these – a larger general store and a *selmag* (the universal rural shop selling goods for other than immediate consumption) in the focal villages – some 50,000 of these, many more than 10 years previously – and finally, in the largest villages, a series of specialised shops forming a business centre, selling foodstuffs, footwear and clothing, cloth, hardware, and so on, or, to an increasing extent, a *univermag* (department store) displaying, on two or three floors, common and less common goods of all types.

Outside the cooperatives, the rural dwellers can still have recourse to some local *kolkhoz* markets that altogether represent about 5 per cent of all the retail sales in rural areas; and also more importantly, since 1959, to the mail-order agency *posyltorg*.

'Commission' trading.   Another task of the SELPOS since 1953 has been to collect and store the harvested crops sold by the peasants and destined for the supply of neighbouring towns. Compared with their retail function, this wholesaling activity is of minor importance, and in 1973 it only employed 160,000 persons. The task was entrusted to the SELPOS partly to relieve the peasants of time-consuming journeys to the urban markets. The SELPOS arrange contract prices that are higher, when transport costs are deducted, than the *kolkhozniki* would get by direct sale in the town. This commission trading, in accord with government principles, has the advantage of reducing the free market and diverting towards the centralised sector an important part of private produce; the purchases in 1974 represented one-third of the transactions still carried out in the *kolkhoz* markets.

Urban trading   This is dominated by state undertakings, run by the Ministry of Internal Trade. In 1974, they represented 88.5 per cent of all urban sales; the rest was effected by the remaining *kolkhoz* markets (2.9 per cent of sales) and, especially in the smaller towns, by cooperative shops (8.6 per cent). The state shops and consumer cooperatives continue to increase their role, at the expense of the *kolkhoz* markets, which in 1965 still represented 4.4 per cent of the sales. Thanks to the rapid growth of small towns, the turnover of the cooperatives, which in addition to other goods, sell the same products as are allowed in the *kolkhoz* markets, is progressing at a faster rate than that of state shops.

State shops   Of all the Soviet commercial structures, state trading has the longest and most complex hierarchy. The *torg*, the municipal body responsible for the organisation of distribution, is an essential link in the chain. There are more than 1,000 *torgi* in the USSR. Each *torg* is concerned, in its particular area, with the organisation and administration of retail trade, as well as with its supplies, thus undertaking some wholesaling operations. Large cities have two separate *torgi*, one for food and the other for non-food commodities; the largest conurbations, and particularly Moscow, may even have several, specialising in different types of consumer goods.

Each *torg* is responsible for the establishment and management of retail shops. As consumption increases, the *torgi* multiply the undertakings, giving a greater weight to specialty shops. Obviously there is a greater variety of shops than in the rural areas. The small shops are the least specialised, but have a very limited range of food and non-food goods; they represent under 10 per cent of state trading and have been disappearing at a regular pace since 1960, when they still formed 15 per cent of urban shops. Among the food stores that still represent over half the total, about 55 per cent are non-specialised, like those called *prodmag* (small-scale provisioning from local sources), and the branches of two enterprises, 'Gastronom' and 'Bakaleia', that offer a wider choice; and finally the specialised shops – bakeries, butchers, dairies, fruiterers and sweet shops, all of which, as in western countries, are tending to decline, though perhaps less rapidly. On the contrary, in the non-alimentary sector, which is expanding rapidly, specialisation is increasing as the standard of living rises and a greater variety of consumer goods becomes available. This movement, we may remind ourselves, is the converse of what is happening in the capitalist industrialised countries with a high living standard. Other than the big department stores, there were only 38 per cent non-food shops in 1960, and not far short of 50 per cent now; at the earlier date, 69 per cent of them were specialised, but by 1966 this percentage had risen to 75 per cent, and it is over 80 per cent now. Pharmacy goods, books and magazines are also distributed through *magaziny* which somewhat resemble small drugstores.

All these shops must obtain their stocks through the medium of the appropriate *torg*, which itself will set in motion the hierarchy of services provided by district, province and republic (that will respond to 40 per cent of the requirements), or by the Ministry of Internal Trade for most other goods, the Ministry of Health for pharmaceutical goods, or the Ministry of Communication for books and papers. At this federal stage, in accordance with the directives of GOSPLAN, and thus of national availability, the requests are redirected either directly to the producer-undertakings, the depots of which may on occasions forward straight to the *torgi* depots or even the shops, or more likely, to wholesale enterprises, the *sbyt*, which through a hierarchical system (always within regional limits) of forwarding agencies, undertake the actual distribution.

The more important the town or the individual shop, the greater the tendency to avoid this long rigmarole by short-circuiting certain territorial stages. Also, the top rung of state shops, the department stores (*univermag*), are in direct touch with the ministerial services of the republics or even, in the conurbations, with the appropriate federal ministries. It is true that the *univermag* of the large cities, like GUM and TSUM in Moscow, or Gostinyi Dvor, the largest of them all, rebuilt in 1965 in Leningrad, are gigantic sales organisations employing thousands of people. In view of the reforms that we shall deal with anon, and because there is a gradual increase in the average size of shops, direct deliveries from factory to shop are becoming less uncommon than hitherto. It is difficult to say precisely where this movement towards concentration in state trading is taking place, but between 1960 and 1966 the average number of employees in ordinary food shops rose from 2.7 to 3.3, and in non-food shops from 3.1 to 3.6, while in the *univermag* the numbers rose from 57.9 to 71.6.

State trading assumes a guiding role in everything pertaining to distribution. First in the matter of price: this is fixed so as to direct demand and to cause the other markets, cooperative and *kolkhoz*, to follow suit. Also in the introduction of new techniques, all the more so since these are mostly imported from western countries – such as sales equipment (refrigerators, cash registers, pre-packing of goods to replace the open-counter sales that are still widespread, and special display fittings), and sales techniques (credit and sampling, introduced in 1959, self-service, for which a food store opened in Leningrad in 1954 set a fashion that had so multiplied that in 1976 the cooperatives alone had 10,000 of them, and vending machines that have become popular in the last 15 years).

Consumer cooperatives   In the small towns there are about 70,000 shops belonging to cooperative societies, that differ from the SELPOS only in their name, which is *gorpos*.

The Kolkhoz markets   The sale by the peasants of part of their produce directly to urban markets is to a degree successful in all parts of the world, even if the components of this success may vary somewhat. In the USSR, the collective farms, held to a certain yield per hectare, can sell only their surpluses as they wish, and to these may be added the produce from industrial members of the *kolkhozy*. The state tolerates this private enterprise, not only for political and social reasons but especially for economic reasons: this local trading, that brings the producer close to the ultimate consumer, avoids the loss of perishable commodities, reduces transport costs, and acts as a safety-valve for the provisioning of the towns.

The part played by this free market is most important in the case of perishable foodstuffs: within this sphere it provided 30 per cent of the national food sales, way back in 1940, but the proportion fell to 15 per cent in 1960 and is now below 5 per cent. It clearly affects the towns most, but to a very varying degree; some towns are still very dependent on their local countryside, like Odessa, which in 1955 derived 60 per cent of its supplies therefrom and still gets 10 per cent.

In 1961, despite the abolition of large numbers, there still remained 9,000 *kolkhoz* markets in the Soviet Union, often located close to crossroads and to stations: in 1965 Moscow still had 30 or so, and Odessa 8.

As in the West, these markets have an advantage, from the citizen's viewpoint, in the quality and freshness of their products; above all, they supply articles such as meat, milk, eggs, green vegetables, potatoes and fruit, of which the state shops have insufficient quantities. On the free market, prices are generally higher than in the controlled shops, and in conformity with the laws of supply and demand, vary with the scarcity of the articles.

The *kolkhoz* markets are administered by a branch of the local *torg,* that is charged with the task of attracting the *kolkhoz* peasants, and helping them, for a small charge, to transport their produce and set up their stalls; the service includes sanitary supervision.

Nevertheless, the relative importance of the *kolkhoz* sales in feeding the urban populations has not ceased to decline during the past 30 years, even though the total volume of produce sold continued to rise until 1958; but since the beginning of 'commission sales', the volume of produce entering the markets has declined, except for two types of goods – fruit and butcher's meat.

The reform of a distribution system ill-adapted to the growth of demand

The above description of this centralised commercial organisation, that was already cumbersome during a period of economic poverty, should enable the reader to understand the difficulty, when the volume of goods for sale increased in size and variety, of ensuring the speedy and satisfactory regulation of internal trade flows necessary for economic development and thus, in principle, to a rising standard of living for the population. The Soviet rulers have been all the more tardy in remedying the deficiencies of the distribution system because they have been obliged to call into question the very principles upon which the system was based.

The increasingly felt deficiencies of the commercial system
Lavigne (1970) has clearly analysed the faults in the distribution system for capital and consumer goods in the USSR. We shall base our study in part on his reflexions, before describing the expansion of consumption that rendered reform inevitable.

The weight of local bureaucracy and the absence of local initiative   In the matter of the demand for *consumer durables,* the activities of undertakings are hindered by the long delays in delivery resulting from the ordering procedures, that also seriously increase production costs. The whole economy suffers from the inadequate coordination of the multiplicity of administrative services that control trade – between the federal offices of GOSSNAB and those of other territorial organisations, between GOSSNAB and the ministries that despite the reform of 1957 have continued to hand out purchasing certificates. On the other hand, the planning of GOSSNAB proving to be less rigorous than that of GOSPLAN when it had charge of the entire distribution system, it is frequent to find that goods delivered do not correspond precisely to what was ordered. Finally, in the face of real needs, there are many excesses or deficiencies of production due to the slowness of communication between producers and consumers (it frequently takes several months to go back and forth through the official channels, even using the services of semi-official 'representatives' whose task is to ferret out the purchase tickets). 'The market is not organised to relate supply to demand: the plan does that' (Lavigne, 1970).

This aspect of the inconvenience of the system is even more serious in the case of *consumer goods.* In the former condition of poverty, the problem of matching supply and demand did not exist. Consumers absorbed all that producers (whose only constraint was to conform to the plan) were willing to supply. Consumption increased; but the planners tended to revise their plans from one year to the next, foreseeing neither a change in the nature of the goods consumed, nor any variation either upwards or downwards in the quantities consumed per capita: 'only when stocks attained massive volumes was the plan altered' (Lavigne, 1970).

The slowness of the procedures often prevented seasonal products from appearing in the shops when the customers needed them: when it became necessary to buy winter clothes in summer, and vice versa, the consumer was placed in an uncomfortable situation! We may add that the lack of coordination, at the production stage as well as in distribution, sometimes submitted the unfortunate consumer, if we may judge from the contemporary press, to some degree of torment – from tape-recorders without magnetic tapes, or suspender-belts with no suspenders!

It was not only the bureaucracy of the bodies engaged in planning distribution, and their lack of contact with the reality of consumer requirements, that were called into question in the 1960s, but also the passive role attributed to the business of trading in the Soviet system, and the functioning of that business.

The commercial apparatus is evidently too passive in that not only has it never been given the role of effectively apprising the producers of the wishes of the customers, but all initiative of this kind would have been regarded as out of place, or even subversive, because all such initiative in the flow of trade was the province of the single supplier. It is too passive, also, because conversely it has never been able to mould the customers, to entice them and teach them how to take account of technical information that would enable them to appreciate the relative value of the commodities on offer. Considered as a passive organ of transmission, trading, paralysed by its supply difficulties and by the officialdom of its controllers, seems so fixed in its passivity that it cannot always perform its tasks with normal efficiency. The technical qualifications of the personnel leave much to be desired, the spirit of initiative is lacking and the capacity for adaptation to situations not covered by the rules is non-existent. It is also true that commercial employees have always been, like those in health and social security services, at the lower end of the salary scale in the USSR – 104.5 roubles a month in 1974, when the national monthly average was 140.7 roubles; there has thus been little incentive for dynamism!

In retailing, with the obvious exception of self-service, slowness is the rule in shops; it is necessary to stand in three queues before obtaining one's purchases, the first to state one's requirements and be able to examine the goods, another to pay at the cash-desk, and a third to receive the packages. And almost everywhere, but especially in areas of expanding population, the waiting queues get longer while the sales counters get emptier, for supplies to the shops are very irregular.[4] In 1972, one retail shop served an average of 360 inhabitants (the figure was 324 in 1940 and 340 in 1958); in the same year, there was one salesman for every 62 persons.

Defects accentuated by the growth of demand   In 1965, the Brezhnev government decided to accelerate the implementation of the last of Krushchev's social programmes, and the effective monetary income of the people rose sharply; the annual rate of increase was 8.9 per cent in the period 1965–7, compared with 2.2 per cent in 1962–4 and 7.3 per cent in 1956–8. There followed an upsurge in consumption, the growth rate of which doubled between 1962–4 and 1965–7. True, there has been an easing off since 1970, but the rapid expansion of 1965–7 had rendered unendurable the bottlenecks in the distributive system; consumers resented even more strongly the shortages in the shops, and the supplying of these shops became more difficult as the slowness in the provision of industrial equipment hindered the production of consumer goods. For it was precisely the demand for manufactured articles that was strongest: between 1965 and 1967 the average per capita consumption of all goods rose by 6.2 per cent, but while foodstuffs rose by only 5.5 per cent, textiles rose by 6.6 per cent, and durable consumer goods by 10.5 per cent. Since then, the same tendency has continued, though at a slower rate. Thus, for the period 1965–72, the corresponding figures were 5 per cent overall, 3.9 per cent for foodstuffs, 5.8 per cent for textiles and 7.9 per cent for durable goods.

It must not be forgotten, however, that the growth rate for foodstuffs is actually lower than that recorded by the food shops, for in this still very rural country the rise in the amount of money available to peasant families is naturally accompanied by a sharp fall in the consumption of their own produce. Between 1950 and 1971, for example, the storage capacity for vegetables trebled, cold-stores multiplied twelve times and the output of canned vegetables eight times. As for meat, a growth in demand has remained unsatisfied, so that the price rise on the free market of the *kolkhozy* has been more rapid than that of other products (taking 1960 as 100, the figures for 1966 were 155 for meat and only 119 for other commodities). This was particularly noticeable at the end of the 1960s, and resulted from deficiencies in production rather than in trading.

The sharp rise in consumer demand after 1965, coming at the end of a long period in which individual consumption had been growing after the poverty engendered by the war and post-war reconstruction, had already exposed, at the end of the 1950s, the inadequacy of the distribution system to serve the country's needs. During the long years between 1940 and 1974 it was the trade in non-food goods that progressed most. While food sales multiplied only twice (at constant price), sales of bicycles, furniture and knitwear multiplied 20 times, and of electrical appliances 40 times. In all these cases, half the increase took place between 1940 and 1965, and half after the latter year.

Of course, the rise in the value of sales (at constant price level) does not necessarily imply a corresponding increase in the flow of trade since it is not only the quantity of goods that has risen but also their quality. The fact that commerce does not play an active intermediary role between customers and producers has become more obvious. The rise in the standard of living has rendered families more conscious of the quality and variety of goods on sale: for example, in clothing stores enormous quantities of unsold articles have accumulated. The cost of this kind of neglect has been heavy for the Soviet economy as a whole. All the same, though the peasants have been relatively the greatest beneficiaries of higher incomes, the improvement in the quality and diversity of goods offered by the rual shops has been called in question, bearing in mind that the *kolkhozniki* are going more and more into the towns for shopping – they made one-quarter of their purchases in urban shops in the late 1960s.

Finally, as a last consequence of the rising standard of living, Soviet customers are becoming more difficult to please in the matter of services offered. The retail sale of pre-packed goods, which was quite exceptional before 1950, is expanding slowly but surely; by 1960, 9 per cent of the sugar sold, and 21 per cent of the margarine, were packaged. The virtual nonexistence, until quite recently, of a home-delivery service, of the possibility of telephoning orders, and of any after-sales service has provoked discontent. Credit sale of durable goods, ignored by consumers despite its low (2 per cent) interest rate, while incomes had to be devoted to strict necessities, is becoming more popular – rising from 5.7 per cent of total durable goods sales in 1967 to over 10 per cent now.

Thus, after 1965 it was no longer possible to avoid reforms.

Reform of domestic trade: partial abandonment of marxist principles
Since 1957 there has been a gradual extension of the trading sector of the Soviet economy. Certain equipment that was formerly distributed free has become merchandise: thus machinery now has to be purchased by the *kolkhozy,* and products supplied by the collective farms to the *kolkhozniki* are now sold to them. Thus the rural masses have obtained a foothold in the commercial system. All food and non-food goods had henceforth to be considered as merchandise, and their cost taken more or less into consideration in establishing their price.

At the same time a new system for the distribution of merchandise was tried out, between 1957 and 1965, but it broke down because of its complexity. Then in 1965 the creation of GOSSNAB, followed in 1966 by the federal institute for the study of demand and competition, signalised the advent of a change in the whole commercial system that had remained static for 40 years.

The new bases of commercial organisation   We must once again distinguish between capital goods and consumer goods.

The reform of the distribution of consumer durables   This had two main aspects, the decentralisation of the planning of distribution and the institution of a real wholesaling system.

Within GOSSNAB, the role of regional directorates was reinforced. There were 56 of them at the end of 1969, and they have been gradually transformed into financially autonomous commercial organisations. Their task is to regulate, through their 4,000 local bases, more than three-quarters of the commercial transactions that fall within the province of GOSSNAB. Until 1968, the various regional services existing within the framework of the republics only controlled just under one-third of the trade; they could only, in fact, deal with trade relations within the republics and not inter-regional deliveries which were dealt with by the federal administration. On the other hand, this decentralisation of regional supplies would be accompanied, in another innovation, by the development of direct exchange contracts between industrial undertakings. In fact, however, this extension of direct trading, which applied in 1969 to bulky goods (in order to reap transport economies) has only occurred very slowly, in the face of unwillingness on the part of the relevant administrations.

In another connection, Soviet economists, conscious that what most differentiated their commercial system from that of the liberal economies, aside from the planning of distribution, was organisation at the wholesale level, began to question whether it was not desirable to re-create such a system of wholesaling. Most industrial undertakings apparently believed that a properly managed system for the planning of supplies would suffice, but there was an attempt to create wholesale businesses in the distribution of petrol and spare parts. If this recipe for the development of wholesaling should be more generally applied, the Soviet commercial system, already reformed to the extent of giving economic enterprises more autonomy and more interest in the results of their own management, would have one more trait in common with the capitalist system.

The reform of the distribution system for consumer goods is going in the same direction.

Reform of the distribution system for consumer goods   Here again there are two aspects, the modification of the supply system and the functioning of the commercial enterprises.

As in the case of consumer durables, a policy of direct links has been advocated between suppliers and customers, especially for the large shops which are clearly in a minority. In the case of the cooperatives, direct purchase from the state factories is possible, instead of from the state warehouses. Further, the *oblast* warehouses, which receive the goods, no longer transmit them to the district warehouses, but direct to the cooperative shops. Thus two intermediaries are eliminated, and there is the possibility of choosing an assortment of goods in accordance with the customers' wishes, through direct ordering from the factories. The annual or biennial fairs, which are well developed, allow direct contact between suppliers and customers' organisations, within the cooperative movement as well as in its relations with state industries. It is at these fairs that choice can be made on the basis of samples, and contracts signed (Lasserre, 1968).

As for the reform of retail trading, which comes within the more general framework of the 1965 reform of state economic enterprise, it is intended to restore a certain degree of initiative and thus greater efficiency. In 1972, more than 10,000 state shops had already been so treated, and following this pilot scheme, the cooperatives underwent the same changes.

What is really the essence of this reform? The quest for profit (but, be it noted, only in principle, and not at any price) becomes the official motivation of the undertakings. So that the workers can contribute, a stimulus is provided in the form of bonuses based on the profits, part of which are ploughed back and part divided between the employees and the social services of the undertaking. Moreover, efforts are now made to adapt service to requirements. Regular market research is now undertaken and published.

The basis of this reform reopens the question of the ultimate aim of the commercial function in a socialist system: if undertakings are henceforth to seek profits, they can no longer be content, as hitherto, to remain as passive intermediaries between producers and consumers, nor allow the planning authorities to stifle them with red tape.

Disappointing results so far   The results accruing from this series of reforms are not so far impressive, and commerce, like the whole economy, finds itself disturbed rather than improved. 'The autonomy of management, and the stimulus of the profit motive are counteracted by the whole system of planning and economic direction, that the authorities have preferred to re-touch rather than reject' (Lavigne, 1970).

It is equally true that the commercial personnel accustomed to issuing directives without taking responsibilities, is not anxious to shake off the constraining but protective tutelage of administrations, with which however, they may often be in conflict.

It is also certain that the planning authorities have mounted a considerable resistance to the decentralisation, and that the ministries have likewise opposed the greater autonomy of undertakings: on the one hand because these moves call into question the whole basis of Soviet economic organisation (if commercial enterprises gained full autonomy, the strict planning of production and trade could not survive), and on the other hand because the bureaucracy is unwilling to surrender its power.

In short, to remedy a grave situation, the Russians have introduced (certainly with every endeavour not to contradict marxist doctrine too blatantly) the seeds of principles that Marx himself radically denounced. But this has been done without daring to proceed with the structural reforms that these new principles logically imply, principles that would lead gradually to a market economy supported by a dynamic trading system.

It is difficult, within the framework of the new system, to expect profits from the stimulants, for the realistic gains are derisory. To the extent that retail prices, always imposed by the State, have not risen (though they have done in the case of trade in intermediate goods), profits have oscillated around 0 to 2 per cent, varying in accordance with supply difficulties and from one commodity to another. Under such circumstances the making of a profit and the bonuses that result from it, are more of an incentive to the degradation of the service provided, rather than to its improvement. The proof is that between 1967 and 1970, with retail prices pegged, the flow of goods increased by 27.4 per cent and profits by 57 per cent. The struggle for the division of profits between the wholesaling agents and the retailers only aggravates the situation. Undertakings 'neither act like capitalist shops anxious to promote sales, nor like good socialist businesses that should be engaged in satisfying the needs and demands of the population' (Lavigne, 1970). It is becoming more common for shops to refuse to sell articles that yield little or no profit. Soviet newspapers also denounce a whole series of fraudulent tricks played on customers. Since the problems of undertakings producing consumer goods are somewhat similar, the quality of the merchandise sold does not improve, for the factory has no right to reflect the cost of improving its models in the selling price which is fixed by the State. Often indeed the quality is lowered in order to gain greater profit within the framework of the state-imposed price. The only recourse open to the retailers is to refuse to buy poor-quality goods, and this does nothing to help the problems of the consumers. In 1972, at the wholesale fair, the value of goods unsold because of obsolescence or poor quality amounted to 3 billion roubles. Sometimes indeed, certain goods disappear from the shops because the manufacturers refuse to make articles that yield such tiny profits. It is impossible to put a figure on the 'black market', but its size in the Soviet Union is considerable, and the reforms have done nothing to diminish it.

The 'New China' agency has enjoyed denouncing the errors of Soviet 'revisionism' that reinforce the power of the 'new bourgeoisie' of commercial enterprises. However that may be, the USSR seems very far from having found a satisfactory solution to the problems created by the malfunctioning of its commercial system. If it continues in the direction of the 1967 reforms, it will find itself gradually falling into line with the liberal economies. It goes without saying that that would bring about the evolution of its commercial system in the direction of a spontaneous reinforcement of centrality, a phenomenon that the Soviet rulers were until now forced to contain in order to avoid the formation, at the summit of the hierarchy, of hypertrophic urban concentrations.

They may yet come up with other more radical reforms that are in accordance with pure marxist principles. In any case, sooner or later the introduction of a new distribution system seems inevitable.

The commercial system of other socialist countries

For the 14 states whose ideal is to put materialism into practice, the USSR, the first country to have done so, served as the first point of reference in almost all cases. In respect of the organisation of distribution, the imitation was scrupulous during the 1950s and for the greater part of the 1960s. Everywhere, in conformity with marxist-leninist principles, the function of commerce was degraded, and centralised state services exercised supreme control over most forms of activity. However, it is possible to see slight variations between the various commercial systems, resulting from the historical context of their economic development and the size of the country in question. Since the reforms of the late 1960s, which reverberated through the whole of the socialist world, the divergences from the Soviet model have become more marked. The character of the commercial organisation in the different countries varies with the extent of their relations with the western world and/or their degree of politico-economic dependence on the USSR; and it depends also on the degree of imagination that the rulers and the economists have displayed in the interpretation of marxist ideas. This last factor explains the necessity for distinguishing, for example, the six Soviet-influenced European countries, closely linked for 25 years by their participation in COMECON, from China.

Variations from the Soviet model in the European members of COMECON

Drawn to communism after the Second World War, these countries, particularly the central and northern states, had a standard of living and consequently of commercial equipment, much superior to that of Russia after 1917. The means of comparison at their disposal, and also the different consumer habits of a population already accustomed to a trading economy, rendered them much more sensitive to the inefficiency of a bureaucratic and centralised distribution system. They began by introducing modifications, but in the late 1960s reformed the whole structure much more thoroughly than the Russians had done. It is of course true that the size of these countries renders the decentralisation of supplies less dangerous for national economic unity than in the USSR.

New systems of inter-industrial exchanges
Except in Hungary where most such trading has been freed, the distribution of intermediate goods is always arranged according to a central plan, but these plans are only indicators. 'Enterprise unions' take the place of government departments: these are groupings of branches of industrial activity, charged with the distribution of goods and the arrangement of contracts. They are assisted in inter-sectorial coordination by autonomous commercial organisations.

Supply of consumer goods
There are certain divergences from the Soviet type in respect of the make-up of the commercial apparatus, and the organisation of commercial systems.

Structural variations in commercial apparatus   At first, some of the socialist republics retained a few traces of their former commercial structure, in the shape of small, privately owned shops. There are indeed still a few left (about 8 per cent of the total number) but their part in the total sales activity is minimal (under 1 per cent of the turnover) in Bulgaria, Hungary and Poland; and they have been totally eliminated in Romania (since 1949) and in Czechoslovakia. In East Germany however, they still represent one-fifth of the total retail sales.

On the other hand, except in Bulgaria, which has had difficulty in raising itself from the level of underdevelopment peculiar to the Mediterranean lands, the importance and the structure of commercial activity in the socialist countries of Europe differ noticeably from those of the USSR.

From the available statistics, it would appear that to the extent that retail sales per capita surpass the Soviet figure (as they do by a long way in East Germany, Poland, Czechoslovakia and Hungary), the people's living standards are noticeably more dependent on commercial activities. It is remarkable that even Romania is more devoted to trading activities than the USSR; here the population is living above its means, very largely on credit. Further, the proportion of the total expenditure devoted to non-food goods has everywhere, over the years, exceeded the amount spent on food, and this is so whether the majority of the population is rural (as 60 per cent of it is in Romania) or not; this is the reverse of what was still the case in Russia in 1975. Also, the make-up of the range of shops is dissimilar; for example in 1973, only 35 per cent of Romanian shops sold nothing but food, while 38 per cent were non-food shops, to which must be added 5.5 per cent represented by the 'universal' shops and 21 per cent with mixed sales.

These differences in consumer behaviour between the socialist countries of central Europe and the USSR are largely due to a certain 'European-ness' that derives in part from the recollection of an epoch when the diversity of goods on sale was much greater, and to a large extent from the temptations provided by information filtering in from the trading world of the neighbouring European capitalist countries; there is, too, the policy of western contact adopted by the governments, for various reasons, among which is the wish to respond to the aspirations of the population towards a higher level of consumption. The most tangible proof of these aspirations to a greater choice of available merchandise is the persistence, throughout communist Europe, of a parallel market: thus, together with other rarities, articles clandestinely imported from western countries are bought and sold 'under the counter' for dollars; this practice is condemned in principle, but it exists and is in part tolerated.

The difference in the structure of purchasing expenses also explains why the economists quickly began to reform the distribution system that had been borrowed from the Russians, and why these reforms have gone much further than in the Soviet Union. Indeed, trade in non-food manufactured goods is much more complex than is the case with food products, for it is concerned with a much greater and continually increasing range of articles, and mostly involves long-distance inter-regional exchanges, so that deficiencies in the organisation of distribution become much more noticeable.

How have the reforms in the distribution system gone further than in the USSR? The suppression of hampering administrative constraints; the development of wholesaling; the subordination of production to real needs; effecting a fresh balance between the potential of production and the service of the customer; strengthening the possibility of competition between different forms of retailing – these are some of the varied measures that have been taken in one or other of the countries in question. They indicate the willingness of governments to give internal trading greater flexibility and stability, and thus to permit it to be more efficient and more profitable.

Because their territorial size is smaller, and the mass of bureaucracy less weighty, these countries have had less difficulty in lightening their commercial system than the USSR. They have been able to untie the knots in the chain of command concerning the distribution of goods, by reducing the amount of planning and quota-fixing involved as between state trading and the cooperative movement. It has also been easier for them to depolarise the flow of goods by shortening the supply lines. Until 1965, there were at least two focal stages in the system, that were rarely avoidable: the convergence of goods from the factories towards the specialised collecting-centres run by the state distribution service, and then the collection in provincial warehouses close to the large urban centres, that served the retail shops. At the latter stage, the staircase of territorial levels, necessary in the USSR because of the immensity of the area, was in general already avoided. Of course, orders for putting goods in transit would previously pass through the central administrative machinery. There has been much effort to suppress not only this, but also the first polarisation, and actually to encourage direct contracts between trading and manufacturing organisations. They have not only, as in the USSR, multiplied the links between factories and warehouses or department stores, but have modified the whole system of trade flows. To do this, specialised distribution channels have been set up. The socialist system in fact favours the development of large commercial enterprises, specialised in one or other category of goods and integrating wholesale and retail trading. As an example, from Poland, ELDOM is a national undertaking, created in 1969, comprising a central purchasing agency for domestic electrical appliances (for which it gives direct orders to the factories) and a series of specialised state shops; other similar organisations have been created for the sale of radio and television sets, for optical and photographic goods, for furniture, textiles, and footwear. It is clear that the growth in demand for such goods, as the standard of living has risen, has facilitated these arrangements. This reform of the supply lines, by reducing the polarisation phenomenon, has the effect of restraining the development of rational urban centrality; for it is in the 'capitals' of the various territorial divisions that are concentrated the collecting centres, the packaging warehouses and the administrative services relating to distribution.

For other consumer goods, whether purchased regularly or infrequently, non-specialised stocks are maintained, that help to avoid seasonal crises in the activity of the warehouses. Further, wholesale depots are being multiplied; these are allocated large service areas so as to be profitable: about 100 km radius for non-food goods and less for foodstuffs. Certainly, after having been minimised because of its economically non-productive nature, wholesaling is now considered as a service to be developed in the cause of efficiency. A careful watch is kept so that it does not take on a speculative role: its profit margin is limited to 2 per cent in Romania, for example, as against 5 per cent for retail shops purchasing in the wholesale market (or if they purchase direct from producers, 3 per cent; and as retail prices are uniform, the shops must in this case pay 2 per cent to the State).

Romania is apparently the country that has progressed furthest down the road of reform, especially since the modifications introduced in 1970–1 that marked a real break with the Soviet system. And of all the COMECON countries, it is the one that has diverged politically from the USSR to the greatest degree, and is most open to western commerce: only one-half of its external trade is done with its communist partners, while for Poland the figure has recently been reduced to just over 50 per cent, for Czechoslovakia, Hungary and East Germany it is still 70 per cent, and for Bulgaria 80 per cent.

A novel aspect of the Romanian reform is the way in which, inspired by the Chinese system, at least in theory, it places the accent on the necessity of responding to the needs of the common people. It envisages giving retail trading a greater motivating role in the development of distribution, by making it responsible for seeing that supply matches demand. Previously, retailers had no other task than to sell what was made available to them and send back unsold goods to the warehouse without further ado. Then, just as in the Soviet Union, the accumulation of unwanted articles assumed proportions that were very alarming for the authorities controlling the State's finances. Since 1969, employees of shops having unsold goods have had their salaries reduced: it is for the shops to control their own intake of merchandise. But they have the right to turn round on the wholesalers or producers who have not supplied them with what they asked for. In 1971, a law was passed obliging factories to honour the letter of the requests; that is, to supply the quantities, qualities and varieties requested by the shops. Henceforward industry could no longer dictate to commerce, but had to produce the goods demanded.

However, in order to prevent creative activity in industry from being strangulated by the inability of the retailing business to reflect real consumer demand, several palliatives have been tried. In particular, industrial marketing has been developed, by the creation of retail shops run by producers, who can thus study the market on the spot, analyse consumer behaviour, and put new products on show. The Institute of Market Research has also been given the task not only, as with its opposite number in the USSR, of keeping a watch on market structure, but also of analysing the deep-seated desires of the customers. Further, the responsible minister has taken charge of sales-promotion publicity, through the medium of an organisation known as 'commercial advertising'.

Likewise, to stimulate initiative and efficiency in retailing, some competition has been encouraged: thus, side by side with state shops in the big cities will be found shops run by industrial undertakings, shops dealing in imported goods, and more and more shops belonging to cooperatives (by 1971, 41 per cent of the urban communes had such co-ops); since the reform, 'Centrocoop' has been given the right to build shops in towns, and even, in Bucharest, department stores.

It has been impossible for the authors to discover how far all these measures have been applied and what the results have been. But what makes the measures interesting is the motive behind them – to increase the social and economic productivity of trading by decentralisation and a greater attention to the satisfaction of customer requirements.

Organisation of distribution in the People's Republic of China

Information from Chinese sources on this subject is not abundant, for commerce is but poorly developed. Nevertheless, the character of the system of trading that is evolving cannot escape our attention. It seems to us, after reading such geographical, economic and journalistic information as is available, that the Chinese theoreticians have already elaborated the rules of a completely new and coherent system, that they have attempted to impose upon the country. But all the pragmatic replies given to commercial questions in so far as such questions have been posed, seem to us to outline a system different from those so far considered, by reason of the underlying philosophy.

We have here a collectivist trading system, attentive to the needs of consumers, and in consequence concerned to reduce the inherited social and spatial inequalities, but in a poor country that is still seeking, both at local and national level, to reconcile development and independence.

An organisation that shows a distrust of trading but care for the consumer
It is particularly striking to notice that with a structure, in its first plan, similar in essentials to that developed in the USSR, the Chinese commercial system has functioned for the last 20 years in a manner very different from that which led the Russians to such profound modifications.

From 1949 to 1957, a structure on the Soviet model During the first eight years of its existence, with Moscow's help, communist China began to equip itself with an organisation modelled exactly on that of the Soviet Union. As far as the system of distribution was concerned, this meant a complete distrust of the function of trading, the centralised planning of all supplies, and a range of equipment very similar to that of the USSR of that period, both for external and internal trade. For the latter, for example, there was a Ministry of Commerce and Food, assisted by 22 public corporations, to control the socialised trading businesses, which themselves looked after a host of warehouses supplying the state shops in the towns and the rural cooperatives, spread through a variety of territorial divisions. The struggle against the 'private property' mentality, which however did not go so far as to completely suppress inheritance, was also manifested in the collectivisation of the means of production and of services. In 1949, 'the number of proprietors of a single shop was about 4 millions, of whom 96.7 per cent were petty traders using their own capital and only 3.3 per cent were companies with shareholders' (Han Suyin, 1975). In 1950, 76 per cent, and in 1954, 10 per cent of the wholesale trade was still done by private individuals or firms; the corresponding figures for retail trade were 83 per cent and 26 per cent. From 1957, there was no more private trading, and individual shop-proprietors accounted for only 2.7 per cent of the officially recorded retail sales. However, the elimination of market-cornering has not been so quickly or thoroughly accomplished.

The part played by unlicensed middlemen has remained important, though unquantifiable. It is remarkable that in 1957 it was estimated that there were still as many pedlars as sedentary employees in commerce (Donnithorne, 1967). The exploitation of local differences in prices and supplies, together with the deficiencies of socialised trading, made fortunes for private merchants, and revived interest in a way of life that had behind it a very long tradition.

All the measures taken by the communist rulers at this time resulted in a considerable reduction in the national equipment of permanent shops, and the striking of a new balance. In the countryside, cooperative shops were set up, some of them as a substitute for the now-forbidden rural markets, while the parasitic plethora of tiny shops formerly present in the large towns – such as are still to be seen in the other underdeveloped countries of South East Asia – was replaced by a range of shops that was more rationally functional, at least in its distribution if not in its equipment, that remained at a primitive level. During the period 1952–8 the number of shop assistants fell from 8.4 millions to 6.4 millions (Donnithorne, 1967). But between 1949 and 1952 the collectivisation process had already involved a deflation of the employment roll, and by 1952 half the trade was conducted in the socialised sector.

It must be remembered, however, that trading in China before the civil war had never been as important as in mercantile Europe. The emperors, whose financial strength was derived from land-ownership, had never needed the support of merchants, whose role in the politico-economic life of the country was thus limited. Moreover, the great mass of the population, having generally no choice between self-subsistence or beggary, could hardly provide the basis of a prosperous local trade; outside the towns, only the markets and fairs were of any importance. In fact, it would seem that with a few exceptions, such as Shanghai, the great commercial cities only became so as a result of European influence. In any case, when the communists came into power in 1949, 'commerce was bankrupt or paralysed, government non-existent; hunger, poverty and crime prevailed in the cities' (Han Suyen, 1975); and this in some ways made easier the substitution of the old system by an organisation modelled on that of the Soviet Union, the strongest among the underdeveloped countries of Asia in the first half of the present century.

The imprint of Maoist ideology on the commercial system since 1957   It was in 1957 that Mao Tse Tung, in launching his 'great step forward' campaign, took the first divergent steps from the ideological line followed by the Russians. True, the Chinese rulers continued to beware of any bourgeois-inspired renaissance of commercial activity, with a vigilance even greater than that of the Soviets. But among the innovatory aspects of Mao's 'thoughts', there were several that oriented commercial organisation in a new direction. First was the decision not to sacrifice individual consumption on the altar of national aggrandisement; secondly, willingness to take account of the real needs expressed by the people; thirdly, the idea of the necessity for autonomy at all levels of development; and lastly, the acceptance of a degree of pragmatism in the search for solutions to problems. It must be emphasised that all this did not entail the suppression of structures implanted during the preceding years, but so profound a transformation of their functioning that the Chinese commercial system now appears to be unique.

Let us return to the modifications introduced in 1957. In 1949, taking the helm in a war-torn country in which, over the centuries, more than two-thirds of the population had lived with periodic famines and in a constant state of crisis, Mao Tse Tung deemed light industry, craftsmanship and agriculture of equal priority with heavy industry. A large volume of supplies for human consumption seemed to him indispensible for giving the producers the morale and the energy necessary for the growth of socialism. But until 1957, in conformity with the Soviet conception of national development, priority was given to heavy industry, activity in retailing remained embryonic and the vast mass of the population remained deprived even of most elementary necessities. It was therefore decided to develop as far as possible the provision of consumer goods, both food and non-food, as quickly as that of capital goods. To do this, bearing in mind the extreme paucity of transport facilities, it was necessary to multiply the agricultural basis at local and regional level and the system of small and medium-sized undertakings in crafts and industries; and also to simplify the methods of supplying the local traders, releasing them from the bondage and bureaucracy of state control save for certain essential goods in short supply, and authorising them to get their supplies locally. This done, the producers were given a more direct participation in the feeding of their own locality, thus rendering them more sensitive to their responsibility for raising their own standard of living. From then on, while inter-industrial trading also increased, retail sales never ceased to progress, to such an extent that, with prices remaining stable or actually lowering in accordance with the rhythm of production, wages rose by 50 per cent between 1952 and 1974, and the total volume of merchandise sold multiplied six-fold between 1950–2 and 1973.

Thus Mao's injunction 'stand on your own feet, and accept outside aid only as an extra' has become a reality on the local scale.

Another innovatory idea, introduced in 1958 and much developed since the cultural revolution, concerns the regular two-way flow of information between suppliers and consumers; this is a determining factor in the building of socialism in the widest sense of that term, since in principle it enables customers' wishes to be taken into account. As early as 1958, investigations were undertaken to assess the real needs of the population, both quantitatively and qualitatively, in order the better to understand the discontent within the ranks of the poorly-fed rural dwellers. The enquiries were later extended to the towns. Several years later, much attention was paid to the trading requirements of national minorities. Everywhere, the interviewing was done by groups of workers or by salesmen from the thousands of small craft-shops. Further, exchanges of occupation were arranged, with the object of avoiding or counteracting the traditional divisions between town and country, between 'white collar' and 'blue collar' occupations; and these transpositions often led to workers and peasants taking part from time to time in the business of distribution, and vice versa. Such arrangements had the advantage of bringing producers into contact with their customers, the main object being the best possible social development for all. Thus the quality of many goods and services became modified in various ways, with new varieties of merchandise appearing frequently. Furthermore, it must not be forgotten that commerce, in China as elsewhere, though in this case more openly and actively, fulfils social and political as well as economic functions, and this leads to much discussion between sellers and buyers.

The principle of maximal autonomy put forward by Mao Tse Tung found expression both sectorially and spatially. From 1957, the conception of the relations between administration, production, distribution and consumption began to alter its hierarchical character which involved the domination of the first over the second, and so on, and resulted in ignorance or complete misinterpretation of the wishes and the needs of the consumer. We shall see presently how the burden of bureaucratic control just had to be lightened. As for the relations between production and wholesaling or retailing, they were effected in the following manner: 'the production of the factories is sold to wholesale depots under contracts that stipulate quantity, quality, price and delivery date. Such contracts are obligatory for both parties, and they constitute the main difference between the Chinese methods and the much more rigid system found in the other socialist countries, Romania excepted' (Deleyne, 1975).

Autonomy does not mean anarchy, and it goes without saying that the central planning organisation has retained the power to make the fundamental choices, such as the relation between investments in production and in consumption, the volume of external trade, the fixing of price levels so as to influence demand in the direction deemed to be in the public interest, the regulation of wages, and so on. Also firmly controlled from the centre are the various grades of shops established under the first plan, the trade in certain intermediate goods that are indispensable to the country's economic growth, and such consumer goods as are still rationed (formerly known as 'first-class goods', these are prime necessities of which national production is still insufficient, such as cereals, oils, cotton and their derivatives). On the contrary, the control of the distribution of second-class goods (sugar, eggs, pork, tobacco and certain textiles), the number of which decreases with increased output, only extends to the production quotas imposed on producers and does not concern surpluses; and it may also be confined to certain local or regional cases. Articles in the third class are completely free from all control, and trade in them is at the discretion of local shops. In this way, despite the size of the country and the shortcomings of the distribution system, decentralisation has ensured a better flow of supplies than in the USSR. It would seem also that in easing the flow of trade and restoring to local shops some degree of initiative and responsibility, the Chinese have maintained the lively spirit of the employees, who 'have the same eagerness to do business and to make a profit as the shopkeepers had under the former capitalist regime' (Guillain, 1965).

Neither does autonomy mean total withdrawal into self-sufficiency; measures have been taken to stimulate inter-regional exchanges, which are considered necessary for the consolidation of national unity, and for a more rational distribution of resources. Commercial undertakings having some degree of autonomy at provincial level, may enter into direct supply contracts with producers in other regions. Such exchanges mainly involve industrial goods made in the major urban agglomerations.

The pragmatism and flexibility shown by the Chinese rulers since 1958 contrast markedly with the formal rigidity of Soviet organisation that has resulted, as we have seen, in the over-long retention of formulae ill-adapted to the effective functioning of commercial exchanges. The desire for a radical transformation of society in a fashion peculiarly Chinese has not involved the complete rejection of foreign experience, and has sometimes allowed the regeneration of elements from the past provided that these do not just indicate a surrender to the weight of history and customs, but make some contribution to the general progress. The willingness to establish new, simple and solid commercial structures is seen to be compatible with a functional flexibility that allows evolution to take place. The apparent rigidity of official orders does not prevent a great deal of empiricism. Taking account of practical contingencies, there is a groping search, with perhaps some backward steps, for solutions that are closest to the ideals of communism. One of the best examples is provided by the evolution of the system of rural shops during a quarter of a century. From 1959, before which they were forbidden, a revival of rural markets was authorised, for it seemed more important to allow peasant families who sold produce there to increase their income and rise above the poverty line than to deny, in the name of ideological orthodoxy, any possibility of private profit. Conversely, as from 1966, by which time there was an improvement in rural life, and itinerant peddling seemed to be encouraging capitalist tendencies among the peasantry, it appeared preferable to re-impose a ban on private profits, and the markets disappeared once again from the countryside.

The recent history of these markets is bound up with the system of commercial centres by which they have been replaced. The reaction of the authorities in the face of the difficulties encountered in drawing the map is another witness to the flexibility of the organisation. In 1953, the first steps in the socialisation of rural trading were taken. In the desire to break up the traditional socio-economic structures of the rural areas, it was decided not to locate cooperative shops on former market sites, but to choose the centres of the new politico-administrative divisions. This was to ignore the functional character of market areas. All rural activity was thus profoundly disturbed, and the new system was hardly viable. The supply difficulties experienced by the cooperative shops, integrated in distribution circuits after the Soviet model, succeeded in jeopardising the whole endeavour. A second attempt during the 1960s was more successful, for the collective shops were established in the heart of the people's communes, the limits of which, after the subdivision of the first generation of large communes that took place in 1961, usually corresponded to the spheres of influence of the old markets. All the field studies had apparently convinced the responsible politicians that this framework was no less rational for being traditional. The regularity in the disposition of rural market centres (Skinner, 1965) lent itself to the policy of the harmonious development of the whole territory.

It is clear that it is not always necessary to make a clean sweep of all the inherited structures, if they are comparable with the spirit of the new system that is intended to replace them.

Finally, the commercial organisation developed during the last quarter of a century by the Chinese communists rests on a simple collectivist base, but one which seems to function for the time being with much more success and flexibility than that of the Russians, thanks to a balanced distribution of initiative and a good flow of information between the different sectors of the economic system.

The low level of consumption and trade facilitates actions designed to reduce dependence and disparities in the world of commerce   Unlike most of the present rulers of under-developed countries, who seem to equate growth of gross national product with development, the Chinese in conformity with their communist plan, are certainly always looking for increased production, but match this objective with other accompanying demands that correspond in large measure to the desire to reduce, and ultimately to get rid of, dependences and disparities.

The unequal success of measures to reduce inherited dependences and disparities   Under the leadership of Mao Tse Tung, China decided, as we have seen, 'to build socialism on two principles: independence and autonomy'. This involves basing economic development almost entirely upon the natural and human resources of the country, doing without foreign aid that barely conceals the imperialist aims of those who lavish it, and only trading as an equal partner. For a country whose economic level is already low, this inevitably results in a feeble development of foreign trade. The volume of such trade in 1973 hardly reached a figure equal to 5 per cent of the GNP, compared with 7 per cent in the USSR and 2.5 per cent in the USA. However that may be, the Chinese government is in complete control of this sector, which grows slowly in parallel with the expansion of the national economy.

Translated in terms of domestic planning, the same principle aims not at complete local autarky but at a real inter-regional balance. Hence the policy of modifying the traditional relations between town and country. In order not to leave the big cities dependent on food supplies coming with greater or less regularity from various rural areas of the country, sufficient agricultural production has been planned in the suburban fringes to cover almost all the requirements for fruit, vegetables and meat, and to avoid shortages. Whereas before the Second World War such urban communities as Peking, Shanghai, Tientsin and others, had to import one-half or three-quarters of their food supplies, they now produce enough to provide 500 g of fresh vegetables a day for every inhabitant (Delobez, 1976). By this successful operation, the areas supplying produce to the shops have been transformed, considerably retracted and stabilised. We may note incidentally that this in itself is a factor in whittling down the wholesaling business, which in those countries where it is well developed owes almost as much to distance and the spatial control of supply lines as to its speculative character.

There is another aspect of dependence that the authorities have tried to control, with some success, namely that of urban peripheries on the city centre. Though commercial centrality persists, the suburbs nevertheless have shopping facilities adapted to the demand. In Peking, for example, the suburban areas contain 46 per cent of the city's population, and their shops, which only did 39.5 per cent of the total trade in 1971, were responsible for 44 per cent in 1975. It does not matter that the former great shopping streets of the city centre have retained their attraction thanks to their concentration, their assortment of rarer types of merchandise, and their animation; as in all cities, the central business district has the prerogative of sheltering specialised non-food shops, while the variety stores, whatever their size, are found in other quarters of the city and in the countryside. Centrality will be reinforced as the range of consumer goods, and particularly of manufactured articles, is expanded – but perhaps the authorities will then encourage the diffusion of shops selling the less common goods, as they have done in the case of the basic necessities.

The same principles lie behind the policies of rural development. All the measures taken to encourage the growth of crafts and manufactures in the communes and small towns and to intensify the network of cooperative shops, are in part dictated by the problems of mobility that apply to both goods and people, in the absence of adequate means of transport and freedom of movement. In all cases their result is to hinder the tendency to polarisation through the growth of the large cities, and to prevent the cities from exercising too great an influence on large tributary areas of the countryside. If we reflect on current developments in the capitalist world, where commerce, like all the other tertiary services, concentrates in the cities and disappears from the rural areas, we can measure the weight of political ideology as a factor in the distribution of establishments. It is impossible to know what the communist rulers will do to counterbalance the effect of urban domination, especially since we cannot measure the precise part played in the present situation by political desires and by the constraints imposed by the inadequacy of transport media. In the early 1970s, while the peasantry formed three-quarters and possibly more than four-fifths of the population, rural shops, still inadequate in numbers, despite very real progress in both quantity and quality, only took 40 per cent of the national receipts from retail sales. There was thus much still to be done to limit the dependence of the rural areas on urban shopping facilities.

Much effort is devoted in China to correcting the disequilibrium which is both spatial and social: the very low income of the peasantry makes it very difficult to improve the quality of the shops that serve them. To this end, carefully devised measures that are socially efficient and not just economically profitable, have been taken to revive rural trading. By manipulating the prices to producers in order gradually to narrow the gap between agricultural commodities and manufactured goods, the public authorities have pushed up agricultural wages more rapidly than those of industrial workers. And in taking responsibility for transport charges on light industrial goods moving from urban factories into the rural areas, the State has endeavoured to lighten the cost of distribution in the countryside. It has also instructed the factories in the large cities to send to the rural shops exactly what they have ordered, whereas formerly the goods sent were those that the city-dwellers did not want! All these things help the development of shopping facilities outside the towns and lessen the disparities of quality and variety that in western countries provoke such large influxes of village-dwellers into the urban shopping centres.

How far can they and should they go in improving the standard of village life? In the urban areas the authorities have maintained eight salary scales. Certainly the difference between the highest and lowest is not great, but the inequality in the ability to purchase what is on sale is always there, even though the political theorists regard it as a relic of the hierarchical bourgeois system. A temporary survival, they say, and perhaps they are right. Responsible Maoists, knowing that it takes time to solve all their problems, do not hesitate to mark time or even take a short step backwards occasionally.

Eighteen years after China's political emancipation from the Soviet Union, what most distinguishes the commercial organisations of the two countries is the system of relations that the distribution businesses have between themselves and with both suppliers and customers. This difference is marked spatially in the configuration of the areas of supply, which are smaller and more coherent in China. As for the network of shopping facilities, we lack precise details and it is too soon to say whether these also reflect differences in philosophy. On the one hand, the Chinese policy of correcting spatial disparities has not yet had time to work itself out; and on the other hand the levels of economic development are still too far apart for comparisons to be easy.

Is the apparent uniqueness of the Chinese commercial system due to the low level of internal trade?   The Chinese economy, despite its very considerable development, remains that of a very poor country, all the more so since it abjures foreign aid. The volume of goods traded per inhabitant is still very low. The threshold of sheer necessity has been passed, but only just; no one now dies of famine, but the bicycle, radio and sewing-machine are to the Chinese consumer what the motor car, colour television and refrigerator are for the consumers of western Europe. And the level of consumption of non-food goods reaches these levels in the big cities rather than in the rural areas.

To many western observers, the low level of commercial activity means that the Chinese have not yet confronted, as the Soviets and their satellites have done, the difficult politico-economic problem of the management of trade flows adapted to diversified and abundant production (if not superabundant as in the consumer-societies of the West), in a country covering 9.5 million km² and with a billion consumers. In fact, when China has real economic prosperity and easy transport in all areas, will it be possible to maintain a minimal local autarky? Will not a regional specialisation gradually come about, as in the industrialised western countries, with various production centres becoming completely interdependent? Will not the intensification of trade-flows that results necessitate, as elsewhere, the development of control centres that will gradually become growth poles, exercising a domination hardly compatible with the self-managing organisation of distribution? Will it be possible to continue to regard the socio-political productivity of commercial employees as more important than their economic productivity?

It is impossible to answer all these questions, any more than one can really appreciate the solid realities of the changes brought about within the Chinese commercial system. But whatever may be its ultimate result, the Chinese attempt to modify human society, and through this the ends and the means of commerce, is certainly novel.

Notes

1. The statistics of turnover are broadly comparable since the accompanying para-commercial services are excluded in both cases; but in the USSR the employment figures include neither the management and administrative personnel nor those employed in the transport of goods, so that the discrepancy is exaggerated.
2. In 1976 GOSPLAN only controlled the distribution of a little over one thousand types of intermediate goods that were fundamental to economic development.
3. In the sparsely populated mountain areas, distribution is organised, not by SELPOS, but by RAIPOS, small regional cooperative unions.
4. According to a Soviet press article quoted by H. Smith (*Les Russes,* Paris 1976), the citizens of the USSR lose 30 billion working hours a year standing in queues, just to make everyday purchases.

Part II

The location of commerce

Chapter 1

Theory and practice of commercial location

Location theory

The driving force behind all commercial activity is the existence of a clientele. The word 'clientele' is used in its widest sense to include those who supply the wholesale merchants as well as those who purchase from the retail distributors. The golden rule of localisation is thus theoretically the search for the optimum number of customers and amount of business.

Numerous theoretical studies have revolved around this theme. Many of them have been based on the 'central place' studies of Christaller (1933, English translation 1966) and Lösch (1943). Some authors have been at pains to demonstrate the sound foundation of the theories, others have expressed doubts, not perhaps about the principles, but certainly about some aspects of their formulation, the artificiality of the basic hypotheses (Curry, 1960), and an assumption of economic behaviour on the part of both firms and individuals that everyday experience shows to be fundamentally unreal (Dacey, 1960, 1965). Following the behavioural school, the consideration of behaviour plays an increasingly important part in the general approach (Rushton, 1967, 1969; Goodall, 1972).

It is our intention to evaluate these theories (which we regard as essential research tools since they provide a framework or 'model' without which monographs become simply individual descriptive exercises of little value for the advancement of science) at the same time pointing out their limitations and the necessity of continued empirical studies that show the extent of agreement with, or divergence from, a pre-established model.

The simplest hypothesis – a uniform service

If we take an 'ideal' space, that is uniform in its physical attributes, in production and in the distribution of freely mobile consumers, the best possible location, assuming that there is only one, would be at the geometrical centre. Here, in this basic hypothesis, accessibility is at a maximum for all the inhabitants. But if there is only one centre, there is no comparison possible, and so no competition.

However, though the uniform space may be limitless, there is a limit to the usefulness of the centre. This limit occurs when the desirability of the commercialised product is less than the difficulties to be overcome in obtaining it: the constraints may be in terms of the length or the cost of the journey, or the type of transport available, each of these being interdependent. If we represent the desirability by *d* and the contraints by *t*, it is possible to describe the area served by the centre as a circle whose radius $R = d \geqslant t$.

The next step is to imagine the plain to have several centres of equal importance: each will have a sphere of influence of the same shape and dimensions, but on the ground there will be spaces in between the various circles, not served from any centre (Fig. 2). To minimise these vacant spaces,

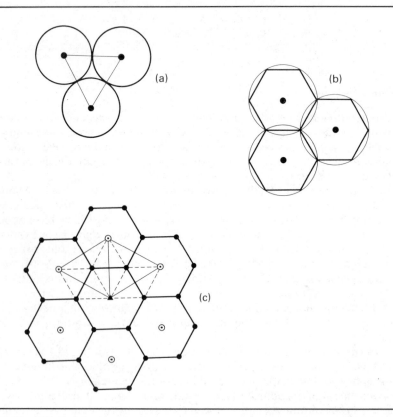

Fig. 2 Theoretical optimal service areas.

the commercial centres must be arranged in a quincunx (one at each corner of a square and one in the middle), in such a way that their minimum distance apart is never greater than 2R; but even so there will remain curved-edged triangular gaps. To cater for these, the centres must be brought closer so that the circles overlap regularly, and then, if the clientele thus doubly served is to be divided equally between the centres, we arrive inevitably at a system of contiguous hexagons (Hartwick, 1973).

The hierarchy of commercial relations

The simple hypothesis outlined above has postulated only terms that are strictly equal and interchangeable; but while retaining the hypothesis, it is necessary to introduce new conditions based on actual experience.

The first is the existence of a hierarchy in the system of commercial centres. This is a less simple notion than might appear at first sight; it is complicated by being both quantitative (number and size of businesses) and qualitative (variety of shops, and type of clientele), as well as by the environmental circumstances in which it exists.

The second is the behaviour of the consumers, and this also has a hierarchical form. The masses satisfy their most elementary needs by frequenting the lowest classes of shop. But as their wants become more complex, these customers begin to use higher-order shops. In this analysis, we are eliminating the incidence of competition and the subjective discrimination that characterise the shopping habits of the clientele. We can however admit that every centre in the hierarchy will have more customers, coming from more diverse homes and having a higher level of consumption, than the centres below it.

It must be strongly emphasised that it is not just a question of the total numbers of the clientele, but of a doubly hierarchised diversification, as one rises in the scale of service centres: if we represent the hierarchy of demands, from the simplest to the most exceptional, by A, B, C, D, . . . , Z, and the corresponding hierarchy of commerical centres by 1, 2, 3, 4, . . . , n, we know that:

Centre 1 offers the possibility of responding to the needs A of the local population, thus:

population p_1 of the centre
population pr_1 of the surrounding rural areas,
but as there may be, for various reasons, some loss, the population concerned is finally:

$$(p_1 + pr_1K \qquad K \geqslant 1$$

Centre 2 offers its own inhabitants shopping facilities at level B (that is, A plus some specialities); the rural population living within the zone of attraction of B also use the same facilities, as in the above formula. But the inhabitants of the small towns of level A are also attracted by the specialty shops. For example, if one is seeking the foodstuffs sold in centre 1, one may purchase clothing and some household goods in centre 2. These kinds of purchases are, as we shall see, more costly and less frequent: customers may therefore be willing to travel further. In sum, therefore, the numbers of people frequenting 2, if we have S dependent towns of rank A, will be:

$$P_t = (p_2 + pr_2) K_2 + \sum [(p_1 + pr_1) K_1] \, \alpha_i \beta_i$$
$$1 \geqslant i \geqslant S$$

But the intensity of shopping visits is different, and this is expressed by the parameter $\alpha\beta$ where the values of α and β vary proportionally to the distances involved and to the overall behaviour of the populations.

And so on: a centre n, with a level of shopping facilities capable of responding to demand X, as well as attracting the local custom and that of its exclusive market area, will 'cream off' some custom from other neighbouring centres, in proportion to the relative levels of their 'equipment'. However, the theory of a simple hierarchy of zones of attraction must be corrected by the probability of cumulative processes. Thus the population of a level-2 centre may go to a level-3 centre for purchases of grade C–B; but it can also go directly to n for everything within grades Z–B, etc. Any general formula, however true it may be in absolute logic, is thus contestable by the actual facts of commercial activity, which is the domain of free-will in countries with a liberal economy. The formula defining the population attracted by centre n is thus only a general indication (we shall see how it works out in practice on p. 116), but it may be useful in cases where local administration is hierarchical in form, or in socialist countries or those of the Third World, because of lack of competition in the former or lack of transport and of advertising in the latter:

$$p_t = (p_n + p_{rn})\, K\, \alpha\beta + S(p_{n-1} + p_{r(n-1)})\, K'\alpha'\beta' + \ldots + S_{n-1}\,(p_1 + p_{rs})\, K'\alpha'\beta'$$

Two conclusions emerge from these considerations: first, that the localisation of more and more complex centres may be so arranged that they offer the maximum possible shopping opportunities to the people from lower-order centres; and secondly that there exists a hierarchy of consumer needs that must be satisfied by a hierarchy of shopping facilities – which is always well understood as part of the general theory.

The hierarchical localisation of complex commercial centres

Starting from the simple hexagonal mesh, how can we envisage the growth of more complex centres? This theoretical proposition has been worked over by many authors, deriving their initial inspiration from Christaller's 'central place theory'. Several possible solutions have been propounded, examples of which are shown in Fig. 2. Berry (1967) has critically reviewed some of them, as has Bailey (1975). Our own point of view is more pragmatic. For while most recent authors are concerned with the study of a hierarchy of 'goods', we prefer 'equipment' as a basis, for this seems, at least in terms of distribution, more representative of the actual situation.

Let us recall schematically one of the possible situations. Starting with a set of grade-1 centres at the points of a hexagon, the most favourable location for a grade-2 centre is the centre of the hexagon. If we accept that all hexagons are thus provided, each grade-1 centre will have a choice of three grade-2 centres, at the apices of an equilateral triangle. On the same principle, from the six grade-2 centres located in hexagonal form, a grade-3 centre appears that controls an area seven times that of the original hexagon, and six grade-2 centres, with the same limitation as before, namely that each grade-2 centre is equidistant from three grade-3 centres.

This scheme corresponds roughly to certain graphical representations of Christaller's theory, with the difference that the theory starts from the upper level of goods distributed, whereas it would appear more logical to start with the lowest level of commercial 'equipment'. This alternative approach was followed by Lösch (1943), who thus established the differentiation of market areas according to the nature of the commodities and types of commercial activity.

Criticism of the theory

There have been many criticisms of the geometrical construction that we have just outlined in its simplest form. Many authors, however, have sought to justify it by studying areas in which it apparently works. We may class the critics in three groups.

In the first are those who criticise the basic hypotheses, including the lack of limits to the space considered, the uniformly distributed population, the problem of the transport system linking centres arbitrarily localised, and the distinction between commercial and central-place functions (Curry, 1960; Dacey, 1965; Bell, Lieber and Rushton, 1974). These are well-founded criticisms, but apparently contradictory. When one seeks to establish a general model, it is usual to express the basic hypotheses as schematically as possible. To introduce limitations like those just mentioned puts the ideas into more concrete form, and this leads to many other criticisms, as we shall see in analysing the examples which follow. It may be an ideal to establish a more complex model, but it is by no means easy!

A second group of criticisms emanate from the unfruitful efforts of many research workers to verify the theoretical schemes proposed, especially the hexagonal plan, the hierarchy of central places as market centres and their lack of locational relationship to variable densities of population (Webber, 1971, 1974; Dacey, 1960, 1965; Rushton, Golledge and Clark, 1966). However, some authors claim to have discovered a more precise correspondence between theory and fact, for example in New England (Johnson, 1971).

It is the third series of critical commentaries that seems best founded and most fertile, however, in highlighting those aspects that make it difficult to construct a general model that will take all aspects of the phenomenon into account. The classical scheme is based on the absolutely rational economy of the consumer, whose sole concern is the minimisation of costs. On the basis, if we admit that the same commodity is available at the same price in two different centres, the consumer must automatically go to the nearest centre, if $t_i < t_j$ because in this case

$$c_i = p + t_i \qquad c_j = p + t_j$$

whence $c_i < c_j$, c being the total cost to the consumer of the commodity, the price of which is p and t_i and t_j are respectively the cost of transport between centres i and j and the consumer's residence.

In practice this is far from being always the case, in the first place because the consumer is in general not seeking only one commodity in one shop but a whole group of purchases (and this underlines our stress on level of 'equipment' at market centres, rather than variety of products), and secondly because he may visit the town for several reasons, shopping being only one of the functions of central places. Mere overall economic rationality renders the model useless because it does not take account of external economies (Bell, Lieber and Rushton, 1974; Golledge, 1970).

The proposal to use a gravitational model based on Reilly's law (see p. 151) would permit a partial improvement of these imperfections by giving a better choice of the indications of urban strength and a more correct index of distance

(Isard, 1967). It is not sufficient to take into account only population; the area occupied by commercial premises, and figures of turnover, would be better, but it would be necessary to formulate a more elaborate expression both of this and of distance.

A more serious difficulty arises from the impossibility of predicting consumer behaviour. Many social, psychological and cultural influences are involved (see p. 116) that would require great courage to attempt to codify. From one degree of technical evolution to another (Berry and Horton, 1970; Marchand, 1973), from one town-size to another (Rushton, 1969), from one perception of the environment to another (MacKay, Olshavsky and Sentell, 1975), the actual behaviour of individuals changes. 'Spatial behaviour, exactly as any other behaviour, is determined by preference only' (Rushton, 1969, p. 400).

The reader may well ask, therefore, why we have attempted this exposition – albeit partial and superficial – of the theoretical approach. The answer is that it occupies such an important place in geographical literature in recent years, particularly in the English-speaking world, and is capable of generating so much conceptual thought, that it would be intellectually fraudulent not to mention it (Böventer, 1969). Besides, it enables us to conceptualise the whole subject and disentangle the fundamental characteristics of commercial structures, including the law of optimum frequency of shopping, the hierarchy of demands, leading to that of the potential hierarchisation of accessibility to markets and shops that themselves form a hierarchy. In the concrete examples that follow, while the geometrical space-relationships are always missing at the local level, they are often found in the underlying structures.

The major constraints on localisation

We must first insist on one type of evidence that has been much neglected by the theoreticians, and that is the importance of *history*. The network of present distributions is in large measure inherited from the past. It reflects technical constraints and economic values very different from those of today, though it tends to adapt itself thereto. It thus cannot be interpreted without taking account of the evolutionary changes, upsets or even extinctions that happen with increasing rapidity in modern times; and to examine it only with the eye of a late twentieth-century economist, is to say the least, somewhat presumptuous. When we refer to the *constraints on localisation*, we are dealing not only with those that are permanent but also those that are inherited from the past and those that are the result of entirely new factors.

Secondly, while it is essential to place emphasis on the location of markets as a function of the hierarchy of commodities and the numbers of customers, we must not neglect another aspect, the availability of saleable goods, which was, and still is over the greater part of the world, the basis of the development and functioning of trading centres.

The difficulties of the analysis would thus appear to be almost insurmountable. While the basic hypotheses that permit the formulation of a schematic model are always intellectually satisfying by their impeccably simplifying logic, actual situations are less easy to understand, define and classify. Every attempt to categorise the external physical, human and economic constraints lends itself to justifiable criticism since account must be taken of internal relationships as well. 'Location cannot be explained without at the same time accounting for trade, and trade cannot be explained without the simultaneous determination of locations' (Isard, 1956 p. 207). We have therefore endeavoured to show how a series of convergent constraints bears upon the three partners in commercial activity, commodities, customers and their meeting-point, the markets.

Availability of goods

All commercial activity, whether related to assembly or distribution, requires the availability of goods that are to form the subject of the transactions. The goods may be available directly, and locally, or indirectly through the medium of transport, from a centre or zone of production (e.g. a factory, a warehouse, or a producing area). The conditions vary with the nature of the goods, the state of development of the country in question, and the type of trading activity.

Some examples may make this clearer. Around the grain-producing area of Beauce, in the Paris basin, there has developed over the centuries a girdle of market towns, such as Chartres, Châteaudun, Dreux, Etampes and Pithiviers, where wheat was exchanged for Perche horses, Loire wines, and the varied products of the Gâtinais. This is how Demangeon (1946, p. 253–4) described it: 'Chartres has always been an important market for the peasantry of Beauce, and every commodity had its own market – grain, cattle, vegetables, poultry, cheese . . . Etampes has for many centuries acted as a distribution centre for Beauce wheat and Loire wines . . . At Pithiviers, on the edge of Beauce and Gâtinais, the peasants come from within a radius of 15 km to sell their harvests of clover and buckwheat from the heathlands of Gâtinais and purchase the cereals of Beauce.' These centres of direct exchange have remained as important service and commercial centres even though the methods of collection and trading in the agricultural industries have radically changed; they are heritages of the past, but in many parts of the world such centres retain their vigour.

Troin's (1975) study of Moroccan *suqs* is another fine example. There are 284 *suqs,* with a weekly clientele of some 1.2 million people. The situation of these *suqs* is interesting: 54 per cent of them are located at points of contact between different physical regions, notably at the foot of mountains; some literally girdle the massifs, as in the western Rif; others lie at the edge of the plateaux and hills that overlook the plains; yet others are found at the limit of the piedmont, and some are on the borders of human regions such as tribal limits. Then 24 per cent occupy focal positions, in the centre of a homogeneous region such as a plain, a plateau, a basin, or a forest clearing, or at a confluence of valleys. And 18 per cent are situated in valleys, about half of them at crossing places (formerly fords, now bridges); only about 15 *suqs* appear to have no particular site features. These *suqs* have been – and still are in many cases – collecting centres for local produce (about half the cereal output, and much more of the fruit and vegetables), as well as centres of exchange and distribution. They express vividly what one might describe as the essence of the country's commercial life.[1]

A study of the spheres of influence of these *suqs,* and of their functioning and transformation, highlights the fundamental role of accessibility, not only in terms of distance and available tracks but also of the facilities offered by transport improvements such as the opening or improvement of roads, and the progress of motorisation. 'The road and the lorry have sorted them out' (Troin, 1975, p. 424). But the nature of the produce also plays a part, and the cattle-markets, dealing in self-transportable commodities, serve much larger areas. In the more remote areas, there are 'subsistence *suqs*' (36 per cent could be so described in 1970 in northern Morocco), proving that trading is still necessary even in the poorest and most backward areas. At the junction of mountain and plain, some local *suqs* simply serve the areas immediately above and below them. On the contrary, the large towns, where wholesale trading is important, serve vast areas: Fez is especially remarkable for its large hinterland; but then it is the focus of many radiating roads and is the principal cattle-market in Morocco and one of the main ones for the fruit and vegetables brought in from northern and eastern regions that are well served by a system of market buses.

The third example is provided by the commercial activities of the port of Bordeaux, for these illustrate the importance of the availability of goods. Indeed, Bordeaux 'owes its role as a trading centre to its position in an essentially agricultural region, to its overseas links and the existence of a transport system that facilitates the distribution of its imports. The role of commerce in the life of the city is testified by the antiquity of its Chamber of Commerce, which was founded in 1705' (Lerat, 1969). Situated thus, at the meeting place of convergent land and sea routes, Bordeaux is the focus of several complex systems of trade; the most noteworthy of these concerns wine, but there are many others based not only on the agriculture and forest products of the region (fruit and vegetables especially), but also on imported products that are processed by local industries (coal, oil, timber and tropical products).

We may draw one major conclusion from these and other similar examples – the essential part played in localisation by 'contact'. Contact is here used in its widest sense; when there is a convergence of lines of communication, or the crossing of a natural obstacle such as a valley or a mountain range, or the break-of-bulk necessitated at a railway marshalling yard or a port, or merely the crossing of two roads in a town, there is a compulsory meeting of two or more ways of life and of different groups of people. There are thus in such areas zones, lines or places where contacts are maximised, thus facilitating the collection, exchange and distribution of a variety of goods. These contacts are helped by the lines of communication and the transport that uses them. Commercial centres – and this applies especially, of course, to towns and regional centres – thus arise mainly in relation to means of circulation.

There are many examples in the modern world of mineral deposits or agricultural potentialities that are poorly exploited by reason of their distance from markets and lack of adequate transport facilities. Conversely the improvement of means of communication 'appreciably reduces the cost of transport, and this leads to a redistribution of market areas, the re-evaluation of resources and a new distribution of industrial production that favours the most efficient and best situated enterprises. In favoured regions great industrial concentrations appear, thus enabling the profits of mass-production to be realised, and provoking a further extension of market zones and new relationships between commercial centres and nodal points' (Isard, 1967).

This quotation admirably sets forth the mechanism of the relations between production and trade and the changes brought about by their evolution. It applies equally – though with due regard for scale – to the Moroccan *suqs* and to the great international markets, for the availability of saleable goods is not merely a function of their existence but of their transportability and competitiveness. The laws of competitiveness seem easy to define; they are concerned with the price of the product and the cost of transport. The general rule is the minimisation of total costs. A wholesaler will decide his location and his area of operation on the basis of the price of the product or series of products in which he proposes to deal; if the distance or difficulty of carriage make the cost of transport too high, the business will no longer be profitable and it becomes necessary to abandon the location and seek another collection or distribution point.

The real world offers several other possibilities. Variations in the means of transport or in freight rates (e.g. for whole train-loads, full wagons, lorries chartered for return journeys, containers) enable modifications to be made in the economic limits, along certain transport arteries or for certain products. Bulk handling and the availability of return loads allow a variety of combinations, all of which may be profitable. More than this: for reasons of isolation, regional development policy or national autarky, or through agreements between industries or businesses, at regional or even international level, there are closed or protected markets where competition is artificial and where the production and marketing of goods are maintained under very unusual conditions.

The availability of goods is thus a function not only of the existence of the goods, but also of the possibility of transporting them and of trading in them in economic conditions that are compatible with the total marketing system.

In the case of goods made available for sale to customers in retail shops, the balance may be delicate. While the price charged to the shopkeeper by the factory or the wholesaler can vary with the quantities purchased, with the frequency of orders, or the mode of payment, there are also variations in delivery charges. In France, petrol costs more with distance from the coastal or inland refineries, and the highest price is found in certain mountain areas where access is difficult; but some garages and hypermarket distributors are prepared to sell at lower rates, particularly for self-service – and similar circumstances prevail in Great Britain. This is a perfect illustration of pricing practice, dependent on the length and difficulty of the transport lines, on the sales policy of the vendor and on the particular state of the market. These price reductions or discriminatory rates are not only found as between small competitive independent shops, but also on a scientifically calculated basis, if one may so express it, between different branches of a chain-store group. Thus the 'X' hypermarket chain in France has different prices that vary with the wealth of the sectors of the Paris suburbs in which the shops are located, with the lowest prices in the poorest areas. In Vichy, another chain-store group competes within itself, as between a hypermarket and several 'junior' department stores[2]; here too the prices, even of identical articles, are different. There is an 'economic' price and an 'arranged' price.

We may go further: there is even a 'perceived' price. 'The general tone of the establishment, the seller's way of doing business, his reputation, courtesy, efficiency, and personal links with customers and employees' (Scott, 1970, p. 85), form a suite of circumstances that may alter the subjective appreciation of the price. Another way of influencing the impression gained by the consumer is to enlarge the range of goods offered and to accept a variation of profit margins; thus certain articles may be sold even at a loss in order to incite the purchase of such bargains and other goods that yield a better profit. The 'price' of a commodity and its impact on the whole commercial operation have thus only a relative value.

The availability of customers

No commercial system can function without its human capital of three kinds: sellers, buyers and merchants. While the first of these play a dominant role in the availability of goods, and the third are responsible for commercial organisation, we must not forget that both of them also in one way or another, form part of the second category, the clients or *customers*.

The first attribute of the clientele is to be sufficiently *numerous*: its size is of prime importance, for numbers mean not only a volume and variety of consumption but also a guarantee of sufficient regularity of custom whatever may be the preferences, antipathies or sheer purchasing inability of certain sections of the population.

The second attribute is a *purchasing power* that will sustain the size and variety of a whole range of trading activities serving the needs of the population. Some authors even suggest that the level of incomes is fundamental. 'Both in the United States and in Britain, the spatial distribution of income has been found to be a more significant factor influencing the structure of shopping centres and retail markets than population distribution' (Scott, 1970, p. 62). A certain degree of wealth is reflected in an expansion in the number of shops, but its distribution between the various social classes also enlarges the range of facilities offered, and a concentration of high-income groups engenders a corresponding improvement in quality; the structure of the income-pyramid thus has important consequences. A chain-reaction is started. The requirements of a rich clientele entail not only an improvement in the quality of the goods offered but also of their presentation (i.e. the quality of the shops themselves), of the personality and the salaries of the assistants, the necessity for increasing the turnover, and so of attracting a larger or a wealthier chientele – or both – and so on. Conversely, the depopulation characteristic of certain parts of France creates difficulties of supply because of the closure of shops that have become unprofitable. The shopping facilities of small centres with a limited clientele do not include the provision of certain types of goods, for which some of the people must go to more important but more distant centres. But at the other end of the scale, the spa towns possess sophisticated stores that serve a much smaller but much wealthier clientele that is prepared to spend lavishly for at any rate some part of the year.

Lastly, the third attribute of the clientele is its *diversity* in age-groups, in tastes, and in culture. The more varied the demand, the more the commercial facilities will respond with a large range of shops and goods. But this clientele, wealthy, numerous and varied though it be, must not just exist; it must frequent the shops, for 'the decision to consume is independent of the decision concerning where the consumption will be made' (Rushton, 1969, p. 393). This well-distributed 'frequentation', that gives life to the whole trading system, reflects the relations between the availability of goods and of the clientele. What are the optimal conditions for this? All depends on the behaviour of the interested parties, that is clients and shopkeepers. But as we have seen, we cannot (despite the opinions of, for example, Brush and Gauthier, 1968) continue to accept the over-simplistic principle that the nearest shop is what matters. The question must be put in another way.

The 'frequentation' of a shop is a function of its accessibility and of the cost of actually getting to it, and its general attractiveness.

Accessibility may be expressed as distance in kilometres, but also as time-distance (that depends on the nature of the roads and of the traffic), as amenity-distance (some routes being more attractive than others), and as efficiency-distance (the possibility of making one journey serve several purposes). It is also a matter of the availability of parking space in the vicinity – and motorised shopping is becoming more and more common all over the world, but especially in the industrialised western countries. It must not be forgotten, however, that the masses, the world over, do their shopping on foot or by public transport. This is almost universal for daily shopping, except in North America and Australia. In this case the distribution of shops and the density of population are intimately related: the distance to the nearest food shop is short (in France, an estimated 300–500 metres; in the United States about 400 m, with 800 m for weekly groceries) (Applebaum, 1968) and the choice is very limited, except in well-provided towns.

For other types of purchase, accessibility is important. It is a question not only of distance but also of the available means of transport; it can thus vary as between individuals (possession of a car, nearness to public services), between the seasons (in countries with extreme climates), and from one day to another. The opening of a vast new road system in Brazil during the last 20 years has completely transformed the movement of goods and people and the main arteries of trade. The movement of the wealthier sections of the population in the United States to the periphery of the great urbanised areas creates completely new conditions for the establishment of shops. It is the same with the daily migratory movements that divide the life of millions of town-dwellers between residence and workplace, with the possibility of shopping at both ends, to say nothing of the time constraints that overwhelm the housewives who have to submit to this rhythm and are thus obliged to make multiple purchases.

The frequency of shopping also depends on *financial considerations*. However, though the absolute rule of an increase of transport costs with distance cannot be neglected, its dissuasive role is probably slight. Customers who are asked about it have often not really given it much thought: they think in terms of journey time or difficulty of access. It has even been suggested that those who confess to being most concerned with selling prices are least concerned with distance (MacKay *et al.,* 1975).

With prices and costs we enter, indeed, into a domain in which the reactions of the clientele are often subjective, rather than founded on precise figures. While the shopkeeper is bound to take costs into account in his calculations, or risk disappointing results, the private individual often makes but an incomplete assessment, for though he may reckon the cost of petrol or bus fares, he omits the cost of his own time and other expenses. The motoring magazines are full of balance-sheets reminding the motorist that one kilometre of travel really costs him (including insurance, depreciation, etc.) very much more than he thinks. This motivation thus has effects that are in general only indirect; either they appear as part of distance, or perhaps they cause some customers to group their purchases more systematically, or maybe encourage two or three families to share a car for shopping expeditions.

The third variable, *attractiveness*, is the most complex since it is the resultant of a series of factors made up of the individual characteristics of the shop (convenience of premises, range of goods, pricing policy and other bargains or special offers designed to suit the needs of customers) and the impulsive as well as the deep-seated motivations of consumers (conservatism or acceptance of change, attraction of novelty or fear of the unfamiliar, acceptance or rejection of advertising publicity, ignorance or information-seeking). All these tastes and tendencies may be encountered. Some are social, some environmental, some economic, with a cultural or ethnic basis, and we could perhaps recognise and classify them. For example, the poorest people are often tied to a shopping sector that offers them prices they can afford to pay, allows them credit and enables them to avoid awkward journeys, and generally lends a sympathetic ear to their daily woes – and in this way, the poorest of the poor often pay the dearest price! An investigation made in London in the early 1950s showed that the East Enders never dared to seek furniture in West End shops where they might have got much better bargains (Morrel, 1956). Besides this 'class' behaviour, there are others of a cultural kind: shopkeepers who serve whites and blacks in the United States are well aware of this; in Canada, in rural Ontario, the service areas of markets are not the same for francophones and anglophones; in the world's great cities, the immigrant communities have created their own commercial ghettoes, and in some cases even their own trading circuits – the Italians and Chinese, for example. But many attitudes reflect more the character of the individual and his momentary impulses. And how can we classify these?

An investigation among housewives in the suburbs of Chicago has endeavoured to categorise their behaviour (Stone, 1954). The author distinguished the 'practical' or 'economic' type, very concerned with price, quality and efficiency, the 'personalising', who attempt to establish close relations with the store personnel (these two categories are found especially among new arrivals, of superior social class in the first case); the 'moralists', whose patronage of shops is based on ethical motives, and the 'apathetic', whose sole concern is the expenditure of the least possible effort (these last two groups being old inhabitants, the less fortunate in the last case). Such subtle distinctions show up the difficulty and uncertainty of these attempts at classification.

In two kinds of circumstances the effects of this apparent anarchy of behaviour are minimised: in the relative isolation and under-equipment of many regions, in particular the rural zones without adequate motorised transport, where the freedom, or even the idea, of choice is reduced to a minimum; and in densely populated areas where there are numerous shops of the same general kind (but not an over-provision), where one customer's fancies are balanced by those of another, and where the very large numbers involved make customer behaviour so predictable that marginal preferences do not upset the shopping structure.

Just as there are localities that are meeting-points for the assembly or distribution of goods, where the establishment of various types of commercial enterprise is possible, so there are localities where customer potential is particularly favourable. The preceding pages have shown that in both cases there must be sufficient concentration, either on the spot or through the medium of efficient transport. Once more it is the crossroads and focal situations that are privileged, because they represent, in rural areas more or less densely peopled, and in urbanised areas with a more or less dense mesh of towns, exceptional gatherings of consumers.

Adaptation of commercial organisms

Before considering actual examples of shopping establishments, their eventual hierarchical organisation and their functioning in spatial relationships, it is useful to examine, as we have done for goods and customers, the constraints which bear on commercial businesses.

The whole organisation, as we have seen, resembles two large cones joined at their apices; the upper cone represents production, its means and location, the lower cone, the mass of retailers and consumers. Between them are the wheels of the commercial mechanisms that assemble, transfer and distribute. This simple model is expressive: it shows that the intermediary businesses can only very exceptionally exercise a constraint that is not reciprocal, whether on goods or customers. On the contrary, they are subject to direct and retroactive reactions with both. Commercial businesses constitute the very heart of the commercial system, as we have defined it, and they behave as such. It follows that we cannot consider their constraints but rather their response to the constraints that limit other elements in the system, in other words their *adaptation* to the functioning of the whole.

To view this question in its entirety would lead us, in fact, to a recapitulation of both the organisation of distribution systems and the spatial distribution of undertakings. We have therefore chosen to give at this point merely a brief account, designed to underline certain synthetic aspects, the details of which figure in other parts of this book.

Adaptation may be by way of localisation, size, or organisation. All kinds of combination are possible, just as the range of situations is infinitely varied, but it is more appropriate to try to identify the average type rather than to study the exceptional cases.

Let us return to our model of two cones. The first consequence is a certain symmetry at the two extremities, the initial assembly and the final distribution, where the product enters and leaves the commercial system. In the classical case, that is still the most frequent, the shops are small, very localised and adapted to the local situation; transport distances are minimal, and can be accomplished on foot or by primitive means such as donkeys or horse-carts. The investments required are small. Such businesses are doubly dependent: on higher-order undertakings and on the local population; their power of pressure and retaliation is virtually non-existent; conversely, the capacity for minimising profits (both individual producers and petty-traders lack organisation and information) and the force of inertia seem inexhaustible in extreme cases.

However, even at this stage, other formulae already exist. The evolution that began a century and a half ago with department stores is continuing, with the development of vast supermarkets and even nationalised retailing organisations. The department stores extend their storeys upwards in city centres, the supermarkets seek peripheral locations; but the desire to remain in contact with the customers, and the dependence on the local environment as well as on higher-order organisations (banks, chains, large companies), remain, though in different forms. There is, in some ways, a spatial concentration of the traditional 'apparatus', related especially to new means of transport, which play an ever-present role in the problem under examination.

Wholesaling can also free itself from fragmentation, even in the initial stages, if it collects its goods from areas of concentrated production. At the intermediate levels, wholesaling is dependent on the quality of the two factors on which it depends to perform its functions, namely transport and the availability of information. It finds the best possibilities either in towns of a certain size, the infrastructure of which it utilises, or in special organisations that it has itself set up. As it operates within the double spiral of the concentration and dispersal of goods, undertakings of larger size and increasing complexity form the links in an organisational chain that adjusts itself to the level of consumption.

There are direct and close relationships between the nature of the goods, the size of establishments, the means of transport and the structure of undertakings. Take two typical examples. Wholesale establishments are usually specialists in terms of products, but they become more and more powerful, and their inter-regional or even international ramifications become geared to mass transportation: ports and inland waterways play an important part, with their accompanying installations (silos, warehouses, special fleets). The trade in grain, oil, ores and phosphates is of this type, playing a part in national and international affairs. Another type involves the assembly of large quantities of goods from many scattered sources. What matters in this case is the size of the warehouse and the possibility of rapid communication with both suppliers and distributors. This type is more usually associated with rapid transport, more diversified but at the same time more constant in service, like the railway, the lorry or even the aeroplane. The proximity of a large city is a great asset, for a large part of the market is thus immediately accessible. The central purchasing depots of the department stores and multiple chain-stores illustrate this type precisely. Thus in France, the warehouses of Printemps, the only large department store in the centre of Paris, were for long in close proximity to the store; but with the establishment of new branch-stores, and the very high cost of renting space in the vicinity of the Boulevard Haussmann, the warehouses have been moved out of the capital and installed in the industrialised zone of the Ile Saint Denis, with intermediate locations in Clichy.

Within the whole range of wholesaling establishments, there are thus those whose main function is to act as a link in the chain of transmission: for these, locations at break-of-bulk points on transport routes is preferable, provided that the machinery exists for organising this function and ensuring its operation. But at the end of the chain, where contact is made between wholesale and retail, the main concern is the service of sales points, and so an expansion of facilities for doing business. In this case, cities of a certain size are preferred, which can support groups of wholesalers and retailers; these will quickly be followed by others who benefit from reliable and rapid business relations. This simple hierarchical advantage introduces a perceptible discrimination between rural and urban environments, between the towns themselves and even between different parts of a single town. This we shall endeavour to show.

Thus, commercial organisms both depend on and create means of transport and of movement in general, and similarly depend on and affect the size and quality of inhabited places. Many authors have tried to demonstrate this parallelism between the size of towns and the number and quality of the shopping facilities. The difficulty is to discover significant comparative values. There are no simple linear correlations or generalisations. Here is another theme that we shall explore in the following chapters.

Notes

1. Since Troin's study is an unpublished thesis, the reader might consult an earlier but much more limited account, containing a map, by Fogg (1932). (Editor's note.)
2. For a definition of 'junior department store' see p. 250.

Chapter 2

The hierarchy of commercial centres

Research into the status of commercial centres

The demands of individuals as consumers are capable of classification. Certain demands must be satisfied daily, in particular that of foodstuffs; they represent frequent and repetitive expenses, and they are generally satisfied by products with some degree of uniformity – bread, milk, meat, and so on, offer few variations other than quality. For most of the population, these needs may be fulfilled in quite simple conditions. But the higher one goes in the scale of requirements, the wider become the choices, the greater the expenditure; and the consumer can seek alternative and competitive supplies, thus involving several shops or even several types of shop (cooperatives, independent shops, department stores, specialty shops) and the devotion of some time and expense in moving from one to another.

The hierarchy of demand has as its corollary a scale of shopping frequency: this is the basis of the theoretical notions suggested in the previous chapter. But as we have already noted, for reasons connected both with the structure and organisation of commerce in particular and space in general, and with consumer decisions, the classification is not necessarily hierarchical in form. Furthermore, centres of different status and progressively greater complexity are in competition with the whole range of lower-ranking establishments; the ranking of their equipment is not exactly paralleled by the size of their clientele, nor by the areal extent of their sphere of influence. These are difficulties that we should do well to remember.

With all these reservations in mind, the study of the relative importance of commercial centres, the principles governing their establishment and the ordering of their market areas, or, in sum, a static view and a functional approach (Beaujeu-Garnier, 1976), appear to be a matter of some difficulty. The more so, since despite an abundance of limited studies, and suggestions for classification or general indices that are often deceptive, the criteria are rarely incontestable. And their authors have all too frequently failed to link research on the classification and hierarchy of centres with that on the areas served, wrongly using the results of the former in the theoretical determination of the latter. This is scarcely surprising if we take account of the mass of local enquiries that are necessary in the absence of any published data.[1]

The bulk of what follows is concerned essentially with retail trade, except for the paragraphs on sources and certain general research; the most notable peculiarities of wholesaling are pointed out in separate paragraphs.

Sources

There are three classes of data that different authors have examined in turn or simultaneously. The first results from direct enquiry. It involves noting, by detailed survey on the ground, the existing location of shops: the number of shops, their nature, their up-to-dateness, and their size are useful points to record; their turnover and other financial details of their operation (rent, value of stock-in-trade, etc.) are also useful but more difficult to obtain. Such a survey is a lengthy, difficult and onerous task, and is thus infrequently undertaken. It has been done for several large cities, notably Chicago (Berry, 1963; Berry and Mayer, 1962; Brush and Gauthier, 1968), for 133 shopping centres in the English Midlands (Lomas, 1964), and for some Belgian cities, notably Liège (Sporck, 1966). In France, certain towns have been the subject of detailed enquiries, notably in Alsace by Nonn (1974–5), in Le Havre (Damais, 1974), in Languedoc (Dugrand, 1963), and in particular at Montpellier (Crouzet, 1975), at Pau (X. Piolle) and in the Paris region, where numerous studies have been made, together with others in the rural areas and country towns of the Paris basin (Angers, Chartres, and in the *départements* of Yonne and Eure-et-Loir). These studies have led to some interesting conclusions. In northern Morocco, Troin (1975) has made a special study of the rural markets (*suqs*).

The second method consists of basing an examination of commerce upon administrative or professional documents which give lists, more or less exhaustive and relatively accessible, and are accompanied by some precise details. In France, the register of business and industrial establishments kept by the National Institute of Statistics and Economic Studies (INSEE) is extremely valuable, but its consultation is subject to restrictions regarding confidential statistics, its information is only partial, and the researcher is sometimes hindered by a superfluity, for the cards relating to defunct establishments are not removed until some time after their demise; but some notable improvements have been made. The great Bottin directory is another possible source because successive editions enable comparisons to be made over time, very accurately for rural areas and small towns, less so regarding the exact numbers of establishments in the large cities, and the information given is rather limited. The original taxation records, when available, are even more valuable. Numerous French workers, including the present authors, have extracted everything possible from these sources. In the United Kingdom, planning surveys have furnished localised information, particularly for Greater London, and similarly in countries with a British tradition, such as Australia. In North America, annuals such as the Dun and Bradstreet Directory have furnished US and Canadian research workers with accurate and much-utilised data. Thus Borchert and Adams (1963) have classified information for the whole of the northern part of the Mid West. In some socialist countries, some annual publications even give sales figures; while some specialist annuals give similar information, like the Market Yearbook in Britain.

The third source comprises distribution censuses. They have been taken in several countries, notably Germany and Italy. They have given English research workers periodic detailed information, not always directly comparable, concerning a number of financial elements in commercial centres defined as having at least four department stores or other large shops selling clothing or domestic equipment. Carruthers (1967) used these data to formulate a national classification. In France the first census of distribution was taken in 1966. It contains numerous interesting elements but has only been published in part. Access to some unpublished tables has enabled the present authors to compile a classification of French towns (see Table 12, p. 140), using also other data extracted from the population census. An analysis of a recent (1970) enquiry by the Ministry of Agriculture enables us to understand certain aspects of the commercial equipment of the villages.

These few examples demonstrate the inequality of the documentation, its fragmentary and often problematical nature (the financial information is often lacking and must be treated with caution; there are no data on the clientele or areas served). And if one resorts to direct enquiries, the field is drastically reduced, and the work lacks coordination with that of other researchers in respect of date and the questions asked. Even the vocabulary is inexact and ambiguous, to say nothing of the classifications: certain goods are considered by some to be 'daily' purchases, and by others to be merely 'weekly'. Quite apart from the subjectivity of the appraisals, consumer habits vary from one country to another (in terms of bread, wine and fish purchases, for example) and even from one region to another, or depending on the standard of living, between different quarters of a town (in terms of visits to the florist or the hairdresser). Even the distinctions between rural and urban, and between the social levels that distinguish one town from another, are subject to debate. All these things must be borne in mind at the outset when considering the difficulties, not only of individual studies but of their comparison and synthesis.

Classification by 'equipment'

The hierarchy of commercial centres is based on certain elements that enable a classification to be made. There appear to be two possibilities: 'equipment' and its fixed characteristics, and 'turnover', which is the result of the functioning of the equipment. Between these two there is not an absolute agreement, but a variable relationship such as exists between the pattern of a road system and the traffic that uses it. In fact, for reasons connected with the history of growth, with perpetuation through sheer inertia, with a sharp rise in population, and with changes in the standard of living, the commercial system may have reached a certain stage, to which the use that is made of it may more or less correspond. It is thus necessary to take account of both elements.

In an ideal world, one might agree with Scott (1970, p. 106) when he states that any classification of commercial centres (on the basis of 'equipment') must include five basic measures: overall importance, composition by types of trade, forms of organisation, size of establishments, size and structure of the market area. In reality one must be content with fewer criteria, or cheat by replacing the missing data by more or less sophisticated indices that are considered to provide equivalent approximations.

To confine ourselves to a classification by status, the main elements are the number, distribution and quality of the shops.

The *sum total* of the facilities may be gauged from the number of establishments, but the limitations of this figure are immediately apparent: a large department store and a small 'corner shop' are each counted as one unit, unless some sort of weighting is adopted. A corrective is applied by the number of employees, provided that both proprietors and paid staff are included and that the proportion of self-service shops is not too high. In France, the statistics usually include only paid staff. The turnover is also an important corrective, together with the surface area of the premises. At Birmingham, in the 1961 census, there were 280 establishments of a certain kind, and in Nottingham, 382 in the same category, but the turnover was four times greater in Birmingham, where chain-stores were more numerous (Scott, 1970, p. 124).

Similar features appear in the distribution censuses of France: if one takes two towns having more or less the same number of shops, one may find overall turnover figures for retail trade that are very unequal; thus Annecy has 851 shops and a total turnover of 334 million francs, while Alès has 908 shops and a turnover of 170 million francs. On a higher level, we may quote Grenoble with 3,153 shops and a turnover of 944 million francs, and Strasbourg, 3,083 shops and 1,297 million francs. This does not make detailed comparisons any easier, but the overall parallelism is striking.

To these overall figures, generally furnished by censuses and allowing us to calculate various indices, may be added others dealing with the *variety of equipment*. In the first place the percentage of non-food shops is particularly significant, for these types of shops have a more than local service area. Within this group one may also introduce subdivisions such as household equipment, clothing, or even finer distinctions such as men's and women's clothing, and footwear.

Another fundamental aspect is the *variety of specialty shops*: and in this also we may distinguish a number of sub-sections. Thus a town like Saint-Flour has 6,200 inhabitants and 55 types of shop, while Agen has 37,500 people and 127 types. This is an aspect that has been but rarely used by writers, but we consider it to be of value. Obviously one cannot take account of the absolute diversity, for the imprecision of the statistics would lead to errors, but it is possible to reckon on regrouping them into a number of categories to see how many are represented in each centre, and in what numbers. This has been done for numerous French towns, and even for the different quarters of Paris (Demorgon, 1975). But of course another interesting factor is the number of establishments in each category of activity. In the case of furniture dealers or women's clothing, for example, it is significant that the activity exists at all, but more important to know whether there are 1, 20 or a 100 shops.

In the same vein, there have been studies of uncommon businesses, which vary from country to country, for example, calculating machines and specialised electrical equipment in France (Hautreux and Rochefort, 1963), oriental carpets in Austrian towns (Bobek, 1968).

Lastly, for a given activity, all its sub-branches must be investigated: thus the feminine-apparel trades of Paris include mass-produced goods, ready-to-wear garments, made-to-measure and *haute couture*. The last two represent a special group that depends on a wide demand base. Conversely, the super-concentration of an activity may reflect an external factor, such as the making of nougat at Montélimar, or copper stewpans at Villedieu-les-Poêles, or the presence of wholesalers, as with ready-to-wear garments and fabrics around Sentier in Paris, or, further, a particular orientation of the economic life, like the *objets de piété* shops at Lourdes or sports goods retailers at seaside resorts. There is indeed a wealth of classification possibilities dependent on this idea of the variety of activities.

There is one other possible factor in the determination of the status of commercial centres, particularly among small centres that are more easily surveyed; this is the *appearance of certain types* of shop in relation to the number of inhabitants in the locality: thus purveyors of meat appear in villages of over 500 inhabitants (Delobez, 1973; Bell *et al.,* 1974); but these thresholds are very variable, for consumer habits change from time to time. The same level of provision is found in Hérault in villages of 2,000 inhabitants as in Ille et Vilaine with 1,300.

The *quality of shops* (and not this time their activities) is another possible theme. It may depend on size, as has often been suggested (Scott, 1970, p. 67), though this may be difficult to prove and is sometimes contradictory. The crude data are often difficult to interpret without taking environment and history into account: the influence of the land parcels in the centre of old European cities acts contrary to the rule which would stipulate that the shops in the central business district, with more custom, should be of larger size (McAnaly, 1965); not to mention the fact that success often means extension, and in the case of these old congested urban centres, removal. If one can relate this crude measure of size, of little significance in itself, to the turnover and number of employees, there is the possibility of a better basis for classification. But these are data that necessitate personal enquiries, and the results are sometimes deceptive.

Personal observation can also be used to record the *condition of the shop*: its degree of modernisation, the quality of its window displays, the standard of maintenance of the premises. The surveys made by Sporck (1971, 1975) in a number of towns, enabled him to formulate a very revealing classification.

Another quantity that is quite easy to measure is the *level of prices,* as revealed by tags attached to goods on display on counters or in windows: this promises to yield interesting results, but it needs much practice, and for non-standard products it is subject to argument. Obviously the comparison can only be made between articles of the same kind, for example, the most expensive spectacle frames in different opticians' shops, the most expensive dress in different female clothiers, the most costly toy or piece of jewellery (Sporck, 1975).

Another somewhat similar idea has been put forward, for investigating the *variety of goods* on offer. This is particularly striking in the case of different shops belonging to the same chain; thus, in Paris, the Printemps chain offers a clear example: the main store in the Boulevard Haussmann is a world in itself, divided into three large premises, but the branches on the edge of the inner city (Place de la Nation) or in the suburbs (Vélizy II) have a much more restricted range, and a further decline is visible in the provincial branches.

Lastly, and still within the realm of static comparisons, the *forms of organisation* should not be neglected; they even figure statistically in the data relating to commercial centres in the United Kingdom census of distribution. Department stores, multiples, single-price shops, cooperatives, independent shops – all of these figure to a greater or lesser degree in accordance with the importance of a commercial centre, its age and its mode of origin.

All these possible ways of differentiating shops and commercial centres find their expression in different rhythms and frequencies of customer visits, that are related to distances travelled. We shall examine them with special reference to areas of attraction (Chapter 3).

We cannot hope, however, to assess the importance and role of a commercial centre without examining the other activities that go on within and around it. All investigations go to show that commerce is accompanied by other closely linked activities: services such as cafés, restaurants, hotels and hairdressers, and also banks; in such cases one may almost speak of symbiosis. In other cases the liaison is much less fundamental – administrative services, amusement centres, clubs and the like; their presence is in the nature of kinship, for they also depend, like shops, on the constant custom of a large body of people. Some authors have thus taken them into account in studying the hierarchy of central places (e.g. Smailes and Hartley, 1961; Andrade 1971), and have even sought to formulate the laws that govern their combination within such hierarchies (Dokmeci, 1973). It is for similar reasons that the sites of periodic markets are usually to be found in close proximity to the commercial quarters of towns (Troin, 1975). The congregation of activities makes for easy contacts, and the concentration of businesses makes for appreciable external economies.

There is thus a mechanism of mutual attraction, at least up to the point at which congestion occurs, thus increasing costs, causing loss of time and money, and internal diseconomies. Whether or not those elements that are not strictly commercial should be introduced into studies of the hierarchy of commercial centres is a matter for some debate. Firstly, because in many cases it is almost impossible to separate certain activities from commerce – to which we have already given a very wide definition. Secondly, because their presence contributes effectively to the sum total of intercourse and it would be hazardous to attempt to identify the parts played by each. And thirdly, because their very existence sometimes generates commercial activity, as in the case of bookshops alongside colleges. It is also true that the two classifications do not coincide absolutely, for it would seem that commerce is the urban activity that has the lowest coefficient of variation. A calculation of this coefficient for 135 Belgian towns gave a value of 0.31, the lowest of 17 groups of activities, followed by building with 0.47, personal service 0.49 and teaching 0.50. Commerce, then, at least in the developed countries of the western world, is an inherent urban function, but other activities are responsible for more marked differentiation, in internal structure if not also in the hierarchy.

Classification by the functioning of the 'equipment'

Another type of hierarchical classification has been used in this book for French towns (see p. 140) and by some other authors. It is based on the sum total of annual turnover. This expresses two notions that are closely linked, even though they do not necessarily vary in parallel: the strength of the 'equipment' and the use that is made of it. Nevertheless, it gives a classification of commercial centres that has some value.

To give greater precision, we may divide the sum total into a certain number of categories: the turnover of food shops is of more importance in small centres, in densely peopled working-class towns, and in the towns of the Third World; that is, wherever the shopping facilities have little diversity, or where food bulks largely in the family budget. Conversely, we may separate out certain specific types of shop (clothing, household equipment), or less common types ('de luxe' shops). But a classification may also be drawn up according to the size of the shops (e.g. no paid assistance, more than 20 staff). And there are other possibilities.

In conclusion, then, we can detect certain characteristics in the trade of commercial centres that are reflected in the nature of their shopping facilities. In the ideal case of homogeneous populations and of facilities exactly matching their rational use by the population, the two hierarchies are identical. But even without taking into account the distortions of the hypothetical conditions that are experienced in practice, there are also two other difficulties: firstly, of obtaining figures of turnover; and secondly, the reliability of such figures diminishes as soon as we cease to generalise from them and try to get down to finer detail. Nevertheless, when the opportunity does occur, as with the publication of a census of distribution, it should be accepted, and the results are worthy of consideration.

Some types of hierarchy of commercial centres

Britain and the USA

Using the various elements mentioned above, or at least some of them, and combining them in several different ways, attempts have been made to establish reasonable criteria for classifying the relative importance of commercial centres, or in other words to formulate a hierarchy. It would require a whole volume to recall all the various schemes that have been proposed, but it is necessary to quote a few in order to show the methods and discuss the results.

First thoughts on methodology suggest not only the difficulty of actually classifying commercial centres (once a certain technique has been adapted), but also of grouping them in a hierarchy that is appropriate to a certain area or country. Absolute values, as we have already noted, are only significant in relation to a given environment, but town A and town B may play the same role (e.g. sub-regional capital) in two different regions, though having a quite different assembly of shops and of turnover figures and even, if the two regions are of opposite types, say, one industrialised and the other essentially rural, with different types of shopping activity that reflect the pattern of social classes represented in the respective populations. The level of 'equipment' and the intensity of sales do not correspond automatically to the spatial function of the centres in question.

Despite these reservations, however, it must be stated that numerous researchers, working in different countries, and using similar but not identical criteria, have arrived at a seven-stage hierarchy. Thus Carol (1960) developed one for the United States, and Thorpe (1968) for Great Britain. The latter author simply took the sales figures for all English centres given in the census of distribution, 1961; using a dispersion diagram, he formulated a division into seven classes: regional centres (e.g. Glasgow, Newcastle), sub-regional centres (Nottingham, Dundee), area centres (Bolton, Shrewsbury), major centres (Hereford, Widnes), district centres, local or suburban centres, and village or small suburban centres. Carruthers (1967) proposed a much more complex method that enabled him to incorporate all the commercial centres of England and Wales, both inter-urban within the national framework and intra-urban within the framework of urbanised areas, into a shopping-centre system. The

Plate 1. *Range of shops*

(*a*) A bazaar in Colombo

(*b*) A 'de luxe' cheese shop in Paris

(*c*) A large department store in Oxford Street, London.

Plate 2. *'Movable' shops*

(*a*) A floating market near Bangkok

(*b*) Temporary fruit-stalls, Warsaw

(*c*) A motorised mobile shop in Mortagne, Gironde, France

Plate 3. *Markets* 131

(*a*) The *suq* at Boumaln de Dadès, Morocco

(*b*) Market at Tepeaca, Mexico

(*c*) Street-market in Kowloon, Hong Kong

(*a*) Pottery in the market at Salvador, Brazil

(*b*) Hot food in the market at Tepeaca, Mexico

(*c*) *Kolkhoz* market-hall at Erevan, USSR

Plate 5. *Shopping streets* 133

(*a*) Main street of Bry-sur-Marne, France

(*b*) In the CBD of Tokyo

(*c*) Shopping arcade in Lyon

Plate 6. *Wholesale produce markets*

(*a*) Traffic chaos in the Washington market at New York in the 1950s

(*b*) Les Halles in Paris, built between 1851 and 1868; abandoned in 1969, demolished in 1971

(*c*) The national produce market at Rungis, near Paris, in 1976

Plate 7. *Future shopping in city centres* 135

(a) Pedestrianisation of main shopping street, the Zeil, in Frankfurt-am-Main

(b) Reconstruction of the CBD in St. Paul (Minnesota); department store in foreground

(c) Building a new regional shopping centre, La Part Dieu, in the heart of Lyon

(*a*) Brent Cross shopping centre, north London

(*b*) A small shopping precinct at Kalamazoo (Michigan)

(*c*) The Northland Shopping Centre in the suburbs of Detroit
(Michigan)

data are also taken from the national 1961 census of distribution, and the author adopts the definition of central places contained therein, that includes almost all towns of over 50,000 population and a certain number of specialised market towns that are characterised by a high proportion of non-food sales. He uses three indices, each of which carries a common graded scale of points values. The first index is based on the proportion of non-food sales in the total; the second is calculated on the difference between the volume of actual and 'theoretical' sales[2]; the third is related to the presence in each centre of six types of shop (boots and shoes; men's wear; female clothing and drapery; furniture and furnishing; radio, electrical goods and cycles; jewellery, leather and sports goods). The second index gives an indication of the attractive strength of the centre, and so of its sphere of influence (cf. p. 152); the first and the third demonstrate the structure of the centre, while a combination of all three permits a continuous classification across which one may distinguish various groups. Thus London is the absolute national centre, there are nine regional centres subdivided into two sub-groups (2B and 2C), and 231 third-order centres in three sub-groups (3A, 3B, 3C if their sphere of influence is wide, 3a, 3b, 3c if it is not).

Two results follow from this that are worth underlining. The regional centres are found within the great industrial zones of the North, the Midlands and South Wales – zones that are well endowed with towns and cities, some of which act as regional metropolises. In the South East, however, there is no intermediate level between the national capital and third-order centres. Exactly the same thing is true in the Paris basin in France, and this conforms to what we have already noted about relationships within the hierarchical system, and that we shall find again in dealing with market areas. It is evident that Carruthers' classification gives only a relative degree of regularity.

A comparison between the simple classification of Thorpe and the more elaborate one of Carruthers does not show the same order for the various centres except at the highest level. But one may also attempt to see whether the classification by commercial importance is very different from the more complex one based on the relative importance of central places. Several authors have addressed themselves to the problem in the United Kingdom (Smailes, 1944; Smith, 1968). We have examined the tabulation presented by Smith, for one of the criteria used in his 36 classes is the commercial function used by Carruthers. The correspondence is as follows: Class (Smith, 1968) 2A, 2B, 2C, 3A, 3B, 3C, 4A, 4B, 4C, 5A (ungraded); Class (Carruthers, based on commerce, 1967) 2B, 2C, 3A, 3B/C. The gradation is similar but not identical.

Among the developed countries, the case of the United States may also be cited, for three reasons: here is an environment which is very different from that of old Europe, and where history began but yesterday and is well understood; the transformation of the commercial structure is already well advanced, accompanying the massive growth in the number and size of towns; and numerous geographers have studied the subject by old-fashioned methods or modern quantitative techniques. The American experience thus merits some attention. The Mid West has for 60 years been the major field for these studies. Numerous criteria have been proposed, and many different results obtained. We shall cite two outstanding works that have been much quoted in geographical literature.

The first of these takes in the Dakotas, Montana, Minnesota, northwestern

Wisconsin and the northern part of Michigan (Borchert and Adams, 1963); it includes 2,532 centres, of which 311, stratified in terms of population, were used as a sample for more intensive study. The Annual published by Dun and Bradstreet gave data for the determination of 52 functional categories; a comparison of classification by size with this range of functions enabled 38 classes to be extracted, corresponding to well-marked demographic series, and this finally led to four types of commercial centres – those selling only a very few commodities, those with all types of commodity, partial commercial centres, and complete commercial centres. This short classification took into account at the one extreme the minimal shopping equipment of small villages, and at the other the differences between the equipment of complete commercial centres, depending on the presence and volume of wholesaling; this last consideration made possible a threefold subdivision of the highest class – so that in effect we are almost back to a hierarchy of seven grades.

Once again, population and the level of 'equipment' appear to be closely related, and it is a question, as it were, of the basic assumptions. As for the spatial distribution of centres, this is related to the physical environment, the types of land-use, the wealth of the population, and the historical background; the fully developed centres are confined to the corn-and-beef areas of southern Minnesota, where the 'twin cities' of Minneapolis and St. Paul, facing each other across the river Mississippi, share a regional function. Centres are more widely spaced in the mainly forested areas around Lake Superior and in the regions of extensive cattle-rearing in the Great Plains. The theoretical geometric pattern is also upset by the presence of population nuclei in the irrigated zones, in the mineral fields and industrial areas, and along the main lines of communication.

Research into the hierarchy of retailing centres has also occupied B.J.L. Berry and several associates. Among his numerous publications, between which there is much overlap, we refer here to only three (Berry and Garrison, 1958; Berry and Mayer, 1962; Berry, 1967) as representing stages in the growth of his ideas. In the first of these the authors express their wish to demonstrate the existence of a hierarchical classification of central places. Field studies in southwestern Iowa, South Dakota and Chicago, and elaborate statistical treatment of the data led to the formulation of a set of rules, clearly set out in the third volume quoted. It is evident that there is a regular connection between different variables for a given group of centres: for example, the population of a centre and the types of commercial activity (correlation coefficient 0.95); 'when urban centres are supported exclusively as

Table 11

	Level in hierarchy	Number of inhabitants	Distance (km) between centres	Functions (number of) Iowa	S. Dakota
Hamlet	0	100	4–5	–	–
Village	1	500	8–10	24	15
Large village	2	1,500	12–15	48	30
Small town	3	6,000	20–25	96	60
Regional centre	4	60,000	50–65		
Regional metropolis	5	250,000			
National metropolis	6	>1,000,000			

market centres by the retail and service functions they provide for surrounding regions' (1967, p. 35). Interdependent, too, are the population of the centre and the population served on the one hand, and the number and type of commercial establishments on the other. But within this continuum of functional relations, it is necessary to introduce some dividing lines; the relationship between the nature of the goods sold and the marketing area permits a hierarchy to be distinguished as in Table 11.

Having discerned in these two examples a regular increase in functions, Berry proposes a formula to measure the number (N) of types of activity at different levels of the hierarchy:

$$N = d2^{w-1}$$

where w is the order of the hierarchy and d a number that varies from area to area (1967, p. 38). This study thus points the way to a number of general propositions, that we may apply to French examples.

A comparison of the Berry and Borchert–Adams classifications shows that, in their respective regions, 78 per cent of the centres are assigned to the same level (if we admit at the outset that the villages in the first correspond to the hamlets of the second).

Another proposition, however, is less satisfactory with respect to the 'universality' of the classification. In many regions, while the number of distinguishable categories remains the same, the functional levels do not. In southwestern Dakota, hardware shops appear in the 'villages', whereas in the northeastern part of the state, they only appear at the 'town' level (Scott, 1970, p. 146). This observation, and Berry's care to emphasise the variation in the value of d, show that all these typologies vary with the natural environment (Murphy, 1966). The following examples confirm this.

Some French examples

Studies of the commercial activities of French towns are numerous but not very systematic. They are essentially descriptive monographs, with little concern for general theory, or for a choice of criteria that would permit comparisons to be made. We have therefore decided to include our own researches, which are based on new data and cover the whole country. The statistical sources are the distribution census of 1966, the population censuses (1962, 1968), the card-index of industrial and commercial establishments maintained by INSEE, and the volumes of the Bottin directory.

A preliminary study was made of 91 French urban centres having over 50,000 inhabitants at the 1958 census, but excluding Paris. The towns were ranked according to a number of characteristics: population in 1968, total number of retail shops, total retail turnover, turnover of retail food shops, turnover of retail non-food shops, and turnover of retail clothing shops. The complete lists would occupy much space, and we present in Table 12 the ranking of the top 20 and the bottom 10 (by population).

What conclusions can we draw from this tabulation? The ranking of the towns is fairly consistent on the whole, but with some sharp dislocations in the case of certain towns and certain items. The top 10 are fairly consistent;

Table 12. Ranking of the 20 principal urban agglomerations in France (Population 1968 and other commercial criteria 1966)

Rank of towns and cities 1968	By number of retail shops	By total retail turnover	By turnover of retail food shops	By turnover of non-food shops	By turnover of clothing shops
Lyon 1	1	2	1	2	2
Marseille 2	2	3	3	3	3
Lille 3	3	1	2	1	1
Bordeaux 4	4	4	4	4	4
Toulouse 5	6	6	8	6	5
Nantes 6	8	9	12	8	9
Nice 7	5	5	6	5	6
Rouen 8	9	8	5	9	8
Toulon 9	7	10	9	10	12
Strasbourg 10	14	7	7	7	7
Grenoble 11	13	11	11	11	11
St.-Etienne 12	10	13	14	14	15
Lens 13	11	15	10	22	18
Nancy 14	16	12	13	12	11
Le Havre 15	15	16	16	20	14
Valenciennes 16	17	24	22	21	28
Cannes 17	12	14	17	13	13
Douai 18	20	31	20	41	52
Clermont-Ferrand 19	18	19	21	19	17
Tours 20	21	22	25	17	22

Ranking of the 10 smallest towns (population 1968)

82 Niort	Arras	Périgueux	St. Chamond	Châteauroux	Châteauroux
83 Châteauroux	Agen	Quimper	Alès	Creil	Maubeuge
84 Nevers	Niort	Alès	Montceau	Albi	Bruay
85 Sète	Châteauroux	Albi	Sète	Alès	Châlons/M
86 Albi	Armentières	Longwy	Agen	Longwy	St. Chamond
87 Agen	Montceau	Montceau	Périgueux	Sète	Longwy
88 Longwy	Creil	Menton	Quimper	Montceau	Montceau
89 Quimper	Chartres	Sète	Albi	St. Chamond	Sète
90 Montceau-les-Mines	Chalon/S.	St. Chamond	St. Brieuc	Menton	Menton
91 Armentières	Longwy	Armentières	Armentières	Armentières	Armentières

Source: Census of distribution 1966; census of population 1968.

Bordeaux remarkably so. From calculations of the correlation coefficients made by Bravais and Pearson it is evident that there are very close relationships between the variables, for the values are near to 0.991 between population and the number of retail establishments; 0.982 between population and total retail turnover; 0.986 with the turnover of retail food shops; 0.970 with non-food shops; and 0.944 with the turnover of retail clothing shops. (See Figs. 3 and 4.)

We have tried to discover whether, outside the population, turnover and number of shops, there are similar relationships in the case of other variables such as surface-area of shops and numbers of employees. The data are obtainable from the census of distribution, but it must be noted that the surface-areas have not been recorded with such completeness or homogeneity. We have nevertheless calculated the coefficients in the same way as before, and the results are slightly less high, but none the less remarkable: 0.976 between population and shopping floor-space (Fig. 5); 0.985 between population and

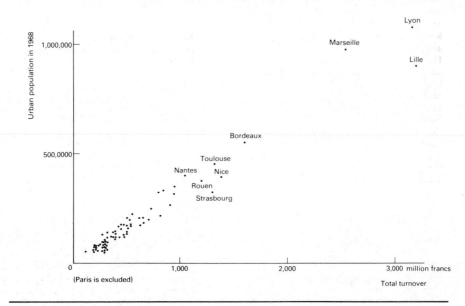

Fig. 3 French urban areas with over 50,000 population in relation to total retail turnover.

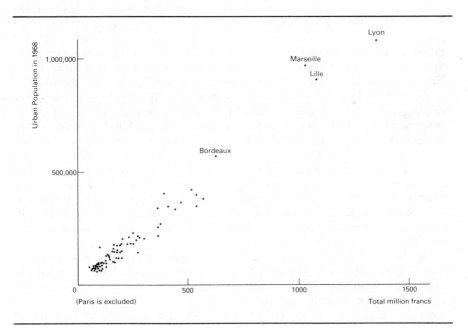

Fig. 4 French urban areas with over 50,000 population in relation to retail turnover in foodstuffs.

the numbers occupied; 0.977 with employment in non-food shops; but only low correlations with salaried employment in household goods shops (0.810); and especially with clothing shops (0.553).

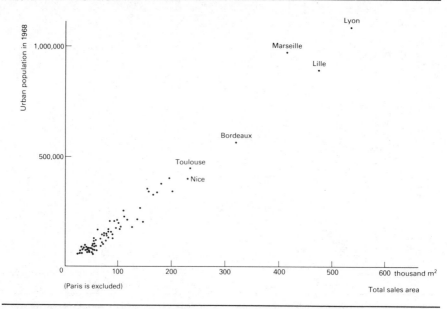

Fig. 5 French urban areas with over 50,000 population in relation to shop floor-space.

The influence of size is here clearly evident, for towns normally have numbers of shops corresponding to the dimensions of their population, and these shops have surface-areas, and a turnover in both food and non-alimentary commodities that is related to the number of consumers. However, the slight differences between the various coefficients makes it worth while to pursue the analysis further. It is curious, for example, to note that the correlation between the total number of employees in household-goods shops and the number of employees and the turnover of non-food shops is in general quite high (over 0.85) while between clothing shops and all the other factors (surface-area, employment and turnover) it hardly exceeds 0.5.

Another result of this approach is that one is led to admit that in order to assess the commercial attraction of a town, one could equally well take the population, the number of shops, the surface-area of sales space, or the total retail turnover. However, though the correlation is high it is not perfect, and if we look into the details, we find that for certain urban centres (Strasbourg and Douai, for example) the choice of criteria is a matter of some importance. We must therefore exercise due caution.

The effect of size is thus important, and as a general rule it ranks the urban centres whether the criteria used relate to numbers (of population and persons employed), to floor-space or to financial matters. And we may add another close correlation with the variety of shop-types.

We have regrouped all the trading activities, both wholesale and retail, under 245 headings, and have counted up all the varieties so defined, for all towns of over 5,000 inhabitants in the *départements* of Cantal, Eure-et-Loir, Hérault, Ille-et-Vilaine and Pas de Calais, and also for certain important towns such as Lyon, Marseille, Bordeaux, Lille, Nantes, for some unique towns such as Nice and Vichy, and for an average middle-class town like Nevers. Plotting the

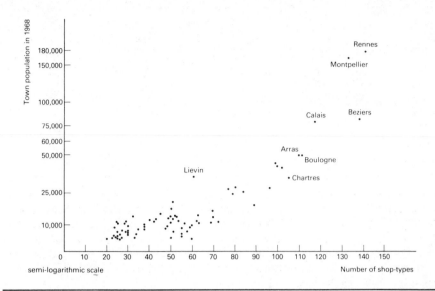

Fig. 6 Relation between population and number of types of shop in towns of over 50,000 population in five French *départements*.

results for the five *départements* on a graph (Fig. 6) we may distinguish two groups: towns of under 18,000 population, that form a cluster that certainly has a 'southwest–northeast' axis (assuming north at the top) though the parallel progression of population and diversity of commercial activities is not uniform. It is true that this conclusion is appreciably modified if we omit the mining towns, the poverty of which in the tertiary sector is well known, and which is occasionally also found in more important towns such as Liévin and Bruay. In the case of the small sample of towns with more than 18,000 population, the correlation is close for the non-specialised examples. But while up to about 15–18,000, the multiplication of types of shop is rapid (from an average of 20 to over 70, or a coefficient of 3.5 for a trebling of population), beyond 20,000 the coefficient falls to 1.5 and stays at that level. There is thus a kind of threshold of general urban 'equipment' that includes about 75 categories for towns of up to 20,000 inhabitants. A study of more examples might very well yield others.

The tourist centres (Nice, Vichy) show positive anomalies that are contrary to those of the mining centres. It would be necessary to pursue the whole investigation much further to demonstrate other facts that we can here only hint at – country-towns are relatively favoured, and isolated towns more so than those that lie close to a higher-order centre; but there could also be regional affinities as well as the functional ones that we have already noted. Lastly, the standard of living also plays a part.

This characteristic of the number of categories also throws into relief another variable, whatever the size of the town: this is the spending capacity of the population, which reflects their standard of living. Table 13 expresses as an index the living standards of the urban population, depending on a number of socio-economic characteristics (the 'Proscop' index).

Table 13

Town	Population	Living-standard index	Number of shop types
Cannes	74,000	2.10	142
Calais	77,400	0.87	118
Poitiers	75,400	1.21	121
Vichy	35,200	1.71	128
Liévin	36,300	0.43	61
Agen	37,500	1.37	127
Megève	5,500	2.11	55
Donges	6,500	0.86	26
St. Flour	6,200	1.11	55

To avoid the influence of size that affects, more or less directly, all the preceding data, we have calculated an index of the relationship between the total retail turnover and the 1968 population (index 1); the retail turnover and the number of shops (index 2); and the surface-area of non-food shops in relation to the population (index 3). The resulting classification yields some surprises. A simple tabulation of the 10 towns having the highest indices is symptomatic (Table 14).

Table 14. Ranking of top 10 towns

Index 1	Index 2	Index 3
Niort	Châlons-s-Marne	Vichy
Châlons-s-Marne	Besançon	Nevers
Vichy	Thionville	St. Quentin
Annecy	Chartres	Chartres
Besançon	Strasbourg	Forbach
Charleville	Niort	Albi
Belfort	Poitiers	Belfort
Chalon-s-Saône	Annecy	Metz
Strasbourg	Colmar	Béziers
Cannes	Mulhouse	Mulhouse

In respect of the first index, Marseille occupies 17th place. Bordeaux is 30th, Lyon 32nd, Nice 65th, Lille 71st (but note that Nevers is 11th). In the list for the second index, Marseille is 16th, Lyon 21st, Bordeaux 23rd, Nice 31st and Lille 51st. At the other end of the first group, there are 9 industrial or mining towns in the bottom 10: Armentières, the least favoured, has an index 3.7 times lower than the top town, Niort. The correlation between index 1 and index 2 is 0.7 and thus not negligible. In the three complete lists, many of the rankings are similar or nearly so, but others show discrepancies. Vichy is by far the best example: well up the list in respect of the relation between retail turnover and population, and between shopping surface-area and population, it is in 79th place for turnover related to surface area; this is typical of a town with an important seasonal population; we find something similar at Cannes, which is in 10th place according to index 1 and 64th in index 2, and also, though less marked, at Nice (respectively 27th and 60th places), where there is a more stable permanent population.

These different approaches show that it is not an easy matter to analyse the commercial strength of a town, which is not only a direct function of the number of permanent consumers but also of their wealth, together with the influx of seasonal customers. It is this last which causes the greatest disparities. But we must also take account of service centres that attract a far greater custom than that of the immediate urban area.

All these considerations may seem very theoretical, but there are also practical conclusions to be drawn: Vichy appears to be a town with a commercial life that is somewhat precarious, and this is confirmed on the ground; the industrial towns, and particularly those dependent on one not very prosperous industry such as textiles or mining, provide examples of obvious under-equipment but also low purchasing power – and this too can be seen in the towns concerned. Conversely, isolated towns, in the centre of prosperous agricultural regions, are relatively well provided.

The socialist countries

While in capitalist countries the hierarchy of commercial centres is based on the competitive development of shopping facilities, and carries the weight of a complex economic history that is not, however, strong enough to disrupt the organisation of the system, in socialist countries the new concepts of economic structure have had upsetting repercussions. It is in the first place clear that studies of the structure and apparatus of commerce appear but rarely in Soviet geography; they figure only among the elements of economic regions in which it is stated that commerce must theoretically lead to the equilibrium of production and consumption (Pokshishevsky, 1974), and it is not in general distinguished from services in the wider sense (Berezowski, 1967).

The authorities have attempted to harmonise systematically, and by a whole range of new establishments, all the services, including commerce, that are necessary to optimise the collection of produce and the distribution of goods in response to the needs of the population, or at least as far as what is available can meet these needs. 'The greater the importance of an urban agglomeration, the larger the range of services it offers to its inhabitants – and that for an area much larger than its own extent. The functional intersubordination in terms of services is based on the fact that higher-order centres, besides their own special functions, have all those possessed by lower-order centres' (Knobelsdorf, 1966). The aim is to achieve the best result with the minimum effort, and this involves service at three levels: as complete a service as possible for 'daily' purchases in the rural areas; service for 'periodic' purchases in sub-regional centres (of 5,000 to 50,000 inhabitants) that can be reached in 20 to 30 minutes and include one department store in the shopping nucleus; and specialty shops in the medium and large cities (of 50,000 to 250,000 population) situated at no more than 1 to 1½ hours' journey time from within their service area and comprising a complex range of facilities including centres of inter-regional trade. Such is the planned scheme: an examination of actual conditions in various regions shows that the weight of historic heritage is appreciable, especially in eastern Europe and European Russia, and that the ideal service in relation to the planned populations is far from being achieved. However, the present developments, or the correctives applied to previous development, are in accordance with the principles (Davidovich, 1960, 1966) and, given the absence of competition and the paucity of individual means of transport, closely reflect the gravity model.

The hierarchy in the USSR is a simple system of five classes: centres of major economic regions, capitals of the federal or autonomous republics, centres of intra-regional or intra-republican regions, centres of lower-order administrative areas, and centres of minor agricultural, forest or mining regions that have not as yet any localities ranking as towns (Knobelsdorf, 1966). That it is not independent of the central-place hierarchy is by the will of the planners. We may consider the organisation of commerce rather like the administrative organisation of western countries: it must offer everyone a minimum of service that we should call 'public'. The few private shops – where they continue to be tolerated as in Hungary and Poland – bring a touch of fantasy to certain large cities, where they are mostly run by foreigners or by privileged members of the local community. But this abnormal element is not sufficient to introduce much differentiation.

The developing countries

While the developed countries of the western world are characterised by a hierarchial continuum of incomes, needs and resultant commercial 'equipment', and the socialist countries are trying to establish equality of satisfaction within an egalitarian regime by the gradual superimposition of a rationally distributed system of trading facilities, in the developing countries there is the maximum amount of contrast. The disparity between the extremes of income is catastrophic, and a 'middle class' scarcely exists or is developing but slowly; even the modes of life are strongly contrasted: while a small part of the population may travel, study abroad and adopt western clothes, food and customs, the vast majority continue in their traditional ways with only odd scraps of 'development' here and there. This division of society is reflected in, and in part provoked by, a marked opposition between the types of commercial structure, from self-subsistence or the native markets to the undertakings of great international organisations that are often not even physically within the framework provided by the local towns: thus the activities of the United Fruit Company, in Central America, transcend the local environment and even international frontiers. But many of these large commercial organisations do leave their mark on the towns of the country where they operate; moreover, a rich and westernised population also lives in these same towns. Thus populous metropolitan centres come into being, whose character differs profoundly from that of the countryside. In nine cases out of ten, such towns have been created, or at least re-created, by the colonial powers. They are therefore not centres sprung from the rural surroundings but staging-posts between two worlds, the colonised and the exploiters. One only needs to look at a map of Latin America, Africa or Southern Asia to be convinced of this.

In all cases where (unlike Egypt and India, for example) an already urbanised civilisation did not exist, or where the post-colonial transformations are still in a rudimentary stage – and that means in fact very many cases – the development of towns results in the phenomenon of 'macrocephalism' that Santos (1971) has so well described. 'Lima controls 75 per cent of Peru's internal trade, San Salvador (in the Central American republic of that name) scoops 77.4 per cent of the trading profits, Casablanca does three-quarters of Morocco's external trade' (p. 179). But outside these swollen giants, where national and international businesses have their offices, warehouses and branches, and where the demands of the population create a flourishing trade in imported goods, what is there? The hierarchical chain is often reduced to a single link. A hierarchy does not in fact exist; either the secondary local centres depend directly and completely upon the national centre, or they depend in some small measure on some poorly equipped regional centre.

However, these are the extreme cases, and not all developing countries have so disjointed a commercial structure. A recent and elaborate work on the Mitidja region of Algeria portrays a situation – transitional perhaps – that is half way towards the developed world (Mutin, 1974). The author made exhaustive enquiries in 23 communes, that in 1966 had 443,751 inhabitants and 6,530 employees in the commercial sector. He uses several criteria in his formulation of a hierarchy. First the total number of shops (group 1); then this figure in proportion to the population (group 2); and finally Christaller's 'centrality index' (group 3) in the form

$$C_t = T_z - (E_z \times \frac{T_g}{E_g}$$

where T_z is the number of shops in centre Z,
T_g the number of shops in the whole region
E_g the number of inhabitants in the region
E_z the number of inhabitants in centre Z.

The second and third criteria allow a five-fold classification: 2 centres well-equipped with shopping facilities, 4 slightly less well equipped, 4 average, 10 moderate, and 3 almost nil. The 10 centres of the fourth level are situated on the edge of group-1 centres to which they are subordinate. Over this assembly, and especially its eastern part, hangs the shadow of Algiers.

We thus have a hierarchy of six groups, including the capital city. But while Blida, the highest-ranking town in the region, is clearly not to be classed on a national scale with major regional centres like Oran and Anneba (its development having been hindered by the proximity of Algiers), we get the impression here of an Algerian hierarchy very similar to those of the industrialised countries but on a much lower level. In the Mitidja there is only one shop to every 65 inhabitants (in France 1 to 47), but the shops are mostly very small (having an annual turnover of less than 36,000 Algerian dinars, or only 400 French francs); in Blida, 45 per cent are of this type, with 64 per cent in a local 'class 4' centre. There may indeed be a hierarchy of shopping facilities, but it must cater for needs that are fewer in number and inferior in quality compared with those of a clientele with higher living standards. In terms of types of commercial activity the level is also displaced downwards. This has also been examined in detail by Mutin, who distinguished nine types of business (food, clothing, domestic furniture, transport, local building, hotels and restaurants, leisure and sports goods, household goods and personal service). Plotting these on a triangular graph yielded the following tabulation (all figures are percentages):

	General average	Group 1	Group 2	Group 3
Food	36.7	<40	40–50	50
Clothing and furniture	22.2	20–30	<20	nil
Other types	41.1	40–50	30 max.	30–50

There is not an absolute correspondence between the two typologies but the final balance gives a classification with eight major urban centres on three levels (with Blida set apart) followed by seven other centres exercising some influence over neighbouring communes, the three highest-ranking of these being better equipped and having a wider sphere of influence (a conclusion confirmed by a study of wholesalers and of markets). Below these three levels, there are the local shops almost entirely concerned with foodstuffs, and the communes that have no shops at all.

This parallel progression in the number of consumers and in the number and specialism of shopping facilities is thus a general rule that applies whenever the structure of the urban mesh, the transport network and the level of resources permit. In the case of Algeria, it is part of the colonial heritage, but in the development programmes of Third World countries it is also an objective to be attained, in the shape of a spontaneous hierarchy, a little ambitious perhaps, recalling that of the socialist countries. Thus Cameroun, in its third plan, offers a very precise version (Morinière, 1975). Over the country as a whole, there is a seven-fold classification of commercial centres, from the rural hamlet to the two national capitals (Yaoundé, the administrative and intellectual capital, and Douala, the commercial capital), through villages, small towns, secondary towns, regional towns and regional capitals. The major villages will have between 500 and 1,500 inhabitants, and their sphere of influence will include 5 to 15,000 people within a radius of 10 to 20 km; the cattle trade and the market retain an important place. The small town is already the headquarters of a district or sub-prefecture; with its 3 to 7,000 inhabitants, and a tributary population of between 40 and 80,000, it is a more diversified commercial centre. The secondary town is an administrative centre of more obvious urban character, with a population of 10–20,000, and serving some 150–200,000; it has a small wholesaling function. There are seven regional towns (such as Maroua and Edea) whose influence extends beyond the department of which they are the centres. Above this level are four regional capitals, including Bafoussam and Garoua, and then the two national capitals. Of course it must be emphasised that at the moment this is merely a plan, a systemisation of what actually exists; nevertheless, the existing urban structure of Cameroun offers a starting base that is not present in all the countries of black Africa.

An undoubted hierarchy

The conclusion clearly indicated by the study of all these examples is this: that the 'equipment' of commerce is distributed in certain functional gradations that correspond to an equally hierarchical spatial distribution based on distances apart and areas served. This is the case in the most highly developed countries, while in the others there is a tendency to copy the model closely, either by strict planning as in the socialist countries, or through normal economic evolution.

But these assertions must not lead us into an improper schematisation of reality. Though it is easy enough to invent a classification for a certain number of important centres, they will differ in detail; and again, the pyramidal structure of inter-relations must always be considered in relation to the country or even region to which it relates, and we must not make invalid comparison of classifications between one country and another, as has often been done. Lastly, the hierarchy of shopping centres does not always correspond to the frequency of customer visits, and the study of market areas or spheres of influence may provide important correctives.

Notes

1. A recent (1970) investigation in France by the Ministry of Agriculture furnished some fascinating data – but except in the Burgundy region the only question asked was 'How far do you go to purchase. . .', and *not* 'Where do you go?'
2. 'Theoretical' sales are calculated by multiplying the local authority population by the average regional turnover per head. 'The difference between the actual turnover in a local authority area and the estimated "theoretical" turnover gives us an estimate of the net trade gained from beyond the administrative boundary, or the net loss of trade across it' (Carruthers, 1967, p. 67).

Chapter 3

Market areas

Research on market areas

Ways and means

While the strength and the quality of the shopping facilities in the business centre are linked to the population of the town in question, as we have just seen, they are also related to the population actually served (cf. p. 116). Some authors have preferred to study the level of equipment; others have concentrated on market areas and have drawn conclusions from this on the strength of the centres. In France, the most famous example – and the only one that gives broadly comparable data covering the whole country – is that of Piatier, (1965–), published by regions and completed or interpreted in many different ways.

We may recall the basic hypotheses. Every commercial centre with facilities superior to that of its neighbours may hope to attract custom from outside; it serves a population greater than that which resides in the town in which it is situated. How can we evaluate the number of people attracted and the area and distance from which they come? On these two questions hang several others: what sort of purchases (and in what kind of shops) are made by the locals and by the outsiders? Why do the visitors come – or not come – to the centre in question? How frequently and how regularly do they come? And so on. The problem is thus a major one in understanding the mechanism of the setting up and development of shops, and so is important in town planning.

There are three approaches to the study of the attractive power of a shopping centre. The first is theoretical, and rests on the use of a gravity model; the second is based on a theoretical formula applied to hypothetical data; the third uses on-the-spot investigation and attempts to draw general conclusions from a series of well-chosen samples.

It must be emphasised that official statistics on the subject are almost completely lacking: there are no censuses, and no annual publications give usable data. If one objects to calculations that are seductive by their logic but have little practical significance, there is no other course but to question consumers or shopkeepers, with all that this entails in terms of labour and the possibility of distorted results. However, confidence may return if one is prepared to make reasonable generalisations, for quite often the statistical procedures and the detailed enquiries seem to lead to the same comforting conclusions.

Following the work of Reilly (1931), and later Stewart (1948) and Zipf (1949), many authors have adopted or have attempted to adapt the *gravity model* which rests on two hypotheses: the interaction between two towns A and B varies directly with some function of their population size, and inversely with some function of the distance between them. If P_A is the population of A and P_B that of B, and d the distance AB, then

Attraction AB $= P_A \, P_B d \, \overset{-x}{_{AB}}$

But now the difficulties begin. Critics have questioned the value to be given to the exponent x of distance d; should it be the first power, the square or some other power? (Isard, 1967); (Reilly himself, in his pioneer study of 255 cases, obtained distance exponents ranging from 0 to 12.5); should the distance be measured in a straight line or over the actual route, and should the time, cost and availability of transport be considered? One might also consider the value of the exponent as a function of these different considerations and even in relation to the spatial environment in which the towns are placed (such as the density of housing and of population). It has even been proposed to give the distance exponent not a fixed value but the form of a binomial function of distance, in order to take account of the stochastic interaction of towns (Andan, Beaujeu-Garnier and Libault, 1975). But what then is the significance of d? It is no longer a distance but something else. Similarly, when it comes to assessing the attractive force in terms of commercial relations, the population seems of little significance (though as we have already noted, in western countries at least there is a parallelism with the importance of trading activities), and one might also use the sales area of shops, their turnover, or the numbers employed.

The model has, however, been used with some degree of success. In his study of spatial organisation in Morocco, Beghin (1974) considered the urban population and the distance to be related by an exponent of 2.5, and he claims a fair agreement between the results thus obtained and those from direct enquiries. Another noteworthy study, although not strictly concerned with commercial attraction, is that of Sporck (1966) on Belgian towns; this, like the Piatier questionnaire, took into account the whole of the tertiary sector. In this paper Sporck traces the actual zones of urban attraction and the geometric polygons obtained from Reilly's law, applied according to a formula that gives a point C marking the dividing line between towns A and B:

$$\text{Position of C with regard to A} = \frac{\text{distance AB}}{1 + \sqrt{\dfrac{\text{pop. A}}{\text{pop. B}}}}$$

For the major centres, the Belgian team took the square of the distance and the population, and for the minor centres, the population divided by 2. The resulting maps are very expressive and the agreement often quite striking; the major discrepancies can easily be explained by elements of a physical nature, the disturbing influence of frontiers or the existence of main routeways that increase accessibility, especially in the south, towards the national capital.

Berry (1967), using the same formula, but representing the strength of towns by the number of shop types, also claims that it works, and one could multiply the examples. Indeed this model has been used by most of the market studies in the United States, and by marketing consultants during the last 30 years or so – and they have not apparently deceived the investors! However, many theoreticians criticise the empirical approximation of this approach and it is evident that it does not entirely satisfy the more exacting research workers.

We accept, therefore, that it has some practical value. The two dimensions involved are important and exert an influence in the sense indicated, but much latitude is possible in their mode of expression and in the weight to be given to them. Distances affected by different exponents retain the same dimensional relativity; and as for the different characteristics of strength, we have already noted that they are closely inter-related. It is sufficient to make the best choice possible, and it is by no means certain that only a single possibility is involved. The formula is sufficiently simple and general to give satisfactory approximations without extended preliminary investigations, and it is easy to explain any deviations.

A second approach is the *calculation of indices* by comparing actual sales totals with theoretical sales (cf. p. 137) – as Carruthers (1967) did, for example. The relevant administrative area may be compared with the urban centre in question, as in the following formula:

$$P_d = P_c \frac{V_r}{V_t}$$

if $\frac{V_r}{V_t} > 1$, the town serves a population P_d larger than its residential population P_r

V_r = real sales volume, V_t theoretical sales volume.

This calculation can be performed for a single shop, for a good, for a group of shops in an urban quarter, or for an entire town. But this hypothetical calculation has two serious disadvantages: it gives an order of magnitude to the clientele for a given district, but does not enable the limits of the area served to be determined, nor the rate at which the attractive power declines; secondly, it requires very precise financial data that are rarely available. Even though turnover figures for a single shop or for a shopping district may be obtained, however (as from the British census of distribution – cf. p. 123), there are no data on theoretical expenses, except in such countries as the United States where values are given for the Standard Metropolitan Statistical Areas and for counties. But in Brazil, for example, the data for towns sometimes lack any solid basis. To have resort to the sum total of expenditure in the commercial sector for a region, to extract from this the individual expenditure, then multiply by the population of the administrative division under consideration, seems a very discouraging sequence of approximations, the hazardous character of which is obvious to all.

Some results, however, have been obtained, and among the most interesting are those published by Waide (1963), who calculated for East Anglian towns the population served in excess of the town population by using the average regional sales per head for each of four commodity groups and total sales. Among the third-order centres (of the Carruthers classification) the population served by each town in excess of the town's population was generally greatest for furniture sales, followed by clothing, total sales, hardware and electrical goods, and foodstuffs. This is a hierarchy resembling the town-types and commodities that Berry, for example, found in Iowa where female clothing followed by male clothing characterised towns of this order.

Different combinations of data are used to compare real and theoretical sales and so to lead to ideas about the attractive power of towns and hence their market areas. Sales figures being lacking, Reynolds (1963) proposed the use of rateable values for shops, and Siddall (1961) the relation between the numbers employed in wholesaling and those in retailing. If this greatly exceeds the national average, it is proof of the city's influence beyond its own boundaries – a credible enough assertion but clearly very imprecise; it would be better to take the national wholesale/retail index for the urban population only, but even so, exceptional concentrations of wholesaling (as in ports) or of retailing (in tourist towns) would introduce distortions.

Some of these calculations – which in principle always give results that are likely to bear some relation to the truth – show how careful we must be. Thus a firm of planning consultants, on the basis of calculations of theoretical sales, tried to estimate the minimum clientele necessary for the establishment of chain-store branches in a proposed new town in mid-Wales. Their figures were 375,000 for a tailoring firm and 150,000 to 200,000 for two footwear chains. Yet shops belonging to these three chains actually existed in a small town in southeast England with a population of only 15,000 and a theoretical shopping population of about 25,000! (Scott, 1970, pp. 157–8).

We are driven once again to the same conclusion – that models, and theoretical calculations sufficiently soundly based to give a 'silhouette' of the real thing and to permit quantitative approximations, are useful in most cases, and certainly to get the general measure of a phenomenon, but are open to criticism if one examines the basis of the criteria utilised or goes into too much detail. For example: we may use one of these methods to calculate the potential clientele of a supermarket (and there are many successful examples of this) – but we may fall into error if we wish to create a new communication link demanding a certain level of passenger traffic between two adjacent towns in a densely urbanised region.

The only certain way of locating these phenomena, and by combining them with certain methods of measurement that we have already mentioned, determining more precisely their value, is the long and expensive one of direct enquiry. But this is not easy. Even if it is not difficult to make a complete census of the shops in a small centre, or perhaps, given sufficient help, in a large town; and even if it is easy, from a good directory, to cover all the establishments in a town or a region, the conduct of a frequentation survey is quite another matter. Whether the enquiries are made in the shops or at the customers' homes, such a technique is very hazardous. All the preferences, and prejudices of customers that we have noted above (p. 116) render extremely difficult the obtaining of a credible sample. However, we can get more valuable data by this method, if it is well executed, than by any other; besides, numerous researchers have used the method more or less systematically, often supporting it by studies of the shopping facilities in the towns considered. It is these twin approaches that yield the richest harvest of material, that accords most favourably with the general method.

Some examples of direct enquiries in the USA and Britain

Studies of the spheres of influence of towns of different importance are numerous, both within countries and within regions, and they shed much light on commercial activities, for they are often concerned with the range of 'services', among which shopping facilities are carefully distinguished. Examples of more precise and detailed studies, however, yielding more than vague generalisations that are sometimes difficult to reconcile, are usually on a smaller scale.

The first example we may quote is the work of Brush and Gauthier (1968), for this treats three types of problem from a conceptual viewpoint: does there exist a regular arrangement in the localisation of commercial centres, and in the disposition of market areas, on the fringes of a great city? The areas concerned lie on the outskirts of Philadelphia. The authors study in turn the origin and development of the various centres from the nineteenth century to the present day, then the actual shopping facilities in quantity, in quality and in their functional arrangement in relation to residential areas and communications, and finally the movement of customers with reference to the private motor car, to food purchases, and to other types of shopping expeditions and their combination.

We may select certain of the conclusions arising from this work. The phenomenon of centrality is confirmed: there is a hierarchy of centres at three levels of 'equipment' (levels, 1, 2 and 3), and a parallel hierarchy of market areas for the first two levels. The most important centre has a sphere of influence extending outwards for 11 to 15 km, with an exclusive zone of 5 km radius. Of all the journeys motivated by the existence of the centre's services, food and other purchases represent between one-half and two-thirds of the total. For food purchases, it is usually the nearest shop that is visited – within a radius of 1,500 to 5,000 m – and this rule is almost universal for the isolated shopping centres on the outer edge of the urban area, though there is more flexibility as one approaches the better-equipped suburbs. Here there are confusing trends that reflect the heritage of a tradition that is in course of transformation.

The already-quoted work of Berry (especially 1967) also takes up the question of the historic evolution of the centres in southwestern Iowa in order to show 'that, at any point in time, the geographic distribution of retail and service business in central places approximates an equilibrium adjustment to the geographic distribution of customers' (p. 4). Included in this work are the results, largely in cartographic form, of two enquiries into consumer behaviour made in 1934 and 1960 among the urban-dwellers on the one hand and the farming community on the other, in relation to the services provided by churches, lawyers, physicians, dry-cleaners, and clothing, furniture and food shops. Berry comes to the categorical conclusion that there is a *central-place system,* and he establishes a hierarchy based on function, shopping facilities and market areas within a single region. Unless industry or other activities create distortions, two classifications are possible. The first concerns the level of goods and services in relation to the size of the market catchment, which is a function of area and the density and wealth of the population living therein. The number of centres with a certain type of shop diminishes, and the size of the market area increases as the consumption of the product in question becomes smaller, either because of its price or because it is not needed so frequently: thus there are no men's clothing shops or dry-cleaners in the villages (which generally have populations of under 1,000). The second classification concerns the proportion of purchases made, by farmers and town-dwellers, according to commodity, in the regional centre, the secondary and the local centre; it appears that for the same type of purchase, the rural dwellers are more tempted towards the major centres than the inhabitants of the medium-sized centres. This is logical enough, but is clearly of interest to planners in the calculation of potential clientele.

Table 15. Percentage of purchases by citizens of Anita (C) and farmers (F) within Anita's maximum trade area

	At Anita*		At Atlantic†		At Omaha‡	
	C	F	C	F	C	F
Men's work clothes	78	47	11	51	0	0
Men's suit	47	31	34	49	13	16
Teenage girl's clothes	0	17	40	83	0	0
Women's coat	3	2	72	74	19	22
Groceries	100	80	0	20	0	0
Furniture	83	50	8	37	6	9

* Anita – small town
† Atlantic – county town
‡ Omaha – regional capital
NB. The figures relate to the *last* purchase made in the category named. The percentages do not add up to 100 because of the interference of other centres, as mentioned above.

Source: compiled from tables on pp. 24–5 of Berry (1967).

From the moment when it becomes necessary to make a journey for shopping, one might as well choose the best locality, even if it is further away. This is equally true for a small town like Anita and a large town like Atlantic. The longest journeys are usually made for expensive durable goods such as furniture, or articles in which fashion plays a part, such as women's clothing.

All these matters must be considered when trying to formulate rules for the extent and transformation of market areas. We may add one final example, this time from County Durham in northeast England (Thorpe and Nader, 1967). Having classified the centres by a combination of criteria into five levels, from regional to local, the authors have compared the types of purchases and the market areas of each centre. Thus the regional level (R) shows the highest proportion of purchases of furniture, footwear, clothing and jewellery; its maximum attraction is exerted within a radius of about 8 km, declining rapidly beyond, to cease almost completely at about 22 km. The A-centres, next in the hierarchy, dominate within a radius of 5 km, especially for food purchases, then the proportion of food purchases declines to about 7 km, and the overall influence extends no further than 10 km (covering an area with 30–40,000 population). And so on. This study is very precise in its details, and apart from showing the way in which market attraction declines regularly away from the centre, underlines once more the relation between facilities and population and market areas that was pointed out by Isard a decade earlier (Isard, 1956, p. 207): 'location cannot be explained without at the same time accounting for trade, and trade cannot be explained without the simultaneous determination of locations.'

French research on market areas

Towns and regions

It is not surprising that the market areas of towns should have attracted the attention of numerous French geographers. This is after all a concrete phenomenon, capable of investigation by direct enquiry, showing the interaction of geographical facts within the framework of the town and its region, and apt for the cartographic illustration of spatial distributions. The movement owes much to the publications of Chabot (1948) and George (1952), in which the notions of an urban system and of spheres of influence, particularly relating to trade, are defined. Chabot (1962) also made the first map of the spheres of influence of French towns (with a population of over 50,000 in 1954), including trade among his three criteria.

Among the many theses devoted to French regions, we only mention two that make a major contribution to our subject. Rochefort (1960), after a series of detailed enquiries in Alsace into the market areas of different types of commercial equipment – shops and services – arrived at a sixfold classification of centres: regional centres, sub-regional centres, industrial towns, market towns, small towns and 'satellite' towns. Within these towns, he examined the shops and their spheres of influence. The physical environment, administrative boundaries and the historical background have created two systems, one based on Strasbourg and the Rhine, and the other on Colmar and the vine-growing area. In response to the question as to whether the localisation and arrangement of the centres corresponds to the Christaller theory, Rochefort says 'I think that the historical factors in the Strasbourg region, are more important to an understanding of present distributions than any geometrical concept' (p. 127). He sometimes recognises geometrical shapes that are more or less hexagonal, but he regards them of little importance. The whole thesis places the emphasis on historic development and on the minute description of actual centres according to a typology that brings together 'functions, population structure and the characteristics of internal organisation' (p. 297).

Dugrand's work (1963) relates to Bas Languedoc. This is a more or less ideal region in which to examine the relations between town and country, for the urban network offers a complete range, while lacking the distorting influences of a super-metropolis or large industries, and exchanges between the urban and rural environments are particularly well developed. The author has also produced a remarkable regional atlas (1969), that complements the thesis in establishing the characteristics of the urban system and the hierarchy of commercial structures.

The work presents a series of analyses and examples that admirably illustrate the wholesale circuits, the influence of middlemen, the function of markets as centres of attraction and distribution, the changing complexity of collection as well as the overlapping areas of consumer attraction, the role of capital – and of psychology. There are maps illustrating all these aspects: market areas are carefully defined in accordance with the nature of their trade, and the type of purchases. The author distinguishes four grades of centre, based on the following types of data: 'the attraction of the weekly market, shops selling common and luxury goods, customer range of retail shops, and redistribution range of wholesalers of food and non-food goods – from which the function of each centre is revealed by the size of its sphere of influence.' By combining these criteria, the centres are classified as follows: 4 regional centres (class 1); 14 major sub-regional centres (2a) and 8 minor ones (2b); 12 major local centres (3a) and 20 minor ones (3b); and finally the rudimentary centres. As a result of the nature of the relief and of the linear arrangement of communications and of the urban network, there is no regional metropolitan centre. For each regional centre, the concentric zones of influence are clearly defined: (i) a narrow inner zone in which the housewives themselves do their shopping in the urban markets; (ii) a zone within which purchases of ordinary goods are still made in the centre; (iii) a zone dominated by sales of less common goods and in part by wholesaling; (iv) beyond 40 km from the centre, where wholesale redistribution and the sale of specialty goods fade out progressively. The spheres of influence overlap at their margins and sometimes enclose or border those of lower-order centres. The patchwork is by no means simple, and the idea of a 'nesting' of market areas, corresponding to the hierarchical pyramid of the theorists, just falls to the ground.

The Piatier enquiry

In arriving at his classification of central places, Dugrand first used a modified version of the questionnaire that Piatier has been employing over the whole of France. A complete *Atlas d'attraction urbaine* ('Atlas of urban attraction') is in course of publication (Piatier, 1965–); the principles and methods have been described in numerous papers (especially 1970). The questionnaire relates to the behaviour of the inhabitants of rural communes (of up to 5,000 population in the northern industrial region); it has been addressed to someone who knows the commune intimately, generally the mayor's secretary or the head teacher; it enquires about the 'equipment' of the commune and especially about the purchasing habits (including frequency of shopping) of the inhabitants, and the marketing of agricultural products. Some final questions relate to the shopping centres most often visited, the centres used for high-order goods, and what the inhabitants regard as their local 'big city'. The examination of trading relations enables purchases to be divided into foodstuffs, and certain other goods such as men's and women's ready-made clothing, household electrical goods, furniture, and so on. In addition, maps were drawn, classifying the centres according to their attractive capacity, in terms of the number of communes served and also the areas within which certain proportions of the total population were effectively served (over 40 per cent, and 10–40 per cent). Despite certain deficiencies in the data, this investigation has no equal for homogeneity, detail and the extent of its coverage.

Some results culled from the Piatier enquiry by Bruyelle (1970) with regard to the northern industrial region are worth noting, for they go beyond the simple, commonplace and inevitable hierarchical classification. While the correlation between the size of the central place and the total population served is high, at 0.881, there are some striking anomalies. For the centres with more than 30,000 population, it is more or less regular, but below this threshold, the slope of the graph is much steeper, and there is a wider dispersion of points, indicating that many towns do not have market areas commensurate with their size (e.g. industrial towns with a stunted tertiary sector). The power of attraction calculated by the formula

$$\frac{\text{Clientele from outside the urban area}}{\text{Population of the town}}$$

shows that there is no correspondence between the size of the town and its relative attractive power. This was indeed a general conclusion arrived at from the national enquiry (Piatier, vol. 19, p. 117): 'The part played by the sector of the market clientele outside the town is more important in the small centres, whose urban population is not sufficient to ensure the full use of the shopping facilities.'

The complexity of the classification – which could be still further elaborated – may be summarised thus: A, regional metropolis; B, major regional centres; C, minor regional centres; D, secondary centres; E, local centres; F, rudimentary centres (and each of these has two or four sub-types). It results from the varied origins of the vigorous urban life, revivified by the industrial revolution and supported by a dense and always prolific population. Though elevation and relief, except in the Boulonnais and the higher parts of Artois, play an insignificant role, the coastline and the presence of large forests exercise some influence. The distribution of centres closely follows the general density of population, which itself is determined by the existence of the coalfield, the Lille conurbation and major lines of communication. The only sectors in which there is any kind of sub-geometrical distribution of centres are the rich rural zones in the northwest and south of the region (Fig. 7).

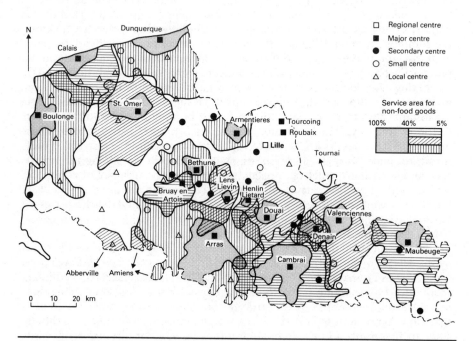

Fig. 7   The hierarchy of central places and urban service areas in the French regions of Nord and Pas-de-Calais. (Source: Bruyelle, 1979.)

A more detailed comparative examination of the different centres shows, however, that only three levels are in fact well defined: the metropolitan centre (Lille) whose influence extends over the whole axial belt of the region, the major peripheral centres whose spheres of influence are well marked, and the micro-centres at various levels that serve the areas immediately around them. The refinement of the hierarchical classification only corresponds to differences in population and not to the nature of the available services. This situation is perhaps peculiar to the northern region where, except in Artois, the commercial equipment is well developed and in great variety: one can even buy motor cars, furniture, electrical goods and female clothing in some small centres (D and even E in the hierarchy) situated in between the market areas of more important centres.

These observations, and many others based on an examination of the numerous publications of the *Atlas d'attraction urbaine* or of the maps in regional atlases that have used the same methods of enquiry, enable us to conclude that the findings of research workers in other countries, and especially in the United States, are quite inapplicable to the French situation, or indeed to other European environments in which a much longer historical development, and a much more varied economic development, combined with much greater population densities in the inter-urban zones, are responsible for a very different localisation and functioning of commercial centres.

Fairs and markets: a particular example of hierarchy

Importance in trade and in social life

In the developing countries, the markets, swarming with people, noisy, smelly and colourful, are one of the most active expressions of commercial life, and sometimes the only one. In the socialist countries, they allow the peasants of the Soviet *kolkhozy* to sell the produce of their own little patch, even if it is only a handful of tomatoes or a few eggs; and they are flourishing in China. Even in the developed countries, they play an appreciable role, and the inhabitants of new urban quarters often clamour for one to be opened. Contrary to some assertions (Harvey, Hocking and Brown, 1974), they are not simply an attribute of the non-western world, though clearly they are much better developed there. Rolph (1932) records that in 1929 the 11 public markets in Baltimore accounted for 11 per cent of the city's retail outlets and 4 per cent of retail sales, chiefly of food. But in Sweden they only represented 0.29 per cent of the turnover in 1975 (Nordin, 1975). They still exist in the United Kingdom, and in most European countries, particularly in France where the weekly 'market day' brings animation and congestion.

In England and Wales[1] there are upwards of 650 markets of one sort or another, about 300 held on one day each week, and another 300 that are open on two, three or even six days in the week. Some are cattle markets, but it is rare to find one of these that is not accompanied, usually on another site within the town, by stalls – in the open air or in a market hall – for the sale of foodstuffs (especially fresh agricultural produce) and a miscellaneous range of other goods such as clothing materials, ceramic ware, and so on. And the vast majority of them, whatever their origin and history, are now simply places in which, because of the relatively low overheads, prices are generally lower than in the permanent shops.

A map of the market towns – which vary in size from large villages to cities like Birmingham and Newcastle – shows clearly that there are two main types: the small traditional market towns of the agricultural lowlands, and here East Anglia is particularly well endowed (see the map in Berry, 1967, p. 113); and the industrial towns of the Midlands and the North, where the existence of a mass of mainly working-class consumers is responsible for the continued prosperity of the markets. It is interesting to note that of 87 towns that have markets open on three or more days in the week, 24 are in the Lancashire–Yorkshire industrial belt. Saturday is by far the most popular day for the market, and no less than 28 per cent of them are open on this day.

Another measure of the present-day significance of markets in Britain may be gained from the 1971 census of distribution. In that year there were 32,000 market traders' stalls and mobile shops operating, although between them they accounted for rather less than 1 per cent of the total retail turnover. Thus despite their local importance, market traders may be regarded as a relatively insignificant fringe of the general retail trade, and as with small shops, their numbers have declined steadily in recent years, with the growth of supermarkets.

There are still nearly 4,000 weekly markets in France, distributed through 2,000 communes and open to the public on a total of more than 200,000 days a year. Some 19.7 per cent of them take place on Saturdays, with 16.8 per cent on Thursdays. The distribution is far from being homogeneous in space and time: thus there are four markets a week at Mazamet, but only one at Albi and Carmaux in the *département* of Tarn; three a week at Gisors, two at Louviers and one at Evreux in the *département* of Eure. But always the relative importance of food sales is noteworthy.

Table 16. Importance of sectors in certain markets*

Commodity group	Courbevoie	Carmaux (market)	Carmaux (ordinary shops)	Louviers
Foodstuffs	57	44	27	61
Clothing	26	50	18	26
Miscellaneous	17	6	55	13

*Percentage of number of market stalls or shops.

These markets provide a necessary stimulus for the revival of local trade, their flexible organisation being readily adaptable to all kinds of constraints; they are held in the open in a central square, in old wooden market halls, or in modern concrete buildings, but whether out of doors or under cover, whether weekly or permanent, they all attract the housewives of France, Italy, Spain, Belgium and other countries.

However, while the almost universal existence of markets is a fact – except in those European countries where their importance has been greatly reduced – their role is very variable. They constitute the main means of exchange in the countryside and even in some towns in Africa, Asia, and Latin America, but elsewhere they are merely relics of the past, auxiliary to trading activities that are largely of external origin, and afford a means of distribution that because of the personal qualities of the sellers, their negligible overheads, and of the way in which they obtain their saleable goods (direct from small farmers and from craftsmen, second-hand articles or old stock), can please a faithful clientele through the cheapness, and perhaps the freshness, of their wares.

While in the western world the market as an economic and social institution is very much on the decline, in the underdeveloped countries it continues to play a vital role. 'The town is permeated by its countryside, and the countryside is supported by the town through the medium of the regional market' (Troin,

1975). 'Systems of rural markets serve as nodal points for the collection and distribution of a large range of goods and services, of both local and external origin' (Good, 1970). Their economic role is well described by these two quotations, which express the bilateral liaison between town and country and further, the evolving relation between the countryside and the outside world. But their importance in the dynamics of development is another aspect: 'They link exchange systems in such a way as to stimulate economic dependence on inter- and intra-regional trading. This, in turn, shifts the socio-economic basis of the community toward constantly expanding production and growth' (Scott, 1972, p. 316). As a medium of exchange, and an agent in economic growth, the market is also an active centre of social life: 'The *suq* is a festival that breaks the isolation of the "douars", the villages and the encampments . . . Relatives and friends are encountered, news is transmitted . . . The *suq* is the standard of time and space for the peasant, defining his place in the system of trade relations' (Troin, 1975).

We may well ask why so vital and important an institution has only recently attracted the attention of geographers.[2] Interest was aroused by a volume by Bohannan and Dalton (1962), and this was followed by a number of books and monographs, some of which were collected in a special issue of *Economic Geography* (1972). The setting up of a special Commission of the International Geographical Union at the Montreal Congress in 1972, concentrated attention afresh on this ancient yet still juvenile phenomenon. One of the most outstanding studies so far is that of the *suqs* of northern Morocco, by Troin (1975). This provides very precise illustrations of the questions of hierarchy and spatial organisation that are the subject of this book. It is difficult and perhaps fruitless to try to compare the incomparable, a survival from the past and a flourishing present-day activity; but a country like France, for so long largely rural, presents a complex picture, varying from region to region, in which, only a few decades ago, some forms of market were very like the most modern of the markets in the underdeveloped countries.

We may glance briefly at some of the latter. What customers want in the market depends on the level of local self-sufficiency. In rural areas where this is high, as in the Ankole region of Uganda, foodstuffs are but little sought (only 2 to 5 per cent of sales): on the contrary, salt represented 10.5 per cent, cattle 15.5, with clothing also important (Good, 1970). In northern Morocco, where the rural areas are 40 per cent self-sufficient, the range of goods is in general more like that found in France, with food and clothing dominant (Troin, 1975). There is also some complementarity between the town markets and the rural *suqs*, as Table 17 shows.

Table 17. Share of certain types of commodity and service in Moroccan trading (per cent)

| | Number of shops (stalls) | | Value of stocks (in *suqs*) |
	In towns†	In *suqs*	
Foodstuffs	36.0	34.6	14.8
Clothing	8.3	16.3	38.1
Raw rural products*	4.4	20.1	40.8
Crafts and services	45.4	20.1	

*Collection and disposal of agricultural products.
†Towns of 2,000 to 50,000 population.

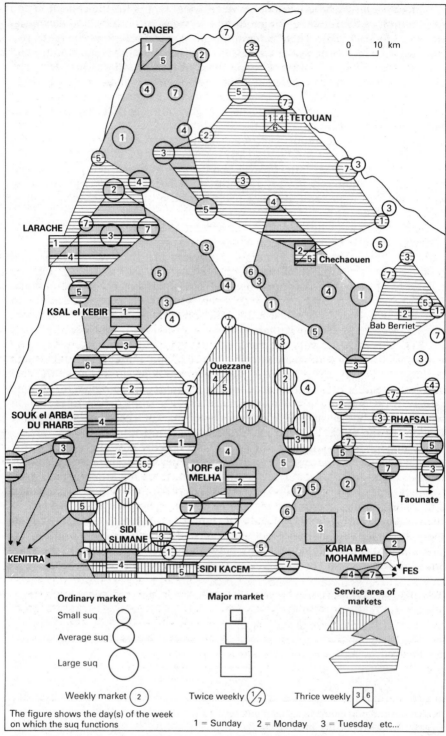

Fig. 8 The *suqs* of northern Morocco; service areas and market days. (Source: Troin, 1975.)

The function of the Moroccan *suq* in the collection of agricultural produce, a function that is to be found in many countries at the same economic level, is one that has obviously disappeared from the markets of developed countries. Furthermore, the proportion of the purchases made by the peasantry is much higher in the food sector than the numbers of market stalls would lead one to suppose: it is about 80 per cent and has shown little change in the last 30 years.

Hierarchy of markets

If the hierarchy of fixed commercial centres is by no means simple to determine, that of markets and fairs – any local non-permanent shopping places in fact – is a brain-racking task.

The most obvious idea is to classify the *suqs* by the number of vendors, but it must be remembered that, especially in those *suqs* where assembly and distribution go on side by side, clients and vendors often change their role during the course of the day, while the number of peasants with things to sell often equals or exceeds the number of genuine tradesmen, and the numbers of vendors varies with the seasons, and with other circumstances such as special events; and further, that there is little in common between the cattle dealers and those who peddle hot water for tea-making. However, overcoming these difficulties, Troin (1975) has proposed a hierarchy based on size and numbers of customers, as shown in Table 18.

Table 18. Size of *suqs* in northern Morocco

	Number of vendors	Number of customers
Very small	<100	<1,000
Small	100–350	1,000–3,500
Medium	350–600	3,500–6,000
Large	600–1,000	6,000–10,000
Very large	1,000–2,000	10,000–20,000

He reckons about 10 customers for one stall, but this is only an average and the variation may be considerable.

Another classification, purely statistical but of importance in the integration of the different forms of trading that contribute to the economic life of a community, arises from the investigation of the relations between the mobile market(s) and the neighbouring townships. In the most elementary cases, the market is the only form of commercial organisation; it appears and multiplies when the population density is sufficient (in the Yoruba district of Nigeria, Hodder and Ukwu (1969) place the lower limit at 20 persons per km²), and generally through some external stimulus (Bohannan and Dalton, 1962); it has a binding effect on the population, well described by Troin (1975): it is above all a catalyst in the formation of a collection of trading activities. The *suq* mushrooms into a rootless village, encysted in the countryside.

A second type may be called the 'town *suq*'. This is an assembly of many more itinerant traders than are to be found in the town to which it is attached. It often occupies a large open square, around which are gathered most of the local traders who also congregate along the adjacent roads. It is in this type of *suq* that the greatest number of peasant-traders is to be found.

The third type, with several variations, comprises the markets of large towns which have a well-developed permanent trading function, in which the *suq* traders figure more or less as supernumeraries. These markets tend to be located outside the town, or in the quarters settled by new arrivals who constitute a clientele of their own; they are specialised, with the specialities often in separate quarters. Thus at Oujda, the food and grain stalls are in the middle, with cattle sales to the north and craft-stalls to the south.

This hierarchy is geographically suggestive since it relates the development and growth stages of the markets to urbanisation and urban growth, but it is difficult to categorise the process because it does not necessarily entail an elaboration of functions. Besides, it frequently happens that an itinerant trader will acquire a local storage space, then a fixed shop, and so gradually cease to be itinerant: this is often the case in West African towns (Hodder and Ukwu, 1969).

The classification that in the end appears to be most useful includes several criteria and rests on the 'balance between collection, consumption and distribution'. This is a compromise between a number of different suggestions (e.g. by Troin, 1975, and McKim, 1972). It involves six types, that are often not very clear-cut.

First and simplest, the *suqs* within regions where self-subsistence is dominant. These are small, and the peasantry buy only a little food from them, plus second-hand clothing and the products of local craftsmen. Little money circulates, for there is little available other than remittances sent from abroad by emigrant members of families.

Next the 'assembly' *suqs*. These dispose of excess agricultural products, which are brought in and collected together by the peasants and then sent out by wholesalers to a single distant market or perhaps to several more local ones. They are often more or less specialised (e.g. in cereals, cattle, ground-nuts). They have almost no retail distribution function, and are located on the cereal-growing plains, at the focus of tracks, or at localities where cattle can be assembled, in the pastoral regions.

Thirdly, the mixed markets; these are both collectors and distributors, at various levels. Some of them, situated at the boundaries of two adjacent agricultural regions (mountain and plain, or in the Andean region, hot, temperate and cool zones) often have relations with both sides; to the exchange of local products is added an external trade, more important in the most accessible places, while part of the produce brought in by the peasants is collected and sent away by wholesalers. In this type, the function is mainly local but there are some external links as well.

The fourth type is made up of markets of the previous type occurring in richer and more developed regions, often closely related to a neighbouring town: these are real relay-stations, as much between the region and the outside world as between different parts of the region. Here, the wholesaling function is more important, and there is a more varied flow of merchandise, part of it serving the local population and part being sent elsewhere. Trading and distribution are diversified and prosperous, and there are wholesaler-distributors as well as wholesaler-collectors. In the markets of Tangiers, Troin (1975) recorded 600 peasants (*fellahs*), 290 rural craftsmen and 420 traders in goods obtained from other towns or imported.

These types lead by transitional stages to the markets of the populous and multi-functional cities. Produce is collected from many sources, and some of it is often destined for export; conversely they are redistribution points for manufactures and imports or for the balancing of inter-regional exchanges. Such markets are often the specialised or eccentrically located rivals of the large local shops, for they act as links with the rural population that feels more at home in them than in the city centre.

All these attempts at establishing a hierarchy, and especially this last one, lead naturally to a consideration of spheres of influence.

Diversity of market areas

The peculiar character of markets makes an appraisal of their spheres of influence difficult. For mobility applies to the market as well as to the clientele, and is almost always closely related to the immediate regional environment. Thus there is not, as with fixed shopping centres, just one area from which customers are attracted and one area for the collection of certain products, but many. We may distinguish the periphery of the area from which the peasants come, either bringing produce or to make purchases, the vastly greater area that supplies produce to the collector-wholesalers, and the area (for which there is no equivalent in the fixed centres) from which the itinerant traders come according to circumstances and the frequency of the market.

Customer patronage and the collection of produce vary in their radius and intensity. The rules are similar to those applicable to fixed centres, but there are differences. In the first place, the flow of customers and produce follow a rhythm (Gould, 1960): the market does not generally function every day of the week; the quantity and the nature of the produce harvested vary with the seasons, and thus there are fluctuations in the flow, in terms of distance, variety, intensity and provenance. The precariousness of the means of transport, and their unequal development (walking and the donkey are found side by side with the bicycle, the small van or even an ancient car or lorry), and the impassable character of some roads in the rainy season, also contribute to the irregularity of customer attendance. Finally, when an accidental shortage of certain products renders supplies difficult to obtain, something like 'market capture' may result: the large cities, better equipped with transport facilities, send out their lorries further and further at the behest of the more powerful merchants, the mobile collectors of produce modify their itineraries, and sometimes these exceptional manoeuvres persist and the traders by-pass their accustomed routes and, with greater flexibility than the fixed businesses, increase and re-orient their own sphere of influence. The absence of investment in fixed premises, and conversely, an organisation geared to total mobility, permit such rapid changes and irregular rhythms. The cost of transport is not considered: the clientele takes precedence.

As for the use made of the markets by the peasantry, the distances involved vary with the facilities provided, the relief of the land, and the possibility of conducting business other than purchasing. On average, the radius is about 2 hours' walking time, but may rise to 8 or 10 hours for special social, economic or administrative reasons. In the Prérif region of Morocco, the average distance is 7.5 km (since 45 per cent of the peasants come on horseback) 10 km in the Rharb plain, and 15 km in the central plateau, with 22 km in the Middle Atlas where the facilities are more sparsely distributed. Over a whole year, the average peasant spends between 48 and 75 days on market expeditions (Troin, 1975). In northern Nigeria, the average distance travelled varies from 5 to 17 km, and in western Nigeria it is about 15 km (Scott, 1972). A theoretical study made with reference to Sierra Leone reckoned the optimum distance at 8 km (Harvey *et al.*, 1974).

For the bulk of the market clientele it is difficult to talk of a hierarchy of shopping visits. According to their needs, the peasants are both customers and vendors, and they go to the nearest place. The necessity for going on foot in any case limits their possibilities of choice. Only those fortunate enough to have some means of locomotion can behave differently (Scott, 1972). For the rest, a small group may occasionally club together to use a small lorry that will take them beyond their customary range for the pleasure of some exceptional purchase. Thus, the great cattle fairs of Feira de Santana in northeastern Brazil, draw crowds from all over northern Bahia – an average radius of 150 km – while the market of Itabuna attracts all the cacao produced within a radius of about 70 km. Cattle markets, which deal in a more valuable and self-transporting commodity, usually have a wider area of attraction.

The size of the town also plays a part in the strength of the *suq* and in the extent of its impact: in Morocco there are three orders that overlap and interlock. The two regional capitals have several overlapping fringes; the sub-regional centres dominate the intervening spaces and are only occasionally and partially included in the primary areas. Finally, the local centres have limited spheres of influence, that are generally enclosed within those of the two higher orders. The hierarchies of importance and areal extent agree, but geometrical disposition is lacking and there is no conforming size-range; the effects of isolation (as in the case of Nador, which has an enormous area of attraction) and of history (Tangier has but a limited zone, Meknès and Fez compete, as do Rabat and Salé) are apparent.

Another spatial subdivision involves 'chains' of markets. The itinerant merchants move systematically from one locality to another in a circuit that depends on the days of the week. These are major centres, that are the merchants' base, surrounded by others of less importance that are visited successively. Webber and Symanski (1974) have attempted to define such 'cycles', and Harvey *et al.* (1974) have tried to find a theoretical optimum rhythm. It is noteworthy that two neighbouring markets are rarely held on consecutive days, in order to avoid too direct a competition, but clearly this is not in the interests of the travelling salesmen. It would seem that the sequence of opening days among neighbouring markets is a matter of compromise between two opposing demands (Hill and Smith, 1972). This leads to another form of spatial organisation, that depends on a residential base for the itinerants and a circuit of markets that they visit: the study of *suqs* in northern Morocco, (see Fig. 8) provides a very striking example.

Markets and urbanisation

Markets are organisms of varying degrees of importance, more or less integrated with a neighbouring centre of population, and showing a great variety of characteristics, influence and activity; they have a role not only in the conduct of commercial relations but also in the dynamism of the urban system. Many a European town had its origin in a market, and the same thing is occurring in the developing countries. 'The gathering of people round a *suq* does not precede its development but establishes its vitality' (Troin, 1975). Such markets are appearing at an increasing rate with population growth and the expansion of production, needs and incomes. The development of meat consumption since the Second World War has been followed by a rash of new markets in the pastoral zones of east Africa (Good, 1970); the arrival of a road or a railway also encourages both markets and urban growth (Morinière, 1975). The founding of new markets represents 'an indigenous phenomenon expressing an intelligent appreciation of mutual interest on the part of the chiefs of neighbouring villages' (Hodder and Ukwu, 1969), often quite independent of the district administration.

But where is this movement leading, with current technical progress and the great upsurge of urbanisation? There are some success stories, in Morocco for example, where a market based on a new road during the colonial period became first a straggling village, and then a town. But now there is a new trend: 45 per cent of the *suqs* in northern Morocco are in a state of decline, especially near the large towns, while in the mountains and remote zones they stagnate

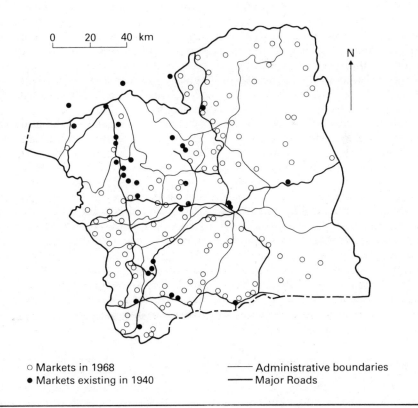

○ Markets in 1968
● Markets existing in 1940

—— Administrative boundaries
—— Major Roads

Fig. 9 Evolution of markets in western Nigeria. (Source: Eighmy, 1972.)

and disappear; but they are holding their own especially in the zones of contact between prosperous regions and about a quarter of them are really flourishing, in the countryside where harvests are plentiful, new roads have been built and the towns are dynamic. This evolution corresponds well with the schematic model put forward by Eighmy (1972) after studying markets in western Nigeria (Fig. 9). The model involved the growth of the better situated and more important markets, backed up by an upsurge in urban growth, a decline in those close to the towns, but the maintenance of those further afield or of more specialised function. In a word, the appearance of a grading – a hierarchy perhaps – in which the observers are looking for a geometrical centrality, recalling Christaller's theory, that is difficult to see in the distribution of markets as exemplified in the genuine and spontaneous patterns of the present day.

Notes

1. Editor's note.
2. Apart from earlier descriptive works such as A. Allix 'The geography of fairs', *Geogr. Rev.*, 1922, 532–69; and W. Fogg, 'The Suq: a study in the human geography of Morocco', *Geography*, **17**, 1932, 257–67.

Chapter 4

Commercial networks

Urban hierarchies

Response to the regional environment

In all the preceding account of research into hierarchies of central places and market areas, the reader will have detected features that are common to the whole subject of commercial phenomena and customer behaviour. The scale of demand, of sales income, of trade fluctuations, of the range of goods, of combinations of shop-types, and of the power of attraction, are recurrent themes that characterise both consumer demand and the seller's response. But their relations do not develop within a uniform environment (Rushton, 1969). Just as we have many times underlined the influence of regional differences on the theoretical framework of localisation, so we must take into account variations resulting from the framework of urbanisation. It would be better perhaps to write 'urban frameworks', for here too, a town of 10,000 and one of a million inhabitants offer very different conditions, as do a European city, an American city and an African city, without mentioning the influence of political regimes.

Whatever the environment, a town is characterised by its relative bulk, in relation to the total dispersion within the region. The bulk is the expression of a concentration of people and buildings, and so of shops, that are sustained by the variety, regularity and extent of the demand. And we have seen that, for equivalent needs, the rural folk will more readily go to a distant large town than to a smaller local centre, which on the contrary will be most frequented by its local citizens. Town size thus opens up the possibility of self-sufficiency that finds expression in a degree of inertia, the more so if the town is large, as Table 19 suggests (Berry, 1967, pp. 24–5).

Table 19. Percentage of population purchasing in their home town

Commodity	Atlantic (county town)	Anita (small town)
Grocery	100	100
Furniture	84	83
Men's clothing	81	47
Women's clothing	73	3

Source: Berry (1967), pp. 24–5.

The second important element is distance. Except in large towns (or in smaller towns that are composed mainly of separate houses with gardens, as is often the case in Britain, America and ex-colonial territories), shopping journeys are possible on foot. When this is not so, public transport, supported by high population densities, allows rapid mass-movement, frequently at a low cost because the local authorities subsidise a service that they regard as indispensable to the town's life. Besides, shopping expeditions are rendered easier by the nature of the urban framework: one goes from shop to shop, down the whole length of the main street; one meets acquaintances, and is attracted by a particular display or bargain. One buys on impulse as well as with deliberate intent; not going about it systematically but window-gazing, dallying and finally purchasing without much premeditation.

Finally, information is more readily and directly available. This is a permanent feature of urban life. It is disseminated in a milieu more ready to receive it and more capable of using it; it has an immediate potential and many repercussions.

These three main characteristics of the urban environment are not, however, uniformly distributed, and this leads us to the highly important notion that urban space is not homogeneous; it is single-centred or multi-centred; the distribution of population and of activity is not uniform, nor evenly balanced. Just as within a region there are centres of different sizes and in different situations, so within a town there may be several nuclei of different kinds. The study of the shopping facilities is an essential part of any examination of urban space. In particular, can we apply the elements of the hierarchical theory of commercial centres, within the towns themselves? Most authors would agree that we can. 'The hierarchy of business centres within cities is consistently related to the hierarchy of market centres in rural areas' (Berry 1967, p. 42). 'A hierarchical system offers the most efficient means of affording to the citizens the range of goods and services that they require, for the higher-order functions are concentrated in the most accessible centre, the CBD, and those of lower order are scattered through the suburbs to cater only for local needs' (Johnston 1973).

How is this hierarchy of commercial structures arranged within urban areas? Of what does it comprise? What areas does it serve? These are the three questions to be examined.

Intra-urban commercial structures

It is customary, when considering the localisation of commerce within cities, to recall the three classical schemes developed by Burgess (1929), Hoyt (1939) and McKenzie (1933) (the last of these popularised by Harris and Ullman, 1945) on the general distribution of activity in towns. In fact, they each contain some truth and some deficiencies.

In the simple general theory of urban space, it is clear that commerce is to be found in a central position, as defined by Burgess. Often linked with the very foundation of the town, or at least with its early development, it is, so to speak, its very backbone. Besides, as an activity linked primarily to the maximum flow of people, and so the greatest accessibility, it finds, in the heart of the town, its most appropriate location, where, however, the rents payable for sites and floor-space are at their highest levels.

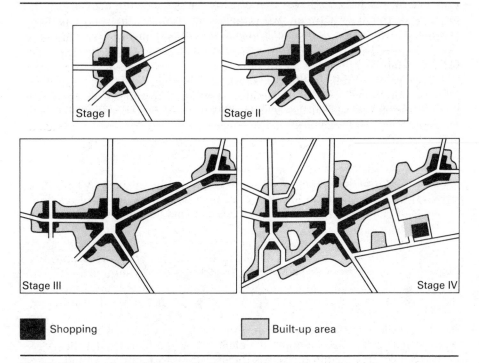

Stage I

Stage II

Stage III

Stage IV

■ Shopping   ▨ Built-up area

Fig. 10 Stages in the development of towns and their shopping areas.

But as the town grows, buildings spread, with a tendency at first to congregate along the principal radiating roads – where again accessibility is at a maximum (Fig. 10). These roads are the easiest ways to the central core, and carry the most traffic – and so we get the development of sectors, as suggested by Hoyt (who, however, placed the accent on industrial and residential development). Berry enlarged on this concept of the ribbon development of shopping streets. It is characteristic of all medium-sized towns that their shopping streets radiate from the main centre; in larger towns, such arteries are not only branches but also links between one centre and another.

Beyond a certain size, the single-nucleus structure of urban commerce is inadequate. So little swarms of commercial activity appear, with several peripheral centres, as in the polynuclear scheme of McKenzie. But where exactly are these secondary centres? Once again, at points of maximum accessibility and traffic movement – at crossroads or where two roads converge; and two types may be distinguished: first, at the junction of an incoming road leading to the town centre and a transverse road used either by residents of other parts of the town or by country-dwellers coming in from a different direction; secondly, where a particularly densely populated quarter develops (e.g. an old village engulfed by suburban expansion, the site of a new housing estate or of dwellings concentrated through some relief feature, or the appearance of a new form of activity as around the nineteenth-century railway stations). As the town grows, the same theme is repeated with variations according to the nature of the site (linear growth, splitting into two, or radial-concentric), the density of the peripheral population, the previous presence or absence of villages that already had small shopping centres, the intensity of the links between two neighbouring centres, that may isolate or box-in the town centre, or the creation of new transport lines (e.g. extensions to London's underground or the Paris métro during the present century), or of new or 'satellite' towns.

The location of the business centres in Istanbul, a city of 2.2 million inhabitants, on a particularly fragmented site and with a spatial development inherited from many periods of history, may be cited as an example (Fig. 11).

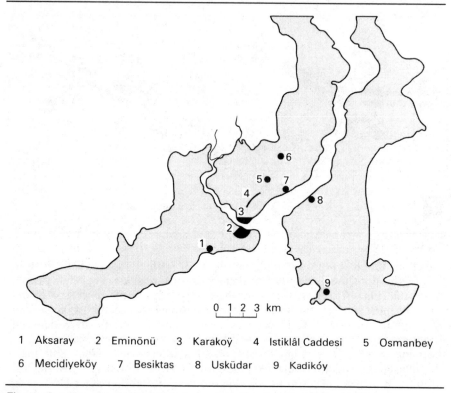

0 1 2 3 km

1 Aksaray	2 Eminönü	3 Karakoÿ	4 Istiklâl Caddesi	5 Osmanbey
6 Mecidiyeköy	7 Besiktas	8 Usküdar	9 Kadikóy	

Fig. 11   Location of business districts in Istanbul. (Source: Tumertekin, 1968.)

Nine separate centres may be distinguished (or a central business district split into nine nodes). Indeed, the real heart is divided into two, on the low banks of the entrance to the Golden Horn, crossed here by a bridge. Eminönü, on the southern shore, is the more picturesque, while Karaköy, on the north bank, has a mixture of hotels and shops, flanked on the north by banks and specialised quarters (e.g. Galata with its leather industry). These two parts of the main centre, hard pressed by the old city, and easily accessible from the Asiatic shore, are now only partly surrounded by residential quarters. On the contrary, all the other secondary centres, whether they are commercial thoroughfares like Istiklal Caddesi (with apartments, restaurants and entertainments) or local business centres in course of transformation in other parts of the European city or on the other side of the Bosporus, show the same mixture of shops and traditional and modern services, and are in close contact with residential areas whose needs they satisfy almost completely. A third type is coming into being, with numerous small local shopping centres, located at crossroads in the most populous areas; these owe their origin and custom to the growth of new residential quarters. But since 1962 the growth of consumer demand has initiated a transformation in their numbers and quality: 'groceries and butchers have doubled or trebled very rapidly in many localities. Businesses normally occupying the ground floor premises have migrated upwards. More and more dyers, pastry-cooks, estate agents and many other types of undertaking are gathering around the food markets' (Tumertekin, 1968).

In towns of this type, with a rapidly expanding population, where economic resources are often limited and planning non-existent or ineffective, one can appreciate in the flesh, so to speak, the process that in western Europe took centuries to develop and has only exploded in the twentieth century. Many examples can be found in the great surge of urbanisation that brought numerous cities in developed countries to a state of gigantism, and is swelling those in the underdeveloped world. This is the theory that we have just described, exemplified in practice.

Though we may debate the relative value of the three schemes cited above, as far as the general organisation of urban space is concerned, we must admit on the other hand that they express three stages in the development of the spatial distribution of commerce. But how far does this progressive spread correspond to a functional hierarchy, and does this once again follow the famous 'central place' theory?

Proudfoot (1937) was apparently the first author to propose a hierarchical classification of the structure of retail commerce within towns, based on the study of many actual cases. He distinguished five types: the main central business district, the outlying business centres, the principal business thoroughfare, the neighbourhood business street, and the isolated store cluster. Each type of locality corresponded to a more or less complex organisation and a different response to the clientele. Murphy (1966), reviewing the results of research on United States towns, suggested the retention from the previous work of only the two opposed morphological types: the 'nucleus' and the 'ribbon', which is perhaps a rather too formal distinction.

It is evident that differences in organisation vary with several elements, first and foremost with the size of the town or urban agglomeration. Berry (1963), in a study of metropolitan Chicago, which then had 7 million inhabitants, described the following zones: a hierarchy of commercial centres comprising, below the level of the Loop (the central business district), the main regional centres, smaller local centres, community centres, and neighbourhood centres (the hierarchy being somewhat different and less complete in the lower-income zones); together with commercial ribbons along certain streets, especially at the beginning of streets leading out of the city, and zones with specialised trading (e.g. automobiles, furniture).

In the great cities, like London or Chicago, the main regional centres are located either within the web of the inner city itself or else they form business concentrations outside the area that comprises the real central business district (cf. p. 179, on Paris), or within the agglomeration where they may be of two types: centres of secondary towns, often with an historic past, or new 'shopping centres', maybe quite outside the traditional urban area and associated with new planned towns. Examples may be found in Nord-West Stadt, outside Frankfurt-am-Main, and in many instances in the outer suburban areas of London, Stockholm or Paris. Around London, Carruthers (1962) distinguished two rings of service centres, the first comprising centres of medium rank, tending to decline with a decrease in population, and the second studded with shopping centres of sometimes greater importance, and in course of expansion. But Smailes and Hartley (1961) in a contemporary study of the same material, found a hierarchical classification that only occasionally corresponded to that of Carruthers. This disagreement highlights the great difficulty of finding objective and indisputable criteria for a hierarchy of business centres within towns or urban agglomerations. The difficulties are even greater than in investigations of regions, for the interactions are more numerous, the overlaps more confusing, and the concomitant activities often badly assessed or even badly documented. But one may attempt very large enquiries, perhaps profiting by the availability of exceptional statistical information, in order to make more precise analyses, should the opportunity arise.

Racine (1973), taking advantage of the national Canadian census of 1966, which presented precise and homogeneous data on the commercial activities of municipalities and census districts within towns, used retail sales figures and the value of salaries paid in commercial services to make an analysis of Greater Montreal. By quantitative analysis he showed that the city itself did 80 per cent of the total trade within the agglomeration; 'the remaining 20 per cent reveals a fairly regular concentric structure around the city centre... Though the overall distribution of commercial activities closely follows the distribution of population ... we see that in detail the main concentrations are directly related to the importance of motorway junctions and roads leading to river crossings, that is to the hierarchy of traffic flows, or in the last analysis, to the relative centrality of places in the urban system, which is a function of accessibility.' He goes on, with a remark that is useful for future studies, 'an eventual model of the localisation of commercial centres should therefore be based on an analysis of intra-urban circulation, which is the best means of understanding the hierarchy of conditions of access.'

It is evident, as we shall see later on when looking at studies of Parisian commerce, that new methods of research now being used by some geographers may yield the possibility of classification and correlation that a mere descriptive analysis of the phenomena cannot achieve.

Discussion of some criteria of intra-urban hierarchy

Many criteria are possible and many have indeed been used. They fall into three groups: those that refer to the actual characteristics of commerce, those that consider their degree of association, and those that take account of the flow of customers.

The schematic presentation of information about the small French town of Beauvais (Thibault, 1977), which has a population of 40,000 and 735 commercial sites, is very revealing (Fig. 12). The two cross-sections follow the two diagonal axes formed by roads RN1 and RN31 which cross at the town centre: 358 premises representing 54 per cent of town's shopping floor-space

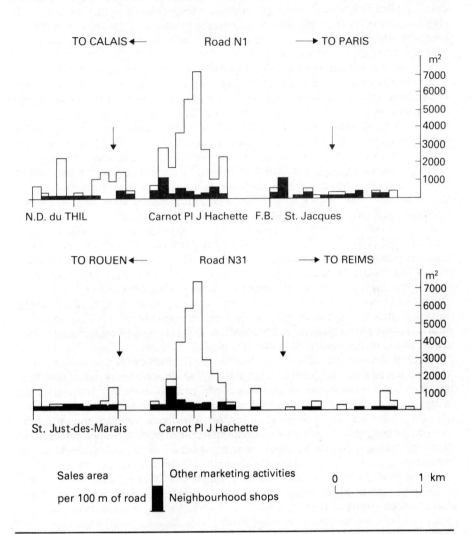

Fig. 12 Distribution of shops in Beauvais. (Source: Buildings Census, 1970.)

lie along these axes. The graph shows the number of square metres of shopping space per 100 m of road. A major centre is apparent, at the crossroads of the Rue Carnot and the Place Jeanne Hachette (6,000 m² per 100 m) but the proportion of local shops is small (only 4 per cent) while a large department store (Nouvelles Galeries, with 7,900 m² in two separate premises) occupies the most important site. Outside the main centre is a ring of mainly food shops. This is a picture of the traditional commercial nucleus. The commune of Beauvais was enlarged in 1943, and on the first cross-section one can trace the secondary suburban nodes, just inside or straddling the former boundary; on the second section, the auxiliary nodes are outside the boundary but at about the same distance from the centre, except in the direction of Reims. The disposition of shops on these axial roads outside the centre suggests ribbon development, with minor concentrations corresponding to old village centres (N.D. du Thil, St. Just-des-Marais) or the suburb of St. Jacques beyond the bridge. Outside the area covered by the two sections is a 'shopping centre' of recent origin, on the RN1, covering 8,300 m².

This spatial pattern corresponds to differences in specialisation. While the main centre contains the great majority of the non-food shops, the axial roads are getting more and more businesses related to automobiles, agricultural machinery, and road traffic. As for the food shops, they vary in quality: in the centre, the pork-butchery is of high quality, and the bakers' shops have a varied assortment. But the price of a square metre of space does not reflect the apparently clear-cut hierarchy. In the centre, the minimum value is about 50 francs per square metre, but with variations: lowest in the hyper-centre, where shopkeeping families live, with businesses handed down from father to son (45 per cent own their shops), well established and living on their reputation and their 'class', rather than on their modernisation; higher (over 70 francs) on the edge of the centre where food shops are more numerous, and often rented (only 11 to 22 per cent own their shops), competing for the custom of a clientele that has a choice. On the other hand, the value falls to 45 francs in the suburban nodes, and to 10–30 francs on the outer fringes of the town, away from the main roads; but it rises again to 84 francs in the new shopping centre.

This analysis of commerce in Beauvais has the great merit of epitomising both the theme, explored in its many aspects (spatial, historic, qualitative, functional), and the difficulty of the research. The census of buildings, 1970, is a valuable French source of information.

It seems that we must first fasten on the importance of the business centre – the number of establishments, or better still, the floor-space occupied, and the numbers employed. But the urban way of life introduces variations even within a single town. The example of Leeds shows the importance of social values. Davies (1968) studied two suburban centres in which the average income of the people varied in the ratio 1 to 2.6. In the first, there were fewer establishments but more functions, or in other words, specialisation was greater in the wealthier area. On the other hand, the wealthier clientele made more frequent visits to florists, hairdressers, shoe-repairers and banks, while the poorer customers made more visits to the cake-shop. Shopping journeys varied likewise (see Table 20).

Table 20. Suburban centres in Leeds

	Wealthier population	Less wealthy population
Number of shops	78	65
Number of functions	101	134
Clientele using nearest shop for groceries (%)	57	81
Number of different shopping centres visited	23	13

Source: Compiled by Johnston (1973) from information contained in Davies (1968).

These findings show clearly the difficulty of defining hierarchies. Even if they seem to be based on valid and objective elements, the social context may introduce major distortions.

Another difficulty with hierarchical classifications results from changes in the urban make-up – changes which, depending on the period of their occurrence, may take place under very varied technological conditions. The older suburbs, the extent of which was dependent on pedestrian transport, are often characterised by a network of shops, strung about almost continuously, especially along the main roads that also carried horse-drawn vehicles. Thus the centres of large European towns have an intricate web of shopping streets linking the numerous market-places, indicating a slow growth over the centuries. The residential quarters that were built in the late nineteenth and early twentieth centuries arose during the railway and tramway age; stations

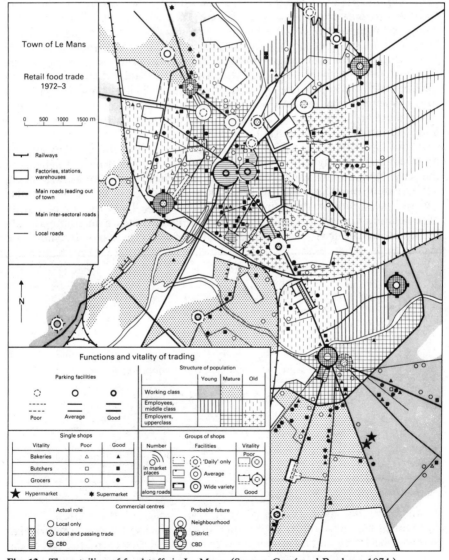

Fig. 13 The retailing of foodstuffs in Le Mans. (Source: Carré and Rouleau, 1974.)

and halts attracted new and more loosely-knit communities that were still, however, closely tied to the transport media. But the coming of the motor car has upset all these arrangements: its liberating influence allows individual movement and so a widespread diffusion of dwellings, with a more flexible and concentrated development of shopping facilities. For the dominance of the relatively immobile pedestrian it has substituted the rule of free choice and greater distances. The commercial structure of such French cities as Pau, Le Mans (Fig. 13), Lille and Paris illustrates the process perfectly; a city like Salvador, in Brazil, is only now passing into the third stage after having experienced the other two, but especially the first. It may almost be suggested that the medium-sized towns of the American Mid West (Minneapolis for example) had an accelerated first stage and then passed directly to the third. Certainly the city centre, where every street is lined with shops, is very small compared with the size of the agglomeration, in which, on the contrary, ribbon development and recent peripheral nodes are strongly developed.

The superposition or juxtaposition of two civilisations may also upset the urban structure, with the development of two centres, and a duality of shopping facilities with perhaps some mixture of clienteles. This is typical in colonial towns, where it may persist even after independence. Even in large western cities, there are Chinese, Mexican and Italian quarters, each with its own style and functioning of retail marketing.

A final difficulty arises from the relation between population density and the hierarchy of shopping centres. Theoretically the main centre is in the heart of the city; but to an ever-increasing extent these core areas are being depopulated: this is certainly so in London, Paris or New York, but it is also true of Lille, Leeds or Minneapolis, and many others. The variation in density of population from the centre towards the periphery is shown diagrammatically in Fig. 14 by curve A; the importance of commerce by curve B. Shops are

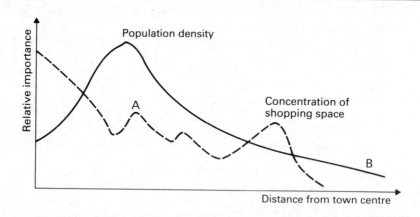

Fig. 14   Relationship between population density and concentration of shopping facilities.

dominant in the main centre (this is indeed part of the reason for the depopulation), while immediately surrounding the centre is a zone of high population density that forms part of the clientele of the centre, the rest of the customers coming from the remainder of the urban agglomeration and beyond.

The developmental process described above results in the main centre being surrounded by a number of secondary centres: since population density is still high, with a dense network of streets, these centres, which do not benefit from convergent accessibility like the main centre, are smaller in size, and they also suffer competition from numerous small shops along the main roads or in clusters, which attract customers for daily purchases. Further out from the main centre, densities are lower and cannot support a scatter of shops; there must thus be a concentration of shopping facilities in order to attract sufficient custom, so that, somewhat paradoxically, 'the lower the density, the greater the size of the centre' (Johnston, 1973). There is, in fact, a sort of counterpoint between densities of population within an urban agglomeration, and the distribution of commercial structures, especially with the changes in distribution that are now taking place.

These statements show not only the existence of several types of commercial concentration, and the reality of a graduated difference corresponding to the level of shopping facilities, but also the impossibility of establishing a simple hierarchy between the various groupings within an urban space, and even more so of relating this either to population density or to localisation.

Example: an analysis of commerce in the city of Paris

The analysis of trading within a city like Paris, numbering nearly 2.3 million inhabitants and 115,000 shops, and exercising commercial dominance not only over its own agglomeration but also part of the entire French population and even including a world-wide clientele, necessitates considerable research. The results here presented were arrived at in two stages, the first empirical and the second using a computer, a large data bank and factor analysis.

The first stage was carried out for the *Atlas de Paris et de la région parisienne* (1967). From a survey of the addresses of all Parisian shops from the INSEE card-index of commercial and industrial establishments, and a field check in every street, sheet 81–1 of the *Atlas* was prepared. The general criterion was the number of shops per 100 m of road. From this information the second stage was performed by the Atelier parisien d'urbanisme (1975), using the data bank that had been assembled there from documentation by INSEE. This work was done by the information unit and some geographers (Demorgon, 1975). All the blocks with a retail-shop density of more than 3.5 per cent per 100 m of road were selected (the average for the whole of Paris is roughly 2.6). On the basis of this spatial selection, that revealed 1,560 such blocks, further analyses were conducted.

The simplest was to determine, for the 1,560 blocks, the proportion of food and non-food shops. Three classes emerged: 60 per cent or over of food shops (very rare, this), 50 to 59 per cent, and 40 to 49 per cent (the average for the whole of Paris is 25 per cent). The distribution is very striking. The blocks with food sales dominant disappear almost completely from the main commercial centre as from the main administrative centre (the 6th and 7th *arrondissements*); those that do occur are about 1 km (in a straight line) from each other. They are also virtually absent from the major boulevards. On the contrary, in the districts where residential accommodation is dense, food shops predominate, as in most of the peripheral *arrondissements* and those of the historic centre on the right bank of the Seine – Montmartre is very characteristic, bordered on the south by Clichy boulevard where food retailing gives way to other activities. In these residential districts, the groups of food shops are seldom separated by more than 300 m, and often less.

The second study was an attempt to establish a typology of the shop groups according to their functional classification. All the data were used in the form of percentages in order to avoid the effect of size which would have caused distortion. Significant criteria were sought by the successive elimination of variables that appeared redundant or useless. Out of 40 variables, 21 were finally retained, combining the nature of the customers (daily food purchasers, customers from the vicinity, exceptional customers), the size of the establishment (estimated as a function of four grades of wage-bills, with a special category for specialty shops and department stores), the density of employment (in relation to the number of inhabitants and to the length of the street containing the shop-cluster), the proportion of employees in very large shops (over 20 wage-earners) and shops with a peculiar clientele, the presence of ancillary activities (cafés, restaurants, entertainments), the density of residential population in 1968, that of residents plus daytime working population in 1968, the proportion of employment in shops to total employment, the density of all establishments and of all employees – all these last data for each shopping nucleus considered. Factor analysis was then used to

Table 21

Structure	Area served

Dominance
– of specialty shops
– of shops with more than
  20 assistants
	1. *Very large radius*
	   Champs-Elysées, St-Michel, Madeleine-Tronchet,
	   Chaussée d'Antin, Opéra, Hôtel-de-Ville-Rivoli.

	2. *Regional*
	   Passy, St-André-des-Arts, Barbès, Nation,
	   Rue St-Denis, Ternes, . . .

High Density
– of shop assistants
– of employees in businesses
  other than shops
	3. *Sectoral*
	   Général Leclerc, Av. des Gobelins,
	   Fbg. St. Antoine, Victor-Hugo, Rennes,
	   St Germain-des-Prés, Rue de Sèvres, . . .

Transition	4. *Local, but with extra functions*
	   Lorette-Martyrs, Du Four, Marché St. Germain,
	   Aligre, Alichy, Rue des Dames, . . .

Dominance
– of 'daily' shops
– of neighbourhood shops
– of shops with no assistants
	5. *Local, with diversified shops*
	   Pte de Versailles, Rue du Commerce, Croix Nivert,
	   Gros Caillou, Rue St-Antoine, Rue de la Chapelle,
	   Rue de la Convention-Vaugirard, . . .

Low Density
– of businesses other than
  shops
	6. *Local, with 'daily' shops dominant*
	   Rues Lecourbe-Blomet, Raymond Losserand,
	   Belleville, Abbesses, Mouffetard, Goutte d'Or,
	   Damrémont Ordener, Poteau-Duhesme,
	   Clignancourt-Marcadet, . . .

	7. *Neighbourhood*
	   Rue de Patay, Glacière, N. d'Italie,
	   Ménilmontant, Panoyaux, Claude Decaen,
	   Pl. de la Réunion, Rue Myrrha, . . .

identify eight factors that explained 80 per cent of the characteristics of the selected areas. The resulting typology is shown in Table 21, and represented in Fig. 15.

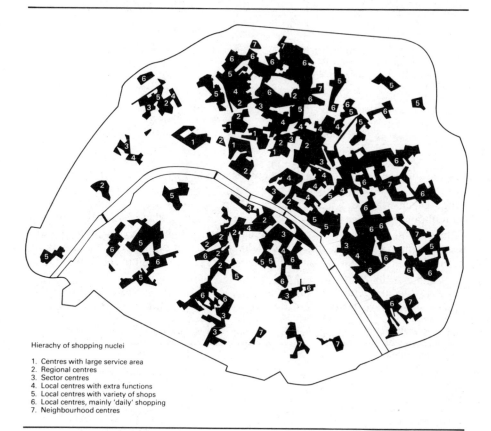

Hierachy of shopping nuclei

1. Centres with large service area
2. Regional centres
3. Sector centres
4. Local centres with extra functions
5. Local centres with variety of shops
6. Local centres, mainly 'daily' shopping
7. Neighbourhood centres

Fig. 15   The shopping framework of Paris.

Of course for a complete picture of Paris shopping it would be necessary to add to this list all the shops in small groups, at crossroads, and on the ground floor of houses, that are scattered through the urban area, but were omitted at the outset as not being in the 'clusters' category.

The distribution of the different types of shopping centre within the urban framework is not without interest, as Table 22 shows. Need we underline the disequilibrium in the way in which different sectors of the capital city are served by shops? While the ancient nucleus – and particularly the right bank – is served by shopping centres and ribbons that are almost continuous, the peripheral districts have real 'nodes' of shops, each quarter or neighbourhood behaving more or less like an individual urban entity. But the main streets, and especially those radiating outwards, form the links between them.

These studies illustrate and bring into focus a number of matters relating to intra-urban commercial structure: the general coincidence between the 'business centre' and the highest levels of commercial activity; the virtual absence of local centres (classes 5–7) within the perimeter of this business

Table 22. Distribution of Types of Shop-Clusters

			1	2	3–4	5–6–7	Total
Paris before 1860	Right bank	West	12	12	9	5	38
		East	1	6	9	17	33
	Left bank	West	1	1	10	10	22
		East	1	0	5	11	17
	Total		15	19	33	43	110
Peripheral *arrondissements*			1	4	8	91	104
Total Paris			16	23	41	134	214

Source: Demorgon (1975).

centre, and conversely of regional centres (class 2) within the peripheral areas of the city; the wide spread of a whole hierarchy of centres with ever-decreasing range of custom, and a multiplicity of small shops serving daily needs or 'neighbourhood' needs;[1] the persistence of old village centres, suitably transformed (e.g. Passy). These conclusions, reached by the use of new methods, confirm the results of the field studies that preceded the production of the *Atlas*: the classification of commercial types (as given in the volume that accompanies the *Atlas*, p. 674 ff.) is almost identical.

Using the elements employed in the factor analysis, Table 23 shows the precise characteristics of the different types of shopping clusters.

Table 23. Characteristics of different types of shop-clusters (per cent)*

	1	2	3	4	5	6	7
Number of shops with no assistants	15.3	27.9	29.1	57.7	33.1	41.4	43.9
Number of shops with more than 20 assistants†	4.7	2.6	2.2	1.8	1.0	0.6	0.2
Number of employees in shops with over 20 assistants‡	73.7	38.8	29.9	27.4	20.8	16.8	6.9
Employment in 'daily' shops‡	13.7	27.6	20.8	40.0	37.0	38.5	39.0
Employment in unusual shops‡	44.6	34.9	37.0	19.1	20.5	16.7	14.6
Residential density (persons per ha)	376	659	724	906	800	899	851
Employment density (all employees) per ha	1,721	843	448	485	339	248	197
Employment density (in shops) per ha	353	110	77	83	55	45	35

* For the zones, see Table 21. The figures are from Demorgon's study '*Le commerce à Paris, 1976*.
† Shops of the type quoted in proportion to total number of shops in the zone.
‡ Employment in shop-type quoted in proportion to total employment in the zone.

The differences have many aspects, involving both type and size of establishment, the frequency of custom, and degree of specialisation. The central sectors, enjoying the custom of visitors from afar, coincide with an area where residents are fewest and employment is at a maximum and vice versa.

A third investigation, still using the same data on shop-clusters, concerned types of shop (e.g. food, clothing, sports, household equipment). Thirty-six categories were distinguished. Here a rather curious fact appears – that the maximum diversification is found in the peripheral nuclei (20 out of the 36 classes represented); on the other hand, in the central nuclei that have large areas of attraction, not more than 24 of the categories are to be found: notably, the 8 classes of food shops are absent. Other studies reveal interesting relations, especially between the areas of customer attraction and the population served. It is also possible to measure the relative attraction exercised by the major shopping centres: thus more than one-third of the customers in the department stores in Boulevard Haussmann are from abroad; the 'regional' centres (class 2) exercise an influence within a radius of 60 km from the capital; the new peripheral centres compete with those in the centre (Parly II for the clientele in the western part of the city, Velizy II and Belle Epine for Avenue Général Leclerc-Orléans).

Wholesaling within towns

While retailing serves the population, wholesaling is an intermediary service between producer and retailer. Its localisation and functions within the urban area depend on quite different forms of activity. For wholesalers are necessary to provide inter-industrial and inter-commercial business links, and to supply raw materials to craftsmen and merchants. Wholesalers thus find themselves in a dual role in towns, being both receivers and providers. On the other hand, their role can usually only be exercised in towns of a certain size; to a greater extent than in retailing, the characteristics of wholesaling show a well-structured hierarchy of inter-dependence – as we have already seen in the case of markets (Troin, 1975).

In view of the paucity of studies of wholesaling in towns (Murphy, 1966) the following observations may more appropriately be regarded as suggestions rather than as conclusions. Once again we can fall back on the detailed spatial and functional analysis made for the *Atlas de Paris* (1967, plates 81 and 82), as well as on information contained in monographs on various towns and on the current research of A. Delobez.

Five types of localisation emerge, more specifically diverse than classifiable by their relative importance, for the criteria are very varied. The *first type* is linked with the functions of the town centre: here are located the offices of the big national or international wholesaling businesses, and the agencies representing the commercial sections of industrial groups; the offices may function for the whole concern, or may be linked with warehouses on the urban periphery, in the provinces or even abroad. They are essentially concerned with communication, meetings, discussions and orders. The *second type* comprises less powerful companies, or individuals, who need to be close to their stocks of merchandise, and must have more space at a lower price; they are thus located in the peripheral districts, sometimes isolated, sometimes to be found in the midst of zones of economic activity where they occur in groups and may have small factories where processing or repairs may be done. A variation on this forms the *third type*: these are wholesalers specialising in a well-defined product such as cloth or wood, or in making for sale goods based on such products (e.g. ready-made clothing, or furniture). They occupy decrepit premises just outside the central business district, in more or less decayed parts of the old centre, where warehouses, shops, workshops and dwellings are inextricably mixed. They sell to wholesalers from other towns or from abroad, to retailers near and far, sometimes to individuals or to each other. They are often foreigners (e.g. Puerto Ricans in the ready-made clothing trade of New York, nationals of central and east European countries in the Paris clothing and fur trades). The *fourth type* deals in bulky products; for them, what matters is access to means of communication giving the best transport facilities (such as waterfront quays, railway goods stations, or road transport depots); they usually seek large spaces, carefully planned, with offices or processing plants adjacent to stockpiles, transhipment facilities and special equipment for handling heavy and bulky goods and for turning and parking the lorries that carry them. Extreme examples are oil tank-farms, timber-yards and dumps of building materials. Lastly, the *fifth type*, found in some very large cities, comprises the agglomerations of food wholesalers. Les Halles in Paris, and Covent Garden in London, were gigantic examples of this type, before being expelled from the inner city to Rungis and Nine Elms respectively. Les Halles used to be known as 'the stomach of Paris'; it attracted prostitutes and revellers as well as genuine merchants and private buyers seeking a good bargain. Rungis is a voluntary reconstruction of this great assembly: somewhat far out, perhaps, but situated near two motorways; it seeks the custom of ordinary buyers and lovers of good food. This wholesale organisation thus differs from the other four types in requiring a very large and varied clientele.

Such are the five types of wholesaling. They are easily distinguished in the Paris region. They might be compared with the detailed schedule given by Murphy (1966) in his account of wholesaling in Columbus, Ohio: wholesaling in the centre, in secondary centres, along main streets, near railways, near roads, and warehouses outside the city.

Several of these types are subject to evolutionary change: thus a wholesaler whose business develops while the city is growing will be interested in moving further out from the centre, so as to pay less rent for larger and more modern premises; he may sell his old premises and take advantage of the improved communications. But there are also disadvantages, in the greater distances involved and the depolarisation of the journeys necessary to serve the customers. In Paris, Rungis and Gennevilliers (now the seat of many wine merchants banished from the Halle aux Vins or from Bercy) provide good examples (Delobez, 1964, 1966). Modifications in transport routes and technology affect such enterprises very rapidly. The circumstances of competition and prosperity are much more closely linked with costs than in retailing, where personal and psychological factors play a greater part. Systematic studies of the mechanisms and localisations of wholesaling ought to make it easier to establish models of structure and evolution within the framework of economic laws.

Commerce in the central business district (CBD)

Characteristics and limits of the CBD

The CBD is a unique environment: in all towns of any size it is the pulsating heart of the organism. It is the assembly point for activities that inform, direct and report, and an area in which the population may derive the maximum satisfaction of its many demands in the minimum of space and with the greatest facility. Everything, in ideal circumstances, must be within walking distance (so that one only needs to park the car once), or better still perhaps, as in modern American-style centres, so that many different calls can be made by merely using the elevator from one floor to another of a giant skyscraper block. Concentration is the key-note of the CBD, permitting the greatest economies, both external, by reducing distances, and internal, by the combining of functions, the reinforcement of potential attraction and so the maximisation of profitability – in time for administrative businesses, in value for services that depend on the flow of money such as banks and merchanting, or in a word in efficiency and power for all things connected with organisation, culture, information, and equally, trade.

There is no need here to attempt any more precise definition of the CBD, nor to analyse its functions. Whole volumes have been devoted to this, particularly Murphy's synthesis published in 1972. But it is important to recall certain features that are particularly important for commerce. Just as the town itself is a privileged concentration within its region, so the CBD is the super-centre of the town. This concentration of activities has certain consequences – spatial, financial and functional.

Space in town centres is always restricted. In towns with a long history, the street network is older the nearer one gets to the original site. This centuries-old inheritance is so constricting that in some cases it has forced the CBD off-centre, towards the more spacious streets and squares of the seventeenth and eighteenth centuries – as at Pau and Le Mans, or in the nineteenth century in Lille and Paris, or in the twentieth century at Oxford or Rouen. In cities in the New World that are only 300 or 400 years old, or sometimes less than a century, a similar displacement has occurred – as in Salvador (Brazil), Mexico City, and New Orleans; and in ex-colonial cities that had an ancient nucleus, like Algiers, Tunis, Bombay and Delhi, there has also been a splitting of the centre. These well-known facts can only serve to emphasise, by their many implications, the fundamental point, which is that the centrality of the urban core confers an enormous privilege, for the roads that radiate from it give an exceptional degree of accessibility – but also a grave handicap, for it becomes boxed-in and thus subject to severe constraints.

In view of the congregation of activities that can profit by a central situation, the town centre tends to become densely built-up, often with multi-storeyed blocks that can accommodate the greatest amount of business on a restricted site. This creates financial pressure resulting from competition; this has been described by many authors, and it has sometimes been suggested that the focal point of the CBD is where land values or rents, or both, are at their peak (Olsson, 1940). It follows that land occupation is a function of the importance attached by the contenders to a privileged central location. Those for whom this is the optimum are disposed to pay for it, and are capable of doing so (Simmons, 1964). The 'economic rent' falls between two thresholds: that beyond which the anticipated profit falls below the increased costs (d_0 in Fig. 16) and that below which the decreased costs would be more than balanced by a rapid decline in profit (d_1 in the diagram). This law also controls the subdivision of functions within the CBD (see below), and it explains the decline and then the disappearance of typical CBD activities at a certain distance from the centre.

This distance, however, is not constant, for as with all market areas or

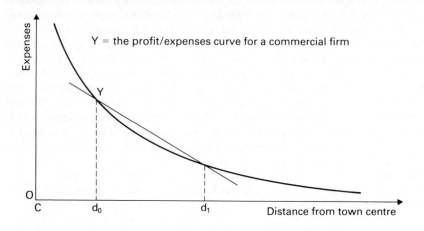

Fig. 16 Business location as a function of expenses.

spheres of influence, the environment is not uniform. In relation to the density of population in different sectors of the town, to the quality of that population, and to access roads, the centre may be deformed, with spatial specialisation within it and prolongation along the major communication arteries, which become lined with shops that derive benefit from the passage of those who, for whatever reason, use the central area: this is one of the reasons for the ribbon development of commercial activity.

Alongside these positive factors, town centres also offer much less favourable conditions, which reciprocate the former. The agglomeration of businesses pushes out residential accommodation and results in the daily commuting of more people over longer distances as the congestion in the centre grows and the area of the town expands. This daily travel also generates custom, however, for some of those employed in the CBD, and especially the women, will take the opportunity of doing a little shopping; but at the same time it contributes to the congestion. Congestion, indeed, is the main bugbear of the CBD; it increases costs, paralyses accessibility, renders parking impossible. In the towns of continental Europe, for long confined within their walls, this phenomenon is particularly marked and dangerous. In other countries such as the United States, there is another peril facing the CBD: the wealthier population is living further and further out, leaving the inner city to the poor, often to the blacks, and the cross-section of incomes across the city is unfavourable to the maintenance of the pre-eminence of the centre, even though recent slum-clearance and rehabilitation policies may have gone some way to counteract this tendency.

There is thus a peculiar situation in city centres as far as commerce is concerned, as well as a problem for the future that is becoming more and more acute in many countries.

The position of commerce in the CBD

Though the CBD houses many activities, commerce always occupies a special place. An examination of 10 medium-sized towns in the USA showed that the proportion of the land occupied by retail trading varied between 25 and 40 per cent, averaging about 30 per cent (Murphy, 1972). But there is no uniformity within centres: some authors have distinguished four sub-zones, the first of which is the nucleus, the hyper-centre; in this, commerce is absolutely dominant, reaching a maximum productivity per square metre (Hotwood and Boyce, 1959); clothing shops and department stores take pride of place, and there is a tendency for the clustering of the non-specialised shops such as department stores, drugstores and single-price shops, with a suite of small shops devoted especially to clothing (but the 'small' ones are the largest of their kind). On the other hand, food retailing is but poorly represented. In the second and third sub-zones that encircle the shopping centre, banks, offices and commercial services are more important, and in the fourth zone, car sales and wholesaling, which are completely absent from the first zone, take the lion's share, together with shops selling furniture and household equipment.

Numerous studies of European cities such as Liège (Sporck, 1966). Montpellier (Crouzet, 1975), Le Havre (Damais, 1974), Paris (Atelier parisien d'urbanisme, 1976, and the *Atlas de Paris*, 1967), lead to two main conclusions. In towns of moderate size, the CBD is divided into differentiated sectors and is surrounded by a 'zone of deterioration'. The case of Liège is typical: there is a southern sector with high-quality shops, and a northern, more popular sector with department stores that sell goods in more frequent demand, with peripheral tentacles in which shops selling food and other daily requirements multiply. In many cases a traditional food market remains in the centre for historical reasons, as at Montpellier. In very large cities such as London or Paris, the sectors are sharply defined, both in terms of specialities and socio-economic level. It is possible to buy the same articles in several sections that offer the same range of goods, but at different price-levels – as in the Rue St.-Honoré, Rue Royale and Rue de Rivoli, and Avenue de l'Opéra. There are several centres within 'the' centre.

We can go further with this micro-analysis of the CBD and determine 'areas of compatibility'. These may take two forms: in the first, shops with the same speciality are strung out along one street, or in small groups – such as antique shops, glassware shops, jewellers, furniture stores; this system recalls the sectors of the *suqs* in North Africa and the Middle East, the subdivisions of the markets in most countries of the world, and the clustering of cloth stalls and leather retailing in Latin American towns. In the second form, shops serving a particular class of customer, or a particular frequency of demand, are found along a single street or around a crossroads. The degree of proximity of all forms of clothing shops (tailoring, men's and women's footwear) of perfumery shops, of fancy-goods shops, is very noticeable. Often a large department store or a non-specialised store may gather around it a number of small shops selling individually some of the same or similar articles. These two forms of clustering are a response to the law of cumulative attraction, either by reinforcing the choice available within a single product or by the multiplication of the opportunities offered by the variety stores. In each of these two cases there are the possibilities of changes or additions: the pushing out of food shops as the general tone of the shopping area rises, the accentuation of specialisation in a street that is doing well, or the insertion of new types of shop into an already flourishing medium – such as sports shops and discotheques.

Within the main centre, the subdivisions are numerous, the more so as the town becomes more important. But the phenomena of micro-centrality are constantly developing, and permanent fluctuations enrich and modify them continually. Any simple and fixed schematisation is a dangerous mistake.

A study of Zurich by Carol (1960) emphasised the specificity of the CBD in commercial terms by considering price, choice and frequency of custom, and so quality and influence. He took four products – champagne, cigars, wrist-watches and jewellery. For the first two, he counted the number of varieties, and for the last two, the price range. He also sought the market areas of the last two, as a function of sales points in the CBD, in a regional centre and a peripheral neighbourhood centre (within the city). His results are shown in Table 24.

Table 24

	CBD	Regional centre	Neighbourhood centre
Varieties of champagne	20	3	1
Varieties of cigars	501	205	112
Price of watches (Swiss francs)	100–20,000	60– 950	40–200
Price of jewellery (Swiss francs)	100–30,000	50–1,050	30–210

The neighbourhood shopping centre received 80 per cent of its custom from the local area (which had 13,000 inhabitants); the regional centre, 50 per cent from the local area, 30 per cent from within a radius of 4 km except towards the south where the main centre was located, and 20 per cent from more than 25 municipalities strung out from northwest to southeast over a distance of up to 40 km. As for the luxury jewellery trade of the CBD, its custom came not only from the whole of the urban agglomeration but from the whole of eastern Switzerland, and by reason of the importance of tourism, from the whole of Europe, North America and even South East Asia. This underlines both the appearance of new functions, and the greater specialisation and more varied range of goods that respond to the demands of a clientele coming from an ever-widening sphere. (Everson and Fitzgerald, 1972.)

One other aspect must be mentioned: since the frequency of custom varies from one type of goods to another, it is interesting to get some idea of the distribution of activities according to this criterion. In their study of Norwich (Everson and Fitzgerald, 1972) the authors classified one-third of shops in the CBD as 'shoppers' shops' (referred to earlier in this book as of weekly frequentation), visited from one to four times a month, and one-fifth as 'specialty shops', visited several times a year (furniture, electrical appliances, household goods); in all more than half the shops were the subject of only infrequent visits. On the contrary, in the secondary shopping centres, daily shopping, which only represented 10 per cent of the CBD trade, rose to over 40 per cent, with the other two types reduced to less than one-fifth. Along the streets linking the two types of centre, the figures lay in between the extremes.

In Rome, the commercial centre has only 11.2 per cent of the population but 38.5 per cent of the non-food retail trade and 52 per cent of the city's employment. In the most specialised sector (Condotti Street) 67.5 per cent of the shops are in the 'specialty' class, 15.9 visited occasionally and 16.6 in the 'daily' category (Seronde, 1975).

It is interesting also to enquire about the perception that customers have of the objective criteria that characterise the city centre. We refer to a study of

Liège by Merenne-Schoumaker (1974) because it has the merit of being comprehensive and concerned with a city of sufficient size but not too vast to examine the problem thoroughly. Two questions may be asked: what characterises the city centre from the visitor's point of view, and what are its advantages?

In answer to the first question, 40.7 per cent of the persons asked mentioned commercial activities (36 per cent said simply 'the shops'); but two other items merit attention: the general activity, the life and the atmosphere received 20.1 per cent of the votes, and the site and traditions, 19.7 per cent. Those questioned, selected at random, thus appreciated the characteristics of the city centre as outlined by the research workers, but the analogy does not stop there: their approval or criticism was also motivated by arguments that stress the evidence of the role and the difficulties of commerce. In answer to the second question, 57.5 per cent in their replies mentioned advantages connected with the commercial function (presence of numerous shops, greater choice, cheapness, department stores, specialty and luxury shops, etc.) and auxiliary features that help or augment that function (public transport, concentration of activities and the general bustle). On the contrary, 54.1 per cent of the criticisms related to movement (traffic hold-ups, parking difficulties) and 32.8 per cent to the general environment (pollution, noise, crowds). The balance-sheet of this study thus gives psychological confirmation of the economic findings on the subject of the city centre.

But the arguments advanced by the persons questioned show clearly that the attractiveness of the centre that indeed holds all the trump cards, also encounters some opposition, the arguments for which are of serious import.

The evolution of commerce in the CBD

If we write that the great enemy of the commercial supremacy of the CBD is the motor car, we are only expressing a little harshly the result of the evolution that makes itself felt all the more as the general mechanisation of a country becomes more advanced. The motor car is indeed responsible both for the congestion and pollution of the overcrowded streets of the centre and for the almost indefinite sprawl of the suburbs; but further, it carries with it the almost unlimited possibility of movement in all directions and the necessity for its users, eager for a certain standard of comfort, to be able to go where they like, park near to their destination and satisfy as many of their needs as possible with the minimum inconvenience. Though this description may be idyllic in relation to reality, it is psychologically true.

A study of Columbus, Ohio, made in 1955 (Murphy, 1972) at the beginning of the new era of competition from suburban shopping centres, attempts to balance the two attractions and we can see that the criticisms then made on the subject of peripheral commerce have since been overcome, so that these outlying developments have now become a danger to the CBD. In the centre, one finds a better selection of goods, and the possibility of buying most of one's requirements in one place – but the crowds and the congestion are annoying; the suburban shopping centres are much nearer home, parking is easy and opening hours are more convenient – but the variety of goods is smaller, and the higher prices and the lack of other activities are unfavourable factors.

The results of this rivalry can be measured financially. It is in the United States that the phenomenon is more advanced than elsewhere, and some urbanists are already talking of the disappearance of town centres, and the uselessness of towns. Though this extreme view is contradicted by the policy of rehabilitating city centres, officially applied since the late 1960s, it nevertheless expresses a marked tendency, particularly in respect of commerce. Since the United States pioneered the creation of vast peripheral shopping centres, it has been the first to suffer their consequences.

An examination of the map of retail trade in the *National Atlas of the United States* (Washington 1970, plates 222–3) yields much of interest. This double map-sheet shows the total volume of retail sales in each of the Standard Metropolitan Statistical Areas (SMSA) and for certain selected counties. Within the proportional circles, one quadrant shows the part played by the CBD, and colours indicate the extent of the gains or losses in percentage of sales in the two types of area (CBD and the remainder of the SMSA) during the period 1958–63. It is noticeable at once that the share of the CBD in the total sales is less than 20 per cent in all the large cities (save in New Orleans, San Antonio and Lubbock), and is below 10 per cent in Detroit, Chicago, Los Angeles, Boston, Dallas and San Diego. Further, the share of the CBD had diminished during the period except in Washington, Atlanta, San Francisco, San Jose, Sacramento and about 20 other cities of less importance (about one-sixth of the total of the SMSAs that are mapped).

The phenomenon has been described by Berry (1963) in a study of the situation in Chicago; he distinguishes four types of deterioration affecting the CBD: economic deterioration (disappearance of shops, many vacant premises, lowered level of shops that remain, with diminished turnover); functional deterioration linked with the economic run-down; deterioration of the environment (litter, pollution); physical deterioration (neglect of buildings). In the same paper, Berry suggests parameters of the consequences of decline, with relation to United States towns: a modification of 1 per cent in the number of inhabitants will result in a 1 per cent change in the number of shops in the same sector; a variation of 1 per cent in real incomes will provoke a 0.9 per cent change in the number of shops; the growth in size and efficiency of the commercial units, combined with the increased mobility of the consumers, will produce an annual reduction of 5.9 per cent in the number of shops. By combining these variations, he suggests that in the wealthier sectors, the growth in size compensates for the reduction in numbers, and that in fact the position of retailing is more or less stable; but in the poorer parts, the decline may be as much as 4 per cent per annum, increasing if the income level is itself lowered. We quote these figures, for what they are worth, but would suggest that such precise correlations seem hardly credible.

That quantitative relations exist between these variables cannot be denied; it is much less certain that they are constant and directly proportional. There is in any case a difference between local shops, which may be affected at once by such factors, and those of the business centre, that benefit from a much more varied clientele and where the interplay between different types of shop is of some importance.

Some western European examples show both the continued strength of the town centre as the privileged location of shopping facilities, and also the modifications that are taking place.

The business centre of the reconstructed town of Le Havre (Damais, 1974) shows the persistence of tendencies that could be regarded as derived from the historic evolution of the town. The hyper-centre close to the Town Hall contains only 6 per cent of the population, but 21 per cent of all the shops and 31 per cent of the commercial floor-space in the entire urban area. It is linked by two major axes, along which the town grew, and which are now lined with shops, to two secondary nuclei within the central area (the Rond Point and the station); the whole forms the commercial centre, which, with only 14.5 per cent of the population, has 37.4 per cent of the shops and 47.5 per cent of the shopping floor-space. The average size of the shops is 54.6 m², compared with 28–30 m² in the peripheral areas of the town. High-quality and luxury shops are particularly concentrated (Table 25).

Table 25. Business centre of Le Havre

	Percentage of all town shops in hyper-centre	Percentage of total shopping floor-space in hyper-centre	Average size (m²)	
			Hyper-centre	Whole town
'Leisure and culture' shops	31.6	47.1	56	37.7
Luxury goods	38.0	55.2	–	–
Clothing	38.4	53.8	64	45.7

Source: Damais (1974).

During the course of recent years (1970–3) the evolution has followed the recognised pattern: there has been some progress in the shopping facilities of the town as a whole (about +3.5 per cent), but a slight decline in the centre (−0.6 per cent), especially noticeable in food and clothing, though with stability, or even an increase, in a variety of other types including luxury goods. The apparent stability of the hyper-centre results from the balance of two trends: closures are more or less matched by new openings, and the closure of small shops by an expansion of the big department store Nouvelles Galeries; but the secondary centre at Rond Point, which only became a somewhat artifical urban nucleus after the war, is in decline (−8.9 per cent).

Studies of the commercial structure of other town centres – notably that of Sporck *et al.,* (1975) concerning Liège – confirm these conclusions in respect of older European towns: the CBDs are holding their own, and are improving and even developing some of their activities, especially in the luxury sector in which there is least competition. On the contrary, the middle-level shops within the centre are suffering severely from the competition of shopping centres in the expanding sections of the town, and more particularly from the new forms of trading being developed on the outskirts.

A detailed survey of the urban area of Montpellier (Crouzet, 1975) has drawn up a balance-sheet for the decade 1962–72: while the population increased by 40 per cent, the number of shops went up by only 8 per cent, and in the centre there was a decline of 4.5 per cent. The centre's share of the total fell from 63 to 55 per cent; this was due mainly to a major fall in the number of food shops (by 29 per cent; in the town as a whole, food shops fell from 45 to 33 per cent). On the contrary, the centre was upgraded by the establishment of more high-quality shops (a 2 per cent increase in 'leisure and culture' shops, and a rise of 13 per cent in household and office equipment, of 20 per cent in clothing and footwear, and of 22 per cent in medical and sanitary goods). But these generalised figures conceal variations: thus groceries, especially in small family shops, have suffered greatly (−32 per cent), pharmacies and hardware shops almost as much (−30 per cent); sales of drapery and cloth have also diminished (−9 per cent); but specialised food products have not changed; and shops selling radios and television sets have multiplied (+16 per cent); tailoring and clothes have taken a sharp upward trend (+40 per cent), while the record would appear to be held by photographic and music shops, of which 64 per cent are situated in the centre. The localisations along the main axial streets are unchanged, while secondary shopping streets are developing. The balance between openings and closures, however, conceals a much more unstable situation, for the changes are many, and renovation and modernisation have altered not only the nature of the shops but also to a large extent their standing, their character and their clientele. It is sufficient to walk through several of the older but renovated streets to appreciate how the old town centre has maintained its commercial strength.

In the rest of Europe, the city centres have suffered, both financially and functionally, a diminuation in their commercial activity. At Strasbourg, for example, though the sales turnover rose by 10 per cent in five years, it diminished in the CBD.

In countries where the possession of a car is less common, and where the majority of the population is poor and ill-informed (with many recent arrivals from the countryside, often illiterate, forming a miserable underemployed proletariat), the decline of the city centre (the function of which, it is true, differs from its role in the developed countries), has not yet begun. The first hypermarket in black Africa only opened in 1975! The example of Salvador, an important city in northeastern Brazil, will illustrate this alternative development, which we may follow from 1956 to 1973. In 1956–60, the centre was of mediocre importance and relatively low order; it clustered around the Praça da Sé, close to the old city, and only served the local population, whose wealthier members did their shopping in Rio (1,300 km distant by air, or several days' uncomfortable journey by road!), São Paulo or abroad. Two events changed the situation: the discovery of oil in the Reconcavo and the establishment of the important Petrobras services that created a local middle class; and the growing importance of tourism with a clientele of wealthy Brazilians from the south, and of Americans and Europeans who create a demand for high-quality specialty goods. At the same time the proper surfacing of a system of radiating roads facilitates access, not merely for the peasantry fleeing from the misery of life in the rural areas but also for the wealthier clientele that is making money out of cattle-raising and improved agriculture. The business centre is expanding, and developing two nuclei, one in the old town on the hill and the other near the port; its strength is reinforced by the banks, offices and company headquarters, and the shops multiply and grow larger and more modern. In 15 years, the area of the business centre has trebled, but its quality and turnover have risen much more. However, during the same period urban expansion has taken the population from 300,000 to one million, and commercial development along the main axial roads has gone on apace, with shopping centres in the suburbs, and the first supermarket, reached only on foot or by bus (for there are almost no car parks), was opened in 1971, about 6 km from the main centre.

In the socialist countries, despite the desire for a rationalised equality, important cities like Warsaw and Budapest, or even lesser cities like Gdansk or Iasi have central nuclei with specialty shops, an inheritance from the past importance of their sites and a reflection of their present position as national or regional capitals. Certain types of shop, like those run by shop-keepers with a special status (private craftsmen for example), tourist shops selling antiques, imported goods and works of art, and shops of department-store type are located in close proximity to hotels, historic sites, and government buildings. The reconstruction of the centres destroyed during the war has had due regard for the location and organisation of the old nuclei, even though the composition has been modified as a result of a new political ideology. In these countries, too, the central commercial function is confirmed, though in a less dominant form than in western Europe.

This brief comparative review enables us to take a more balanced view of what is now being called the 'city-centre crisis'. The phenomenon is most serious in the United States; it is discernible also in other extra-European 'British' countries where the automobile dominates personal transport; it should be taken into consideration now in western Europe if the authorities are not to be confronted by it later on.

Elsewhere, for many different reasons, it is not yet noticeable and in most countries where urbanisation is still in full swing, this is accompanied by the growth of CBDs that have so far no rivals.

The renewal of the commercial centre

In those types of urban civilisation in which the town centre is threatened with decline or even extinction, the responsible authorities have sought palliatives. The central focus of the town, as much by reason of its position in the urban web as by its traditional functions, cannot easily be abandoned without grave social consequences, as the United States have discovered through the racial disturbances of the 1960s. Measures must certainly be taken in many of the most urbanised countries of the world, either to rehabilitate the centres or to prevent their decay. It is certainly not a question of reconsidering the whole policy relating to urban centres, for much of their activity revolves around offices, public or private services, transport organisation, and efforts to recover or maintain a certain amount of life through clubs, shows, lodgings and restaurants. We shall restrict ourselves to the description of several examples to show the revival and integration of commerce into the more general policy.

In the United States, there is a widespread view that retailing has but little chance of retaining its place in city centres. The competition of peripheral shopping plazas is indeed very strong (see below, p. 216) and the old idea of a living community in the centre has become outmoded, for the wealthier sections of the population are living further and further out. Most planners are convinced of this, and the relatively small and decreasing part played by the CBD in the retailing turnover of the Standard Metropolitan Statistical Areas (SMSA), that we have already noted, offers little cause for optimism. However, personal observations in several towns that are replanning their centres, and conversations with housewives (mainly middle class, it is true) suggest a rather less negative approach.

The example chosen is the Twin Cities (Minneapolis – St. Paul), which have

1.8 million people within the SMSA and dominate the northern part of the central plains. While St. Paul, capital city of Minnesota, on the east bank of the Mississippi, has scarcely begun to think about the renewal of its centre, the process is already well advanced in Minneapolis, on the west bank, where the urban population is now twice that of its twin. Drastic measures were taken to permit the pulling-down of all the ordinary buildings in the central blocks, which had been completely built-up, and to turn the areas into car parks, while investors were encouraged to concentrate their resources on the CBD proper, to increase its density of occupation and give it an architectural and functional dominance (Beaujeu-Garnier, 1972). What room is left for commerce in all this? In addition to the office space allocated in recent skyscraper blocks to wholesaling and general commercial business, three possibilities are offered. Department stores and specialty shops (ready-made clothing, tailoring and some kinds of personal service such as hairdressers) continue to line the central streets, and the special or communal car parks that give ready access to these are well patronised. Secondly, shopping floor-space has been provided on the ground or first floors of office blocks and a system of covered ways, at first-floor level, permits shoppers to cross roads and make their way around without having to encounter motor traffic and its accompanying atmospheric pollution. Finally, a mall, arranged as a promenade with seats, flower-beds, and artistic decorations, is provided in the heart of the centre as a link between two business nuclei; it is bordered by new shops, with alluring window displays, mingled with restaurants, cafés and banks. Compared with the vast size of the suburban shopping centres, this is certainly small, but it exists and is all the more appreciated by contrast with the run-down blocks and old traditional shops that still characterise the centre of St. Paul, side by side with some new developments.

How much use is made of this centre? Numerous visits enabled the author to see that in fact it was very well patronised, despite the existence of about ten shopping centres or hypermarkets on the city's perimeter. But enquiries showed that the wealthier customers actually preferred the city centre for three types of purchases: personal clothing of high quality; children's wear, because of the range of goods offered and the possibility of choice from several adjacent shops; and finally for personal services such as female hairdressing.

The use of modern rapid-transit means of mass transport, that is so important in the location of peripheral shopping centres, may also favour city centres. Montreal is a good example, where the Place Bonaventure centre contains shops at several levels, with underground car parks, the whole complex forming a veritable commercial fortress, linked to the Place Ville Marie business centre in the heart of the city, with the underground railway and walkways giving access to other shopping centres, hotels and places of entertainment, completely sheltered from the harsh Canadian winter and from street traffic. A whole township of underground services follows the street pattern above. It is obvious that the city centre benefits considerably from these facilities. A somewhat similar situation may develop in Paris, at the great Châtelet-Halles crossroads, where two métro lines and the rapid-transit line cross (with the eventual possibility of linking with main-line trains); here the works at present being undertaken will permit a traffic of 50,000 passengers an hour.

All these reconstructions are primarily for the benefit of the life of the city in general rather than for retail shopping in particular, but the latter benefits from its symbiotic relationship to the whole organism. The rehabilitation of some moderate-sized centres can also offer the same double benefit.

At Montpellier, the plans are already made (Crouzet, 1975) to graft a new centre on to the old in a vast redevelopment scheme that will use former military land about 300 m east of the town centre. The new town hall, the regional government buildings and a large hotel jostle a commercial centre with 35,000 m² of floor-space. This will comprise two large sections, one occupied by the department store Galeries Lafayette (transferred from the old centre), and the other by 60 separate shops on two levels; 3,000 parking spaces will be provided. One might well think that Montpellier, whose population grew by 68 per cent in 20 years, had an inadequate shopping centre, and that the numerous peripheral developments did not sufficiently compensate this. But can the two parts of this new double centre co-exist and continue to grow in harmony? There must be some complementarity, and already the old centre, by cleaning up its historic buildings and picturesque old streets, is turning towards arts and crafts and antique shops side by side with those dealing in goods more constantly in demand; some streets are specialising in leisure equipment, or jewellery, for example. On the other hand, strong measures are being taken to speed up traffic without creating dangers for the dawdling pedestrian, by creating large car parks, and an underground shopping mall connecting the two centres. One innovation follows another, and the example of Montpellier is certainly one to be followed.

In addition to the national and municipal policies that are being pursued in many countries and many towns, we should notice the initiative of the shop-keepers themselves. These latter have not always been as prompt in seizing or in creating opportunities as one might have imagined. Thus in the case of Montpellier, of the 60 shop-spaces on offer in the renewal operation, only 15 were taken up by local citizens, 14 by individuals living in the *département* of Hérault, 18 by people from within the region and 21 by Parisians. When a comparable operation was proposed at Strasbourg for revivifying the centre, 150 shop-proprietors were interviewed, of whom 84 per cent were unaware of any problem, 53 per cent saw no reason for taking any positive action and only 15 per cent were really concerned and ready to act (Nonn, 1974).

Besides general and radical measures, partial solutions may be accepted. One of the principal grievances voiced with regard to traditional town centres is the difficulty of movement. One solution of the conflict between vehicles and pedestrians may be to prohibit vehicular traffic from certain streets in the centre. Although there was some initial hostility from shop-keepers, this solution has now been widely applied in France: Rouen and Strasbourg were among the earliest towns to experiment with it. Here and elsewhere the results have been very favourable; thus the reconstructed centre of Cologne is forbidden to vehicles for most of the day, and is a shoppers' paradise. In Munich, a rapidly expanding city, with 2.6 million people in its urbanised agglomeration, the hyper-centre, which sheltered only 40,000 inhabitants, received 72,000 visitors a day in 1965. Because of the resulting congestion, it was decided in 1966 to limit vehicular traffic; the experiment was subsequently extended, rationalised and embellished with the provision of sitting-out areas and street decorations. The published turnover figures issued by the Chamber of Commerce showed increases of between 40 and 60 per cent, and even of 20 to 30 per cent in parallel streets that were still open to vehicles (Lottman, 1974). The hundred or so French towns that have pedestrianised centres have nothing to complain of, either, it would appear. But some modifications take place, such as an increase in shops catering for personal needs (clothing, leisure), and the disappearance of 'technical' shops (hardware, electrical goods, house furnishing), together with modernisation, more window-dressing, and lengthening of opening hours.

Central area redevelopment in Britain*

Despite the widespread attention given to various forms of suburban and out-of-town shopping locations in recent years, it is quite clear that it is the traditional city-centre shopping areas which have seen the greatest concentration of investment in post-war Britain, and as Schiller (1977) has shown this was reflected in the superior growth rates of town centres between 1961 and 1971. The decentralisation of certain functions has left many inner-city districts in an impoverished state, but within the CBD itself there has in many cases been an intensification of economic activity, the demand for prime locations has grown steadily and the city centre has not disintegrated, despite many predictions to the contrary. In general terms the activities which are being squeezed out of central locations are the large space users, or those with a non-commercial basis, such as industry, community facilities and housing, whereas profit-oriented activities such as shops, offices and hotels are on the increase (Alexander, 1974). This process is very much in accordance with Alonso's principle of rent-paying ability.

Although direct comparisons are difficult, the 1961 and 1971 censuses of distribution permit us to estimate the importance of the central shopping area in towns of different sizes. Table 26 indicates the proportion of total retail turnover accounted for by the central area in metropolitan areas of different size classes. The Standard Metropolitan Labour Areas (SMLA) are as defined by Hall *et al.*, (1973), the central areas are as defined by the relevant censuses, and although there were boundary changes between 1961 and 1971 it is considered that the figures give a valid representation of the situation.

Table 26. Proportion of total SMLA turnover in central areas

Population size class	% of turnover accounted for by central area (median)	
	1961	1971
100,000–250,000	40.1	45.7
250,000–500,000	28.9	30.7
500,000–1 million	20.0	25.3
> 1 million	25.9	24.9

The proportion of total turnover accounted for by the central area declines with increasing SMLA size, a point noted by Thomas (1975) and attributable to such factors as increased competition from larger suburban centres and higher travel costs for journeys to the CBD in larger urban areas. Perhaps more

* This section has been contributed by Dr. P. T. Kivell

significant for present purposes is the fact that in all size classes, except the largest, the median figure increased between 1961 and 1971, indicating either a real increase in the central area's share, or an enlargement of the defined central area between the censuses. Both of these can of course be interpreted as a strengthening of the trading position of the central area. To a large extent central-area redevelopment schemes must be seen as a natural part of the process of urban growth and change, taking place against the background of ageing and decaying buildings and changing economic and social demands. Retailing is by no means the only component of this process, commonly it is a part of a wider programme of change which embraces many other activities, notably office development and traffic-management policies, but it is significant that Britain, unlike the USA and much of Europe, decided to build new regional shopping facilities in established centres. In general terms, the factors which form the background to central-area redevelopment are fairly well known; they include the wartime damage inflicted on certain city centres, the spread of motor-car ownership, changing retailing and land-ownership patterns by multiple organisations, the decentralisation of industry and population, and changing investment opportunities. There are also, however, a number of specific landmarks which need to be examined briefly in order to understand the process of redevelopment.

The 1947 Town and Country Planning Act gave local authorities extensive powers to designate Comprehensive Development Areas, complete with the ability to undertake compulsory purchase in order to assemble coherent blocks of land. In the same year the Ministry of Town and Country Planning published *The Redevelopment of Central Areas,* which pointed the way towards tidier, more carefully zoned and rigidly controlled central areas, and in 1962 further guidelines were produced jointly by the Ministry of Housing and Local Government and the Ministry of Transport (*Town centres: approach to renewal,* 1962).

The changing pattern of transport has had a profound effect upon central area planning and this aspect was dramatically brought into focus by the Buchanan Report (Buchanan, 1963). The report prompted such a fundamental re-think among planners that Percival (1965) suggests that it resulted in many city-centre schemes being outdated before they were complete. Since then private motor-car useage has increased inexorably while public transport everywhere has continued to lose both passengers and money.

In the early 1950s a change of government and a relaxation of financial and building controls (building licences were abolished in 1954) led to a return to free market conditions. The resulting property speculation boom had its main impact upon the office sector but retailing too was affected. The implications of this process, which reached its peak between 1955 and 1965 have been well documented by Marriot (1967) and Ambrose and Colenutt (1975).

Some of these trends were apparent in most of the countries of the western world, and Britain was not alone in developing new and redeveloping old established shopping centres. Among the better-known early examples is the Lijnbaan in Rotterdam (Part I opened 1953) a redevelopment scheme in which an open and airy pedestrian mall replaced congested mediaeval streets. In 1954 Stockholm opened the Vallingby centre, suburban in location but none the less setting an example for future central-area schemes. In America too, early experiments resulted in the pedestrianisation of two blocks of traffic-laden streets in Kalamazoo in 1959, to be followed in 1962 by the Midtown Plaza, a fully covered mall in Rochester, New York. British planners and developers were extremely active during this period: Hart (1968) identified 178 central-area schemes embracing 3,240 ha in 1964, and it seemed to the casual observer as if every town and city in the land was intent on augmenting or at least remodelling its central area.

Because of the widespread occurrence and varied nature of post-war redevelopment schemes, they do not readily fall into a simple classificatory framework. For our purposes, however, it will be useful to consider four informal categories: reconstruction, substantial addition, piecemeal redevelopment and reorganisation.

Within each of these categories there is considerable variation, and an individual city may well show examples of all types. The reconstruction category is perhaps the most fundamental, for within this group we must include those towns and cities which experienced substantial wartime damage. Many cities suffered extensive damage to their shopping centres, but two in particular, Plymouth and Coventry, stand out in terms of the scale of damage they sustained. Initially there are many comparisons: both cities had populations of approximately 200,000, both had important regional shopping roles, both suffered extensive damage concentrated in their central areas and both made an early start on reconstruction. The results of these reconstructions, however, show many contrasts.

Plymouth's reconstruction plan, produced jointly by the City Engineer, M. J. Paton Watson, and the well-known planner, Sir Patrick Abercrombie, was adopted in principle in 1944. The previous tangle of small streets was replaced by a series of bold, rectangular shopping blocks despite substantial difficulties over land ownership, compensation payment and the understandable reluctance of traders to take new sites with unknown trading potentials. Originally covering a combined business and shopping centre of some 31 ha, the plans were reviewed and extended on several occasions, and at the formal approval of the development plan in 1956 the city-centre Comprehensive Development Area embraced 93 ha. The new shopping centre was largely enclosed by a ring road which intercepted the main radial routes into the city, but in retrospect it is easy to criticise the lack of separation of pedestrian and vehicular traffic. The major areas of the new centre were Armada Way (a 54 m wide, landscaped pedestrian thoroughfare) and Royal Parade, which was effectively a part of the inner ring road with the major department stores fronting directly on to it. In addition Armada Way was interrupted by two other major traffic thoroughfares. The Plymouth Plan, in common with many others of the same period, did not accurately predict the rise in traffic volumes. The 1950 prediction of a 75 per cent rise by 1970 was in fact reached by 1957 and a revised estimate, produced in 1956, to forecast 1974 levels was attained by 1960.

The Coventry plan on the other hand saw the separation of pedestrians from vehicles as an essential component. The city, which had been one of the fastest growing areas in Britain in the first half of the twentieth century already had pre-war plans for a redeveloped shopping centre, but the war, and the legislative changes of the 1940s made possible a more ambitious approach. The redevelopment of central Coventry has been well documented elsewhere, especially by Gregory (1973), so a brief summary will suffice here.

A reconstruction plan for Coventry was approved by the city council in April 1941, only months after the bombing, and from the very beginning a pedestrian precinct within a ring road and a girdle of car parks was outlined. The council itself started the reconstruction by building Broadgate House at the traditional focus of the city centre, together with a number of shops and offices between 1948 and 1953. Immediately to the west, a new pedestrian shopping precinct was subsequently developed, with department stores strategically located at each end; this was the core of the post-war plan, but eventually the precinct became but one element in a larger redevelopment of the whole area, a plan which provided for other pedestrian shopping streets, extensive office space, a higher-education precinct and the rebuilt cathedral, now Coventry's most famous landmark.

Between 1948 and 1972 Coventry's plan was reviewed by central government on eight occasions, and one of its strengths has been its flexibility. It has also benefited from a fruitful cooperation between the city council and private development interests. The former provided the infrastructure, assembled the land and the majority of the finance (£32 million out of a total investment of £44 million in the years 1948–71), whereas the private developers provided office and retailing expertise, building skills and the balance of the finance, a pattern of cooperation which has since been replicated in a large number of schemes throughout the country.

With the subsequent pedestrianisation of adjacent streets, it is clear that the precinct has become integrated within a considerably larger central-area redevelopment scheme than was originally envisaged. The precinct has acted as a nucleus within the core formed by the inner ring road, and other specialised areas such as the cathedral and the polytechnic result in a clearly segregated land-use pattern. The amount of office space existing in 1971 was double the 1957 plan estimate and as Davies (1972) has shown, Coventry substantially increased its central area retailing floor-space during the 1960s, and, unlike many other British cities, has even experienced a net increase in the number of establishments since 1951. Specialist shops figured particularly prominently in this growth but clothing and household goods shops also increased substantially.

The second category of central-area change includes those cities which have undertaken major additions to their established shopping centres. Within this category there is considerable variation, particularly with respect to size, degree of integration with the established centre and with transport nodes, range of facilities and the extent to which they are designed as covered, controlled environments. Many are large enough to be included in the category of regional centres, having over 100 shops and one or more department stores, and are designed to serve catchment populations of well over 100,000. Such centres as Eldon Square in Newcastle, the Victoria Centre in Nottingham and the Arndale Centre in Luton all exceed 50,000 m² of shopping floor-space and are comparable in scale and facilities with the large American out-of-town regional centres.

It is not only the centres of provincial cities which have undertaken this kind of development, for there are in addition many examples within the metropolis of London. Developments such as the Whitgift Centre in Croydon and the Riverdale Centre in Lewisham may appear to have suburban locations in the context of London itself, but they are truly central areas in the context of the London boroughs to which they belong.

Normally developments of this type are located immediately adjacent to established central shopping areas, and indeed it is sound planning and commercial practice to ensure a high degree of integration between the old and the new. A major new development can have the effect of totally altering the centre of gravity within an established centre, but it is still desirable to capitalise upon existing patterns of customer flow and traffic nodes. Location with respect to these factors is critical in the success of a new centre. Thus Nottingham's Victoria Centre, which is heavily used, is well linked with the old central area and incorporates a bus station, whereas the Greyfriars Centre at Ipswich, built in 1966 and separated from the traditional centre by 200 m and a dual carriageway road, had only one of its 52 shop units let a decade later.

Although conceived mainly as shopping centres, many of the larger developments contain a range of other facilities. Sometimes these are of a genuinely commercial nature, such as restaurants and cinemas, but often they are community facilities of one kind or another which have been included as a part of the bargaining process between developers and local authorities. One good example of this is the Arndale Centre in Poole, developed jointly by Town and City Properties and the local authority. Above the shopping area of 93 shops, a public house, restaurant and bus station, there is a sports centre financed jointly by the developer, the local authority, the government and local sports organisations, and now run by a sports trust. In addition there is a large, modern library, and in the covered shopping area there are periodic fashion shows, art exhibitions and charitable events.

Design details vary widely from one centre to another, but many aim for a covered, controlled environment in which heating, lighting, ventilation and security can be carefully monitored and controlled. The running costs of such a sophisticated system are high, and it already seems that the viability of some of the more elaborate centres is threatened by service costs which can reach 15–20 per cent of rental income. In the freedom of access which is naturally encouraged during shopping hours it is easy to forget that many centres are in fact totally private enclosures. With centralised ownership and management they operate almost as enormous department stores, in which separate departments are sub-let to individual traders.

Two developments which illustrate many of the aspects noted above, as well as some of the problems of these schemes are the Victoria Centre in Nottingham, and the Cardiff Centre plan. Nottingham's Victoria Centre, which has been described as the first of the American-style shopping malls in the UK (McDougall *et al.*, 1974), is a multi-level complex developed on an 8-ha disused railway station adjacent to the city centre by Capital and Counties Property Co. Ltd. Its 54,000 m² of shopping floor-space includes two department stores (Debenham and John Lewis Partnership) at opposite ends of the main shopping deck, and a carefully controlled mix of 86 other retailers. Other facilities include an underground car park for 1,750 vehicles, a partially covered market of 11,000 m² and a new bus station. With the exception of 464 council flats which rise high above the centre the whole development is very much privately owned and controlled. Although an undoubted commercial success, the development is not without its critics. Attention has been focussed upon the lack of control exerted by the local authority, who were only minimally involved in the development and management of the centre, but in addition it has been suggested that no comprehensive assessment of future shopping needs was undertaken, anchor shops have been lost from the old city centre and overall the city receives no financial return from what is one of the largest developments of its kind in Britain.

Cardiff's Centre plan differs in that it was a later development, more ambitious in that it involved new urban motorways, cultural and educational facilities in addition to shops and offices, and it was from the beginning a joint venture between the city corporation and Ravenseft, a subsidiary of Land Securities, one of the largest property development companies in the world. A public enquiry was held in 1970–1, but in the meantime inflation was pushing up the cost estimates from £43 million in 1969 to £83 million in 1974. This scale of inflation severely stretched the financial resources of both developer and corporation, and the scheme has been further threatened by the non-realisation of the consultants' forecasts of growth in population and jobs within the area. Some of the scheme's problems have been identified by Dumbleton (1974) and it seems likely that a much more modest proposal for new shopping facilities south of the recently pedestrianised Queen Street will be pursued.

Perhaps the most widespread form of city-centre change which has been undertaken is the piecemeal redevelopment of individual buildings or small numbers of adjacent sites. Redevelopment of this kind has taken place in virtually all centres on a very individual and sporadic basis according to the varying ages of buildings, lengths of leases and the requirements of owners and tenants. At its best it can represent a sympathetic and gradual replacement of obsolescent buildings and infrastructure while maintaining the essential mix of land uses and site values of the traditional centres. As standards of conservation and architectural awareness have risen, so too have the aesthetic qualities of many of these smaller redevelopment schemes, and most town centres afford both good and bad examples.

Piecemeal redevelopment along these lines has played a very significant role in the attempts of retailers to increase their store sizes and maximise their site efficiencies. During the 1970s many food retailers have been developing new central-area supermarkets of between 2,322 and 4,644 m² and this too is a size range which many multiples and variety-store operators are aiming for.

An alternative to redevelopment, and one which has been almost universally successful, is the re-organisation of existing centres, most commonly through the process of creating limited access or pedestrian-only streets. The idea is an old one stemming from nineteenth-century examples such as Burlington Arcade in London, or the Galerie d'Orléans in Paris; in modern times it was re-established in the British New Towns and the post-war reconstruction of such streets as Princesshay in Exeter, and subsequently it has spread to many old established shopping areas. After 1960 there came a general recognition of the need to improve conditions for the pedestrian, and the Buchanan Report (1963), which suggested that the degree of freedom for pedestrians in the central area was a useful guide to the civilised nature of a town, provided additional stimulus.

This general trend was more formally reinforced by the 1967 Road Traffic Regulation Act, and the Town and Country Planning Acts of 1968 and 1971 which made it easier for local authorities to restrict vehicular access to selected streets.

Among the many problems which have to be overcome in pedestrianisation schemes are those of delivery vehicles, bus routes, car parking, the re-orientation of through routes and the frequent opposition of traders. Many of these depend upon local circumstances but the latter point, the fear by traders that they will lose custom, most often proves to be ill founded. When London Street in Norwich was pedestrianised in 1967, 28 out of the 32 shops reported an increase in trade in the first summer.

The pattern of pedestrian schemes also varies and the reader is referred to a comprehensive bibliography prepared by Dalby (1973). Some, such as Newcastle-under-Lyme in Staffordshire, aim to ban all private traffic from virtually the whole centre; others, such as Oxford Street in London, compromise by banning private cars while allowing buses and taxis continued rights of access; and others, such as Portsmouth's Commercial Road ban all traffic, public and private, from selected shopping streets. In most cases there is also some degree of environmental improvement such as cobbled surfaces, tree planting and changes to the street furniture.

The overall rationale behind this concentration upon central-area development is not entirely clear, but certainly it is explained in part by the desire of towns to protect their standing investment and rating base, and by the nature of post-war British planning which has tended to protect the *status quo*. Despite the increasing sophistication of the planning system and the battery of techniques available to the retailer for the assessment of shopping needs and market potential, there has been a surprising amount of guesswork involved, even in some of the largest developments. Relatively few comprehensive studies to assess shopping floor-space needs or overall levels of demand have been undertaken, and during the hectic period of development, in the 1960s in particular, many elaborate schemes were based largely upon the availability of suitable land. Compared with the attention paid to the detailed design aspects such as maximising pedestrian flow, ensuring adequate parking facilities, the size and flexibility of units and the correct mix of traders, very little consideration was given to the integration of new schemes into the local or sub-regional retailing environments.

In addition to their duties as planners, many local authorities have been more closely involved in shopping redevelopment through partnership schemes with property developers. In the early post-war schemes such as Coventry, Plymouth and Bristol, local authorities normally owned the land which they then leased for development, the actual development undertaken by the local authorities themselves being mostly confined to roads, car parking, public buildings and other community facilities. The idea of local authorities assembling land which could then be leased to developers was strongly recommended by central government in the 1960s, and with the passing of the Community Land Act in 1975 the role of the local authorities with regard to development land has been further strengthened.

The conditions under which property development companies operate in the 1970s are very different from those of the previous two decades. Against a background of high rates of inflation, a commercial rent freeze, rising building costs, the collapse of the secondary banks, high interest rates and the institution of a Development Gains Tax, many developers have withdrawn from direct involvement in new shopping schemes. To some extent they have been replaced by retailers themselves acting as developers and new investment funds have also been made available by insurance companies and pension funds. For example the I.C.I. (Imperial Chemical Industries) pension fund has investments in the Victoria Centre, Nottingham, and joint schemes for town-centre development have been arranged between the Norwich Union Insurance company and the boroughs of Woking and Horsham.

Although it is difficult to speculate on future developments in such a dynamic field, there is already evidence of a changing emphasis in central-area shopping development. In America closer attention is being paid to smaller developments (McCahill, 1976) and it seems that in Britain too, both planners and commercial interests are likely to focus upon cheaper, less ambitious projects in the immediate future.

The future of commerce in town centres

In the preceding pages we have several times referred to variations in the situation as between different types of town. From the examples quoted, and others, it would appear that there is some sort of relation between the influence of history, the intensity of current urbanisation and the extent to which the population is motorised.

In countries where the past is expressed in ancient towns in which historic monuments, fine buildings and old houses bear witness to stages in development, there is an urban tradition that weighs heavily in terms of space and ways of life. The people are faithful to this instinctive reaction that is often centuries old and comes to life again on the occasion of certain official ceremonies or popular festivals. But such a centre may become cramped and inadequate. Conversely, in the town that has but a short history and a very commonplace centre, the business core has no solid foundation. There are thus two extreme cases: strong centrality and weak centrality (and in the second case, congestion or lack of organisation of the centre).

On the basis of this fundamental aspect of the centre, the other two factors come into play – the present state of urbanisation and the degree of motorisation (that is in itself a reflection both of living standards and habits). In other words, the past may act as a brake, and the other factors as a motivating force:

$$\text{Evolution of centre} = \frac{\text{Present urban development. Degree of motorisation}}{\text{Strength of inheritance from past}}$$

The following may be regarded as characteristic situations: if present development is stagnating, there will be stagnation or a *decline* of the centre; if it is rapid and there is little motorisation, there will be a *growth* of the centre; if it is rapid but with strong motorisation, the centre will *burst*; if it is moderate, with a solidly based old core and moderate or strong motorisation, a *transformation* of the centre will take place. One could apply these situations regionally or nationally – but it would be foolish and hazardous to try to sum them up in a single formula.

Rural commerce

What is rural commerce?

The expression is ambiguous, for three reasons. The term 'rural' invites consideration of the countryside population as opposed to that of the town –

but what is a town? Each country has its own definition, which ranges from a population of 500 in Denmark to one of 12,000 in the USSR; in France the threshold is 2,000 inhabitants. But it is obvious that such an arbitrary limit can lead to argument and to an evaluation that varies widely according to the human environment under consideration. Thus in the Scandinavian countries, where population is sparse and dispersed, it is normal to retain a low threshold, but the reverse is true in Sicily or in Hungary where huge, predominantly agricultural villages may house 30–40,000 people.

The second ambiguity arises from the question of function: where are the shops that serve the rural population? They are generally not in the open country but in places where people congregate, that is in villages and towns. Thus the clientele of a small town surrounded by a rural population may come mostly from outside the town itself: are the shops in the said town then part of rural commerce? The reply to this question depends on the population thresholds and on the proportion of the customers coming from the two environments. Another example: it was discovered during the course of an enquiry that certain restaurant proprietors in Beauce, and certain retailers in Picardy, got their supplies from Les Halles in Paris. All of which goes to show that it is very difficult to place a limit on what may be called the commercial servicing of the countryside, and further, that there is more complementarity than antagonism between towns and their surrounding local areas.

Lastly, what is covered by the expression 'rural population'? This depends on the country in question. In certain areas of black Africa, 80 or 90 per cent of the rural population is agriculturally occupied. In France, 15 million people are classified as rural, but only 3 millions are active in agriculture; some 'villages' near to Paris and other large French cities are populated almost exclusively by civil servants, by retired former city dwellers, and by people who live in improved cottages and work in the town. In Beauce, there are villages of 200–300 inhabitants, of whom only 4 or 5 are in agricultural employment; in regions further removed from the big urban agglomerations the proportion of agricultural workers may sometimes rise to 40 or 50 per cent. In the United States there is a further complication in that part-time agricultural employment is becoming more and more common, and is indeed encouraged by the government that sees this mingling of agriculture and other sectors of the economy as a useful contribution to the social evolution of the community. Since 1970 more than 50 per cent of the American agricultural workers have devoted less than half their time to working on the land, and this proportion has been growing fairly constantly at about 1 per cent per annum in recent years. Not only do certain smallholders hold on to their farm simply as a residence, or retain the status of agriculturist for reasons of taxation, but many farmers also have another job. The case has been quoted of the state of Kansas, where 22,000 wives and daughters of 43,000 farmers are employed in teaching, as secretaries or in health services.

For these three reasons, then, great care is needed when dealing with rural commerce; there must be a study of individual cases after the general outlines of the problem have been identified.

General conditions of rural commerce

The first really specific influence on rural commerce is the relative dispersion of the population, which contrasts with urban concentration. The rural population may be quite dense, but even the 500–600 per km² of the Nile delta, the Japanese plains or the great deltas of South East Asia cannot compare with the 10–30,000 per km² of the world's large cities. Numbers and disposition are fundamentally different. So in the main characteristic of rural commerce is that it has to face the fact of dispersion.

This is accentuated by the arrangement of the means of communication, which do not converge, as towards urban centres, but merely traverse the space concerned, serving it in linear fashion. Places where roads happen to cross have advantages of access that are often marked by the presence of small corner shops. Since it is impossible to serve every dispersed household individually, the vital question is what is the best location possible, and it is from the study of this type of service in a relatively homogeneous agricultural plain that the geometrical constructions of Christaller's central-place theory emerge.

The first idea that comes to mind is the importance of the characteristics of the population in question, especially their density and purchasing power, the one being capable of more or less completely compensating the other. In an individual country, density is of prime importance; figures for China, shown in Table 27, are especially revealing.

Table 27. Extent and population density of market areas

Average area (km²)	Average density (per km²)
158 and over	under 19
97–157	20–59
30–96	60–299
16–29	300–499
15 and under	500 and over

Source: Skinner (1965).

While in towns the size of the population is of most importance, for rural commerce the way in which the land is occupied is of greater concern, for example, isolated farms and small hamlets as in areas of dispersed population, or collected in villages and small market towns.

A study of shopping facilities has been made for about 100 communes in four French rural zones, one in the vicinity of the metallurgical centres of northern Lorraine, one in the purely rural area of southern Lorraine, and two in areas of dispersed settlement, the first in eastern Brittany, in the Rennes basin, and the other in Haute-Vienne, near Limoges. The two Lorraine examples come from areas of strongly nucleated settlement.

The average population of these communes was around 1,000. The opposition between types of settlement is very striking, and the situation in relation to large towns is similar (see Table 28). The average number of shops per commune is larger in the areas of dispersed population, but the variety of shops is more or less equal in all cases. It is evident that the grouping of the population favours service from compact groups of shops, in village centres, and that this spatial concentration reduces the possibility of competition due to the dispersed character of the settlement. This is even more marked if one takes communes having more or less identical populations: thus in the Limousin, where relief accentuates the difficulty of communication, the number of shops in communes of between 900 and 1,100 inhabitants averages 25, whereas in Ille-et-Vilaine the figure is only 15 and in Lorraine 12.

Table 28. Shopping facilities in relation to population dispersal

	Total population	Percent of dispersed population	Average number of shops per commune	Number of shop types
Haute-Vienne (14 communes)	13,917	77	22	10
Ille-et-Vilaine (10 communes)	11,885	79	21.3	9
Meurthe-et-Moselle* (20 communes)	18,483	9	10.6	6.6
Meurthe-et-Moselle† (16 communes)	17,819	3.2	13.3	8.3
Moselle (15 communes)	14,966	11.4	15.6	9.3

* All the communes in the area between Longwy and Briey.
† Omitting 4 communes with no shops.

While this influence of population distribution is already noticeable in countries like France with a high standard of living and plenty of motor transport, it is even more important in countries where the density of population is low. But these levels of consumption and mobility are the controlling factors in the organisation of rural commerce.

The diversity of consumption is much more varied than in the towns. In the first place there is a fundamental opposition between two extremes. In the rural areas of the most primitive countries, the needs of the inhabitants are few and simple; self-subsistence is the rule as far as food is concerned. The lack of monetary income results in barter or a system of compensatory exchanges: in the morning, scraps of surplus agricultural produce are sold, and the few coins so gained are spent in the afternoon on household necessities. At the other end of the scale is the specialist farmer who sells but one product and has to buy all the rest. Thus the cereal farmer sells his grain but must purchase many more items than the city-dweller: for he must indeed acquire not merely all his food (even milk, butter, eggs), and all things necessary to clothe himself and equip and maintain his house, but also all the things that enable him to till the land and reap abundant harvests, such as fertilisers, seeds and implements. Such exploiters of the land thus have more numerous and varied requirements than those of the townsmen. When a single farm can yield a revenue of more than a million dollars – and this is not uncommon in California, for example (Gregor, 1974) – one can imagine what a purchasing power this represents!

Indeed, the commercial system of the rural world is quite different from that of the urban dwellers. While the latter are mainly consumers, served by a very wide variety of producers, the proportions are generally reversed in the countryside, where the farmers are both producers and consumers. However, as we have already noted, this class does not constitute the entire rural population, and its relative importance is less in the more developed countries. Here, therefore, is another constraint on rural commerce: it must serve a complex variety of people: as well as the farmers there are the civil servants, the retired, the shopkeepers, and the citizens who reside temporarily or permanently in the countryside. For a long time, and to this day in the underdeveloped countries, craftsmen-shopkeepers were an important element in the community. They worked on the spot. Certain activities that in the town are undertaken by businesses because the concentration of customers makes this possible, are done in the village by men who are half producers, half salesmen.

The weight of history and tradition bears heavily on rural areas, which are only slowly freeing themselves from established habits. All the French geographers who have considered rural commerce have borne this out. Thus Brunet, writing of the rural areas around Toulouse, paints a vivid portrait of this often picturesque archaism: 'the network of relationships favours the multiplication of middlemen who, in return, contribute to its perpetuation . . . It is the kingdom of small individual enterprises' (Brunet, 1965, p. 258). And he goes on to describe these middlemen as horse-traders, brokers, carriers, itinerants of all kinds.

It would be fruitless to attempt to characterise in a single formula the whole wide and changing range of the clientele of rural commerce. We may, however, note several general features: incomes, and thus purchasing power, are on average lower; birth rates are higher than in the towns, but as many of the young folk leave the land, and numerous retired people migrate to the villages, the average age is often higher (especially in France); habits of consumption and tastes are more rustic, tending towards comfort rather than sophistication. For the country folk, the town is the centre of attraction that enables them to break their isolation, to see new things, to meet other people, to escape from their limited workaday world, and to enjoy a little social life – provided that it is sufficiently near to be easily accessible, and small enough to prevent their being swallowed up in it. This is the reason why 'markets' are so successful, for they provide a meeting-ground on the edge of, or within the town, and they combine the possibility of a gathering of country-folk with the opportunity of using the resources offered by the town. One has only to visit the cafés around the market places to see (in France at any rate) the mint tea, the rough red wine or the cups of coffee that accompany or follow the business deals, light up the faces, loosen the tongues and cast a warm glow on the days of isolation to which the parties will return.

We must not conclude without underlining the difficulties that arise from the fragmentation of rural commerce. A limited clientele, high prices because of the nature of the organisation, and small profits are the general rule. But in certain extreme cases the difficulties may be even greater, for the dispersion may be such that the small shopkeepers can no longer get in fresh supplies because of the disproportionate cost of transport. Some sections of the Massif Central, in France, have reached this stage because of depopulation, and the same thing is true of certain former mining regions like the Sierra Diamantina in northeastern Brazil. When costs pass certain limits, the system can no longer function. A similar situation arises with regard to the collection of agricultural produce, when tonnes of fruit and vegetables must be destroyed or ploughed-in, and thousands of litres of wine poured down the drain, because there is no means of selling them economically; at the distribution stage there are whole sectors that run the risk of ceasing to be served at all.

Characteristics of rural commerce

In response to these peculiar demands, rural commerce may adapt itself in three ways – spatially, morphologically, functionally – that may overlap according to the circumstances.

Spatially, the adaptation takes the form of a search for the optimum amount of contact between vendor and customer. At the embryonic stage this consists of little more than a stall at a crossroads, even where there are no dwellings in the immediate vicinity. Such are the wooden huts that one finds in the interior of Brazil – counters at which one may have a drink and purchase such things as tobacco and sweets, while waiting perchance for a bus or to hitch a lift. Similarly, there are the isolated 'gas stations' that punctuate the road system in the great plains of the United States: they comprise petrol pumps, a drugstore and perhaps a motel or a restaurant, and maybe a silo. Berry (1967) calls them 'hamlets' and says that they may have up to 100 inhabitants and six or seven small shops.

As the population becomes more concentrated and less dispersed, groups of better-appointed shops may appear, for the clientele is more numerous and is fixed and not itinerant. Localisation depends on means of access. In Europe, with its long history of human occupation, it is difficult to trace the processes that resulted in the present carefully balanced range of centres, but in the United States, especially in the central plains where the whole settlement and road pattern is not much more than a century old, it is possible to follow the evolution very precisely and to appreciate the part played by settlement from the east, crystallised by railroad penetration, the development of a hierarchy resulting from the choice of local government centres, and finally the flexibility introduced by the motor vehicle. 'Political centrality provided added reasons for farmers to visit one centre rather than another' (Berry, 1967, p. 7). In quite another context, similar developments have taken place. The progress of colonisation depended on administrative centres, the opening of the interior through communications and ports, the encouragement of agricultural production – all of which gave rise to the growth and eventual sorting out of rural trading centres, as in the countries of black Africa such as Togo and Dahomey (Hetzel, 1974), or in other areas like Morocco (Troin, 1975). Zones of dense population, and points of contact between countries, ethnic groups and different agricultural production were especially favoured.

In all cases, if the physical environment is more or less homogeneous, the centres have a tendency towards regularity of distribution. But if there is a hospitable valley, or a much-used route, the centres will multiply. A good example is to be found in the areas west of the Missouri. Along the railways, duplicated later by modern highways, communications and activities are strung out: telephone lines, high-tension cables and sometimes belts of irrigation. Railway stations formed the first villages, that later became towns and centres of rural commerce and life. Kraenzel (1953) gave the name 'Sutland' to these 'more densely occupied zones that form a corridor enclosing the main communication arteries, the principal establishments for wholesaling, business and industry, the major schools and hospitals, and the centres of government and the social services . . .; the areas in between are the "Yonland", that is the areas devoid of all such equipment.'

Morphologically, the adaptation of rural commerce is complex. It appears both in the particular characteristics of sedentary commerce and in the appearance and growth of certain new forms. In traditional commerce, the size of shops is small; they are localised in the oldest and most cramped sections of villages or small towns; they often occupy the ground floor of houses that were not designed for this purpose. The modernisation of such shops is difficult because of the limited capital resources of the owners. However, improvements may be made by branches of chain-stores or by other business groups and in some countries by professional developers, who have had special training in commerce and have their own or borrowed capital available for the necessary investment. Another characteristic of such improvements is de-specialisation. In the most primitive rural shopping situations, the basic shop is the grocery, which may also be a café, and may sell tobacco, bread and pharmaceuticals, so as to be, in effect, a miniature 'bazaar'. The American 'drugstore' sells everything and one finds such shops, more or less flourishing and well stocked, at many levels of the hierarchy. Besides these 'hold-all' establishments – which may be either Aladdin's caves or mere junk-shops – most rural shops are multi-functional – butchers with the purveying of cooked meats, drapery with clothing. They make up, by the variety of articles, for the small sales of any one type; but as their resources and their space are very limited, the assortment is crude and serves the needs of only the poorest customers or those in a hurry. This marginal position is reflected also in the relatively high prices, because the shopkeeper can depend on only a small turnover and is often himself hard pressed to support his family. His activities are thus vulnerable, but at the same time conservative, because his needs are few and his initiative small.

Rural folk have nevertheless some alternatives, even without journeying to a town that is better provided with shopping facilities. Though the local shops may be lacking or poor in quality, other more flexible means of trading may be available. First of all there are the markets, that we have already dealt with (p. 159). These generally follow a weekly rhythm (or in China, every 10 days), and thus for certain types of purchases attract a clientele six or seven times larger than that of the fixed shops. Their presence fulfils a local need and stimulates trading activity, at the same time helping to foster good relations in the rural community. Market-day is the occasion for meeting people, and the very dispersal of population is conducive to its prosperity (Brunet, 1965). Over vast regions of the globe, the market is the only means of trade for the rural population. Thus China, where there were 80,000 'commercial markets' in 1958, the market is the basis of the rational integration of economic life within the new political regime (Skinner, 1965). But the shop can come to the customer in two ways, by travelling salesmen and by the delivery of goods; these are similar, but differ in respect of who takes the initiative. In the first case, travelling salesmen (or roundsmen) serve remote localities, villages that are poorly equipped, and people who cannot get out in the normal way. This method of the 'mobile shop' enables the tradesmen who employ it to extend their clientele and thus increase their profits and attain a better measure of financial stability. It is also the only way of serving areas where the rural population is too sparse to support a permanent shop (as happens in many French areas at present), or areas in which commercial activities are rudimentary. In the Douar area of Algeria, the arrival of the cotton-goods pedlar, the pot-seller or the grocer is a familiar sight. He uses an old wagon, harnessed to a donkey, and sometimes does his journeying on foot. In the Mitidja, this sort of thing makes up 10 per cent of the total trading activity (Mutin, 1974).

In the case of deliveries, it is the consumer's initiative that sets the process in motion: by telephone, by post, through a catalogue or a trade show, he can make his wants known, place his orders and have the goods delivered to his home. While the travelling salesmen is to be found in all countries, from the most developed to the most backward, ordering for delivery is mainly characteristic of the most advanced countries: in Sweden, the United States and West Germany the system is very common and is spreading.

Finally, rural commerce adapts itself *functionally,* by the shopkeepers adjusting to the particular circumstances of their environment. The adaptation may be either spontaneous or voluntary and deliberate.

Of their own volition shopkeepers, to a much greater extent than their urban counterparts, seek to please their customers: through their hours of opening, their pleasant conversations about personal affairs, and the relaying of news, they attract and retain their custom. In backward countries, the shop is often the only possessor of a light, that acts as a rallying point. Pedlars, with an inexhaustible gift of the gab, gather there and offer goods of a traditional kind such as herbal medicines, charms, local craft products, food prepared in time-honoured ways, like the *carne do sol* (sun-dried meat) in Brazil, or dried fish in Africa; or goods to be sold to the poorest of the poor, like utensils made from old tin cans, or second-hand clothing. The formation of associations of shopkeepers, the establishment of direct relations with wholesalers, and the setting up of cooperatives, are other measures designed to counter the problems resulting from dispersion and small turnover.

As for spontaneous adaptation, this results from the very nature of the environment. The setting-up of a shop carries with it its own penalty. There is a minimum clientele, below which certain types of trading cannot subsist. If such shops are in fact established, for the sake of tradition, for family reasons or even by chance, they wilt and disappear unless by their own initiative they can penetrate other local market areas and so increase their clientele. Berry (1967) has proposed a tabulation relating resident population to the population served and the quality of facilities in terms of numbers and varieties of shops, and degree of specialisation.

Table 29. Levels in the hierarchy of rural commerce in southwestern Iowa, 1960

	Population	Number of shops	Categories of shops	Population served
Hamlet	100	5–6		
Village	500	40	22	1,200
Town*	1,100–1,600	100	45	4,000
Small city*	6,500	450	90	30,000

* Berry's terminology; the English equivalents might be 'larger village' and 'small town'.

Source: Compiled from Berry (1967, p. 14–15). The figures give the general order of magnitude.

Another kind of functional adaptation is related to the types of goods sold and the pricing policy. There is attention to the current requirements of the local clientele rather than to a large assortment of goods that will only find a few buyers among a large body of customers.

The part played by food sales is very large, for these are goods that are indispensable daily requirements. Even in regions that are more or less self-contained, the food shop is the first to arrive and often the only one. The larger the centre, the smaller the proportion of foodstuffs in the total sales, as

Table 30. Shop-types in the Mitidja, Algeria (per cent)

	Total Mitidja	Blida	El Arba
Food	37.7	26.0	45.2
Clothing and household equipment	22.2	31.2	23.7
Services	41.1	42.8	31.1

Source: Mutin (1974).

Table 30 suggests. Mutin's detailed study of the 23 communes in the Mitidja (Algeria) is very instructive: 84 per cent of the total trade is concentrated in the 10 largest centres; many villages have no shops at all. Commercial organisation is dominated by 91 wholesalers; of these, 54 per cent are concerned with foodstuffs, and they have 73 per cent of the turnover.

Some notes on commerce in rural France

The French situation is unique because it combines three aspects that are more usually unconnected. Population densities are relatively low compared with neighbouring European countries; the accelerated decline of rural population came later in France than in most other industrial countries; and the force of tradition, the reluctance to move and the antipathy towards things new, that are part of the peasant heritage, hinder development. Further, the shopping facilities are often ill-adapted, hopelessly out of date (a feature constantly mentioned by authors describing the situation), or, on the other hand, lacking by reason of the serious decline in the number of inhabitants that results from a long period of rural exodus.

It is difficult to give precise figures. One may nevertheless hazard a guess that communes of under 2,000 inhabitants contain 15 million people, or 30 per cent of the national total, and that this figure diminished by 12 per cent between 1962 and 1968; but these communes had only one-quarter of the total number of shops. The facilities are thus below the French average, and their recent decline is more rapid and more obvious than that of the population (see Table 31).

Table 31. Evolution of rural shops, 1966–71

	Non-food (%)	Food (%)
Communes with under 2,000	−17	−20
Communes with 2,000 to 10,000	+ 5.8	− 1.2
Whole of France	+ 5.5	− 7.1

Source: Les Comptes commerciaux de la Nation.

At the end of 1971, there were 53.3 food shops per 10,000 inhabitants, and 34.1 non-food shops in communes of under 2,000 people, as against 55.4 and 63.6 respectively for the whole of France. These figures emphasise once again the relatively poor service provided in the countryside and the importance of food shops. But there is some compensation in the small towns (of 2,000 to 10,000 population) where the figures are 68.5 and 84.6 for the two types; it is interesting that there should be this degree of resistance to high-order shops in the larger villages and small towns.

Apart from these generalities, a number of enquiries and measurements have been made to determine more precisely the characteristics of French rural commerce.

A careful study of shopping facilities in towns of under 5,000 population in 14 varied *départements*, combined with direct enquiries about shopping frequency, led to a classification of the lower levels of the hierarchy in a rural context. Five levels were distinguished (Delobez, 1973): villages with no shops; those with one or two sorts of food shops; those having the basic trio of food shops – general foodstuffs, butchers, bakers – which in fact form the first level of the hierarchy of commercial centres in rural areas; those having the food trio plus either clothing or household goods; and those with the food trio plus clothing and household goods and one or two others giving a total of 6 to 10 types of shop.

Next, in order to examine the upper classes of rural service centres, a computer was used to classify the 327 communes having more than nine types of shop. Forty-four types of retail shop were considered. The resulting matrix enabled several levels of shopping facilities to be distinguished, but it also demonstrated the absence of any sharp discontinuities between the communes. The gradation of facilities and the arrangement of types were such that it was difficult to define any precise and absolute breaks in the sequence. In the case of the hierarchy of facilities, after the elimination of four food-selling types of almost universal distribution, three groupings appeared. The first included drapery, novelties, hardware, pork-butchery, shoes, cakes and pastries, cycles, watches and clocks, and books and stationery: more than 73 per cent of the communes had a shop within this group. The second group of 8 types – drugs, radio and TV, photography, cheap store, fruit and vegetables, fish-mongery, furniture, florists – was present in 34 to 60 per cent of the communes. Lastly, the 13 types in the third group were much rarer in occurrence (only 8.5 to 21 per cent of the communes); this group comprised creamery, horse-meat butchers, sports goods, household appliances, crockery, weapons, confectionery, men's ready-made clothing, leather goods, opticians, electrical goods, gift shops, cutlery. But the commune centres could not be classified on the basis of this hierarchy of shopping facilities. The reality is much more complex: for example, a commune well provided with shops of the third group might have none from the second group.

In analysing the arrangement of shopping facilities in communes of under 5,000 population (other than those lumped together as 'towns'), seven types were distinguished. The first related to villages with no shops at all (type 0) and the second (type 1) those with only one shop, or maybe several, but too widely separated to form a centre of attraction. With type 2, characterised by the grouping of shops catering for indispensable daily needs, we can begin to talk in terms of 'commune centres'. Types 3 and 4, rather more advanced, having groups of ordinary shops, with perhaps three of four serving other than daily needs, and usually including a chemist's, with type 3 sometimes having no shops selling household equipment, sometimes none dealing in personal requirements. Types 5 and 6 characterise the large villages (*bourgs*) and small towns. Type 5 includes several specialty shops as well as those serving ordinary needs; finally, type 6 includes a remarkably wide range of commercial

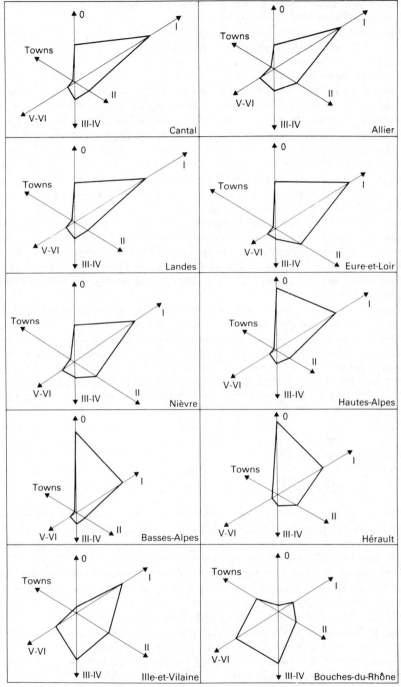

The six axes total 100% of the communes in each *département*
1 axis = 1 type of commune   1 mm = 2%

Fig. 17   The framework of rural shopping in ten French *départements*.

activities, bearing in mind that the communes in question have under 5,000 people (see Table 32).

This twofold classification, though handy and informative, may seem superfluous; but it does reveal all the variations in shopping facilities – variations that field study shows to correspond with specific types of consumer habits or shopping frequency.

The details of this research have been given in order to demonstrate the complexity of the hierarchies and to show that all such classifications are disputable; and they provide an additional argument for veering away from rigid schemes of central-place analysis. In Fig. 17 is displayed in graphical form the hierarchical order of rural communes in 10 French *départements,* based on shopping facilities. It reveals a great variety of structures. True, one can speak of a type-structure, represented here by Eure-et-Loir, Landes, Nièvre, Cantal, and perhaps Allier. But to anyone who knows France, it is clear that in the existence of high population densities (as in Ille-et-Vilaine), strong density contrasts (as in Hérault), the presence of a large city (as in Bouches-du-Rhône), or a mountain environment (Hautes-Alpes and Alpes-de-Haute Provence – formerly known as Basses-Alpes), there are elements that upset this structure-type. Besides, any map of the distribution of these hierarchised centres shows that the spatial distribution differs from the geometrical scheme (Delobez, 1973).

Other results of the above research concern the structure of the shopping facilities; they would appear to be of sufficient general import to be worth recording here. A detailed analysis of the communes in Eure-et-Loir since the end of the nineteenth century suggests two trends in the development of shopping facilities.

Table 32. Evolution of shopping facilities in rural communes in Eure-et-Loir

Level	1911	1936	1969
0 (no shops)	105	64	113
1 (Type 1 – at least one shop)	243	259	207
2 (Type 2 – hamlet-centre)	18	44	45
3 (Type 3 & 4 – central village)	34	34	25
4 (Type 5 & 6 – large villages & small towns)	4	4	5

The facilities increased at all levels between 1911 and 1936; this inter-war period represented something of a shopping explosion, and the number of communes without shops fell markedly. The years following the Second World War produced another burst of shop-creation, but since the late 1950s there has been a decline. Overall, between 1936 and 1969, there was a strong contrast between the most poorly served communes, which are becoming depopulated and even further deprived of their shops, and the large villages, where the facilities are becoming concentrated, especially above a certain level. This is in conformity with the selection process already mentioned. This difference in the evolution of shopping facilities is a function not merely of population size but of types of shop.

Food shops are affected; the increased consumption of fresh meat is reflected in the sales figures, despite all the indications to the contrary in the shape of population decline, improvements in long-distance transport and means of preservation; though the trade is concentrated in fewer shops. Home refrigerators are an important reason for this. Clothing shops are on the decline while new shops selling electrical and household goods are appearing, often accompanied by other services, such as banks, that seek closer contact with the rural clientele.

Table 33. Evolution of some shop-types in the rural areas of Eure-et-Loir

	1892	1912	1955	1969
Butchers	5	16	22	18
Grocers	–	76	80	66
Drapery	–	19	7	5
Clothing	–	12	5	5
Electrical and household appliances	0	0	0	9
Banks	0	0	0	10

Source: Abstracted from Bottin directories.

Another systematic study may be cited, to show other characteristics of rural shopping facilities in a different region. The region is the Franche-Comté (an area in eastern France focusing on Besançon), of no great population density (62 per km² compared with 92 in the whole of France, in 1968), and still largely rural (43 per cent as against 33.8 per cent). Robert (1975) has proposed nine types of simple central functions to characterise the villages. On this basis there appear to be 239 complete village centres (CVCs) and 167 incomplete village centres (IVCs) having less than four out of the nine functions. It may be noted that as with the researches quoted above, the author admits that the groups that he has distinguished are arbitrary, since there is in fact a continuum of variations. Thus there is one CVC for 70 km² on average, but the density is greater in the more populous areas, along the main highways and valleys, and less on the more sparsely peopled plateaus. A calculation of relative isolation shows that the distance to the nearest centre in three directions has a median value of 10 km (falling to 4 km towards Montbéliard, where the area is only 15 km², and rising to 17 km on the isolated plateaus). Relating nucleated population to type of centre, Robert shows that in the 500–699 population range, 47.4 per cent of the villages are CVCs, a figure that rises to 90 per cent for the 1,000–1,999 range, and 98 per cent for villages of over 2,000 people. On the contrary, most of the IVCs are in the 300–399 population range (34.8 per cent). As for groupings of less than 200 people, 98.2 per cent of them are simple hamlets. The average size of the CVCs is 600 inhabitants, and of the IVCs, 350, but on the urban fringes, the CVCs disappear, even though the village populations may rise above 700. As regards spheres of influence, only 4 CVCs cover no more than their own commune; in 40 per cent of the cases, 4 to 6 communes are involved. The population served averages 1,437 for the CVCs and 785 for the IVCs. The author concludes that it is necessary to have at least 1,500 inhabitants to maintain the vitality of rural commerce; even if one reckons on some contribution from tourism, which provides a one-third increase in the clientele during a couple of months, the provision of shopping facilities appears excessive.

Above the level of the villages, Robert distinguishes *bourgs* (small towns) characterised by 20 selected activities that include specialty shops, private services, public services and administration. By regrouping the minimum combinations so as to eliminate chance localisations, he arrives at 32 complete and perfect *bourgs,* 37 complete but imperfect *bourgs* (87 per cent of these two series being the 'capitals' of cantons), and 20 incomplete *bourgs* (only 54 per cent of which are canton capitals). Among these *bourgs,* 25 have more than 4,000 inhabitants, but in the depth of the countryside some of them have no more than 750. Once again, the distances separating two *bourgs* vary from one part of the region to another: from 3 to 5 km in the vicinity of Montbéliard to 15 km in the vineyard area, and more than 20 km on the plateau. The general conclusion in respect of the Franche-Comté region is that, except when there is urban competition, the *bourgs* serve areas of between 100 and 200 km², containing 4 to 5,000 people. The spheres of influence, generally corresponding to a canton, or to half a canton, appear to be frequently conditioned by the nature of the physical environment.

The next stage above the villages and *bourgs* comprises the urban centres, 21 in number. The author presumes to emphasise the existence of a hierarchy: 1,800 communes, 406 key-villages, 92 *bourgs* and 21 towns, 'in each case including both complete and incomplete centres', giving a coefficient of $K = 4$ – but we must avoid being bemused by this as is the concluding section of the study itself.

All these examples taken from the French countryside lead to the same conclusion as we have already mentioned, namely, that there is undoubtedly a gradation in the provision of shopping facilities. Much ingenuity has been used to establish levels within this gradation, but the classifications are weak and often open to question. Furthermore, the centres within these hierarchical levels are not spatially localised according to regular geometrical patterns. Besides, analyses of shopping frequency, where they exist, show short-circuits or inflexions that add still further to the irregularity of the theoretical pyramid. It is thus only by fabrication of averages and generalities that one can find any analogy with the theories of Christaller and Lösch. It is easier to demonstrate this in the case of the rural environment than by using towns and cities, for which the detail of trade flows and shopping equipment is more complex and difficult to ascertain with any degree of precision.

The new shopping types of the urban fringe

Needs and constraints

The recent outburst of urbanisation and the widespread diffusion of the private motor car have been accompanied in the industrialised countries by a rapid and often uncontrolled extension of suburban tentacles. In the United States, for example, while the population in 1960 was still in three more-or-less equal sectors, at the present time 40 per cent are in suburbs as against 30 per cent in towns and 30 per cent in rural areas. Having grown in a few decades, these suburbs find themselves in an uncertain situation: too far from the centre, to the congestion of which they contribute, assimilating former villages with shopping centres that were often decayed and ill-adapted to the quantitative and qualitative characteristics of the new clientele, they have experienced great difficulties, both in respect of service and the means of transport. The inhabitants of these new quarters have often had no other recourse but to go to· the central business district, on which all the traffic flows converge, resulting from the heritage of the road system. For daily needs, the local shops, whether inherited from the old village or built in among the new housing, were often primitive and inadequate. Between the parent city and the rural areas there was a girdle of varying width that was almost devoid of commercial activity.

The Paris conurbation gives a picture, on a very large scale it is true, of this situation. In 1962, there were 70 people occupied in retail trade for every 1,000 inhabitants in Paris itself; in the suburban fringes (within a radius of 15 km) the proportion fell to 35 per 1,000 but with variations of from 17 to 30 in the interstitial zones and 30 to 50 along the main highways. These figures compare with 46 per 1,000 calculated for separate French towns of roughly the same size as the new suburbs, namely 10 to 50,000 inhabitants. Beyond, in the outer circle, within a radius of 15 to 30 km, the figure averages no more than 19.6 per 1,000, despite the presence of several more favoured localities distributed in broadly radial fashion (Delobez, 1973). The growth of the suburbs has taken place without an equivalent development of shopping facilities, which are 'few in number, three or four times less than the French average, and lacking in variety. . . For all purchases other than daily needs, the people go to an older centre, such as Choisy or Juvisy, or go into Paris, and some of them even go outside the suburb for food purchases'; this is a picture of the southern suburbs of Paris, that have sprung up since 1945, according to Bastié (1964, p. 428). The same phenomena have been described in reference to many cities in other parts of the world, notably in the big cities of the United States, where the whole process has been carefully analysed (Vance, 1962).

The multiplication of shopping facilities in the urban fringes is thus a response to an absolute necessity. It has taken several forms that are dependent on a certain number of prerequisites and constraints. Situated as they are on the periphery, these new shopping facilities cannot profit from the convergence of routes, nor from the variety of attractions, nor from the high residential densities that characterise the city centre. On the other hand, they have the advantage of the availability of space at a reasonable price, freedom of choice in the selection of an exact site, the existence of good-quality roads that are not congested, and the presence of a relatively young clientele, motorised and with considerable purchasing power, and not set in its ways. There is further the possibility of building from scratch to suit the particular purpose, using materials and cheap constructional methods that permit alteration, adaptation, and perhaps even transfer to another site after a certain time, as the urban area develops (thus the Carrefour de Créteil, covering 6,750 m², was built and removed after only 10 years). They come into being and live in an atmosphere of dynamic expansion, while the commercial centres within the city are often paralysed by environmental constraints, and may indeed be struggling for their very existence. There is thus great opposition between shopping in the centre and shopping on the periphery. The only thing in common is the profit motive, which is very important. In countries where the standard of living has risen sharply during the last few decades, the consumer appetite is strong, and is easily excited by advertising and fashion changes; the shops wish to participate in the general prosperity, and to that end must constantly increase their turnover, by attracting an ever larger and more covetous clientele.

This being so, the course is marked out: the establishments must be of large size to make a good profit; they must display a wide range of goods so as to satisfy and retain the custom of a clientele of heavy spenders; their location must be such as to permit rapid and easy accessibility from a wide peripheral area where the population is generally spread out rather than concentrated.

The formula has been progressively modified, as residential areas have spread, incomes have risen, more families have cars, and sales techniques have developed, with better planning and rationalisation of the facilities. The quality of freshness possessed by these new establishments derives from the absence of an inherited past; generally established after more or less careful market research, they have opportunities of choice and of innovation that are denied to the traditional shops; they are located in or adjacent to developing residential areas, with a population that is young if not very wealthy, dynamic and abounding in children. However, they do not benefit from the advantages of a central situation, an established reputation, the company of other attractions, and in some cases the beauty of the setting and the pleasant appearance.

Types of development

We may now consider this vast movement towards the establishment of peri-urban shopping facilities, using four overlapping criteria: contents, size, period and localisation.

The shopping facilities of the suburbs may take one of three forms: the strengthening of the centres of villages engulfed by the tide of urban expansion; the setting up of small neighbourhood shops designed to serve, for better or worse, the local residents, mainly with daily requirements; and the establishment of large complexes offering a variety of resources to the clientele in the vicinity. The first formula is not always possible, for very often, especially in the newer countries, the suburban expansion does not encounter a pre-existing village network; and when it does, as in Europe, what exists is often old and confined, picturesque maybe, but unsuitable for large-scale expansion and improvement. The second solution has the disadvantage of responding only to a very limited demand, and in poor conditions. It is also rendered increasingly maladjusted by modern car transport and by technical progress in home storage (refrigerators and deep-freezers). And it does not dispense with the necessity of going to other better-served centres for many purchases. The third possibility is thus the establishment of new kinds of shopping facilities, sufficiently large, varied, attractive and accessible to bring in the large volume of customers that, under the capitalist system, are necessary for them to be profitable.

To do this, there are two possibilities: one very large emporium with many departments, or a group of shops with as wide a variety as possible. In both cases, the management is constantly preoccupied with seeking the range of goods that will attract the greatest number of customers, either to maximise the profits or from a desire to give the best possible service to the maximum number of people.

While the department stores, born in the nineteenth century, and later the multiples, between the First and Second World Wars, have always sought sites in the heart of the most central business quarters, and often in the absolute centre of the town or city, the new types tend to follow, or even to precede, the development of the suburbs.

The theorists can easily distinguish and classify these new forms of trading. As in most studies of localisation, they have been concerned more with models of ideal planning networks than with the real developments that are going on daily under our very eyes. In both North America and Europe, the projects that have been completed may be divided into three grades (Mérenne-Schoumaker, 1974; Careil, 1967; I.A.U.R.P., 1968). At the lowest level, the *local centre* or neighbourhood centre has a sales area of 3–5,000 m²; it consists of a dozen or so specialty shops grouped around a supermarket or a chain-store; it has 500–800 parking spaces, and serves 10–30,000 people. The *medium-sized centre* offers a wider range, with a surface area of 10–20,000 m². It has at least two poles of attraction, that may be a department store, a multiple, one or two supermarkets or a hypermarket; its service extends to 40–100,000 people, 3,000 parking spaces for cars, and some services as well as shops. The *regional centre* has an even larger function. Its sales area is greater than 25,000 m², with more than 50 specialty shops around several poles of attraction, and a number of services; the population served may be well over 100,000, and there may be as many as 10,000 parking spaces.

These are the general rules that have been followed in recent years, with variations, regarding suburban shopping developments in the most highly developed industrialised countries. In the United States, where the regional centres have had quite a long history (see p. 21), three stages have been recognised (Careil, 1967): the first generation, before 1950, were of limited area, linked to existing roads and often to an already established shopping centre; the whole group had little coherence and but few parking spaces. One could hardly speak of 'shopping centres', of which the first was really the one opened in Seattle in 1950 (Michel and Vander Eycken, 1974). Between 1950 and 1960, a second generation saw the light of day, with the expansion of the suburban motorway system; the characteristics remained the same, but the overall size increased. After 1960, a third generation made its appearance; Careil calls them 'huge'. They were established further and further from the city centre, anticipating future urban development, and always alongside motorways; the 'shopping centre' became an architectural entity with covered ways, decorations and amusement arcades: a city within a city, a place of leisure, spending and diversions, with ample parking, and not only supermarkets but department stores, branches emanating from the city centre, adding their magnetic attraction to that of the individual shops.

In Europe the first shopping centre was probably that at Main-Taunus, near Frankfurt, opened in 1954 (Fig. 18).

How can we characterise these new shopping centres? We may be content with the raw data given in all the publicity relating to them: number of shops, extent of sales floor-space in square metres, and the proportion of department stores, supermarkets and hypermarkets. Such figures have their value but they are formal and descriptive. A centrality index has been proposed by Thorpe and Rhodes (1966), that takes account of the number of non-food shops (M) in relation to the number of branches (which themselves are divided into three categories: A, branches of non-food multiples; B, banks; C grocery multiples and cooperatives; that are weighted according to their number – thus over three banks counts four points, one or two banks, two points). To adapt this to more recent circumstances it would be necessary to introduce a coefficient for the presence and extent of really large supermarkets.

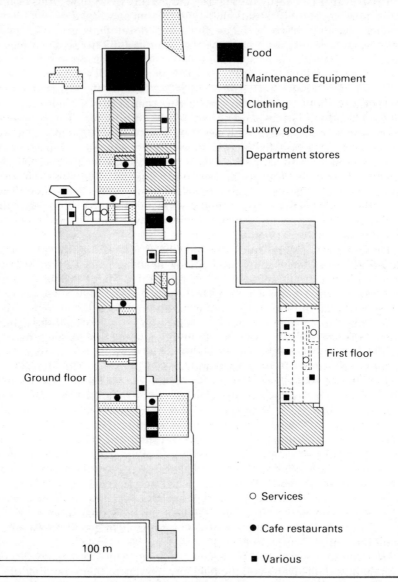

Fig. 18 A modern shopping centre; Main-Taunus Zentrum, W. Germany. (Sources: Wolf, 1966 and Brunet, 1972.)

It must be noted that two kinds of establishment appear in these new centres, the 'progressive', which, according to the period, are the supermarkets, the department stores and multiples, and then the hypermarkets; and the 'complementary', which are the smaller specialty shops that line the roadways or arcades that surround and enclose the big ones.

Supermarkets have existed in the United States since 1937, but, as Applebaum (1968) remarks, they were then located in the central business districts, and there is no mention in contemporary reports, of planned shopping centres, nor of motorways, for such things did not exist at that time; likewise, special car parks were a rarity, and lines other than foodstuffs (such as pharmaceuticals and hardware) had scarcely entered the picture. This type of establishment, officially defined in France as having between 400 and 2,500 m² of floor-space (though in some countries, such as the United States, the distinction is based on annual turnover), specialised particularly in food products, and had features that were obviously appropriate for serving the shopping needs of the suburbs, as they were at that period. Their rapid spread in the United States is thus not surprising; at the end of the Second World War they were located mainly along the road arteries leading to the city centres, if possible at crossroads, and they began to develop their own car parks. This uncontrolled spread often led to cut-throat competition and the elimination of the weaker elements. It took some time for the supermarket chains to realise the value of the close physical proximity that constituted 'shopping centres'.

This movement was a veritable revolution in retail trading. The example of a grocery chain in northeastern England is indicative of the early stages in the transformation (Thorpe and Rhodes, 1966, p. 53): the initial expansion was most rapid in the suburban fringes, especially around the great conurbations. 'Thus, in 1964, comparing the share of the regional supermarkets in the national retail sales with the same region's share of the national population, there was an excess of 1.9 per cent in London, of 1.8 per cent in the London suburbs, and of 0.4 per cent in the Tyneside towns, but a deficit of 1.5 per cent in the remainder of the North East, and of 4.1 per cent in Scotland.'

The *department stores and multiples* belong to another era, and their presence in the new centres indicates the willingness of these older types to take part in the new strategy. The branches remain associated with the main store, which is better stocked and more luxurious. In the United States, this has been a veritable explosion, and all the main chains have taken part in it (Sears, Wards, Dayton, etc.). The Parisian example is also typical: Printemps, Samaritaine, and Bazar de l'Hôtel de Ville have spawned new shops in the suburbs, and then in new centres further out.

The *hypermarket* is the newest arrival on the scene. The first was a French one, established by Carrefour (see p. 49). The United States gradually came to appreciate its merits (see p. 22) and in 1973 the first American one was opened, in a Chicago suburb. Like the supermarket, the hypermarket can stand on its own, but it can also become part of a larger complex, of which it remains the central core.

Combinations of these three forms of retail trading are so varied, in the countries that have taken part in such new development, that it is impossible to suggest a firm classification. But the most important factor seems to be accessibility. In Belgium, only 27.6 per cent of the super- and hypermarkets in the big cities are on major routeways, but those that are so situated are by far the largest, and they contain 50.9 per cent of the floor-space. Further, the turnover and so the profits also vary widely in relation to the characteristics both of the clientele and of the centres themselves – not merely the composition of the centres in terms of variety of shops represented, but also their arrangement within the chosen sites, the quality of the management and the reputation of the leading shops. Finally, spatial distribution is not unimportant, as Table 34 shows.

Table 34. Sales and profits of supermarkets according to type of location (average for the chain is 1).

Location	Turnover	Profit
Major planned regional centre	2.6	1.3
Planned Local Centre	1.7	1.3
On a major highway	1.4	1.1
Unplanned major centre	1.3	1.2
Unplanned local centre	1.1	1.0
Isolated location	1.0	1.1
Small town centre	0.8	0.9

Source: Appleton (1968), p. 48.

Some French examples

An inspection of the maps in the French *Atlas urbain des commerces de grandes surfaces,* edited with commentary by Coquery (1972), leads to a number of general conclusions. The towns referred to all have more than 50,000 inhabitants; they are distributed throughout France, except in the Paris region and the northern industrial zone (Nord and Pas-de-Calais).

Twenty towns had *supermarkets,* which numbered 185 in 1971. Fourteen of these had appeared before 1963; among the pioneers were those at Bayonne (1955), Bordeaux and Lyon (1962). By the end of 1968 there were 128, with 57 more opened between 1967 and 1971. These creations had an average surface area of 793 m². Their distribution was so uneven that no simple conclusions can be drawn regarding the sizes of the towns served or their geographical location. The average distance from the traditional urban centres was 1.8 km.

Thirty-six urban agglomerations had 74 *hypermarkets* between them. All were situated either on the outer edge of the suburban zones, or some distance beyond the built-up area, but always on major roads. The straight-line distance from the traditional CBD averaged 4.2 km (with a minimum of 1.5 km in Limoges and a maximum of 8 km at Marseilles, Nantes and Toulouse). The surface area averaged 7,311 m² and was still growing. The first versions of this new type were of modest dimensions, that at Bordeaux in 1968 (slightly later than the first one in Paris) having no more than 2,500 m² floor-space. But gigantism soon appeared, and the Carrefour hypermarket at Marseilles in 1970 had 20,000 m², and that of the same company at Toulouse in 1972 had 24,459 m². For the whole of France, other statistics give 147 hypermarkets in 1971 and 292 in 1975.

The same *Atlas* also shows 55 *shopping centres* in 27 towns, indicating (on 1 : 50,000 scale maps) their total surface and year of creation. The period covered is 1958 to 1972. For the years 1958–68, the average size of these shopping centres was 2,654 m² – an advance on the 1,000–1,200 m² of those established at the beginning of the period. Almost all these centres were within already existing suburbs, or at the junction of older and newly developing suburbs. Of the 29 centres built before 1968, four-fifths were under 2,200 m² in area. After 1968, the dimensions took an upward turn: for 28 new centres, the average rose to 13,479 m², and in 1971, 69 per cent of the centres were over 6,000 m². But the characteristics are changing, and many of the newest centres are located in zones of planned urbanisation, in which the development revolves around a hypermarket, a department store or both of these; they are invariably adjacent to important roads, either on major radial routes or better still at the junction of two radials or a radial and a peripheral motorway either existing or planned – for anticipation is part of the new strategy.

In 1975, there were 238 shopping centres of which 9 had more than 50,000 m² of floor-space. Sixty-seven centres were located in the Paris region, which also had 7 out of the 8 'regional centres' (the eighth being in Lyon). Most of them had been opened between 1972 and 1974.

It is possible, from the data contained in Coquery's *Atlas*, to make a graphical model of the commercial development of the average French town (Fig. 19).

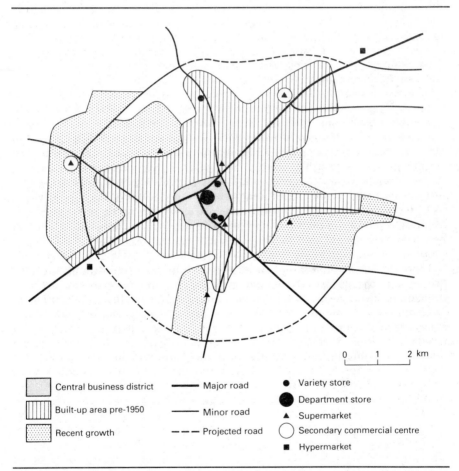

▦ Central business district	▬▬ Major road	● Variety store
▥ Built-up area pre-1950	▬▬ Minor road	⬤ Department store
▨ Recent growth	- - - Projected road	▲ Supermarket
		◯ Secondary commercial centre
		■ Hypermarket

0 1 2 km

Fig. 19 Schematic map of the location of shopping facilities in an average French town.

The traditional central nucleus is based on several department stores and multiples dating generally from before 1940. The older quarters, built up before 1950, are relatively poorly served, but the creation of a number of supermarkets and chain-stores has supplemented the local shops, which were often deficient. The newer establishments are generally to be found along the main axial roads that cross the town, or on the boundary between the older and newer built-up areas. The newer suburbs are served by supermarkets, with or without accompanying shops, and by shopping centres containing services as well as shops, supermarkets and multiples. Finally, at the edge of the existing urban area, and on major highways, are the new hypermarkets.

The regional shopping centres built in the Paris region represent a highly integrated type of organisation, whether or not they form the centre of new towns. We may site the example of Rosny II, which cost 160 million francs to build and covers 88,000 m². It is served by a railway station (17 minutes from the Gare de l'Est), two motorways (the radial A3 and a feeder road A86), and six bus routes, and has a car park with 5,000 spaces. It is all under cover and air-conditioned, and has two department stores (Bazar de l'Hôtel de Ville and Samaritaine), four smaller companies (C & A, La Redoute, Prisunic and Casino) and 125 specialty shops, the rents for which are based on their turnover. Besides the shops there is a whole range of services, such as dry-cleaning, travel agencies, temporary employment bureaux, pharmacies, six restaurants, six cinemas, several clubs, and information centres.

In other cases, the shopping centres, accompanied by other forms of business, are designed as the structural nuclei of new towns in course of development, with one large one in the centre and smaller ones in the various quarters. In the new town of Evry, the main shopping centre was opened in 1975. It is a real functional heart of the future city; it has a surface area of 70,000 m² with over 4,000 parking spaces: there are two large department stores (Printemps and Nouvelle Galeries) and over 100 shops with cafés, restaurants, cinemas, swimming pool, skating rink, leisure services, conference hall, etc. It is the real 'agora', the meeting place, a centre of life and amusement as much as – or more than – a shopping precinct; its designers have given full play to the complexity and the integration of central-place functions in which shopping has an important role.

There is thus a whole range of new developments that result either from private initiative or from communal effort. In total, the floor-space area of all the centres having over 2,000 m² in the Paris area alone reached 500,000 m² in 1970 and one million in 1973 – an explosion indeed, that has brought about considerable changes in the movement of people as well as in the balance of retail trade. Table 35 summarises some turnover figures to give an idea of the returns from different urban and peri-urban establishments.

Table 35. Comparative turnover

Company (and date)		Turnover (million Fr)	Turnover (Fr) per m² of sales area
Samaritaine	1971	547	11,072
Galeries Lafayette	1971	700	14,799
BHV Centre	1971	534	16,700
BHV Flandres	1971	34	6,800
Parly II	1972	420	7,562
Belle Epine	1972	365	5,214
Carrefour, Créteil	1972	315	46,700
Carrefour Ste. Genev.	1972	169	38,148

Source: Bulletin Information de la Région parisienne: *Les Commerces,* 1974.

It is instructive to compare these turnover figures. They show that the large single establishments (of the traditional department-store type) have a larger turnover per unit area because they are more compact, with smaller circulating areas. Food sales, that characterise the Carrefour centres, are top of the list (and it is these vast areas devoted to this activity that place this firm in the front rank nationally). The department stores in the centre, which can develop no further, still have a large turnover compared with either their own extensions in the suburban centres (BHV Flandres), or with the sum total of the peripheral shopping centres. It is evident, however, that a relative rather than an absolute value must be attached to these comparisons between turnover figures for some of the data, notably on floor-space, are not strictly comparable for department stores, shopping centres and other types with large sales areas.

Suburban and urban-fringe retailing in Britain*

In many aspects of retailing, Britain has played a pioneer role, but when we look at recent changes in the locational pattern of shops we can see that Britain has been far more conservative than most west European countries or North America. Large British urban areas have important suburban shopping centres, and extensive shopping facilities have traditionally been common in the suburbs, but the overall locational pattern, dominated by the central area, has remained basically unchanged for half a century. Until the 1960s the only major departures from the established pattern were the New Towns and a few district centres associated with rapidly expanding suburban areas such as Yate near Bristol and Cowley on the outskirts of Oxford.

In most other western countries there has been a much greater development of planned shopping centres in new locations on the urban fringe and beyond. Generally this is a trend which has been prompted jointly by the impact of the private motor car and the movement towards mass merchandising; in the USA this trend was especially strong in the period 1938–58 whereas in Europe, it is the succeeding 20-year period which has been important. Today in North America a hierarchy of planned shopping centres can be recognised as follows:

Table 36. Shopping centre hierarchy

	Typical size characteristics			
	Floorspace (m²)	Site area (ha)	Car spaces	Population served
Regional centre	40,000+	16	4,000	100–250,000
Community centre	9,000–14,000	4–12	1,300	20–100,000
Neighbourhood centre	2,500–4,000	1.5–4	360	7–20,000

Although it is possible to find plenty of examples to fit this hierarchy from recent developments in mainland Europe, the British case shows few similarities. Excluding the abortive Haydock Park scheme between Manchester and Liverpool, only one example of the planned regional shopping

---

* This section has been contributed by Dr. P. T. Kivell

centre can be cited in the UK. This is the Brent Cross centre, one of 29 designated strategic shopping centres in suburban London, and the only one which is completely new in both design and location (Blake, 1978). Built on a 21-ha site which was previously allotment gardens and open space, the centre occupies an advantageous location at the junction of the North Circular Road and the A41 spur from the M1 motorway. Although aimed primarily at car-owning shoppers – there are an estimated 1.25 million within 20 minutes driving time – the centre is also served by nine bus routes. The centre, which was opened in 1976, is a joint development between the Hammerson Property Group and the London Borough of Barnet, and it has had a protracted gestation period. The site was originally considered in 1963, by 1968 a public planning enquiry was held and building actually commenced in 1972. Today there are some 90 shops providing nearly 75,000 m² of floor-space arranged about an enclosed and air-conditioned mall. Food and convenience shops play only a minor role and the emphasis is firmly upon fashion and consumer durables, with John Lewis, Fenwicks, Marks & Spencer, Mothercare, Miss Selfridge and Austin Reed being important magnets. Although the project is now successfully established, changing economic circumstances make it unlikely that this style and scale of development will be repeated elsewhere in the foreseeable future.

As far as the second category is concerned, Britain has relatively few developments which match the American Community Centre. In terms of size and facilities, the Hampshire Centre on the outskirts of Bournemouth would fit this description, so too would the development at Thornaby, a suburb of Teesside, but for the most part Britain's restricted experiments with such new schemes has involved the construction of free-standing superstores or hypermarkets which fall somewhere between neighbourhood and community centres in size and facilities. Although there are still some minor differences of opinion, a 'superstore' is normally accepted as a single-level, self-service store offering a wide range of food and non-food merchandise, with a sales area of at least 2,500 m² and supported by its own car parking. The term 'hypermarket' is generally confined to developments which exceed 5,000 m², although in view of many planning appeals and public enquiries the word itself carries certain emotive overtones and it is completely eschewed by some developers. The other common feature of such developments is their site, although given that a non-central site is often only a means to cheap building land or adequate space for car parking, it is not surprising that superstores and hypermarkets are to be found in a variety of locations including greenfield, urban fringe, suburban, inner-city redeveloped sites, and in the notable case of Telford, a hypermarket forms the anchor store for the town centre itself.

There is no doubt that Britain has adopted a more cautious approach than many of her neighbours: by the early 1970s hypermarkets were an established part of the European retail scene as Table 37 shows, but Britain had barely started. Undoubtedly developments in Britain lagged far behind at this date, but the solitary hypermarket accredited to Britain by this table, the French-sponsored Carrefour at Caerphilly, is certainly an underestimate. The suggestion that the Caerphilly hypermarket was the first in Britain when it opened in 1972 is often repeated but in fact several developments of a comparable nature had already been trading for a number of years without actually using the name 'hypermarket'. Probably the first was the 6,500 m²

Table 37. Hypermarkets in western Europe (1973)

	Belgium	France	W. Germany	Netherlands	UK
Number of hypermarkets	46	212	406	7	1
Total selling area (m²)	306,868	1,238,803	2,595,825	33,816	5,202
Average selling area (m²)	6,671	5,843	6,394	4,830	5,202
% of retail trade	4.6	4.8	6.8	< 1	N.A.

Source: Smith (1973)

GEM superstore opened at West Bridgford on the outskirts of Nottingham in 1964. Although built originally by an American company, this store was taken over in 1967 by the Leeds-based Asda (Associated Dairies) group. By 1972, when the first Carrefour hypermarket started trading, Asda were operating 18 large stores, mainly in the north of England. Although the majority of these were below the hypermarket size threshold of 5,000 m², other companies, notably Woolco, had larger units. The first Woolco, a store of 5,850 m² of selling space was opened at Oadby, near Leicester, in 1967 and by 1972 it had been joined by five others at Bournemouth, Thornaby, Killingworth, Middleton and Hatfield, each with between 6,000 and 7,000 m² of selling space. Subsequent developments have been fairly slow, for reasons outlined below, and the most recent figures available from the Unit for Retail Planning Information (1977) suggest a total of 139 superstores and 38 hypermarkets trading or with planning approval in the UK.

To a large extent the factors encouraging the decentralisation of retail activities have been similar throughout the western world; it is only the time-scale and the political and planning responses that have differed. There are many rapidly changing conditions tending to favour suburban and out-of-town retailing locations. These have been discussed at greater length elsewhere (Kivell 1972; Mills 1974) and a summary will suffice at this stage. Firstly, the urban environment has changed in physical terms as well as demographic. Congestion and high land prices in the centre coupled with lower land prices and better road access on the fringe have provided a physical stimulus to decentralisation. In addition, the population of most cities has experienced a marked decentralisation in recent years. The Department of the Environment (1976) has shown that between 1951 and 1961, more than half of the standard metropolitan labour areas in Britain experienced either relative or absolute population decentralisation, and that by 1971 this proportion had risen to four-fifths.

Secondly, a number of social and economic changes have encouraged decentralisation. Of prime importance is the motor car, both for its general role of encouraging suburban growth and for its specific role as a large motorised shopping basket, but many secondary factors such as the number of wives at work, the increasing importance of convenience foods and the use of freezers must also be taken into account.

From a retailer's point of view the large development on a suburban or fringe site is the most practicable way in which to achieve economies of scale, room for expansion, efficient deliveries and adequate parking space.

In summary then there are three groups of factors affecting the urban environment, the consumer and the retailer respectively, but all working in the same direction, in favour of large retail units with generous parking facilities located in suburban or urban-fringe areas. Certainly there have been other forces working in the opposite direction but the centrifugal pressures have been strong enough to provoke a considerable degree of interest in decentralised retailing.

Overall there is little difference between the operation of these factors in Britain and in other urbanised western nations. Similarly, there is little difference between most indicators of personal affluence in Britain and her EEC partners. The explanation for the difference in the scale and distribution of supermarket and out-of-town shopping developments must therefore be sought elsewhere.

The most obvious difference lies in the greater rigidity of planning restrictions in Britain. Even without discussing specifically retailing issues, it is easy to see that a planning philosophy which is based upon the containment of urban growth, the prevention of sprawl, the protection of the countryside and the creation of self-contained communities will discourage retail developments in peripheral locations. In addition to these general issues, most planners and local politicians assume an obligation to protect the central shopping-area of their town.

By the early 1970s the argument between those in favour of hypermarkets and those against became intense. The main issues have been listed elsewhere (Thorpe, 1974) but basically they revolved around the promised advantage of greater convenience and lower prices and the implied disadvantages of the threat to the viability of central-area shopping, the encouragment of urban sprawl, the traffic-generation problem and the distribution of benefits disproportionately upon wealthier car-owning shoppers. Although shopping provision is basically a local planning issue, many planning authorities were almost overwhelmed by applications for superstore and hypermarket developments. In 1972 the government purported to give the local authorities some guidance by the issue of *Development Central Policy Note No. 13* (on out-of-town shops and shopping centres). This note briefly listed some of the advantages and disadvantages and effectively discouraged greenfield and urban-fringe developments. Unfortunately it failed to provide the one thing which most local planners needed, and that was precise guidance on how to handle this major new issue. In the same year the Secretary of State for the Environment decided to call in all applications exceeding 4,645 m² for decision at central-government level.

The result was that superstore developments of less than 4,645 m² went ahead, albeit slowly, but larger hypermarket developments were subject to lengthy and expensive planning application, public enquiry and appeal procedures. Planners and local politicians were seen to be adopting negative attitudes, judging an application not upon its merits, but upon its lack of demerits. Delays of up to five years occurred and meanwhile the economic situation had changed, bringing with it tighter investment conditions, declining personal affluence and increasing travel costs. Planning restrictions, however, are not the sole factor in accounting for the slow growth of off-centre locations. Sweden, with equally restrictive planning laws, has been among the leaders in developing new retail centres, and even France, a hypermarket pioneer, has experienced tight controls since the Royer Law of 1973. Consequently we must identify additional factors such as the greater significance of multiple retailers in Britain (especially food supermarkets), the greater strength of town centres, a different political climate and the effects of the upheaval and reorganisation of local government in the early 1970s. Finally, during this period many local authorities were in the midst of preparing new structure plans and while this may have given them the opportunity to undertake a comprehensive review of their shopping provision, it was not an ideal situation under which to make speedy *ad hoc* decisions about superstore or hypermarket applications.

Largely as a result of planning strictures, either real or imagined, the rate of development has been slow and the schemes approved appear to be something of a compromise both in size and location.

Only one-fifth of the 177 superstores and hypermarkets in the UK exceed 5,000 m² and the typical development appears to be a free-standing store of approximately 3,000–4,000 m² in a suburban or urban fringe rather than greenfield location. Only half a dozen stores exceed 7,000 m². Geographically there is a fairly distinct pattern, with the North, North West and Yorkshire/Humberside regions having the greatest amount of development, and particularly notable concentrations in the Greater Manchester area and the West Yorkshire conurbation. This regional pattern is very much in line with the suggestion of Schiller (1974) that the major innovations in retailing have taken place outside of the South East, and in this case is probably explained by the greater availability of land and the rather weaker position of large-scale multiple retailers outside of the South East of England.

Most of the large retailers have expressed an interest in fringe or out-of-town locations, with only Marks & Spencer being firmly wedded to central locations. Many national food retail chains, including Fine Fare, Tesco and Sainsbury, have undertaken superstore developments and the Co-op movement has been active. Four operators stand out in particular; Woolco because of the large size of their stores (average > 6,000 m²) and because they were one of the earliest developers; Asda because of their numerical supremacy (30 stores in 1977); the Co-op because the superstore appears to be a major factor in their revival; and Carrefour because they have uncompromisingly promoted the hypermarket name and image.

Perhaps the most contentious issue in the whole hypermarket debate has concerned the effect which such developments would have upon established centres, and this objection has been responsible for more planning refusals than any other. Widely varying estimates have been made at planning enquiries but clearly a large hypermarket, which is expected to generate up to 30,000 customers per week and achieve an annual turnover comparable with that of an established town like Durham, Cirencester or Sevenoaks, is bound to have a significant impact. Hypermarkets have been blamed for the closure of small shops, but few comparative studies have been done and it is clear that many small shops are closing in areas without hypermarkets or superstores. In America the growth of out-of-town centres has been cited as the major factor in the decline of the CBD but studies such as that by McDonald (1975) suggest that there is not a direct causal link, but that both CBD decline and out-of-town growth are due to the suburbanisation of population and greater personal mobility.

Much obviously depends upon local circumstances, but it is difficult to find hard evidence which supports the viewpoint that hypermarkets will have a disastrous impact upon established shopping centres. Although it is too soon to be conclusive, the consensus of evidence tends to suggest that carefully controlled developments of this nature will have only a modest impact. Thorpe *et al.* (1972) suggest that the Hampshire Centre, a large development, has usurped an estimated 8 per cent of Bournemouth's town-centre trade; Bridges (1977) shows that a smaller Asda superstore at Huntington has taken only 2 per cent of York's central-area trade, and Eastleigh district council suggest that their town-centre trade has been virtually unaffected by the presence of a 5,200 m² Carrefour hypermarket. Several studies have been reviewed by Mills (1974) and there seems to be large measure of agreement with the view expressed in the impact study of the Caerphilly hypermarket undertaken by Donaldsons (1973) that changes in the shopping pattern have been subtle rather than gross and that the effect was dispersed among many centres. The impact will normally have a differential effect according to location and type of retailer and as Thorpe *et al.* (1976) suggest, the multiples and Co-ops are hit harder than independent retailers, and nearby suburban shops are more severely affected than central shopping areas. The significance of relatively small changes in turnover should not however be underestimated, for as Pickering (1972) has pointed out, a large proportion of a retailer's costs are fixed, and a 10 per cent reduction in his volume of trade can result in a 75 per cent reduction in profits.

Finally there is evidence that hypermarkets/superstores and conventional town-centre retailers can co-exist; the Telford Carrefour has a Sainsbury supermarket as one of its nearest neighbours, at Eastleigh Carrefour and Tesco both thrive, in North Staffordshire four peripheral Co-op superstores have been followed by large new Tesco and Sainsbury supermarkets in central locations, and in Bradford the development of eight superstores totalling 25,500 m² in the decade 1966–76 has been paralleled by the addition of 23,225 m² of additional floor-space in the town centre.

The evidence relating to the impact of superstore/hypermarket development is still not conclusive. Many concurrent and interacting variables have affected the pattern of retailing in recent years and it is often not possible to separate completely the input of a specific hypermarket scheme from the broader pattern of change due to other factors. The cautious approach adopted in Britain has certainly avoided some of the worst problems of saturation development that have occurred elsewhere and it seems that continued modest development will ensure that the superstore/hypermarket (of under 9,290 m²) will have an important but by no means dominant position in the hierarchy of retail centres.

Location of the new forms of retailing: chance or rationality?

In reading some of the literature on these modern commercial establishments, one might be led to believe that rational planning, either by the major sales organisations or by the public authorities, had completely dominated this sphere. It seems logical enough: there were underequipped suburbs, and there are urban extensions continually in progress and in which public investment in the infrastructure is considerable; one might imagine that both to improve the situation of the inhabitants of the older suburbs and to anticipate the future, an overall programme had been adopted that would have the effect of satisfying the consumers and avoiding the risk of wastage or failure on the part of the businesses. But what is the situation?

It was in the United States, in the early years of the present century, that the first researches were undertaken to permit the rational determination of the most favourable locations for commercial development. Done at the request of certain chain-store firms, they related to tobacconists and were mainly concerned with pedestrian traffic; later on, motor-car traffic was analysed in order to rationalise the location of petrol stations. After 1930, the investigations multiplied and became more precise, sponsored by grocery chains; areas of attraction were mapped, together with their population. But still most new installations were located by chance. It was after the Second World War that market research expanded rapidly and developed its own methodology, at the same time retrospective and prospective, not only for the location of retail shops but also for the assessment of the security of the investments that were becoming even larger. An enquiry made in 1963 showed that the cost of the research represented almost 1 per cent of the amount invested.

W. Applebaum, one of the pioneers of this research, who was first a practising businessman and then a theoretician at the Harvard Business School, has emphasised its interest and importance (Applebaum, 1968). Of course, the object is to inform and protect private capital, but Applebaum insists that this kind of research is necessary in any kind of economic regime. Indeed, one might well think that the profitability of state enterprises is just as important as that of privately financed undertakings.

It is interesting to compare this confession of faith in the necessity for market research with experience in France, where large organisations and companies often fight shy of this procedure. 'Is it really responsible to waste time in market research when the Parisian suburbs are suffering from a severe underdevelopment of modern shopping facilities? The hypermarkets at weekends are as congested as the métro in the rush hour.' So wrote the managing director of one of the great stores. This is an extreme view, and many investors are less bold.

It must be admitted, however, that in many cases the situation in the suburbs, and particularly in the new towns, is such that success is guaranteed in advance. This certainly does not mean that all market research is useless, nor that every success is unaffected by set-backs.

In the type of country where these developments are taking place, and within the framework of the society that lives there, social relationships are no longer only of an economic nature, or concern only individuals. It is therefore necessary to consider the facts in the context of the whole system rather than on an individual basis.

This represents a major change, characteristic of our times. In place of an urbanisation that went on day by day, by rule-of-thumb methods, there has been substituted an urban explosion, usually planned or at least under control, using hitherto unknown techniques. Four groups thus confront each other – the developers, the public, the existing shops and local government.

For those responsible for the new commercial developments themselves, whether a colossal hypermarket or a composite shopping centre, the tying up of capital demands the best possible choice of site, bearing in mind the whole conception of the centre and the actual and future risks of competition. For the population concerned, it is a question of basic facilities, for which there is no equivalent or substitute, that will give them satisfactory service at any price so

that their mode of life does not suffer. For the traditional shops of the locality or neighbourhood that do exist, however inadequate they may be, it is their disappearance or adaptation that is involved. Finally, for the public authorities, through the medium of democratic institutions and the ballot box, it is their maintenance or separation, and eventually perhaps a change of ideological outlook, that is in question. These different interests, that affect life in the new suburbs, also have their effect on commerce. What is now called 'commercial urbanism' is an important element in town planning.

The choices are fraught with consequences, and in European countries in particular there are several options. Take as an example the location of shopping centres (Fig. 20). Is it necessary to place them at the end of suburban transport lines so as to encourage the growth of secondary urban nuclei away from the main city, as in Stockholm? Or should they, as in Liège, be located in a

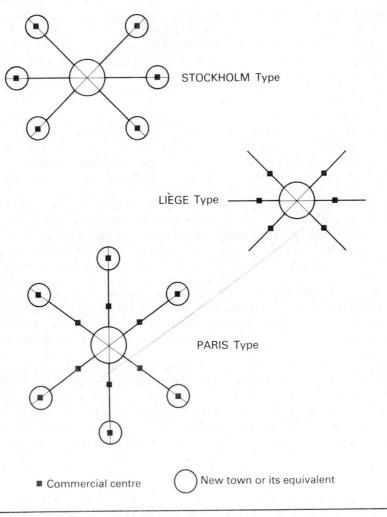

Fig. 20   Theoretical location possibilities for commercial centres.

girdle immediately outside the city, forming a kind of screen to catch the traffic converging on the centre? In the Paris region, much larger and more complex, there is a mixed response: to the shopping centres planned on greenfield sites in the new towns, that are situated at the extremities of the urban region, are added those of the outer circle (Parly II, Vélizy II, Rungis, Créteil, Rosny), while those of the older absorbed villages are maintained (Saint-Germain-en-Laye, Versailles, Saint-Denis).

The Paris example gives food for thought. While an overall development plan for the city and its region was formulated in 1965, and fully equipped urban centres have been created in the four or five new towns in course of construction (together with smaller centres in these towns), the vast developments initiated by private promoters have not always respected the plan.

One is thus led to the fundamental question: should complete freedom in the matter of shopping provision be left to private enterprise? In France, the Royer Law of 27 December 1973, through its restrictive powers (cf. p. 54), put a serious brake on the development of vast shopping areas. But it is still obvious that the existing organisation of retail business is somewhat archaic: there are too many small shops, often badly distributed. The clientele suffers because this entails the existence of a series of often parasitic middlemen and high prices that result from undue stretching of the link between producer and consumer, and low sales figures. Changes are certainly necessary, but if they are made too abruptly the social upheaval may be great. On the other hand, it must be admitted that the gigantic hypermarkets already in existence totally dehumanise the business of shopping. This is not the case with well-planned shopping centres which have an undeniable power of attraction – and distraction! – and create an atmosphere conducive to human intercourse; however, the fact that they are enclosed and encysted in the midst of residential quarters denies them one of the more agreeable aspects of the old town centres with their shop-lined streets, so easily accessible for daily purchases without demanding a special expedition.

Competition or complementarity

This 'revolution' in the distributive trades stems largely from two important facts: the increase in the number of urban dwellers and the growth of incomes. Surely here are developments that could hurt no one? But we must also take note that part of the turnover and profits realised by the new shopping facilities is at the expense of the older shops. When the new facilities are implanted in the heart of the suburbs, it is the older centres that are affected; many small and isolated shops can only subsist on the basis of chance custom and daily purchases; the competition may even extend to the main business district which is visited less frequently and only for exceptional purchases (in Paris, for example, there is competition between the Rue de Passy and Parly II). When the new centre is situated outside the urbanised area, the shops in the neighbouring countryside feel the effects (thus the Carrefour at Chartres has shaken the whole commercial foundations of the rural area of northern Beauce).

In certain cases there is complementarity , but it is more usually competition, between the older and newer types of shop. In more and more countries the

Table 38. Large supermarkets in the Paris region

	Carrefour Ste. Geneviève	Mammouth Montfermeil	Carrefour Créteil	Montréal Chambourcy
Characteristics:				
Date of opening	1963	1967	1968	1968
Sales area (m²)	4,430	2,910	6,750	4,073
Employees	260	199	495	240
Turnover per 1,000 m² (million francs)	37.7	22.3	34.9	142
Turnover per employee (thousand francs)	599	355	470	241
Clientele:				
Population of market area 1968	199,000	105,000	416,000	168,000
Population increase 1962–8 (%)	+50	+28	+18	+15
% Working-class population	13	12	15	20
% Wealthy population	41	34	24	19
Accessibility within 5km	Fairly good	Moderate	V. good	Good
% Working class in clientele	29	30	30	14
% Upper class in clientele	20	20	32	48
% Motivation of clientele:				
Price	31	36	39	26
Grouped purchases	22	22	11	37
Range of choice	17	10	24	10
Good parking	6	8	15	15
Impact on pre-existing shops:				
Number of shops in 1968 per 1,000 population	5.1	5.6	6.7	6.1
% change in shops per 1,000 population 1962–8	−50	−27	−28	−24
Number of medium-large shops (M.L.S.) pre-existing (self-service area over 120 m²)	16	33	97	57
% increase in sales area of M.L.S. 1968–71	+21	+56	+64	+98
% of small shops with reduced turnover in last 6 months	79	72	62	56
% with > 20% decrease	37	20	23	14
% of communes not having regained their 1970 turnover	62	36	28	28

Source: A. Delobez (1973) (based on 1970 figures).

newer forms are coming to predominate: in 1970, integrated commerce represented more than 50 per cent of the total in the United Kingdom, 36 per cent in West Germany and in the United States, 35 per cent in Sweden and Switzerland; though it only stood at 24 per cent in France and 6.3 per cent in Italy (Michel and Vander Eycken, 1974). The rapidity of the change explains the discontent of the traditional shopkeepers and the massive changes in the spatial and functional distribution of trading profits. Two examples will suffice.

With the help of the Ministry of Commerce, some investigations were made in France some years ago of the effects of the establishment of several types of supermarket on the pre-existing shops. It was found that the area of customer attraction varied according to several criteria: the number of new establishments offering equivalent facilities, their accessibility, the aggressiveness of their sales policy, the distribution of the outer suburban population and its characteristics, and the quality and adaptability of the shops that were there

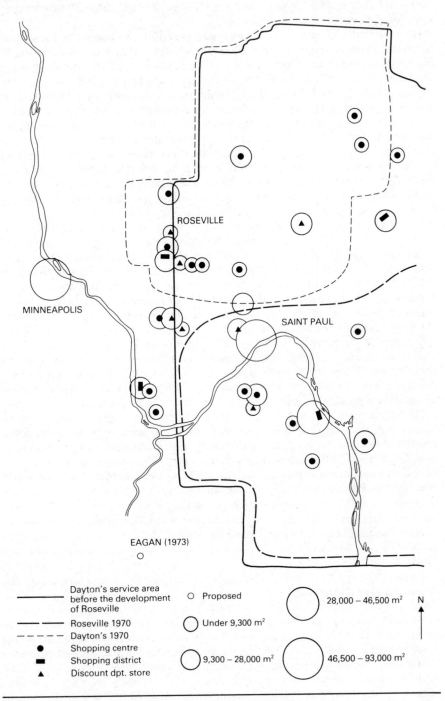

Dayton's service area before the development of Roseville
Roseville 1970
Dayton's 1970
● Shopping centre
▬ Shopping district
▲ Discount dpt. store

○ Proposed
◯ Under 9,300 m²
◯ 9,300 – 28,000 m²

⬤ 28,000 – 46,500 m²
⬤ 46,500 – 93,000 m²

N

Fig. 21 Service areas of Dayton's stores in St. Paul (Minnesota) as indicated by credit cards.

already. The clientele was primarily middle and upper class, while the working class and lower income groups were poorly represented. Table 38 summarises some of the results.

However difficult it may be to evaluate precisely the impact of these new creations on other shops, there is no doubt whatever that it is considerable, as the table demonstrates. Nevertheless, the conclusions of this detailed study shed a good deal of light on the possibility of defending the small shops. 'The supermarkets themselves are already vulnerable, especially by reason of their own multiplication, that has already created difficulties for some of them (as in the southern suburbs in particular) and has forced others to become no more than neighbourhood shops (for example Mammouth at Montfermeil); further, even when they are isolated, they maintain themselves only with difficulty in the face of competition from old and flourishing shopping centres (such as St. Germain), or more modern ones; and if the retailers knew how to face the competition this could be more frequent, unless the supermarkets react by improving their own services' (Delobez, 1973, p. 54).

Another investigation, this time in the twin cities of Minneapolis and St. Paul, in 1971, also produced some interesting results (Bongars, 1971). One of the main features of the reconstruction of the city centre of St. Paul was the rebuilding of the Dayton department store. This flourished until 1968, when the building of another Dayton branch, in the outlying business centre of Rosedale, in the northern suburbs, resulted in a 13.6 per cent fall in its turnover between 1968 and 1970. An examination of the credit cards of customers showed clearly the formation of two different market areas, and gradually the city centre store came to dominate only the city itself (Fig. 21).

The new forms of retail establishment thus appear to be very disturbing in their effects. They not only change people's habits, but undoubtedly reduce ordinary expenditure while exciting new appetites; this in all probability does not lead to a more favourable balance-sheet for the customers, but it enables them to purchase more. The new establishments have upset former trading habits, both spatially and functionally. Contrary to some expressed opinions, they create employment opportunities in the distribution sector – but of course to the detriment of the independent shopkeepers. They respond to a new type of society in which mass-production, the artificial creation of needs, the general rise in purchasing power, and the increasing population of consumers inevitably result in mass distribution methods.

Note

1. In this study, this means daily – or almost daily – requirements of non-food goods provided by chemists and hardware stores.

Conclusion:
Marketing systems and regions

Our examination of the differentiation of commercial equipment, as well as the extent and disposition of spheres of influence, has involved frequent reference to the notion of hierarchy and a description of trade flows converging on selected centres surrounded by more or less interlocking aureoles. The whole system appears on a map as a kind of net, in which the market areas are represented by the threads and the centres of attraction by the knots that join them.

Without attaching a magical importance to the geometrical regularities, we may yet note certain characteristics of these arrangements: the wide spacing of the more important centres, which are surrounded by secondary centres more or less regularly disposed; the spheres of influence of these major centres, juxtaposed and completely covering the area which itself is subdivided into numerous smaller cells that join, intersect and often overlap. This spatial disposition influences the form of the commercial systems, and the relations established through the medium of the elements of these systems result in a subdivision of space that it is as well to emphasise.

Commercial systems

A system has been defined as 'the distribution of the elements of an organisation in different localities; the elements so distributed' (Robert, 1975). In geographical literature, the expression 'urban system' is already well established. It has been defined as 'the organisation of towns of all types in a given area. The towns always appear to be linked to each other and to their hinterlands by various relations or contacts of a technological or commercial nature, or concerned with labour supply, and so, whether or not their arrangement is hierarchical, and whatever their functions, they always form a system' (Kostrowicki, 1967).

Observations and research on the distribution and functioning of commercial centres leave no doubt about the possibility, indeed the necessity, arising from the preceding definitions, of considering 'commercial systems'. There are the elements, which are the establishments or groups of establishments, and there is their distribution, which results in the servicing of the population and thus in a kind of organisation of trading patterns arising from these elements. But while the existence of commercial systems is not in doubt, there are three subsidiary questions that must be answered: Is the structure of these systems hierarchical? What are the major factors influencing the structures? And to what deformation are they subject?

Hierarchical structures

A hierarchy, as we understand it, is the 'organisation of a whole in a series, in which each term is greater than the following one by a symbol of normative character' (Robert, 1975). It is important to place due weight on the terms of this definition: hierarchy implies classification and not subordination. This is a fundamental notion.

In a system of administrative or educational establishments, for example, there exists an inevitable hierarchy of establishments, in parallel with the degree of use to which they are put. It is quite otherwise with commerce in all free-enterprise countries. In the first place, the classification is not simple: we must distinguish, within the hierarchy of establishments (from small one-person shops to hypermarkets and large department stores), a variety of organisational mix, and of groupings within urban centres, and finally the flow of consumers. Secondly, neither at national nor at regional level is there any competent central authority, but a multitude of grouped or independent organisms, often in competition with one another; concentrated to a greater extent in the big cities, but also widely disseminated in other centres, down to the very smallest. The general organisational structure is thus atomised, and is based primarily on the principle of competitiveness. What assures the gradation is thus the size and the selectivity of the consuming population, and its needs.

Bearing this in mind, one cannot deny that, whatever aspect is considered, there are in fact hierarchies, of individual establishments, of commercial centres, and also of the size of service areas; while there is often a more or less universal correspondence between the three classifications, however great may be the difficulties, already referred to in passing, of finding appropriate and unquestionable criteria. But the subordination of these various elements according to their classification only exists in certain very particular types of organisation, for example, all the shops in a large chain, all the distributors who depend on one company, and collection and distribution in some countries with planned economies. In general, the relations are more subtle, and it is often only by a misguided projection of the administrative relations between two towns that authors have been led to regard one as subordinate to the other.

The centres are real, each has a certain strength, a certain organisation, a certain sphere of influence; one may place them in categories or at different levels, but that is all.

The only fixed elements are the two ends of the scale. The principal business district of the regional centre, which is at the same time the seat of the highest concentration of urban commerce and the main focus, for a large part of the regional population, occupies an undeniably primate position. At the other extremity, there is the basic shopping equipment (the village store, or the neighbourhood shops on the periphery of a major town) which serves only the local population's most elementary needs. Between the two, all kinds of relations are possible – direct or indirect and at various levels. All the same, even the most simple classifications can be upset: a cooperative serving a large agricultural area may be implanted in a small parish if there is an important transport artery nearby; a hypermarket may be installed in a peripheral community, close to a large city, and thus upset all the commercial traffic flows; spa towns have a seasonal clientele that lies outside the traditional shopping routine. But these are exceptions.

In addition to these exceptions, there is the fact that the behaviour of consumers towards the hierarchy of possibilities offered could call into question the classification based on a hierarchy of commercial centres. The law of averages entails that a majority of people, in almost all situations, behave in accordance with statistical expectations, at least in clear-cut situations.

If we accept these reservations, we can nevertheless still talk of a commercial system, and even of a hierarchical commercial system. This implies a scattered distribution of elements that are classifiable in terms of their relative importance; it does not imply, in most cases, a condition of subordination. This view does not conform to the ideas introduced into geographical literature by certain specialists, with whom all do not agree, but we believe it is always dangerous to read into words more than they imply.

Elements in the differentiation of commercial systems

These are no different from those that apply to urban systems. We may briefly recapitulate.

The maximum differentiation of systems, in respect of the complexity of their structures and the number of categories that compose them, is linked above all with the economic and social development of the country or region concerned. This is evident particularly from the first part of this book. Three correctives may intervene: the influence of political organisation, the historical background, and the average density of population.

Political organisation cannot wipe the slate clean of the past in areas where history has left a strong imprint, but it tends to modify the inheritance, and in new countries to impose a rationally formed structure. We may recall in this connection a remark concerning Poland: 'the economy is planned, and the extent of a large part of the regional or local functions is fixed and determined in advance by administrative arrangements' (Kostrowicki, 1967). Conversely, free enterprise allows undertakings to flourish that may be superfluous, or, on the other hand, when the anticipated profits are too low, it may result in an insufficient service to some parts of the territory. The system may thus reflect something that is quite different from economic equilibrium.

All the authors who have studied this question, often with penetrating analysis, come to the same conclusion, and we may quote Dugrand (1963, p. 320): 'this analysis of economic life leaves, with regard to the structural plan, a curious impression of disorder, even incoherence, so abundant are the contradictions'.

Even China, though profoundly revolutionised, has not escaped this dominance of history (cf. p. 101): the regime decided in 1958 to modernise the traditional trading zones by suppressing the small ancient markets and replacing them by a single shopping unit attached to each people's commune. This simply had the effect of disorganising the rural economy, and it was abandoned in the summer of 1958, with a return to the old customs. It has been impossible to close down and constrain this system of natural markets within the limits of ill-established administrative units (Skinner, 1965).

The role of history and of economic development may have opposing effects in some instances; thus, in Europe, where the historical network is firmly established and of ancient origin, and where the siting of many of the major cities goes back to prehistoric times, local attachments and currents of trade are very strong, and the industrial revolution merely adapted modern transport to an ancient framework, thus reinforcing it, at the same time creating new towns alongside old ones. In the United States, especially in the central plains, the opening up of the land and the creation of towns are quite recent and reflect the development of a transport network, especially of railroads; when the conditions that brought them into being no longer applied, these creations, less firmly rooted, more superficially functional, and serving a much less dense population that was more scattered and more mobile, faltered and declined except where their nuclei were sufficiently solid. Berry (1967) demonstrated this in the case of Iowa, and Hodge (1965) has described the vicissitudes of the urban system in Saskatchewan, where three movements are discernible – reinforcement of medium-sized and large centres, decline of small centres, and the continuance of slight progress in the newest creations. The study of commercial organisation has shown that, with a roughly similar standard of living, a difference is apparent between certain Asian countries, which have a long tradition of trading, and others in black Africa where this was absent: this is reflected not merely in the structure of the existing commercial systems but even in the characteristics of trade. In many black African countries, most of the trading is done not by the native people, but by Syrians and Lebanese.

As for population density, this may or may not be balanced by the standard of living. Thus a sparse population, motorised and well-off (as in the United States) may guarantee an adequate return for a commercial enterprise that could not survive in a poor area that had a larger population, such as one finds, for example, in parts of southern Europe. The distribution of commercial centres in the former is thus no less dense than in the latter. But if the standard of living is equal, population density plays its part. A study of the Philadelphia region, from the urban fringe to the peripheral rural areas, shows this clearly (Brush and Gauthier, 1968): in the rural zone, with a density of 300 households per km^2, the distribution of shopping centres is such that it is necessary to travel more than 3.2 km to the nearest one for the simplest purchases; while in the suburban zone, where the population density is more than twice as great, the shopping centres are less than 3 km apart and the consumers, for similar purchases, need travel less than 1.5 km.

Apart from these general factors, there are other occasional or more localised modifications, such as the presence of lines of communication, the existence of industrial areas, the attraction of a great regional metropolis; all these introduce variations in the system that may be described as accidental.

To illustrate more precisely what may be called anomalies in the system, we have studied systematically the maps resulting from the Piatier enquiry, already cited (p. 157), for a series of French regions. These are some of the conclusions reached: the sphere of general influence of a higher-order centre (such as the regional metropolis of Lille, for example) is more extensive on the one hand if it is located at some distance from other comparable centres, and on the other hand if its pre-eminence over the secondary centres is well marked. Save under exceptional circumstances, large centres disappear around the regional poles which in some ways sterilise their development within a certain radius (the obvious case of Parisian pre-eminence is in fact repeated around other great cities). When several centres of a similarly high order are relatively close, the secondary centres disappear (as for example around Reims, Epernay, Châlons). The major centres exercise an influence over an area with an average radius of 25–30 km in a mainly rural environment; intermediate centres are situated at an average distance of 10–15 km from the major centre – always assuming, of course, that the system is not disturbed by industry. On the other hand, the presence of a great industrial area (like the Nord coalfield) alters the regularity of the hierarchy. Regions of sparser population (e.g. Artois) have centres that are weaker, and lower down the hierarchy, but which still offer an adequate service thanks to a range of shopping facilities that is diversified though not quantitatively or qualitatively well developed (cf. pp. 203–216 and Fig. 7 on p. 158).

The natural environment exercises a major influence on the distribution of shopping centres, on the deformation of their spheres of influence and, to the extent that it determines a growth of population or a diminution of resources, on the general level of the elements in the commercial system. An excellent example is furnished by the study of Barbier (1969).

Transformation of commercial systems

The growth of population, and economic and social development, are favourable to commercial activity, but this does not mean that all parts of the system benefit equally. This will depend on the distribution of the existing centres, the solidity of their background and the technological changes that accompany the general growth. Here, as in many other spheres, the changes vary according to the previous circumstances.

In the developing countries, the traditional system is severely upset by all forms of progress, particularly in transport. Witnesses abound: 'the often rapid evolution of the transport network facilitates the unification of the market to the advantage of the country's most progressive centre. . . The rise of "middle-tier" towns thus depends largely on the organisation of transport' (Santos, 1975). In Morocco, Troin has remarked how facilities for movement increase spheres of influence, reinforce the growth poles, and devitalise the intermediate centres, which become mere staging-posts (Troin, 1975). In Cameroun, Morinière describes the progress of the north–south road and rail route: when the first trunk line reached Belabo, in the east, in 1967, forest-exploiters, transport firms and merchants rushed in; 'with the trans-Cameroun rail-link, and new roadways, products hitherto consumed only locally could be exchanged between north and south'. But paradoxically, the effect was not the same over the whole country: trade encouraged by the new transport media and the growth of monetary income, favoured the northern towns, while the trading system of the south suffered a spectacular decline, evidenced in the small towns through the substitution of local trading for the large firms which closed their branches, while the Europeans retreated into the more important centres (Morinière, 1975). All these issues are in accord with the results of a theoretical study by Eighmy made from data for western Nigeria that reached the following conclusions: when income and demand grow, the most important and the best sited of the temporary markets become permanent; those situated in the vicinity of these more-favoured centres see their activity reduced, even to disappearance, if the rural population declines. The development of transport and the relative decline in the cost of movement entail in the smaller centres a loss of their functions. The mesh of the system widens, and while the most important nodes develop, some of the intermediate centres disappear, leaving only the small and more distant centres which have a better chance of survival (Eighmy, 1972). The same evolution has taken place in the Chinese countryside (Skinner, 1965).

But after this early upsetting of the pre-existing trading structure, eliminating the parasitical intermediate centres that owed their existence to the poor communications and the primitive character of the trade, there comes a second stage in which the trading economy progresses under the combined effect of an increase in population, of the rural–urban drift, and of the development and use of resources, and the system grows, not in the number of centres but in their size and quality; new market centres appear along the new transport axes or within newly exploited areas. A new system thus comes into being, based not on close proximity and the elementary needs of underdevelopment but on the facts of economic progress.

In developed countries also, modifications occur. Berry (1967, pp. 3–25) mapped the markets of a certain region in the United States' Mid West in 1879, 1904, 1914, 1956 and 1960, and the variations in the shopping habits of the clientele between 1934 and 1960. It is possible to detect a series of stages that in some ways resemble those quoted above: a multiplication of centres resulting from increasing population density and the improvement of transport, and the disappearance of the less well-placed centres and of the small shops with a purely local clientele. With the advent of the automobile and the asphalt-surfaced road, there began 'a process of differential growth in which the smallest centres vanished, the intermediate-sized places suffered a relative decline, and only the larger centres grew' (Berry, 1967, p. 8). We have been able to make similar observations in France, through the mapping, in some 15 *départements*, from the most urbanised and industrialised, like Rhône and Bouches-du-Rhône, to the most rural and mountainous like Eure-et-Loir, Yonne, Landes, Cantal and Basses Alpes, of commercial centres and their 'equipment' in 1892, 1912, 1955 and 1969.

Other comparisons can be made within the surroundings of metropolitan cities, from the rural to the suburban. Studies made by Brush and Gauthier (1968) in the Philadelphia region enabled the authors to draw a series of schematic graphs showing the possible variations (Fig. 22). The peripheral rural girdle, studded with small village centres, has increasingly given way to an urbanised zone, provided with a succession of secondary commercial centres that increase in number with the rising density of population.

We can thus establish a certain parallelism between the overall development of an area and the kind of commercial system that serves it; questions of persistence and of renewal are linked in a complex fashion with the previous state of the system, with the spacing of the centres, and with the modes and conditions of demographic and economic change.

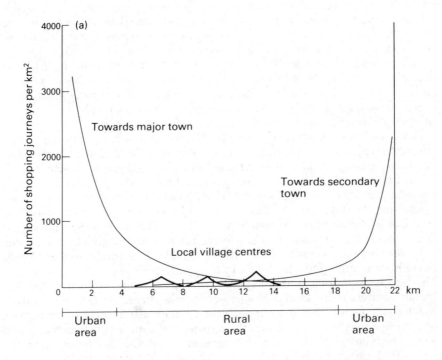

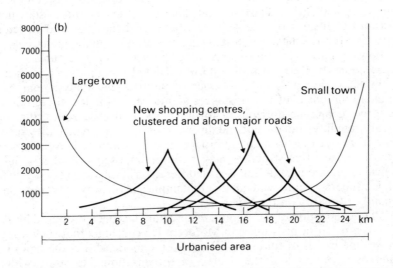

Fig. 22 Development of shopping facilities on the edge of a large town.

Commercial regions

The term 'region' is used with some reserve, for many geographers have used it with reference to types of interactions, whether spatial in character or not, engendered by commercial activities. We must not, however, use the word only in its restrictive sense of 'part of organised space', but must accept a wider definition such as that used by Perroux (1950) or Boudeville (1961), for example, when they distinguished types of 'economic space' – the area that is the 'economic horizon of a firm', the area of attraction, the homogeneous area. It is precisely these three notions that appear over and over again in the analyses of commercial relations made by different authors.

These authors, using various methods and approaches, have described different types of 'commercial areas'. We here give three particularly instructive examples that invite critical evaluation and further research.

The first example is taken from the work of Berry (1966a). In this analysis he examines the flow of 63 types of consumer goods in relation to 36 areal units comprising the states and the major cities of India, and uses factor analysis to establish a classification of functional regions. This shows the convergent flow-systems from producing areas to the great consuming cities, with some links also between certain of the cities (Fig. 23). In a further paper (1968) Berry is more ambitious, for he seeks to superimpose two types of structure. The first is a synoptic study of spatial structure, taking for each of the 325 Indian districts more than 100 socio-economic characteristics; the analysis isolates nine factors that show up the urban and industrial regions, the regions of intensive irrigated agriculture, the agricultural contrasts between east and west, the Ganges valley, the dry agriculture of the northwest, and the specialised mineral-producing areas. Across this spatial structure, goods circulate, and the second analysis thus seeks to discover the 'functional relations', using the 63 types of consumer goods, between sections of the territory, and so to define 'behavioural space'. The relations between the two systems, studied by a conventional analysis, 'reveal three statistically significant dimensions of inter-relations between behaviour and structures' (Berry, 1968). It is a means of displaying types of functional regions, based on trade flows, separately from regions categorised by their structure.

These studies by Berry, based on statistical data by methods of classification using in succession different processes of multivariate analysis, emphasise functional relations over long distances and in various fields; these relations explain the 'economic horizon' of towns, ports, industrial zones, that draw necessary supplies from distant and diverse sources-areas, which they serve in return. It concerns a form of interdependence dominated by commercial relationships, but this structure may be superimposed on other schemes, statistical or functional, but founded on different criteria. One may say, in fact, that it is a superstructure, with all that that implies in the way of tyranny on the one hand or fragility on the other.

Another conception of the 'commercial region' has been proposed by Troin (1975) as a result of his studies in Morocco. He considers that such a region expresses the trends of trade flows but also the mode of life, the nature and volume of resources and the degree of urbanisation. He starts with the observation that 'structures and localisations rapidly reflect types of consumption' (Troin, 1975, p. 561). Relations between resources and trade

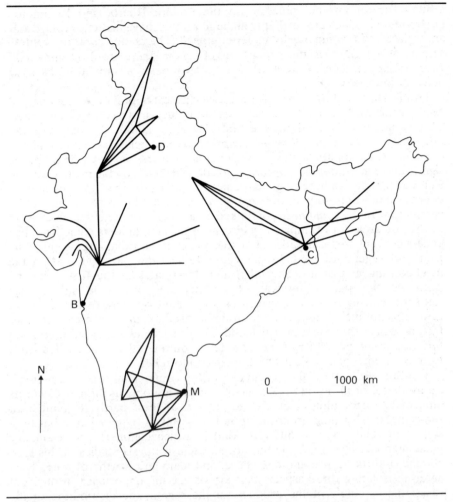

Fig. 23 Flow of consumer goods into Bombay, Dehli, Calcutta and Madras.

are much more evident than in developed countries: the *suqs* reflect the level of
the local economy. The towns accentuate the disequilibrium between the rural
and urban worlds by their spheres of commercial influence. The author uses six
elements in his classification: the size and number of markets, the functions and
specialisation of these markets, the articulation of the system of *suqs,* the single
or multiple polarisation of these systems, the dependence or commercial
autonomy of the sector studied, and the regional level of development and its
evolution. He first develops a classification of *suqs,* and then, using the last four
factors, divides northern Morocco into 25 commercial zones, of four types:
regions of intense polarisation depending on a powerful internal centre that has
no outside competition (10 regions, including Tetuan, Tangier, Rabat-Salé,
Meknès, and Fez); regions of external polarisation, that are close to the
previous zones, and are attracted by their centres (in western Morocco and
around Fez, Meknès and Rabat); articulated autonomous regions, organised

around several internal poles as in the eastern Rharb, and Zemmour; buffer-regions which are further from large centres, have no major centre and are isolated and commercially under-equipped (Ouezzane, Taza, the central Middle Atlas). Between these four types of regions, there are also commercial vacua, areas difficult of access that are slowly being absorbed as the road network improves.

Troin's study is thus at variance with the classical notion of the commercial region conceived essentially as the sphere of influence of a commercial centre. This variation is twofold. In the first place, the author demonstrates the difference between the *domaine propre* of commercial attraction and the *domaine lié*. As applied to the Fez region, these expressions have the following significance: in the *domaine propre,* everything depends on the main town; the stall-keepers of Fez here reign supreme; the provisioning of the Fez market depends almost entirely on the area, and the market buses serve the district completely. In the *domaine lié*, or 'linked area', there is more independence; in the Sefrou area, for example, 17 per cent of the stall-holders come from Fez and 68 per cent are local traders, but 46 per cent of the grain, 20 per cent of the fruit and vegetables, and 35 per cent of the cattle are still sent to the neighbouring metropolis. Secondly, and this relates to the first point, he describes the partial survival of autonomous structures, still largely self-sufficient, in zones where centres are distant or non-existent. In some cases, it is not the existence of a central nucleus that limits the area, but other factors such as the extent of tribal lands in the Zael and Zemmour areas, and this despite the proximity of the large towns on the Atlantic coast. Thus two forms of commercial solidarity are thrown into relief.

The third example is the classic one of the commercial role of a regional centre that is of sufficient importance to ensure not only its influence over its immediate surroundings but also to shelter, at least partly, a number of sub-centres; the whole group being not only linked by commerce but by a system of relations of a different kind in which commerce, an economic phenomenon, plays a notable but not an exclusive part. Studies of this kind abound both in France and elsewhere, and many are worthy of note. They agree in isolating three aspects that are of varying importance in different cases: the assembly of the products of the region, the distribution of the products fabricated in the town or coming from elsewhere, and the supplying of some goods to the outlying population through local retailing. These three functional aspects may be in step, and in some cases may represent a systematic organisation (e.g. multiple chain-stores, wholesalers, specialised distributors). We here quote the analysis of two French towns, each with its own characteristics – Toulouse and Rennes.

Rennes is the only large town in the interior of Brittany, and its position at the base of the peninsula, eccentrically placed from the rest of France, gives it an exceptional importance in a region where agricultural production is dominant and markets are distant. The Breton capital reflects exactly the model of three functions. 'Wholesaling is most important, geographically. Rennes collects and distributes all kinds of commodities for the whole of Brittany: commodities such as motor fuels, foodstuffs, iron, textiles, and about half its trade consists of groceries and metal goods. The wholesalers also collect the products of the region for distribution elsewhere. Several wholesale markets control the business. The market for hides and skins deals with the offerings from all the abattoirs in Brittany (St. Brieuc, Vannes, Lorient, Quimper, Lannion, Redon and Landerneau). The nationalisation of the wheat trade has not stopped the business of the commercial bank. Other organisations specialise in goods destined for the town itself – such as the milk cooperative.' (Meynier and Le Guen, 1966.) Retailing, which includes a host of small and often old-fashioned shops and three large stores, also depends on some newer establishments, and on the 10-day annual fair that attracts visitors

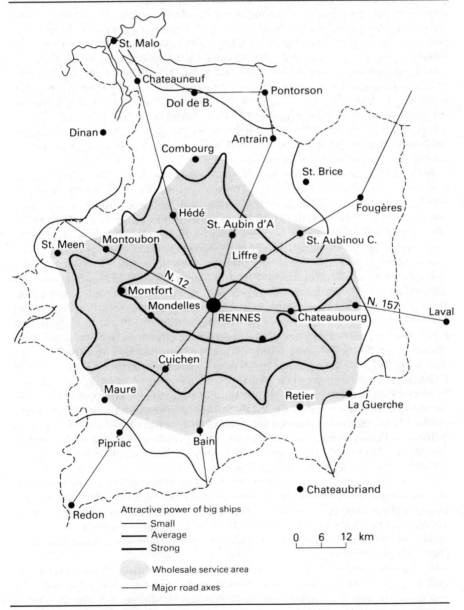

Fig. 24 The pull of the big shops in Rennes.

from the whole of Brittany. The authors of this study have tried to define a number of zones, based on different criteria, but the boundaries are difficult to draw. They distinguish a zone in which the retailers of commonplace produce may supply themselves in Rennes without the intervention of a middleman; another from which customers come for certain types of purchases in Rennes; another from which small farmers come to offer their produce directly in the regional centre; yet another zone that supplies the big traders such as butter factories and abattoirs; and a larger zone from which customers come into Rennes to purchase household equipment, furniture, and so on. We may quote the conclusion of the study: 'finally, many commercial operations necessitate one or more staging-posts between sellers and buyers, and this constitutes an urban "system". We may consider Rennes as a first-order centre within this system, depending directly on Paris and related to local buyers and sellers through second-order centres (Brest, Lorient, St. Brieuc) then third-order centres (St. Malo, Dinan, Fougères, La Guerche, Redon), and finally the smallest centres such as Combourg, Dol, Montfort, Janzé. It comes into competition as a regional centre with Nantes, Angers, Le Mans; it maintains only with difficulty its supremacy over Brest or even Lorient, which tend to rise within this urban hierarchy' (Fig. 24).

Toulouse has been the object of a study by Pechoux *et al.* (1966). It occupies a crossroads position between the Atlantic and the Mediterranean, between Bordeaux and the towns of Bas-Languedoc, and encounters much more active competition, especially in the assembly of agricultural products, a field in which 'its competence is shown to be more limited than in wholesaling'. Certainly there are active private wholesalers in the agricultural business, but they have encountered opposition in the form of new commercial systems, the multiplication of market depots in the valley of the Garonne, and the regulations of the national market depot at Toulouse-Lalande, opened in 1964; the situation is thus complex and fluctuating. Conversely, however, some Toulouse wholesale businesses redistribute textile products, foodstuffs and many other types of consumer-goods, over an area that may be very large; cloth sales may reach the Atlantic coast, Périgueux, Aurillac and Montpellier; one company, L'Epargne, spreads its network of 250 branches from southern Landes to Lot and western Aude. 'The system of distribution in the Toulouse region is thus mainly within a radius of 60 to 100 km from the city; on the outskirts of this region, the city's influence spreads unevenly and is less marked; the quantities distributed decline in inverse ratio to the increasing influence of competing centres'. The system is evolving, with the imposition of sales zones that modify the shape of the traditional spheres of attraction. As for retailing, the present superabundance is in course of reorganisation; its clientele varies 'in an area of greater or less extent according to the nature of the purchases – for normal and current needs or for exceptional requirements. In the first case the essential factor is distance; in the second, the influence of Toulouse extends into neighbouring *départements,* especially the Castres area, and is only limited in its own *département* by the competition of Saint Gaudens' (Péchoux *et al.,* 1966).

The importance of these commercial relations – in whichever of the forms that we have just described – is considerable, for their value is not only economic. If we refer back to previous chapters, and recollect what has been written about the ancillary functions of commerce, we shall be conscious of the transformations that they can bring about in the areas in which they operate; and the reverse is also true: that spatial changes can influence commercial functioning. This indeed is included in the 'commercial system' that we have defined, and which is expressed here in its spatial aspects.

Glossary

Consumers' cooperative. A voluntary union of persons organised to supply members with goods and services. In Britain the movement started in 1844, and there are now 243 separate societies operating 14,000 outlets. Each society is controlled by its members (consumers) who receive the profits in the form of a dividend or trading stamps. (S & W, 417; Davis, 53)

Convenience goods. Products purchased regularly, in relatively unvarying quantities and available in the same quality and price in most outlets and areas. (S & W, 417)

Department stores (Fr. *grands magasins*). Large shops selling, in separate departments, at least five different merchandise groups, one of which must be women's and children's wear. The store must also have at least two of the following three characteristics: more than 175 employees, more than 2,000 m² of selling space, more than 1.5 million dollars annual sales. (J & K, 146–7). The British Census of Distribution 1971 stipulated at least 25 employees.

Discount houses. In the USA, these are retail shops offering branded, fixed-price merchandise at substantial discounts. (S & W, 417).

Discount stores (D. Shop: D. Centre). Mass-merchandising stores selling durable goods at low prices, particularly electrical equipment; characterised by low staff costs and sites outside the CBD or in peripheral locations: e.g. 'Trident', and 'Comet'. (Mills)

Hypermarket. Similar to superstore (q.v.) but over 5,000 m² of selling space and appropriate car parking. (URPI)

'Junior' department store (Fr. *Boutique 'junior'*). A term not in common use in Britain. It refers to enlarged variety stores (q.v.), enlarged not only in terms of selling space but also in the variety of goods offered. The traditional variety store lines – toiletry, stationery, toys and smaller hardware, are supplemented by women's, men's and children's clothing and footwear, items of furniture and household equipment, sports and travel goods, etc., as well as the food trade. (J & K, 112)

Mail-order houses. Organisations selling direct to the consumer, either by means of direct distribution of catalogues or by agents calling on customers in their houses, or by a combination of both methods.

Multiples or multiple-shop organisations. Organisations operating 10 or more retail branches (but excluding consumers' cooperatives, q.v.) (J & K, 146)

Retailing. All establishments, fixed or not, and all persons – owners, family workers, employees, full-time or not – engaged wholly or mainly in the sale of goods, in a state ready for final consumption or use, to private consumers. *Excluded* are units that sell primarily services, e.g. cafés, restaurants, dry-cleaners, laundries, and repairers of various sorts if repairing represents the greater part of their trade; also excluded are dealers selling raw materials, agricultural supplies in bulk, machinery and building materials. *Included* are all retail outlets coming within the above definition, whether they be fixed shops, kiosks or market stalls, or itinerant traders selling on street corners or selling from door to door. (J & K, 143–4)

Supermarket. Self-service establishment of 400 m² or more selling space, with a sale of non-food as well as a complete range of food goods. (J & K, 106)

Superstore. Single level self-service store offering a wide range of food and non-food, with at least 2,500 m² net floor-space, supported by car parking. (URPI)

Variety stores (Fr. *Magasins populaires*). Variety chain-store organisations are multiple-shop organisations that sell in their retail establishments a wide range of commodities, usually by open display with no physical barriers between different types of merchandise, except in some instances in the case of foodstuffs (J & K, 146). British examples are Marks & Spencer, and Woolworth's; Marks & Spencer had over 100 'Penny Bazaars' in the UK by 1914, and Woolworth's '3*d* and 6*d* stores' started in the UK in 1909.

Voluntary association (group). In these, independent retailers undertake to buy from a wholesaler in return for a discount and supporting services. In Britain voluntary groups rarely comprise more than a few hundred retailers, and their sphere of operations tends to be restricted to a region or a group of towns. (Scott, 44)

Voluntary chain. Comprises two or more wholesalers each with its associated independent retailers. In Britain voluntary chains, which first appeared in the 1950s and are now well established in the grocery trade, have typically several thousand member retailers and are either regional or more usually national in coverage. (Scott, 44)

Sources

Davies. Davies, R. L. (1976) *Marketing Geography,* Corbridge.

J & K. Jefferys, J. B. and Knee, D. (1962) *Retailing in Europe,* Macmillan, London.

Mills. Mills, E. (1974) Planning Research Applications Group, Technical Paper No. 3, London.

Scott. Scott, P. (1970) *Geography and Retailing.* Hutchinson, London.

S & W. Stacey, N. A. H. & Wilson, A. (1965) *The Changing Patterns of Distribution,* Pergamon, Oxford.

URPI. Unit for Retail Planning Information (1977) *List of U.K. hypermarkets and superstores.*

Bibliography

This bibliography includes only works and articles cited in the text.

Adams, T. F. M. and **Kobayashi** (1969) *The World of Japanese Business,* Ward Lock, London.

Alexander, I. (1974) 'City centre redevelopment', *Progress in Planning,* 3.

Ambrose, P. and **Colenutt,** (1975) *The Property Machine,* Penguin, Harmondsworth.

Andan, O., Beaujeu-Garnier, J. and **Libault, A.** (1975) 'L'accessibilité des grandes villes françaises', *Geoforum,* **6,** 137–50.

Andrade, M. C. de (1971) 'Considérations sur la division de l'espace de Pernambouc en régions homogènes', *La Régionalisation au Brésil,* C.N.R.S., Paris.

Andrieux, P. (1972) *Le Commerce Indépendent,* Dunod, Paris.

Annaert, J., Goossens, M. and **Van der Haegen, H.** (1967) 'Les zones d'influence des centres et la structure des activités urbaines', *Atlas de Belgique, Commentaire des planches 28A–B–C,* Bruxelles.

Anuarul staistic al republicii socialiste (Romania) (1974).

Applebaum, W. (1967, 1968) *Store Location Strategy Cases,* Addison-Wesley, Reading, Mass.

Applebaum, W. *et al.* (1968) *Guide to Store Location Research,* Addison-Wesley, Reading, Mass.

Arita, K. (1973) 'Japan's general trading companies', *Toyota Quarterly Review,* No. 2.

Atlas de Paris et de la région parisienne (1967), ed. Beaujeu-Garnier, J. and Bastié, J.

Bailly, A. S. (1975) *L'organisation urbaine',* Centre de recherche d'urbanisme, Paris.

Bank of Tokyo, *Yearbook,* 1973, 1974.

Barbier, B. (1969) *Villes et Centres des Alpes du Sud,* Aix-en-Provence.

Bastié, J. (1964) *La Croissance de la Banlieue parisienne,* Paris.

Bataille, R. (1964) *Structures du Commerce au Japon,* Office franco-japonais d'études économiques, Paris.

Beaujeu-Garnier, J. (1965) 'Méthode d'étude pour le centre des villes', *Ann. de Géog.,* No. 406, 695–707.

Beaujeu-Garnier, J. (1972) 'Comparaison des centre-villes aux Etats-Unis et en Europe', *Ann. de Géog.,* No. 448, 665–96.

Beaujeu-Garnier, J. (1973) 'Réflexion sur le problème des centres-villes', *Chronache Economiche,* Turin, No. 3–4, 1–6.

Beaujeu-Garnier, J. (1976) *Methods and Perspectives in Geography,* Longman, London.

Beghin, H. (1974) *L'organisation de l'espace au Maroc,* Academie Royale des Sciences d'Outre-Mer, Bruxelles.

Bell, T., Lieber, S. R. and **Rushton, G.** (1974) 'Clustering of services in central places', *Ann. Assoc. Amer. Geog.,* **2,** 214–25.

Berezowski, S. (1967) 'Le rôle du secteur tertiaire non polarisé dans la formation des villes', *Geographia Polonica,* **12.**

Berezowski, S. (1967) 'Méthodologie de l'étude des lieux centraux en Pologne', *R. Géog. de l'Est,* No. 3, 365–76.

Berry, B. J. L. (1959) 'Ribbon developments in the urban business pattern', *Ann. Assoc. Amer. Geogr.,* **49,** 145–55.

Berry, B. J. L. (1963) 'Commercial structure and commercial blight: retail patterns and processes in the City of Chicago', Univ. of Chicago, *Research Paper,* 85.

Berry, B. J. L. (1966a) 'Essays on comodity flows and the spatial structure of the Indian economy', Univ. of Chicago, *Research Paper,* 111.

Berry, B. J. L. (1966b) 'Interdependence of spatial structure and spatial behaviour', *Papers of Regional Science Assoc.*, **21**, 205–27.

Berry, B. J. L. (1967) *Geography of Market Centres and Retail Distribution*, Prentice Hall, Englewood Cliffs.

Berry, B. J. L. (1968) 'A synthesis of formal and functional regions using a general field theory of spatial behaviour', in *Spatial Analysis*, 419–28, Prentice Hall, Englewood Cliffs.

Berry, B. J. L. and **Garrison, W. L.** (1958) 'The functional bases of the central place hierarchy', *Econ. Geog.* **34**, 145–54.

Berry, B. J. L. and **Horton, F.** (1970) *Geographic Perspectives on Urban Systems*, Prentice Hall, Englewood Cliffs.

Berry, B. J. L. and **Mayer, H. M.** (1962) *Comparative Studies of Central Place Systems*, Washington, D.C.

Berry, B. J. L., Parsons, S. J. and **Platt, R. H.** (1968) *The Impact of Urban Renewal on Small Business*, Univ. of Chicago Urban Studies.

Berry, R. A. (1977) *Small Unit Retailing in Urban Britain*, St. David's College, Lampeter.

Blake, J. (1978) 'Brent Cross: a regional shopping centre', *The Planner*, **64**, 115–7.

Bobek, H. (1968) 'Die versorgung mit zentralen Diensten', *Mitt. Osterr. geogr. Gesell.*, **110**, 143–58.

Boddewyn, J. J. and **Hollander, S. C.** (1972) *Public Policy Toward Retailing*, Heath, Lexington.

Bohannan, P. and **Dalton, G.** (1962) *Markets in Africa*, North Western Univ., Evanston.

Bongars, S. (1971) *L'avenir de la rénovation urbaine du centre de St. Paul'*, Unpublished thesis.

Bonnefonds, A. L. (1968) 'Le commerce de traite en Côte d'Ivoire', *Cahiers d'Outre-mer*.

Borchert, J. R. and **Adams, R.** (1963) *Trade Centres and Tributary Areas in the Upper Midwest*, Upper Midwest Res. and Devel. Council. Minneapolis.

Boudeville, J. (1961) *Les espaces économiques*, Paris.

Böventer, von. E. (1969) 'Walter Christaller's central places and peripheral areas: the central place theory in retrospect', *Journ. Reg. Science.*, **9**, 117–24.

Boyer, J. C. (1976) 'L'évolution de l'organisation urbaine des Pays-Bas', Unpublished thesis.

Bridges, M. J. (1976) *The York Asda*, Centre for Urb. & Reg. Res., Univ. of Manchester.

Bronson, D. W. and **Severin, B. S.** (1974) 'Le niveau de vie du consommateur soviétique de 1ère de Brejnev', *Problèmes économiques*, No. 1379.

Brunet, R. (1965) *Les campagnes toulousaines*, Publ. Fac. des Lettres et Sci. hum. Series B, vol. 1, Toulouse.

Brush, J. E. and **Gauthier, H. L.** (1968) 'Service centres and consumer trips', Univ. of Chicago, *Research Paper*, 113.

Bruyelle, P. (1970) *L'influence urbaine et milieu rural dans la région du Nord*, Paris.

Buchanan, C. (1963) *Traffic in Towns*, HMSO, London.

Buchanan, I. (1972) *Singapore in southeast Asia*, Bell, London.

Buchanan, K. (1973) *L'espace chinois*, Colin, Paris.

Burgess, E. W. (1929) *Urban Areas*, Univ. of Chicago, Research Series.

Busaka, A. (1975) 'Les effets économiques et sociaux de la concentration de la population dans la ville de Kinshasa', Unpublished thesis, Paris.

Careil, S. F. (1967) *Confort collectif, urbanisme et commerce*, SEPAIC, Paris.

Carol, H. (1960) 'The hierarchy of central functions within the city', *Lund Studies in Geog.*, **24**, 555–76.

Carre, J. P. and **Rouleau, R.** (1974) 'Le commerce dans le tissu urbain', *Espace. Geogr.*, **4**, 311–17.

Carruthers, I. (1962) 'Service centres in Greater London', *Town. Plann. Rev.*, **33**, 5–31.

Carruthers, I. (1967) 'Major shopping centres in England and Wales', *Regional Studies*, **1**, 65–81.

Cas, G. (1975) *La défense du consommateur*, CERF, Paris.

Chabot, G. (1948) *Les Villes*, Paris.

Chabot, G. (1962) 'Les zones d'influence des grandes villes françaises', *Lund studies in Geog.*, **24**, 197–200.

Christaller, W. (1933) *Die Zentralen Orte in Suddeutschland*, Jena; English translation by Baskin, C. W. (1966) *Central Places in southern Germany*, Prentice Hall, Englewood Cliffs.

Clarke, W. A. V. and **Rushton, G.** (1970) 'Models of intraurban consumer behaviour and their implications for central place theory', *Econ. Geog.*, **46**, 486–97.

Claval, P. (1962) *Géographie générale des marchés*, Génin, Paris.

Claval, P. (1966) 'Le théorie des lieux centraux', *Rev. Géog. de l'Est*, No. 1–2, 131–52.
Claval, P. (1973) 'La théorie des lieux centraux révisitée', *Rev. Géog. de l'Est.*, No. 155, 225–51.
Claval, P. (1976) *Elements de géographie économique*, Génin, Paris.
Conduche, R. (1960) 'Marchés et tournées', Unpublished thesis; summarised in *La Vie Urbaine* (1960).
Coquery, M. (1972) *Atlas urbain des commerce de grande surface en France*, Comité de la recherche commerciale, Paris.
Coquery, M. (1976) 'Contribution a l'étude de la géographie du commerce de détail en France', Unpublished thesis.
Costes, J. (1961) *Les supermarchés, une révolution?*, SNEREP, Paris.
Coville, G. (1974) 'Le développement des grandes surfaces commerciales en Europe et les problèmes qu'il pose', *Problèmes Economiques*, No. 1396.
Crouzet, R. (1975) 'Evolution de la centralité urbaine et translation du centre d'une ville', Unpublished thesis.
Curry, L. (1960) 'The geography of service centres within towns', *Lund Studies in Geog.*, **24**, 31–53.
Dacey, M. F. (1960) 'Analysis of central place and point pattern by a nearest neighbour method', *Lund Studies in Geog.*, **24**, 55–73.
Dacey, M. F. (1965) 'The geometry of central place theory', *Geografiska Annaler*, **47b**, 111–124.
Dacey, M. F. (1970) 'Alternative formulations of central place population', *Tijds. v Econ. en Soc. Geog.*, 10–15.
Dalby, E. (1973) *Pedestrians and shopping centre layout*, Transport and Road Research Laboratory, Report LR 577.
Damais, J. P. (1974) 'Le Havre: structures commerciales du centre-ville', *Soc. Et. urbaines de la région du Havre*, No. 672.
Davidovich V. G. (1960) *Settlement in Industrial Nodes*, Moscow.
Davidovich, V. G. (1966) 'On the patterns and tendencies of urban development in USSR', *Soviet Geography*, No. 1, 3–31.
Davidovich, V. G. (1968) *Town planning in industrial districts*, Jerusalem.
Davies, R. L. (1968) 'Effects of consumer income differences on the business provisions of small shopping centres', *Urban Studies*, **5**, 144–64.
Davies, R. L. (1970) 'Variable relationships in central place and retail potential models', *Regional Studies*, **4**, 49–61.
Davies, R. L. (1972) 'Structural models of retail distribution', *Trans. Inst. Brit. Geogr.*, **57**, 59–82.
Davies, R. L. (1972) 'The retail pattern of the central area of Coventry', in *Inst. Brit. Geog. Occ. Pub.* No. 1.
Davies, R. L. (1973) *Patterns and Profiles of Consumer Behaviour*, Univ. of Newcastle.
Davies, R. L. (1976) *Marketing Geography with Special Reference to Retailing*, Retailing and Planning Associates, Corbridge.
Dayan, A. (1975) *Manuel de la distribution*, Les Editions d'Organisation, Paris.
Deleyne, J. (1975) *L'économie chinoise*, Seuil, Paris.
Delobez, A. (1964) 'Les entrepôts de Bercy', Préfecture de la Seine.
Delobez, A. (1966) 'Le commerce de gros du vin à Paris', Unpublished thesis.
Delobez, A. (1973) Three papers in *Analyse de l'Espace*, **4**, pp. 28–56, 107–31, 132–9.
Delobez, A. (1976) 'L'organisation de la distribution dans la république populaire de Chine', *L'Information géographique*, No. 1.
Demangeon, A. (1946) *La France économique et humaine*, Vol. VI of *Géographie Universelle*, Colin, Paris.
Demorgon, M. (1975) 'Recherches sur les structures commerciales de Paris', Atelier parisien d'urbanisme.
Demyk, N. (1975) 'Le systeme des échanges commerciaux au Guatemala', *L'Espace géographique*, No. 3.
Dept. of the Environment (1976) *British Cities: Urban Population and Employment Trends, 1951–1971.*
Dokmeci, V. F. (1973) 'An optimisation model for a hierarchical spatial system', *Journ. Regional Science*, **3**, 439–451.
Donaldsons, Ltd. (1973) *The Caerphilly Hypermarket Study*, London.
Donnithorne, A. (1967) *China's Economic System*, Allen & Unwin, London.

Doyère, J. (1975) *Le combat des consommateurs,* CERF, Paris.
Dugrand, R. (1963) *Villes et campagnes en Bas Languedoc,* P.U.F., Paris.
Dugrand, R. (1969) *Atlas du Languedoc-Roussillon,* Paris.
Dumbleton, R. H. (1974) 'Cardiff's centre plan', *Town & Country Planning,* **42,** 119–24.
Dupuis, J. (1972) *Singapour et la Malaysie,* P.U.F., Paris.
Dwyer, D. J. (1974) *China Now,* Longman, London.
Eighmy, T. H. (1972) 'Rural periodic markets and the extension of an urban system', *Econ. Geog.,* **48,** 299–315.
Ellul, J. (1956) *Histoire des Institutions,* P.U.F., Paris.
Etienne, G. (1974) *La voie chinoise,* P.U.F., Paris.
Everson, J. A. and **Fitzgerald, B. P.** (1972) 'Inside the city', *Concepts in Geography,* No. 3.
Fetjeanu, G. (1971) *La coopération de consommation en Roumanie,* Centrocoop.
Fogg, W. (1932) 'The suq: a study in the human geography of Morocco', *Geography,* **17,** 257–67.
Fuji Bank Bulletin, 1972–5.
Fustier, B. (1975) 'L'attraction des points de vente dans des espaces précis et imprécis', I.M.E. Document de travail, Univ. of Dijon.
Geertz, C. (1963) *Peddlers and Princes, Social Change and Economic Modernisation in Two Indonesian Towns,* Univ. of Chicago.
Gentelle, P. (1974) *La Chine,* P.U.F., Paris.
Gentelle, P. (1975) 'Les villes en Chine, une stratégie différente', *L'Espace géographique,* No. 1.
George, P. (1952) *La ville,* P.U.F., Paris.
George, P. (1973) *L'économie de l'URSS,* P.U.F., Paris.
Gibson, M. and **Pullen, M.** (1972) 'Retail turnover in the East Midlands: a regional application of a gravity model', *Regional Studies,* **6,** 183–96.
Goldman, M. I. (1966) *Soviet Marketing Distribution in a Controlled Economy,* Free Press, New York.
Golledge, R. G. (1970) 'Some equilibrium models of consumer behaviour', *Econ. Geog.,* **46,** 417–24.
Good, C. M. (1970) 'Rural markets and trade in East Africa', *Research Paper* 128, Univ. of Chicago.
Goodall, B. (1972) *The Economics of Urban Areas,* Oxford.
Gould, P. R. (1960) 'The development of the transport pattern in Ghana', *Northwestern Studies in Geography,* No. 5.
Gregor, H. F. (1974) 'An agricultural typology of California', in *Geography of World Agriculture,* Budapest.
Gregory, T. (1973) in Holiday, J. (ed.), *City Centre redevelopment,* Knight, London.
Guillain, R. (1965) *Dans 30 ans la Chine,* Seuil, Paris.
Hall, M., Knapp, J. and **Winston, C.** (1961) *Distribution in Great Britain and North America,* Oxford.
Hall, P. *et al.* (1973) *The Containment of Urban England,* Allen & Unwin, London.
Han Suyin, (1975) *Le premier jour du monde,* Stock.
Harris, C. D. and **Ullman, E. L.** (1945) 'The nature of cities', *Ann. Amer. Acad. Pol. & Soc. Sci.,* **242,** 7–17.
Hart, T. (1968) *The Comprehensive Development Area,* Oliver & Boyd, Edinburgh.
Hartwick, J. M. (1973) 'Lösch's theorem on hexagonal market areas', *Journ. Reg. Sci.,* **13,** 213–22.
Harvey, M. E., Hocking, R. T. and **Brown, J. R.** (1974) 'The chromatic travelling salesman problem and its application to planning and structuring geographic space', *Geog. Analysis,* **1,** 33–52.
Hautreux, J. and **Rochefort, M.** (1963) *Le niveau supérieure de l'armature urbaine française,* Min. de la Construction, Paris.
Hautreux, J. and **Rochefort, M.** (1964) *La fonction régionale dans l'armature urbaine française,* Min. de la Construction, Paris.
Hetzel, W. (1974) *Handel in Togo und Dahomey,* Kölner Geographische Arbeiten.
Higgins, B. (1956) 'The Dualistic theory of underdeveloped areas', *Econ. Devel. and Cultural Change,* **14,** 99–115.
Hill, P. and **Smith, R. H. T.** (1972) 'The spatial and temporal sychronisation of periodic markets', *Econ. Geog.,* **48,** 345–55.

Hodder, B. W. and **Ukwu, U. I.** (1969) *Markets in West Africa*, Ibadan Univ. Press.
Hodder, B. W. (1972) 'Urban growth and markets in West Africa', in *La croissance urbaine en Afrique Noire et à Madagascar*, CNRS, Paris.
Hodge, G. (1965) 'The predictions of trade center viability in the great plains', *Papers and Proc. Reg. Sci. Assoc.*, 87–115.
Horton, F. E. (1968) 'Location factors as determinants of consumer attraction to retail firms', *Ann. Assoc. Amer. Geog.*, **58**, 787–801.
Horwood, E. M. and **Boyce, R. R.** (1959) *Studies of the CBD and urban freeway development*, Seattle.
Hoyt, H. (1939) *The structure and growth of residential neighbourhoods in American cities*, Washington.
Hoyt, H. (1964) 'Recent distortions of the classical models of urban structure', *Land Economics*, **40**, 199–212.
Institut d'aménagement et d'urbanisme de la région parisienne (1968) 'Centres commerciaux périphériques aux USA; un exemple, Northland, Michigan'. (*Cahiers de l'IAURP*, vol. 10.)
Isard, W. (1956) *Location and Space Economy*, Wiley, New York.
Isard, W. (1967) *Methods of Regional Analysis*, 5th edn, MIT Press, Cambridge, Mass.
Japon-Economie (1973) Special issue, 'La distribution au Japon', Office franco-japonais d'études économiques, Paris.
Jeanneney, J. M. (1954) *Les commerces de détail en Europe occidentale*, Colin, Paris.
Jefferys, J. B. (1954) *Retail Trading in Britain, 1850–1950*, Cambridge.
Jefferys, J. B. and **Knee, D.** (1962) *Retailing in Europe*, Macmillan, London.
Jetro (Japan External Trade Organisation) (1971–4) Marketing Series, No. 4, 'Planning for distribution in Japan'; No. 5, 'Retailing in the Japanese consumer market'; No. 7, 'Sales promotion in the Japanese market', Tokyo.
Jetro (1972) *How to approach the China market*, Tokyo.
Johnson, L. J. (1971) 'The spatial uniformity of a central place distribution in New England', *Econ. Geog.*, **47**, 156–70.
Johnston, R. J. (1973) *Spatial Structures*, Methuen, London.
Jones, C. S. (1969) *Regional Shopping Centres*, Business Books, London.
Kagan, M. and **Bergé, C.** (1972, 1973) 'Les conditions de vie des ménages en 1970 et en 1971', *Collections de l'INSEE*, M 16 and M 21.
Kerblay, B. H. (1968) *Les marchés paysans en URSS*, Mouton, Paris.
Kirby, D. A. (1974) 'The decline and fall of the smaller retail outlet', *Retail and Distribution Management*, **2**, No. 1.
Kivell, P. T. (1972) 'Retailing in non-central locations', in *Inst. Brit. Geogr. Occ. Pub.* No. 1.
Kniazeff, I. (1960) 'Le commerce de détail en URSS', *Et. et conj.*, **10**, P.U.F., Paris.
Knobelsdorf, E. V. (1966) 'Le rôle des villes et des grosses localités rurales dans la formation des régions', *Geografia Naselenija*, Leningrad, 69–89.
Kostrowicki, J. (1967) 'Le réseau urbain, sa notion, ses éléments, ses types, son aménagement', *Geographia Polonica*, **12**, 249–59.
Kovalov, A. (1966) 'A geography of consumption and a geography of services', *Soviet Geog.*
Kraenzel, C. F. (1953) 'Sutland and Yonland communities in the Great Plains', *Rural Sociology*.
Lasserre, G. (1968) 'Les coopératives de consommation en URSS', *Annuaire de L'URSS*, CNRS, Paris.
Lavigne, M. (1970) *Les économies socialistes soviétique et européenne*, Colin, Paris.
Lefranc, G. (1972) *Histoire du commerce*, P.U.F., Paris.
Lerat, S. (1969) 'Bordeaux et la communeauté urbaine de l'agglomération bordelaise', *Documentation française*, No. 3565–6.
Letang, E. (1972) 'Les centres commerciaux Haussmann, Opéra et Rivoli', Unpublished thesis.
Lomas, G. M. (1964) 'Retail trading centres in the Midlands', *Journ. Town. Plann. Inst.*, **50**, 104–19.
Lösch, A. (1943) *Die raumliche Ordnung der Wirtschaft*, Jena; English translation by Woglom, W. H. (1954) (2nd edn 1967) *The Economics of Location*, Yale Univ. Press, New Haven and London.
Lottman, H. (1974) 'Munich: une expérience de rue piétonne', *Métropolis*, **3**, 57–63.
McAnaly, (1965) 'Grocery trade in shopping centres', *Journ. Industrial Econ.*, **13**, 193–204.
McCahill, E. (1976) 'Downtowns welcome back small shopping centres', *Planning*, **42**, 15–18.
McClelland, G. (1964) *Studies in Retailing*, Oxford.
McDonald, J. F. (1975) 'Some causes of the decline in the Central Business District retail sales in Detroit', *Urban Studies*, **12**, 229–33.

McDougall, M. J. *et al.* (1974) 'Nottingham's Victoria Centre', *Town and Country Plann.*, **42**, 124–8.

McGee, T. G. (1970) *Hawkers in selected Asian cities*, Univ. of Hong Kong.

MacKay, D. B., Olshavsky, R. W. and **Sentell, G.** (1975) 'Cognitive maps and spatial behaviour of consumers', *Geogr. Analysis*, **1**, 19–34.

MacKenzie, R. D. (1933) *The Metropolitan Community*, McGraw-Hill, New York.

McKim, W. (1972) 'The periodic market systems in northeastern Ghana', *Econ. Geog*, **48**, 333–44.

Makanishi, C. (1973) 'Physical distribution in large cities', *Toyota Quarterly Rev.*, No. 2.

Marchand, B. (1973) 'An introduction to the topological analysis of geographical spaces, the topology of central place theory', *Geog. Analysis*, **4**, 205–13.

Marriot, O. (1967) *The Property Boom*, Hamilton, London.

Menguy, M. (1971) *L'économie de la Chine populaire*, P.U.F., Paris.

Mérenne-Schoumaker, B. (1974) 'La perception du centre-ville: le cas de Liège', *Bull. Soc. Géogr. de Liège*, **10**, 135–51.

Mérenne-Schoumaker, B. (1976) 'Evolution récente des grands "centres commerciaux" en Belgique', *Bull. Soc. Géogr. de Liège*, **12**, 51–63.

Mersey, B. (1973) 'What's happening to the grocery symbol groups?', *Retail and Distrib. Management*, **1**, 44–8.

Metcalf, D. (1968) 'Concentration in the retail grocery industry in Great Britain', *Agric. Economist*, **11**, 294–303.

Meynier, A. and **Le Guen, M.** (1966) 'Rennes. Les grandes villes françaises', *Documentation française*, No. 3257.

Michel, M. and **Vander Eycken,** (1974) *La distribution en Belgique*, Duculot, Gembloux.

Mills, E. (1974) 'Recent developments in retailing and urban planning'. Planning Research Applications Group, *Technical Paper* No. 3, London.

Mitsubishi Bank Review (1972–75)

Morinière, J. L. (1975) 'Le Cameroun: l'organisation de l'espace dans un pays en voie de développement', *Cahiers Nantais*, No. 9–10.

Morrel, J. G. (1956) 'Furniture for the masses', *Journ. Indust. Econ.*, **5**, 24–9.

Murata, S. (1973) 'Distribution in Japan', *Toyota Quarterly Rev.*, No. 2.

Murphy, R. E. (1966) *The American City*, McGraw-Hill, New York.

Murphy, R. E. (1972) *The Central Business District*, New York.

Mutin, G. (1974) 'La Mitidja: décolonisation et espace géographique', Doctoral thesis, Algiers.

National Atlas of the USA (1970) Washington.

Nikolskiy, I. V. (1973) 'Problems in the study of the domestic commerce of the USSR', *Soviet Geography*.

Nonn, H. (1974–5) *Les commercants dans les opérations de restructuration urbaine*, Univ. of Strasbourg.

Nordin, C. (1975) 'Market places and social change', *Choros*, No. 85, Univ. of Göteborg.

Office belge du commerce extérieure (1975) *Les canaux d'importation au Japon.*

Olsson, W. (1940) 'Stockholm: its structure and development', *Geog. Rev.*, **30**, 420–38.

Papageorgiou, G. J. and **Brummel, A. C.** (1975) 'Crude inferences on spatial consumer behaviour', *Ann. Assoc. Amer. Geog.*, **65**, 1–12.

Partigul, S. (1967) 'Le commerce dans le plan quinquennal', *Annuaire de l'URSS.*

Pechoux, P. Y. *et al.* (1966) 'Toulouse. Les grandes villes françaises', *Documentation française*, No. 3262.

Percival, R. N. (1965) 'Shopping centres in Britain', *Journ. Town Plann. Inst.*, **51**, 329–33.

Perroux, F. (1950) 'Economic space: theory and applications', *Qu. Journ. Econ.*, Cambridge, Mass.

Piatier, A. (1965-) *Atlas d'attraction urbaine*, Gauthier-Villars, Paris.

Piatier, A. (1970) 'L'influence urbaine en milieu rurale dans la région du Nord' (Introduction to *Atlas* sheets), Paris.

Piatier, A. *et al.* (1964) *Les formes modernes de la concurrence*, Gauthier-Villars, Paris.

Pickering, J. F. (1972) 'Economic implications of hypermarkets in Britain', *Europ. Journ. Marketing*, **6**, 257–69.

Pokshishevsky, V. V. (1974) 'On the Soviet concept of economic regionalisation', *Progress in Geography*, **7**, 1–52.

Poland: *Maly rocznik statystyczny* (1977) (Statistical abstract), Warsaw.

Problèmes économiques (1973) Special issue No. 1352: *Information et défense des consommateurs.*

Prost, M. A. (1965) *La hiérarchie des villes en fonction de leurs activités de commerce et de service*, Paris.

Proudfoot, J. M. (1937) 'City retail structure', *Econ. Geog.*, **13**, 425–8.

Quin, C. (1964) *Physionomie et perspectives d'évolution de l'appareil commercial français, 1950–1970*, Gauthier-Villars, Paris.

Quin, C. (1971) *Tableau de bord de la distribution française*, Grédimo, Paris.

Quin, C. (1973) 'Les circuits de distribution en France', *Coopération,* Paris.

Quin, C., Boniface, J. and **Gaussel, A.** (1965) *Les consommateurs*, Le Seuil, Paris.

Racine, J. B. (1973) 'La centralité commerciale relative des municipalités du système métropolitain montréalais', *Espace géographique*, **2**, 275–89.

Reddaway, W. B. (1970) *Effects of the selective employment tax*, HMSO, London.

Reilly, W. L. (1931, 2nd edn 1953) *The Law of Retail Gravitation*, New York.

Reynolds, J. P. (1963) 'Shopping in the North West', *Town Plann. Rev.*, **34**, 213–36.

Rivet, D. (1975) *Les relations commerciales: du marketing au merchandising*, Chotard, Paris.

Robert, A. (1975) 'Les hiérarchies du monde rural: centres ruraux de commerces et de services en Franche-Comté', *Eléments de géographie comtoise*, 149–89.

Rochefort, M. (1960) *L'organisation urbaine de l'Alsace*, Univ. Strasbourg, Paris.

Rolph, I. K. (1932) 'The population pattern in relation to retail buying: as exemplified in Baltimore', *Amer. Journ. Sociology*, **38**, 368–76.

Rushton, G. (1969) 'Analysis of spatial behaviour by revealed space preference', *Ann. Assoc. Amer. Geog.*, **59**, 391–400.

Rushton, G., Colledge, R. G. and **Clark, W. A. V.** (1966) 'Some spatial characteristics of Iowa's dispersed farm population and their implications for the grouping of central place functions', *Econ. Geog.*, **42**, 261–72.

Santos, M. (1965) *A Cidade nos Paises subdesenvolvidos*, Rio de Janeiro.

Santos, M. (1971) *Les villes du Tiers-Monde*, Paris.

Santos, M. (1975) *L'espace partagé. Les deux circuits de l'économie urbaine des pays sous-développés*, Génin, Paris.

Sapirot, A. and **Lendrevie, J.** (1973) 'Les mouvements de défense des consommateurs dans cinq pays', *Problèmes Economiques*, No. 1352.

Sawadogo, A. (1975) 'Le développement de l'agriculture en Côte d'Ivoire', Unpublished thesis.

Schiller, R. (1974) 'Retailing and planning', *The Planner*, **60**, 744–9.

Schiller, R. (1977) 'What the census says about shops', *Chartered Surveyor*, 190–2.

Scott, E. P. (1972) 'The spatial structure of rural Northern Nigeria', *Econ. Geog.*, **48**, 316–32.

Scott, P. (1970) *Geography and Retailing*, Hutchinson, London.

Seronde, A. M. (1975) 'Rome, croissance d'une capitale', Unpublished thesis, Paris.

Setogawa, T. (1973, 1974, 1975) Three articles in *Japon-Economie:* 'Pour une stratégie de pénétration de marché japonais'; 'La distribution au Japon'; 'Structures économiques de Japon'.

Siddall, W. R. (1961) 'Wholesale-retail trade ratios as indices of urban centrality', *Econ. Geog.*, **37**, 124–32.

Simmons, J. (1964) 'The changing pattern of retail location', Univ. of Chicago, *Research Paper* No. 92.

Skinner, G. W. (1965) 'Marketing and social structure in rural China', *Journ. Asian Studies*, **24**, 3–43, 195–228, and 363–99.

Smailes, A. E. (1944) 'The urban hierarchy in England and Wales', *Geography*, **29**, 41–51.

Smailes, A. E. and **Hartley, G.** (1961) 'Shopping centres in the Greater London area' *Trans. Inst. Brit. Geog.*, **29**, 201–13.

Smith, B. A. (1973) 'Retail planning in France', *Town Plann. Rev.*, **44**, 279–306.

Smith, H. (1947) *Retail Distribution, a Critical Analysis*, Oxford.

Smith, R. D. P. (1968) 'The changing urban hierarchy', *Regional Studies*, **2**, 1–19.

Sporck, J. A. (1964) 'Etude de la localisation du commerce de détail: aspects méthodologiques', *Bull. Soc. d'Etudes Géog.*, **33**, 63–70.

Sporck, J. A. (1966) 'Le commerce de détail à Liège, aujourd'hui et demain: implantation, structure et qualité', *Habiter* (Bruxelles), **36**, 20–37.

Sporck, J. A. (1967) *Problèmes industriels, rénovation urbaine et centres commerciaux*. Excursion guidebooks, International seminar in Applied Geography, Univ. of Liège.

Sporck, J. A. (1968) 'Réalisation et projets de rénovation urbaine a Liège'. *Congrès et colloques de l'Université de Liège*, **48**, 409–18.

Sporck, J. A. (1969) 'Problèmes du commerce de détail en Wallonie', *Bull. d'information de l'institut économique et sociale des classes moyennes*, Bruxelles, special issue No. 5, 40–51.

Sporck, J. A. (1971) 'Qualité du commerce et valeur du paysage urbain', *Geografisch Tijdschrift,* **5,** 341–4.

Sporck, J. A. (1972) 'Les nouvelles implantations commerciales dans la métropole liègoise, à la lumière de réalisations récentes: americaines, européennes, japonaises', *Rev. de la société d'étude et d'expansion,* **250,** 193–203.

Sporck, J. A. (1973) 'Le shopping centre: une conception positive d'intérêt général' in *Rénovation commerciale par le shopping centre,* Comité belge de la Distribution, No. 2, 55–60.

Sporck, J. A. (1976) 'Aspects structurels et qualitatifs du commerce de détail', Comptes rendues, 94th Congress of the Assoc. française pour l'avancement des sciences (Bruxelles, 1975).

Sporck, J. A. *et al.* (1966) *Hiérarchie des villes et leur structuration en réseau,* Min. des Travaux Publics, Liège.

Sporck, J. A., *et al.* (1973) 'Une activité en mutation: le commerce de détail, son évolution dans les cantons urbains de Chenée et de Flero, 1964–71', *Travaux géographiques de Liège,* No. 11.

Sporck, J. A. *et al.* (1975) 'Le commerce de détail à Liège-ville; évolution quantitative et qualitative 1964–1973', *Bull. Soc. Géog. de Liège,* No. 11.

Stacey, N. A. H. and **Wilson, A.** (1965) *The Changing Patterns of Distribution,* Pergamon, Oxford.

Stewart, J. Q. (1948) 'Demographic gravitation', *Sociometry,* **11.**

Stone, G. P. (1954) 'City shoppers and urban identification', *Amer. Journ. Sociology,* **60,** 36–45.

Stone, P. S. (1969) *Japan Surges Ahead,* Weidenfeld & Nicholson, London.

Tajima, Y. (1971) *How Goods are Distributed in Japan,* Walton Ridgeway, Tokyo.

Thibault, A. (1977) 'Analyse de la distribution des commerces à Beauvais', Unpublished paper.

Thomas, R. W. (1975) 'Some functional characteristics of British city central areas', *Regional Studies,* **9,** 369–78.

Thorpe, D. (1968) 'The main shopping centres of Great Britain in 1961: their location and structural characteristics', *Urban Studies,* **5,** 165–206.

Thorpe, D. (1974) *Research into Retailing and Distribution,* Saxon House, Farnborough.

Thorpe, D., Bates, P., and **Shepherd, P.** (1976) 'Retail structure and town planning', *Planning and Transport Research and Computation (PTRC),* Publication No. P136.

Thorpe, D. and **Kirby, D. A.** (1972) *The density of cash and carry wholesaling,* Retail Outlets Res. Unit, *Report No. 4,* Manchester Business School.

Thorpe, D. and **Nader, A.** (1967) 'Customer movement and shopping centre structure: a study of central place system in Northern Durham', *Regional Studies,* **1,** 173–91.

Thorpe, D. and **Rhodes, T. C.** (1966) 'The shopping centres of the Tyneside urban region and large scale grocery retailing', *Econ. Geog.,* **42,** 52–73.

Thorpe, D. *et al.* (1972) *The Hampshire Centre, Bournemouth,* Retail Outlets Res. Unit, *Report No. 6,* Manchester Business School.

Town Centres: Approach to Renewal. (1962) HMSO, London.

Tracol, P. C. (1972) *Les canaux de distribution,* Dunod, Paris.

Troin, J. F. (1975) *Les souks du Nord Marocain,* Edisud, Aix-en-Provence.

Tumertekin, E. (1968) 'Central business districts of Istanbul', *Rev. Geog. Inst. Univ. of Istanbul,* **11,** 21–36.

Unit for Retail Planning Information (1977) *List of UK hypermarkets and superstores,* 5th edn.

Vance, J. E. (1962) 'Emerging patterns of commercial structure in American cities', *Lund Studies in Geog.,* Series B, **24,** 485–518.

Vance, J. E. (1970) *The Merchant's World: the Geography of Wholesaling,* Prentice Hall, Englewood Cliffs.

Waide, W. L. (1963) 'Changing shopping habits and their impact on town planning', *Journ. Town Plann. Inst.,* **49,** 254–64.

Webber, M. J. (1971) 'Empirical verificability of classical central place theory', *Geog. Analysis,* **1,** 15–28.

Webber, M. J. (1974) 'Association between population density and the market area of towns', *Geog. Analysis,* **2,** 109–34.

Webber, M. J. and **Symanski, R.** (1973) 'Periodic markets: an economic location analysis', *Econ. Geog.,* **49,** 213–37.

Webber, M. J. and **Symanski, R.** (1974) 'Complex periodic market cycles', *Ann. Assoc. Amer. Geog.,* **64,** 203–13.

Wegnez, L. (1975) 'Le dernier développement de la distribution aux Etats Unis', *Problèmes Economiques,* No. 1438.

Yue Man Yeung, (1973) 'National development policy and urban transformation in Singapore', Univ. of Chicago, *Research Paper* No. 149.

Zipf, G. K. (1949) *Human Behavior and the Principle of Least Effort,* Reading, Mass.

Index